UNLIKE NO OTHER

A Memoir of the Unlikely, Yet Successful Career of a United States Marine Corps Aviator

Book 1 (1965–1974)

The Company-Grade Years

Robert Wemheuer

Copyright © 2022 Robert Wemheuer
All rights reserved
First Edition

PAGE PUBLISHING
Conneaut Lake, PA

First originally published by Page Publishing 2022

ISBN 978-1-6624-7842-0 (pbk)
ISBN 978-1-6624-7843-7 (hc)
ISBN 978-1-6624-7841-3 (digital)

Printed in the United States of America

Dedication

Dedicated to the Officers, Staff Non-Commission Officers, and Civilians I had the pleasure to serve with during my career in the Marine Corps and my loving wife Joanne.

Contents

Acknowledgements vii
Prologue ix

Chapter 1: My First Squadron: Learning to Be a Marine
Company-Grade Officer and Aviator 1
    This tells the story of the path that I took to get into the Marine Corps, finish college, complete flight school, and then to become a CH-53 helicopter pilot and participate in the deployment of the first CH-53 squadron that deployed to Vietnam for combat duty.

Chapter 2: One Long Day in Laos 105
    This describes my second tour flying helicopters in combat in South Vietnam and during Operation Lam Son 719 in Laos.

Chapter 3: Finishing My Overseas Tour with Squadron HMH-462 in Okinawa, Japan, After Leaving Vietnam 251
    The story of life and flying helicopters in and around Okinawa in the 1971 time frame.

Chapter 4: Operation End Sweep—North Vietnam 282
    This defines the airborne mine-countermeasure missions flown by Marine helicopters in North Vietnam waters, which when completed, were a pivotal component in the release of the American prisoner of wars (POWs) from North Vietnam in 1973.

Chapter 5:   Commander of Marine Corps Air Bases, Western Area (COMCABWEST): Marine Corps Air Station in El Toro, California; Essential Subjects Training; and a Transition to Book 2, Which is a Memoir of the Field-Grade Years as an Aviator in the US Marine Corps 1973–1974 362

        This portrays the problems that the military encountered with troops and middle managers (staff NCOs and NCOs) who could not read above the third-grade level. It explains the out-of-the-box solutions to the reading problem.

Chapter 6:   Escape and Evasion for Dummies (An Excerpt from Book 2)...385

Bibliography...395

Acknowledgements

Sergeant William "Whitey" Whitehurst who provided encouragement and technical support in the drafting and publication of this Memoir. Without his support it would not have been possible to complete my quest. I will be forever grateful for his service, Semper Fidelis "Whitey".

PROLOGUE

My story began with my birth on October 16, 1943. My mother worked at the University of Illinois in an office above Stag Field in Chicago. The offices were located above the site of the nuclear laboratory where work was being performed on the first atomic bomb as part of the Second World War effort. She had difficulty all the way through the pregnancy and almost lost me several times.

Arriving from my mother's womb, at a whopping five pounds five ounces, I had a few deficiencies like a sixth finger on my left hand, scoliosis of the spine, eye-muscle problems, just to name a few.

Years later, it was surmised that my pregnant mother was exposed to nuclear radiation while she worked as an editor above Stag Field's laboratories, which could have contributed to my birth defects. My adolescent life was a struggle since I was the butt of jokes by bullies concerning my birth defects and small stature.

The hurdles that were the hardest to overcome were my eye muscle and dyslexia problems, which were not discovered until around the age of seven. That failure in discovering my vision problems caused me to fall far behind my peers in the ability to read and write. After my parents discovered the problem, they put me in a special school for three years, which included physical therapy for my eye-muscle problems and to work to overcome my dyslexia.

I finished junior high school but was lacking self-confidence, and I was preforming far behind my peers in reading and writing. During my freshman year in high school, my father suggested I play football and join the wrestling team. I did as he suggested and played football all four years in high school. I also went out for the wrestling team and competed in my weight class for four years.

It was my good fortune to have a wrestling coach who was a marine veteran who served in Korea. He took a special interest in me. His name was Mr. Mudge, and he became my mentor. He helped me develop my self-confidence and increase my physical strength. He used what he had learned and practiced in the Marine Corps as a basis for his coaching of our winning wrestling team. As part of his mentoring program for me, he taught me all about the Marine Corps.

He started with the motto of *Semper Fidelis*, meaning "Always Faithful." He explained the principles on which the Marine Corps operated, as well as the value of the concepts of never quitting, never exhibiting fear, and accomplishing the mission at any cost. He exhibited, by personal example, what the Marine Corps had instilled in him, how to adopt, improvise, and overcome obstacles thrown in his path. These codes of conduct had served him well during his combat at the Chosen Reservoir in Korea.

He gave me a great start; you could say a push toward a career in the Marine Corps. I had always wanted to fly since I was five years old, so I set my sights on both goals of being a marine officer and a naval aviator. Mr. Mudge always believed in me and pushed me hard to overcome adversity to attain my goals. I owe that man a lot. He helped me recognize, develop, and internalize the concepts of love of God, family, and country, which are hallmarks of the Marine Corps as well as the principles of how to adopt, improvise, and overcome obstacles—principles that I still adhere to today.

Because my career spans over twenty-five years, it was necessary to split this memoir into two books. The reason for splitting the memoir was because of the differences between job assignments, degree of responsibilities, and performance expectations, which differ significantly between company-grade and field-grade officers. An additional consideration was the length of the memoir; in its original form, it was too lengthy to be published in a single book.

The first book is based on my career as a Marine Corps' company-grade officer and naval aviator, starting in 1965 and concluding with my promotion to major in 1974.

The second book highlights my diverse assignments and activities as a field-grade officer in the performance of tasks and in dealing with the challenges that I faced as a helicopter maintenance officer, a commanding officer of two unique squadrons, and the commander of the largest Marine Corps' air station in the corps. I then retired in 1989.

These two sequential books were written for two reasons: first, to highlight the accomplishment of the Marines and civilians who I had the honor to work with during my twenty-five-year career. My hope is that this memoir gives them some of the recognition they deserved for doing an outstanding job day after day, week after week, month after month, and year after year while generally receiving little or no recognition. Second, to give young people who have had problems in their lives either physically or mentally to strive to overcome these obstacles. They should not become victims, not to their afflictions or to the color of their skin or religious choices or their educational background.

I hope my story will give these young people the idea that they can overcome obstacles in their own lives and become productive citizens in the greatest country in the world today, the United States of America.

This memoir is built on newspaper articles, notes, maps, logbooks, pictures, and journals, but it is based mostly on my personal recollections of the people I served alongside as well as the significant events in my career. The people are my primary motivation for telling their and my stories.

The structure of each book containing this memoir is based on a series of stories which follow a normal sequence in chronological order. My stories are laid out based on this order rather than on their perceived importance to me when I was putting the books together.

These memoir stories range from intense combat conditions during my three tours in the Vietnam War to unique escape-and-evasion-training experiences and to my various leadership challenges and achievements, both in command positions as well as in the Marine Corps Headquarters assignments during my twenty-five-year career in the United States Marine Corps.

CHAPTER 1

MY FIRST SQUADRON

Learning to Be a Marine Company-Grade Officer and Aviator

Mid-January 1968, the Republic of South Vietnam

Now flying as an CH-53 helicopter aircraft commander, I participated in the war in the northern part of I Corps in Vietnam as it continued to escalate. The North Vietnamese Army (NVA) had, in fact, moved three divisions of troops into the area surrounding the Khe Sanh Combat Base complex including the airfield used to deliver supplies to the Marines, Army, and Army of the Republic of Vietnam (ARVN) fighters in the region.

During the latter part of 1967 and then continuing in January 1968, the NVA attacked the hills surrounding the Khe Sanh Combat Base and, then finally, the base itself. Marine aviators flew many resupply missions to the hilltop positions as well as Lang Vie, as the NVA closed in, finally overrunning Lang Vie.

Khe Sanh Combat Base was basically under siege starting in mid-January 1968. Our squadron lost a CH-53 at Khe Sanh airfield shortly after an Air Force C-130 transport was hit and destroyed on the ground by rockets while unloading. The two pilots in the CH-53 were killed during the mortar and rocket attack, which also destroyed the fifty-three. We were also involved in repelling the Tet Offensive.

One such mission stood out in my memory above most of the other missions on my first combat tour in Vietnam, and it occurred during the siege of Khe Sanh. We were on a mission to extract ARVN soldiers from the Khe Sanh Combat Base and lift them about sixteen kilometers to Ca Lu Combat Base, which was located just east of the bridge where Highway 9 crosses the Quang Tri River. My aircraft was the second of a flight of two CH-53s. The section leader was Captain Andy M. Tomasko. He was the flight leader since he was senior to me, not because of date of rank, which was the same, but because his last name started with a *T* and mine with a *W*. He briefed us with our mission, saying we were to move approximately 240 ARVN troops from Khe Sanh Combat Base to Ca Lu Combat Base.

We would make two trips each carrying sixty troops on each lift. After the troop movement mission had been completed, we would then move sixty-four thousand pounds of external cargo and supplies from Camp Carroll Combat Base to Khe Sanh. It was a straightforward mission. The intelligence part of our briefing indicated that there continued to be sporadic artillery, mortar and 122mm-rocket attacks on Khe Sanh's airfield as well as the camp itself. The intelligence briefer indicated that during the last twenty-four hours, the airfield had receive over thirty-five 122mm rocket strikes.

The rest of our briefing, preflight, start up, and takeoff were all normal. The weather today was good for being in the monsoon season in South Vietnam. My crew chief on this flight was Sergeant Sullivan, who was an avionics specialist by training but also qualified as a crew chief. As we flew north, I checked the power available from each engine making sure the T5 settings were set to their maximum at 638 degrees centigrade giving us the maximum power available from our two T64-6 engines.

Captain Tomasko led our flight north past Hai Van Pass then to Dong Ha where we refueled. After departing Dong Ha, we headed west, climbing to three thousand feet to stay out of small-arms range, obtained save-o-plane clearance from friendly artillery, naval gunfire, and air attach missions along our route of flight, then we flew past

Camp Carroll, then over Ca Lu to Khe Sanh. We arrived in a loose formation above Khe Sanh airfield just in time to observe several artillery shells hitting the airfield.

We orbited south of the airfield waiting for the bombardment to slow down or stop. We were circling for about ten minutes when we got a call from the tower that the artillery attack had ceased then.

Captain Tomasko called on the FM radio saying that we should split up the flight at this point since the pickup area was not large enough to handle both aircraft safely at the same time, plus he did not want to have two aircraft on the ground at the same time. He indicated he would go in and pick up the first sixty ARVNs, then once loaded and out of the pickup zone, I should go in to pick up the next sixty troops.

After responding by radio that I understood his instructions, he then broke formation heading toward Khe Sanh. We watched him land on the runway, then taxi to the pickup location in the loading area. It took about two minutes to get the ARVN troops aboard. He then taxied to the runway and lifted off just as three rockets impacted the runway area behind where his aircraft had been only a few seconds earlier. As we watched him depart, I started toward Khe Sanh airfield. My copilot and I talked about how much power we had available at this altitude and temperature. He checked the calculations and found we could safely carry sixty ARNV troops with our present fuel load.

As we approached the airfield, I said to Sully (Sullivan, my crew chief), "Be sure to count the number of ARVN troops we put on. We do not want more than sixty on this lift."

"Yes, sir, will do," said the six-foot-four-inch-tall crew chief.

Completing the landing checklist, the tower cleared me to land on the runway and taxi to the pickup area.

Things at the airfield remained quiet as we taxied into the pickup area. Looking out my pilot's window, I could see the ARVN troops coming out of trenches and being lined up in rows waiting to be loaded onto our bird. After stopping our aircraft in the middle of the loading area, Sully started the loading process. He checked the cabin to be sure it was clear of any gear that might obstruct the loading process, then moved to the rear of the bird to lower the ramp. He was in the process of lowering the cargo ramp when the first mortar or artillery round hit about three hundred yards to our rear. This round was followed about ten seconds later by another that was closer to us.

Sully had gotten the ramp down by this time and had signaled the leader of the troops to start loading. I learned later that the loading process had started out orderly but then after the second mortar or artillery round hit, all hell broke loose. Sully was almost immediately overrun by the massive surge of ARVN troops trying to board the aircraft all at once. He was pushed off the side of the ramp as they rushed for what they thought was the safety and protection inside the aircraft.

Sully was knocked to the ground by the force of the surge of troops losing the connection to his long internal communication system (ICS) cord, which had been pulled loose from his helmet. This resulted in him not being able to communicate with any other crew members.

As the troops surged forward, one of the gunners was pushed away from his gun as the troops pushed into the forward part of the aircraft. He had to pull his pistol to get them to move back away from him. I called several times on the ICS for Sully but got no response, then asked the gunners if they could see him in the back of the aircraft. Both gunners replied that they could see only a continuous stream of ARVN troops entering the cabin. While these activities were taking place, the airfield again came under attack. This time, it was 122mm rockets that were falling all around us. I saw one hit the already destroyed Air Force C-130 lying beside the runway, another dropped about a hundred yards ahead of us, and I could hear several more explosions behind our aircraft; fortunately, none were very close. The rockets seem to instill more fear in the ARVN troops who continued to storm ahead to get on board the aircraft. We still had no communications with our crew chief.

I had no idea how many ARVN troops were on the bird, but I knew, one thing for sure, we needed to stop the surge of troops, or we would never get out of there.

Reaching up to close the ramp from the cockpit control switch, I heard one of the gunners say, "The ramp is being closed. I see Sully inside the bird. He closed it. Now he is pushing people back off the ramp that are trying to crawl into the aircraft. We need to move out of here now, sir."

I told the copilot to give me full power just as the next round of incoming enemy fire had arrived. Mortar or artillery rounds and rockets rained down all around us.

I told the tower we were taking off from our present position. Raising the collective, I could feel through the controls that the aircraft was now very heavily loaded. I quickly checked the rotor revolutions per minute (RPM), and it was about 104 percent as I pulled the aircraft off the ground into a very low hover. At this point, the rotor RPM started to decrease rapidly, dropping below the 100-percent-RPM mark, then passing 95 percent RPM as I moved the aircraft slowly into forward flight. In order to miss the crashed Air Force C-130 wreckage, I required more altitude, so I had to raise the collective a little higher as we angled toward the runway. *I also remembered the Naval Aviation Training and Operating Procedures Standardization (NATOPS) manual, the CH-53 bible, that warned pilots that flying the aircraft below 95 percent rotor RPM could result in loss of flight stability and control.*

The copilot raised the landing gear trying to be helpful, as the rotor RPM continued to decrease past 90 percent. It was very apparent we had a very, very heavy load on our aircraft, and we might not make the takeoff safely.

As students at Pensacola, we were taught that rotor RPM in helicopters is just like airspeed in a fixed-wing aircraft. If you don't have enough of either, then you will most likely crash, burn, and die. RPM, RPM, RPM, I thought, *we have to get the RPM up, or we will not make it.*

I heard the landing gear retracting, which was followed by a complete electrical system failure. This failure caused us to lose all the flight instruments that did not generate their own electrical power, electrical inputs to the flight controls, and all internal communications as well as all our radios.

I focused on the rotor RPM that had stabilized at about 87 or 88 percent with my airspeed approaching 30 knots. Since my gear was up, I could not land back on the runway without destroying the bird and potentially killing my crew and passengers in order to abort the takeoff. *Almost to translational lift at about 40 knots,* I thought, *we might make it yet.*

Lowering the bird down over the runway helped me gain some rotor RPM and airspeed as we headed down the runway to the east. We were now doing about 40 knots, with the rotor RPM hovering around 91 or 92 percent. I could feel the FM antenna that had extended beneath the aircraft to its full thirty-inch length, when our landing gear came up, scraping on the runway as we dropped ever closer to it.

At that point, the electrical system somehow restored itself as my rotor RPM climbed back up to 95 percent making it much easier to fly. The airspeed was climbing; the rotor RPM was increasing; and the electrical system was back online.

I thought, *Maybe, just maybe, we are going to make it.*

Then as I looked ahead of the aircraft and down the runway, I saw an unexploded 122mm rocket sticking out of the runway about seventy-five yards ahead of us. I realized that we were still flying down the runway at about eighteen inches above the ground. We measured the antenna after the flight. I knew that if we hit the rocket, we would all be dead, so I continued ahead and pulled up the collective to get a little more altitude, hoping we had enough rotor RPM left to clear it, as I watched it go under the nose of the aircraft and praying it would not explode. After a couple of seconds with no explosion, I assumed we had cleared the rocket. Because of the increase I had made in collective pitch, the rotor RPM had again decreased to about 92 percent, but we were still flying and increasing our airspeed, but now we were about to run out of runway and go over the jungle-covered cliff into the Belong Valley.

Diving over the edge into the valley, we picked up valuable airspeed. I worked the collective, coaxing a little more rotor RPM with each cycle. Finally I was able to get the rotor RPM back up to 100 percent.

After taking a deep breath, I heard Sully come up on the ICS saying, "Captain, we got one whole shit pot full of folks back here. I have no idea how many there are, but it's a lot more than sixty since they're all standing up. I can't count them."

"Sully, I'm glad to hear your voice. Are you okay?" I asked.

"Yes, sir, I'm okay, bruised from being pushed off the ramp, but I am fine now," Sully replied.

"Good, we have to fly for a while to burn off some more fuel, maybe twenty minutes more before we can attempt to land at the Ca Lu Combat Base. Is everyone else okay back there? Please respond on the ICS."

Both gunners responded saying they were both okay but very crowded, still being pushed against their guns by the troops standing everywhere.

We continued to fly down the Belong Valley and went into an orbit over the Ca Lu Combat Base. I asked my copilot to do a power-available calculation based on the decrease in altitude between Khe Sanh and Ca Lu. He did so after regaining his composure.

After twenty minutes orbiting the base, I set up my approach to the extended pad used for cargo and troop drops. My approach was going to be a no-hover-precision approach to the spot about a third of the way up the matting. Calling Sully on the ICS, I said, "Sully, I want to know the exact count of the number of ARVN troops we have on this bird. Count every swinging dick as they exit." Two clicks on the ICS indicated that Sully had receive my message.

We completed the landing checklist as I rolled on final and turned into the relative wind. To my surprise, the no-hover landing went smoothly since we had burned off more than two thirds of our fuel load, which had reduced our gross aircraft weight by a couple of thousand pounds, leaving more power available to work with in the landing process.

Once on the deck, we taxied to the side of the pad and parked, then Sully opened the ramp to the level position and stepped out of the bird onto the matting. Since the distance was about twenty inches from the ramp to the ground, the troops had to jump down.

They could not surge or run out of the aircraft as they had done when they were loaded. This enabled Sully to count them as they climbed off the ramp a couple at a time.

While we were on the ground at Ca Lu, I tried to call my section leader on the FM radio. All I got was static when I tried. We had not received any FM radio transmissions since we departed Khe Sanh. This lack of radio transmission should not have surprised me. Thinking back to our takeoff, I remembered the scraping noise as we were heading down the runway, which may have affected the ability of the radio to function properly.

The off-loading took a lot longer than the loading process. Finally Sully keyed his ICS and said, "Sir, I counted one hundred twenty-nine of the ARVN troops getting off the aircraft. I don't believe that would be possible, but I have to believe my lying eyes. Captain, that is the number of troops I counted."

Before Sully boarded the aircraft again, I asked him to take a look at our FM antenna. Doing so, he said it looked like it had been ground off with about only a third of it left. As he entered the aircraft, my section leader arrived at the Ca Lu Landing Zone (LZ) with more ARVN troops. We would find out later that he brought the last fifty-one of the ARVN troops completing this part of our mission.

While he was sitting on the mat, he sent one of his gunners off to our bird with a written message. It said, "Change frequency on the UHF radio to squadron common so we can talk."

Switching the UHF to squadron common, I called him saying I was up on the frequency. He responded, "I have been calling you on the FM radio for the last thirty minutes. Why have you not answered my radio calls?"

Responding to Tomasko, I told him that my FM antenna had been damaged and my FM radio was down, and that was the reason we had not responded.

Tomasko again responded, saying, "This part of our mission was completed since I only picked up fifty-one ARVNs on this load." He further opined, "That they must have gotten the total number of troops on the mission paperwork wrong. Since your FM radio is down, I want you to head back to Marble Mountain, I will finish the rest of the mission myself since you don't have a working FM radio." I could hear him switching frequencies as he lifted off the mat, not waiting for a reply from our bird.

Once our crew was back inside the aircraft and was ready to go, we took off for Phu Bai to refuel before heading back to Marble Mountain.

Sully climbed up on the jump seat between the copilot, who was now flying the bird on our way home, and myself. I was concerned about the complete loss of electrical power during our takeoff from Khe Sanh.

Sully and I concluded that we had triggered an underfrequency condition in the generators that are driven by the rotor system. This occurred because we had allowed the rotor RPM to drop below 91 percent initiating an electrical shut down of the electrical system.

This would not have occurred if we had had our landing gear down at the time because it disabled the underfrequency switch, but since the landing gear was up, the frequency drop triggered the system to shut down to protect the components in the electrical system from damage.

After discussion with Sully, I had renewed confidence in the ability of the CH-53. It could do almost anything like lift 129 Vietnamese soldiers at one time. *We have come very close to not making it today,* I thought, *but circumstances have forced me to take a chance, and God was looking out for us today.* I concluded as we flew home in a beautiful, clear day in Vietnam.

*****

The mission described above is just one of the many that are part of the story of my arduous path from college to being a combat pilot in my first squadron. It is also the story of how a civilian young man embarks on his journey to becoming a company-grade officer in the Marine Corps.

*****

My journey to becoming a company-grade officer in the Marine Corps and a naval aviator took a lot of hard work and luck in order to achieve my goal.

The hardest of these steps for me in this process was becoming a naval aviator after I was commissioned. However, there were a number of steps that had to be completed before that occurred.

The first of these steps was for me to sign up for the Marine Corps' platoon leaders' class (PLC) with an aviation option right after graduating from high school in 1961. The program required me to become an enlisted Marine while attending college. While in college, I also served in the Marine Corps' Reserve Squadron as an enlisted aviation ordnance man in order to gain additional military experience. After successfully completing two summer training sessions at Marine Corps Base (MCB) Quantico, Virginia—a two-week squadron deployment to MCAS in El Toro—and meeting the academic requirements to be awarded a bachelor's degree from Western Illinois University, I received a commission in the United States Marine Corps Reserve.

My four years at Western Illinois University were, to say the least, chaotic. I had a lot of growing up to do while I attended college. Thank God, I did grow up during my four years at Western, in spite of too much drinking and too many girlfriends, which is about all the good things I can say about my experience at my first college. Partying was the name of the game in those days.

One concept that I did take to Western Illinois University was the concept of *equality*, long before it became a buzz word in our present culture. I had learned a very valuable lesson from my high school wrestling coach, a former Marine, who had served in Korea. He told me several stories of Marines in combat in Korea. The coach spoke from experience saying that the color of your skin, the slant of your eyes, or other exterior differences meant nothing when it came time to being a Marine or fighting the enemy.

"No matter who you are," he said, "we all still bleed red." Never judge people by their color, creed, or religion and always make your judgment based on their character was his bottom line. This concept remained with me throughout my Marine Corps days, and I still believe it today.

Concepts such as loyalty, integrity, honesty, accountability, and family values are a few of these concepts I used in my entire Marine Corps career. In my eyes, all Marines were green in color. Marine Corps' green-skinned bodies cover their red-blooded souls.

The graduation ceremony at Western Illinois University took place in the field house at the university in June 1965. I, along with around five hundred other students, received their diplomas. However, I was the only person who graduated that year to be commissioned in any of the four military services. It was a real interesting experience since the commissioning took place on the stage right after the commencement exercises that gave each graduate their diplomas.

After the last person received their diploma, a Marine captain, in his formal dress white uniform, marched onto the stage, then turned to the gathered graduates, teachers, families, and guests and said, "Ladies and gentlemen, I have a message from the President of the United States." Skipping a beat, he went on to say, "Would you all please rise to hear the president's words and to honor the man who I am about to commission in the United States Marine Corps Reserve."

Everyone in the auditorium rose as I marched to a point in front of him, dressed in my white Marine Corps uniform for the first time. Captain Cliff DeArenelis asked me to raise my right hand and repeat after him as he proceeded to read the words that would start me on a twenty-five-year career in the United States Marine Corps. At the conclusion of the swearing in, the audience broke into applause as the captain and I left the stage.

After the commissioning and then spending some time at home in Mount Prospect, Illinois, I traveled to Naval Air Station (NAS) Pensacola, Florida, for flight school training. Arriving at NAS Pensacola, I checked in with the duty officer, got my orders stamped signifying that I had reported for active duty, and then went to the bachelor offices quarters (BOQ) to get a room. Arriving at the BOQ,

I was told that there was a shortage of rooms, and I would have to share a room with another officer.

It just so happened that another Marine second lieutenant had just arrived at NAS Pensacola, and I would be sharing a room with him. His name was Lucien "Lou" Tessier. He attended Boston College. He and I would not only share a room but would be roommates throughout flight school, becoming close friends all the way through flight training and beyond.

*****

Naval Aviation Flight School is conducted in phases. Phase number 1 is a ground-school-only phase, which is conducted at NAS Pensacola's main side facility. It's the place where your flight school class is formed for the first time and where you receive additional military training and indoctrination. Here, you are also taught to swim if you could not. In order to pass to the next phase of training, you must pass an endurance tread water test, underwater swimming test, then a distance swim in order to continue in the program. You must also pass several physical fitness tests if you are to move along to the next phase. Failure of any of these tests after remedial training had been completed means termination from flight school. For Marines, it means going to another job specialty such as an infantry officer.

Phase 1 also consisted of ground school classes—aerodynamics, weather, aircraft structures, aircraft engines, mechanical engineering—and finally ended with the introduction of basic flying techniques.

Assuming you made it through phase 1 successfully, which I did, the next phase is basic flight training conducted at Saufley Field about ten miles away from main side. In this phase, you continue to learn about the aerodynamics of the aircraft you are about to learn to fly, its engine, its structure and are first introduced to the procedures that are to be learned in order to fly the T-34 training aircraft.

After two weeks of ground school at Saufley Field, you are assigned to a flight or flying group for primary training. You are also assigned to an instructor pilot who will oversee your primary training.

If I remember correctly, my orientation flight was where the instructor pilot demonstrated all the procedures, airfield locations, and maneuvers you would be learning during initial training. This flight consisted of how to preflight, perform control checks, start the engine, radio procedures, taxi, takeoff, course rules, location of outlying landing fields, and acrobatic training areas. The instructor pilot also demonstrated various flight maneuvers, then how to return to Saufley Field and how to perform the landing checklist, how to land the aircraft, all in a one-hour flight. *One hell of a lot to absorb in one flight* was my reaction as I returned from my first flight.

This orientation flight was followed by eight progressively more difficult training flights where more and more maneuvers, emergency procedures, and other tasks were added to the conduct of the flight, with the student being responsible for performing them in a satisfactory manner. The ninth flight was the safe-for-solo check flight. If you passed the check flight, then you were scheduled for a training flight by yourself or solo.

None of my flight schoolmates had any flying experience, so being able to fly solo was a major accomplishment for all of us on our way to earning our wings of gold as naval aviators.

*****

The first instructor pilot that I was assigned to for training was a senior Marine captain who was about to leave the service in a couple of weeks. He did his best to provide professional instruction on the integral processes and procedures for the T-34, but I could tell his heart and mind were elsewhere. I flew my first four flights with him before he checked out of the unit to be discharged from the service. I was then assigned to a Navy lieutenant commander who had the reputation of being a screamer, not a teacher, and disliked Marines. My next four flights were pure hell. I could do nothing correctly according to the lieutenant commander.

The day of my safe-for-solo check with the lieutenant commander was no better. He told me I would never be a naval aviator, and I could not even fly a broom. He gave me a "down," which meant "I was not safe to fly the aircraft by myself." My morale was shattered after that flight. I started to question my abilities to become a naval aviator.

*****

After a student receives a "down," the next step is that the student is reassigned to another instructor pilot and then taken through a remedial flight training syllabus culminating in another check ride. Fortunately for me, I was assigned a Marine instructor pilot who had just returned from a combat tour in Vietnam. The captain, a helicopter pilot, was named W. H. Saward.

The captain went out of his way to help me understand where my problems lay, helping me see what I had been doing wrong, then offering suggestions on how to correct my deficiencies. He coached me in the memorization of procedures, then the implementation of these procedures while flying; it was all part of really learning how to fly the T-34.

His encouragement and understanding helped me through the remedial process, which culminated in being cleared for my safe-for-solo check ride. This check ride was with a different pilot, but I passed the check ride without difficulty. The one thing my Marine instructor taught me that helped me in my future flying career was, above everything else, to remember that you must concentrate on the mission first, fly the bird, make the radio calls, plan ahead, don't think about being scared or the feeling you're going to die, just concentrate on the job at hand, and the rest will work itself out.

This sage advice would help me as I progressed through the various phases of flight training as well as later in my career. Next, I learned to fly the T-28. It was a much bigger, faster, and more complex aircraft than the T-34. We learned to fly the T-28 in multi-aircraft formation, perform aerial gunnery, as well as flying it on instruments in poor weather conditions.

At the cumulation of the T-28 training syllabus was the final challenge of landing on an aircraft carrier at sea. On September 6, 1966, I successfully landed and took off the prerequisite number of times from the aircraft carrier, the USS *Lexington*, to become both day and night qualified in fixed-wing aircraft carrier operations.

These cumulative efforts seem to have become much easier for me after my first misstep.

*****

As I approached the conclusion of the final phase of flying the T-28, I checked my flight school cumulative grades. My flight school grades had gotten much better, and my hopes again rose at the prospect of flying the F-8 fighter, my dream aircraft. However, the commandant of the Marine Corps had other ideas. He did not need additional F-8 pilots or any kind of fixed-wing jet pilots. He needed helicopter pilots. So instead of going to Corpus Christi in Texas for advanced jet training, I and all my Marine classmates were assigned to advanced helicopter training at Ellyson Field just outside of Pensacola.

Just before we were to graduate from flight school, another unexpected event took place. On December 9, 1966, both Lou Tessier and I were promoted to first lieutenant in the United States Marine Corps Reserve.

On the twentieth of December, both Lou Tessier and I along with twelve other Marines received our naval aviator "wings of gold" at a graduation ceremony at Ellyson Field.

My parents and sister made the trip to Pensacola to attend the ceremony. It was another great milestone in my career.

*****

Returning to Mount Prospect, Illinois, for thirty days leave over the Christmas and New Year holidays, I reunited with other family and friends enjoying the new status of being a first lieutenant and a naval aviator.

Early on the morning of New Year's Eve, I got a call from Lou Tessier. Lou said, "There are only four spots open at a new squadron being formed at Marine Corps Air Facility [MCAF] Santa Ana,

California. The new squadron is the first CH-53A helicopter squadron to be formed. If you want to fly CH-53, you better get there quickly. I am leaving in a few minutes to drive out to California. I don't want to fly CH-46s, so I plan to arrive at 0800 on January 2 at the wing headquarters so I can get one of the remaining spots. I suggest you do the same if you want to fly 53s."

I thanked Lou for the information and told him I would most likely do the same thing hoping to meet him there at 0800 on January 2.

My mother and father were not very pleased about my rushed departure, especially driving on New Year's Eve and New Year's Day, but they understood I wanted to fly the CH-53 and not 46s, so they helped me pack my corvette for the trip.

*****

Departing Mount Prospect, I headed southwest for California. Thirty-eight hours later, I pulled into the parking lot of the Third Marine Aircraft Wing Headquarters at MCAS El Toro at around 0630 hours of January 2. About an hour later, I was joined by Lou driving his corvette.

We both checked in to the headquarters' administrative section when it opened and got the last two spots at Marine Heavy Helicopter Squadron 463 (HMH-463), the new CH-53A Squadron. Two other Marines from our flight school class arrived as we were leaving, and I heard them being assigned to a CH-46 squadron as we departed. We looked at each other, and Lou said, "I think we were both lucky today."

We then drove to Marine Corps Air Facility Santa Ana, California, and checked into HMH-463, which was located in hangar number 1. This was one of two very large 1940's blimp hangars located at the base. These hangars were huge measuring over a thousand feet in length and over three hundred feet across and almost two hundred feet in height. Later in my career, I would find out the exact measurements of these mammoth structures.

As we walked into the hangar looking around, I noticed that along with it being huge in size, was the presence of several very large barn owls, well over three feet tall, perched in the rafters high above the new CH-53A aircraft, which were lined up in the hangar.

Hearing a rumble outside the hangar through a small access door, I headed out the door to see where the noise was coming from. Arriving outside, I looked to the east and got my first look at the CH-53 in flight. It was coming back to the base with its retractable landing gear up and at a high speed. "What a beautiful machine" was my first impression of the CH-53 aircraft as it passed overhead. The break maneuver occurred while the bird was out of my sight behind the hangar. The bird reappeared on the other side of the hangar with its landing gear extended as it passed in front of me and made a rolling landing on the runway that was located between the two hangars.

HMH-463 was the first squadron to be equipped and fly the CH-53A. The first six aircraft were ferried from the Sikorsky plant in Stratford, Connecticut, and were sent to Vietnam as Detachment A of HMH-463, which had already occurred. The remaining twenty-four aircraft would be ferried to MCAF Santa Ana, California, as they were completed and test flown. The main squadron had received twelve birds of the twenty-four birds so far.

After checking into the squadron, Lou and I found out we were two of the nineteen first lieutenants in this new squadron.

This new heavy helicopter squadron's composition was a bit unusual. It had two lieutenant colonels. One was already in Vietnam, Lieutenant Colonel Bill Beeler, in charge of Detachment A consisting of six CH-53s; the other was our commanding officer, Lieutenant Colonel Sam Beal.

We had nineteen majors and two captains in the unit when we arrived in January 1967. Middle managers were almost nowhere to be found with only two captains in the unit.

Detachment A departed for Vietnam on December 23, 1966. It was fortunate that the detachment had departed with five majors in its ranks, so that reduced the major pool of people all trying to get a department head position.

Boy, what a nice Christmas present it was for these detachment Marines and families was the thought that passed through my mind as I saw the December calendar for their departure on the side of the bulletin board as Lou and I checked into the squadron.

Being the last two first lieutenants to check into the squadron, we were met by the administrative officer and told to report back to the see the executive officer (XO) at 1:00 p.m., or 1300 hours military time. He also told us where the BOQ (the "Q" was its slang name) was located.

The Q was not far from the front gate. The main part of the Q was a nice-looking brick structure where the office was located. We went into the building and asked for billeting from the clerk behind the desk. He read our orders, then had us sign for our linen, and handed us two keys for our rooms. He then explained that only permanently stationed officers at the air facility had rooms in this building and that our rooms were in the next building over. Picking up our linen and keys, we headed for the next building.

To our surprise, the building was a transit Q. It was an all-wooden building also built in the 1940s as part of the infrastructure and support facilities for the lighter than air base during World War II. It was old and not very well maintained, plus it had no air-conditioning.

You got to be kidding me was my first thought as we walked down the dark hallway to our rooms. *This place is as bad as the Q at Saufley Field where Lou and I shared a room and spent our leisure time throwing our shoes at the large roaches that were almost everywhere. I only hoped that there would not be roaches in this Q. I don't think I will be staying here for long if I can find some off-base housing at a reasonable cost.*

We found our rooms and unloaded our cars before heading back to hangar number 1 to meet the XO.

The XO was a very heavyset man. Some people would call him pleasingly plump major, named Ken Wilcox. His nickname was Cinnamon Bear. Lou and I arrived at the admin office at 12:50 p.m. and waited to see the XO of our new squadron. At about 1310 hours (military time), the admin officer went into the XO's office to remind him we were waiting to see him. Since Lou's last name started with *T* and mine with *W*, he got to go in first.

Lou was in the office about five minutes when he came out and said, "We are free for a week. You're next to see the man. See you at the Q," and he headed out the door.

After knocking on the XO's door, I was told to enter. I was surprised to see the XO in a flight suit. He appeared to be about to leave his office to go flying but was sitting behind his desk drinking coffee. The major did not offer me a seat but kept me standing at attention in front of his desk.

Looking up at me over his coffee cup, he said, "Lieutenant Wemheuer, you are the last pilot that will be assigned to our squadron before we depart for Vietnam. I hope you know how lucky you are to be here to fly the newest helicopter in the corps."

"Yes, sir," I said. "I know how lucky I am to be the last officer to be assigned to this squadron. I wanted to fly the CH-53 and not the 46, so I made the trip here as fast as I could so I could get into this squadron."

The Cinnamon Bear responded, "Well, welcome aboard. Oh, by the way, I need a squadron duty officer [SDO] for tonight. The one that was scheduled is sick in quarters [SIQ]. Can you fill in for him tonight?"

Not wanting to piss off the XO at our initial meeting, I replied, "Yes, sir."

"Good," he said, "go see the admin officer for instructions and welcome aboard again, Lieutenant, who?"

"Wemheuer, sir," I said as he walked past me out of his office into the hangar still carrying his coffee cup.

*****

The admin officer handed me a folder saying SDO on it. The folder was filled with paperwork.

He then said, "Be sure you are back here at 1630 hours to assume the duty, Lieutenant."

Returning to the Q, I finished unpacking and took a short nap trying to catch up on the sleep I lost during my travels to California from Illinois. I almost slept through the alarm I had set but made it back to hangar number 1 just in time to assume the duties as the HMH 463 SDO.

The admin officer posted me, telling me that there was no special instruction for the SDO. Normally this was done by the XO, but he had left for the day after his meeting with me earlier in the day.

At that point, a corporal entered the office and said he was my phone watch. Looking at the corporal, my initial assessment was that he was squared away, which eased my mind some since this was my first time standing the SDO duty. I asked the corporal if he had been to chow yet (slang for meal).

He answered, "No, sir, not yet."

So I sent him to the mess hall for dinner. After he left, I took the folder that contained the list of duties the SDO is required to perform and a list of telephone numbers to call in case of emergencies. I dove into the documents and had just finished reading all of them just as the corporal returned.

Part of my duties were to tour the mess hall, so I headed to it, arriving just before it closed for the evening. Since I had not eaten since noon, I paid the subsistence fee and had dinner at the mess hall. Enlisted Marines eat free at the mess hall; officers pay a fee to eat there. The food was very good, which I recorded in the SDO logbook.

After the good meal, I toured our squadron barracks, then headed back to our hangar, and then to our duty-office space where the duty officer and his phone watch were to stand their duty. The room was small. It had two desks, a telephone, and a set of bunk beds in it.

The corporal looked at me and said, "Lieutenant, you look like you're all done in. Why don't you hit the sack and get some sleep? If you don't mind, I will take the top rack, and you can have the bottom one. It might be easier than climbing up top."

"Thank you, Corporal, I think I will take you up on your suggestion. Are you sure you don't want the bottom rack?" I asked.

"No, sir," he replied, smiling.

Removing my uniform and climbing into bed, I fell asleep almost immediately.

Waking up suddenly several hours later, I had a strong feeling that something was looking at me. Turning my head to the side, I saw two red eyes looking directly at me as I lay in the bottom bunk. Somewhat shocked, I tried to figure out what the creature could be that was staring at me. Then suddenly, it turned away and disappeared. I jumped out of bed and woke the corporal, telling him what I saw.

He said, "Don't worry, Lieutenant, that is just one of the rats we have in the hangar. The owls just love to eat them."

As I climbed back into the lower bunk, I thought, *Now I know why the corporal wanted to sleep in the top bunk. He is a smart Marine, which is why he is a corporal in the Marine Corps, and I am a wet behind the ears first lieutenant.*

So that's how the first day in my first squadron ended, and the second day began. I had a lot to learn about my new squadron, flying the new helicopter, and becoming a real Marine lieutenant in the United States Marine Corps Reserve.

*****

As more CH-53s arrived at MCAF Santa Ana, I got the opportunity to start the copilot training syllabus. It took about twenty-five hours of flight time to complete the syllabus, which occurred over the period of a couple months since we had so many "nuggets," which is what new naval aviators were called, who had just started to fly with an operational squadron.

During this time, I moved out of the Q to an apartment in Laguna Beach about four blocks from the Pacific Ocean. Sitting on the patio of my apartment, I watched the beautiful sunsets. Enjoying the sight of the sun slowly sinking into what appeared to be the ocean was what I remember best. That picture, along with a good martini, made it more enjoyable.

Spending more time after work in Laguna Beach was a pleasant change from BOQ life. One day per week, however, I stayed late to go to the officers' club for Friday night happy hour. This was not a mandatory event, but it was expected. These types of activities were all part of operational squadron life in those days. A good time was generally had by all who attended these events. It was a mechanism that was used to develop unit integrity.

Drinking games were all in vogue during this period. It was hard not to get caught up in the games, then having too many beers under my belt, I could not safely drive home to Laguna. That is when I took advantage of the BOQ lounge couches, which got a workout when I had too many beers or shots of tequila to drive home safely.

*****

As the senior field-grade job assignments were finally sorted out and the pecking order established, the senior commanders got around to giving some lower-level jobs to the junior officers.

I was assigned the job of ordnance officer in the squadron. This assignment was based on my time in the reserve squadron as an enlisted ordnance man, military occupational specialty (MOS) 6511. My main job then was loading 20mm ammunition into the 20mm cannons on the FJ-3 fighter jets. We were also responsible for cleaning and maintaining these weapons during our weekend reserve duty, as well as the two weeks of annual summer training when we normally deployed to MCAS El Toro.

Our heavy helicopter squadron was well on its way to becoming fully combat ready, C-1, and was scheduled to go aboard an aircraft carrier on March 1, 1967. This scheduled deployment plan changed dramatically when our XO flying a training hop after a rainstorm executed a roll-on landing, which resulted in an aircraft accident. The accident was created by the hard landing at one of the outlaying fields called Black Star Landing Zone (LZ), which was extremely muddy that day.

The result caused by the hard landing was that the tail section of the aircraft started to break. There were several stringers, ribs bent and twisted; fortunately, the tail did not break completely off. If it had, then the tail rotor and drive shaft would have departed the aircraft causing a catastrophic destruction of the aircraft. The accident also grounded the entire fleet of CH-53 aircraft until a fix was designed and installed. Fortunately for me, I had completed my copilot qualifications before the accident occurred.

The accident resulted in an emergency repair being required for all the CH-53s. The tail section structure of each aircraft had to be reinforced to beef up the area where it had started to fail. This emergency repair was engineered, then performed by a Sikorsky Aircraft factory team from their plant in Stratford, Connecticut.

The damaged bird was stripped down after it had been inspected and the accident investigation had been completed. It was then lifted externally back to the base by another CH-53 for repair. This was the first recovery of a CH-53 by another CH-53. These repair activities to all our aircraft delayed our scheduled departure for Vietnam until May 1, 1967. Additionally, a Sikorsky Aircraft factory repair team was dispatched to Vietnam to install the reinforcement kits necessary to fix the six Detachment aircraft already in Vietnam.

The sixty-day delay also messed up the schedule for the delivery of the initial issue of weapons and ammunition to our squadron. The Navy had scheduled the initial issue to be delivered directly to our navy carrier or landing platform helicopter (LPH) just prior to our departure. Someone dropped the ball, and no one provided the notice that our departure had been delayed, so the naval weapons storage facility proceeded with the scheduled delivery.

The LPH would not accept the weapons or ammunition since we were not embarked on the ship and could not sign for them. The chief bosun mate on deck watch looked at the paperwork, then told the drivers to proceed to MCAF Santa Ana and find HMH-463 who were going to be the custodian of the weapons and ammunition according to the paperwork that they presented to him.

In my new job for only two days, I had just read a naval message from the LPH that day that indicated that they could not accept the weapons and ammunition. It also said that the shipment was heading to MCAF Santa Ana for delivery to us.

Since I was now the new squadron's ordnance officer, somehow the word that I had this position became common knowledge on base. I knew this was the case when I received a call from the corporal at the back gate of the base saying that there were three trucks with weapons and ammunition waiting to enter the base. The cargo they carried was marked for delivery to the HMH-463 ordnance officer and asked where I wanted them to direct the delivery vehicles.

Having just read the message and getting the call from the back gate, I recognized that I was about to become responsible for the initial issue of all kinds of weapons and ammunitions that were suddenly being delivered here instead of going directly to the aircraft carrier as planned. I told the corporal to hold the trucks there for the next thirty minutes while I scrambled to find a place to safely store the weapons and ammunition. My first call was to the air facility armory on base. I talked to the corporal who was going along with us to Vietnam; he was on loan to the station until we were ready to depart.

The corporal was way ahead of me, like a good Marine NCO. He had also seen the message sending the initial issue to our location and coordinated with the station ordnance officer to allow us to store the weapons in his armory. The corporal had already arranged the storage for the M3-A1 machine guns, M-60, and .50-caliber machine guns in the station armory until we were to embark on the LPH in sixty days. The M-16s and pistols were to be housed in a small armory inside the hangar.

Our big problem was where to store the 50,000 rounds of belted .50-caliber ammo, 75,000 rounds of belted 7.62 machine-gun ammunition along with the 24 light anti-tank weapon (LAW) shoulder-fired anti-tank rockets. These were all part of the squadron's initial issue of armament and ammunition for a newly formed squadron.

The corporal and I discussed the storage of the armament and ammunition recognizing that we needed to find a secure storage space. He said he knew of an ammo bunker located in the middle of the farmer's field on base that had not been used in a long time. He said I should talk to the air facility logistic's noncommissioned officer in charge (NCOIC) about using it on a temporary basis and gave me his phone number. The alternative was to truck the armaments and ammunition another fifty miles north to the naval facility at Seal Beach Naval Weapon Station, which was the closest authorized storage area. I would still have to sign for it, but it would be out of my control.

I called the gunnery sergeant who was the NCOIC of the logistic department. He said the old ammo bunker had not been used for ammo storage in over ten years, but he would meet me at the bunker in fifteen minutes, and we could see if it was usable.

Calling our ordnance corporal back, I asked him to go to hangar 1 on the HMH-463 side and oversee the off-loading of the armaments and ammunition from the trucks that would be arriving shortly. The weapons would go to the armory, and the ammunition would be off-loaded in the parking lot. He responded, he would be there as soon as he could. I then called the back gate and told the sentry to send the trucks to hangar 1 at the HMH-463 side in about ten minutes.

Heading for the bunker and the meeting with the gunny, I took the old paved single-lane black-topped access road that angled off from the main road so I could arrive at the bunker in time to meet him. The access road was partially obscured by a field of sweet corn, but I found it without difficulty. I saw the gunny had opened the bunker and was looking inside it. He heard me arrive and came back out and saluted me as I approached the bunker. We then shook hands as we introduced ourselves.

The gunny then said, "Lieutenant, the bunker appears to be serviceable, but I am not sure it has a current certification by the Navy Command at Seal Beach for the storage of ammo. The one that is posted inside is somewhat out of date, but if you want to use it, that's your call, Lieutenant."

Recognizing that I was taking a chance using the bunker for the ammo storage when it did not have a current certification gave me pause, but it's for only about sixty days, I opined. I thought back to my drill instructor's words at Quantico. He said, "Sometimes you need to adopt, improvise, and overcome to get the mission accomplished." So this was one of these times, I told myself.

Looking at him I said, "I'll take it, Gunny, thank you for making it available to us."

The gunny saluted and headed for his car, saying, "Good luck, Lieutenant. Let me know when you're done with it, sir."

Locking up the bunker with a large padlock I had brought along for that purpose, I then headed back to hangar 1. I arrived there as the trucks with the armaments and ammunition also arrived. I also saw a young corporal climbing out of his car. He stopped the trucks and directed the drivers to start off-loading the ammunition and rockets in the parking lot several hundred feet from any other vehicles. I pulled up next to him as he was giving the orders to the drivers.

Wow, this corporal sure has initiative. I sure could put my trust in this NCO [non-commissioned officer], I thought as I looked at the way the corporal took the initiative to get things organized with a minimum of instructions.

The corporal saw me, just after he finished giving the drivers their instructions, then turned, and saluted, saying, "Lieutenant, it's a pleasure to finally meet you. My lance corporal armorer and I heard you were our new boss. It looks like we have our hands full here, sir. I hope you found a place to put the ammo. As you can see sitting over there, sir, I took the liberty of checking out a forklift from our ground-support section in order to move the ammo."

Smiling at him, I said, "Corporal, thank you for getting here so quickly. Yes, we have a place to secure the ammo until we deploy in a couple of months. Good thinking getting the forklift here ahead of time. Oh, by the way, it's a pleasure to also meet you too."

The corporal knew, as well as I did, that we had a lot to accomplish this afternoon, and I was sure he was up to it.

Continuing, I said, "After you take the ammo and LAWs off the trucks, I will take care of moving the ammo to the storage bunker. After you get it off-loaded, you can then escort the vehicles that have our guns to the armory and see to the off-loading and storage of our weapons. How does that plan sound to you, Corporal?"

"Great, sir," he responded as he climbed on the forklift and started the off-loading process.

The corporal drove the forklift and off-loaded the 50,000 rounds belted .50-caliber ammo, 75,000 rounds of belted 7.62 machine-gun ammunition, and 24 LAW shoulder-fired anti-tank rockets and placed these twelve pallets on the ground in the parking lot. Once this was completed, the corporal climbed into his vehicle, then signaled the drivers to follow him to the armory with our guns. As he departed, I climbed onto the forklift and started moving the ammo and rockets to the bunker.

Since I had worked part-time for my father during my summers through high school and college at his household goods moving business, I knew how to operate a forklift with ease.

Moving the twelve pallets of ammo to the bunker took about two hours since the bunker was almost a half mile from the parking area where we off-loaded the ammo.

I did not elect to have the delivery trucks drive to the bunker since the road was not in very good shape from the main road to the bunker. I also wanted to keep the storage operation as low key as possible.

The corporal returned as I finished moving the last pallet to the bunker. He again saluted and said, "Sir, you handled that forklift very well for an officer. If you like, I will return the forklift to the ground-support area since I checked it out. If you don't have a government license yet, let me know. I have some contacts at the motor pool who can make the process much easier."

Saying thank you again to the corporal, I indicated that I would take him up on the government driver's license help and would drop by the armory later to take a look at our new weapons.

*****

Fifty-five days later, we started to fly some of the aircraft and materials we were going to deploy with to the USS *Tripoli*, LPH-10. Most of the heavy equipment the squadron was deploying with had been delivered to the dock and loaded on the ship, then stored on the hangar deck. There was a fire truck, several jeeps, an ambulance, refueling vehicles, six-by-six trucks, well over a dozen pieces of aviation ground-support equipment to name just a few of the items we were taking to Vietnam.

The day before we were to depart for San Diego, I flew in the aircraft that was transporting our weapons to the carrier. The next two aircraft carried the ammunition and rockets to the boat. I stayed on board that night along with my two ordnance Marines so we could ensure that these items were accounted for and stored properly.

*****

The USS *Tripoli* departed San Diego the next day with our squadron on board heading first for Pearl Harbor in Hawaii. En route, several games were played among the Marines who were not familiar with being on board a naval vessel. A significant number of young officers, including myself, were sucked into falling for the ploys contained in these games.

One of these games involved being assigned to the mail buoy watch. The officer involved was stationed at the bow of the ship and issued a set of binoculars and a chair so he could scan the horizon for the mail buoy. This mail buoy was supposed to contain the mail for the ship's crew, including the Marines on board.

Getting the mail this way, we could get our mail while out in the open sea and not have to wait for the ship to dock in the next port. This posting of the mail-buoy-watch activity was done officially and sanctioned by the ship's captain and our CO.

Another quest was to send a lieutenant off to search the ship for a twelve-inch left-handed adjustable wrench or a night search of the hangar deck for the elusive "sea bats." These games were great fun for all who participated as well as those who watched.

These games and quests were all part of a new marine helicopter squadron persona and a way to deal with the stress as we all headed off to war.

*****

USS *Tripoli* docked at Pearl Harbor, and everyone, with the exception of the duty section, was given shore liberty. The CO called an officer's call at one of the hotel bars. He gave a short speech, stressing that we were going to sail in forty-eight hours and for God's sake to not miss the ship. He also reminded the next duty section of their responsibility to relieve the one on duty so that they can go on liberty too. He concluded by opening the bar and buying the first round of drinks for all the officers who were present.

Drinking games erupted again after the CO finished. No one was very sober when we headed back to the ship several hours later. We all took taxis back to the ship since we had no access to cars in Honolulu. Anyway, no one was in any shape to drive an automobile that night even if we had one.

*****

After leaving Pearl Harbor and while en route to Vietnam, we flew three aircraft, which hot seated crew members in order to get all our pilots and copilots carrier qualified (CQ) both day and night. We were limited to three birds because of the crowded conditions on the flight deck. Additionally, enlisted flight crews were also qualified with the M-60 machine guns that were positioned in the window behind the copilot and the personnel door behind the pilot. The CQ and gunnery operations went well without incident.

*****

On May 23, 1967, the USS *Tripoli* arrived in the waters about fifty miles off the South Vietnamese coast. The ship went to flight quarters and launched the first flight of four aircraft, led by the CO. Each aircraft was loaded with cargo and supplies destined for Marine Corps Air Facility Marble Mountain, located south and east of the city of Da Nang, South Vietnam.

You could tell we were going into combat because for the first time since our gunnery qualification, we had placed guns and ammunition on each aircraft, as well as each pilot and aircrew member having been issued body armor that covered the chest area. We were told that the armor would stop a .50-caliber machine-gun bullet, so you felt sort of invulnerable.

My first flight into Vietnam came that morning. I was assigned to be the copilot for Captain Frank Kennedy. We briefed, preflighted, and manned our aircraft since we were part of the second group to launch after the first four birds departed the ship. After the four birds in the first wave were successfully launched from the flight deck, we were moved by the Navy Green shirts, aircraft handlers, to spot 3 on the flight deck. At their direction, we then unfolded the pylon and then spread the blades as our section leader directly ahead of us had done. Engine starts and rotor engagement and all checklist items were completed. We then were unchained from the deck, and our section leader lifted off first, and once he was clear of the deck, we were cleared for takeoff. I monitored the speed-control levers that controlled the two jet-engine outputs to our bird, as Frank lifted our bird off the deck, checked the power available, and departed the ship.

Frank instructed me to raise the landing gear as we headed up and away from the ship, as he looked to join on our section leader. He caught up with our section leader and easily joined on his left side. We made a wide orbit of the ship waiting for the other two 53s to launch and join on us. After all the aircraft were joined on the flight leader, the flight turned west heading toward the coastline of South Vietnam.

My first view of Vietnam came when I saw a small mountain on the horizon. Looking on the map, we identified the mountain as Monkey Mountain, which lay just east of the city of Da Nang and the Air Force controlled Da Nang Airfield.

Our flight of four CH-53s entered the traffic pattern at our new home, Marble Mountain Air Facility, and we all performed the overhead break maneuvers. Landing on the runway, we were directed to the refueling pits and refueled. We were then directed by the ground crews to an area where we could off-load our cargo.

Frank parked the aircraft in the cargo off-load area but kept the aircraft running as we were off-loaded. At the same time, a major, the operations officer of Detachment A, came aboard the aircraft to talk to Frank. He asked Frank if the aircraft was in an operational ready status or up status.

Frank answered, "Yes, we are up."

The major said, "Good, we have a mission for you. Can you and your crew do it?" he asked.

"Sure" was Frank's reply. "But what about the climatization order for us not to fly combat missions for the first five days after arriving in country?"

"Mission requirements forced us to make an exception to the no-combat-climatization order. You are good to go," the major replied, "and here are the grid coordinates, a map of the area, radio frequencies, and the mission brief sheet. Good luck, Captain." Then he handed the paperwork to Frank and then exited the aircraft.

Looking over my right shoulder toward the rear of the aircraft, I could see we were about three quarters of the way through the off-loading cycle. As the off-loading continued, Frank and I went over the mission briefing, looked at the map, and talked about our first combat mission in the Republic of South Vietnam.

Our mission was not a complex one. We were to fly to Phu Bai airfield, pick up several loads of rice and other supplies and deliver them to three LZs around twenty miles northeast of the airfield. One LZ was close to the South China Sea, and the other two were on the bank of a river inland.

Completing the off-loading, we called for taxi, and then takeoff as we headed north passing west of Monkey Mountain.

This was the first time, I had an opportunity to see the Da Nang Harbor, the city itself, and the sprawling Da Nang military airfield. It was bristling with fighters, bombers, and transport aircraft. Switching radio frequencies to Da Nang tower for Frank before he asked me to do it resulted in a smile and a thank-you comment from him. I tried to stay ahead of things, but it was all new and coming fast. I again remembered what my old flight instructor had told me, "Keep the mission in your mind, focus on it, then do it."

Frank called Da Nang tower and got permission to fly low level, about fifty feet above the water and below their approach corridor as we headed north toward what I would learn was Hai Van Pass.

Clearing Da Nang's control zone, five miles from the airfield, we continued north staying over the South China Sea until we rounded the corner of the mountains, which jutted into the sea.

Frank had me switch the TACAN station (used for aviation navigation) to Phu Bai airfield, then we started to climb to about three thousand feet of altitude remaining over the ocean. He contacted Phu Bai's air traffic control for the sector we had entered, which picked us up on radar, and vectored us toward the airfield about forty miles to our northwest and also providing save-o-plane clearance for our flight.

As we headed toward Phu Bai, I looked down at the flat terrain we were now flying over. It appeared to be made up of thousands of rice patties broken up by rivers and streams. Fishing boats were everywhere I looked. I forced myself to concentrate on the mission and not on sightseeing. I looked up the frequency for Phu Bai tower and made ready to help perform the landing checklist when asked.

At around five miles from Phu Bai, Control turned us over to Phu Bai's control tower. We landed, refueled, and then were directed by ground control to a parking area where we could see our load was staged.

After we parked our aircraft and shut it down, a South Vietnamese soldier approached the bird. Our crew chief intercepted him before he could enter the cargo compartment of our machine.

Frank exited the cockpit first, then exited the aircraft heading for the soldier and our crew chief. At that point, a US Army Special Forces staff sergeant joined the group.

I was the last to arrive and heard only the tail end of the conversation. It was apparent from the discussion that we were going to take the eighteen thousand pounds of rice and assorted supplies to three different locations making three separate lifts to three different LZs. These LZs were located at the same grid coordinates as were shown on the mission order we had received back at Marble Mountain. At that point, the South Vietnamese soldier excused himself, then quickly moved to an area where there were several South Vietnamese civilians seated in the shade. He spoke to them, and they started to move to the stack of rice and other items. It was obvious that this group was going to load the aircraft.

After Captain Kennedy and the Army staff sergeant concluded their discussion, Frank sent me to get the loading process started. Part of my duties as copilot was to keep track of the amount of cargo, we carried from one location to another. It was also important to keep track of the number of bags of rice and the weight of the other cargo that was loaded on the bird. The gross weight of the aircraft was a critical part of our mission calculations, mainly because of the very hot temperatures we experienced in Vietnam, which limited our power available. All these factors, plus a myriad of others needed to be evaluated, so we could safely fly the load to its destination.

Our crew chief had already set up the cargo bay with several pallets that were laid on the rollers inside the cabin so that they could be pushed down the ramp to the ground as we taxied slowly forward. Each pallet was connected to the next one so we could use the first pallet off the aircraft to pull the others off in a daisy-chain fashion. Once in place, he signaled the Army staff sergeant who in turn gave an order to the South Vietnamese soldier, who in turn spoke to the civilians, who then lined up next to the stacks of rice, and the first man in the group climbed on top of the stacks. He then picked up one of the sacks and placed it on the shoulder of the next man in line.

Then that man walked toward the ramp of our bird. Each man in turn was loaded with the one-hundred-pound sack and headed for the bird. The first man arrived at the ramp and stopped. The crew chief signaled him to enter and pointed to where he was to place the rice sack on the pallet. The daisy-chain continued with the pile of rice going down rapidly.

At this point, my job was to keep track of the amount of cargo we were going to carry on each lift. Keeping a running total of the number of sacks of rice that had been placed on the pallets gave me the total weight of the cargo we had taken on board so far.

Checking the mission sheet against what had been loaded, then checking my count with the crew chief's count, we stopped the loading efforts as we had reached the amount of weight for the first load.

By both our counts, we had the six thousand pounds of rice and supplies we were to take to the first LZ

With the first load on board the bird, our crew chief and our two gunners busied themselves strapping down the load. Since we had not briefed for a combat resupply mission on the boat this morning, Frank wanted to conduct an additional briefing.

Captain Kennedy called the entire crew together outside the aircraft, telling them what we might expect on this resupply mission following our naval aviation training and operating procedures standardization (NATOPS) manual for the CH-53A aircraft procedures. He went into detail on when and under what circumstances our gunners could fire their weapons. He indicated that before firing at anything or a potential threat, they had to clear it through him first.

We headed back toward the aircraft. As we were about to enter the personnel door, the Army staff sergeant came walking up to the bird, indicating to Frank that he needed to go with us to the first LZ to check on the Army Special Forces advisors he had left in the village near the LZ. The South Vietnamese soldier also indicated that he would like to make the trip to ensure the cargo went to the right location and people.

Captain Kennedy made the decision that taking these two people was okay, and they were loaded into the rear of the aircraft.

Preflight checks, start up, and rotor engagement were all routine. We then taxied for takeoff to the runway. After making a hover check to see how much power it took to hover out of ground effect, we departed Phu Bai airfield.

Captain Kennedy then asked me to calculate again the maximum power available based on the outside air temperature and pressure altitude from our NATOPS charts. Frank headed our aircraft toward the east, climbing again to around three thousand feet which was generally out of small-arms range of the Viet Cong gunners. Completing my calculations, it was apparent that we had about 20 percent more power available than was necessary to hover out of ground effect at the LZ location.

Our first load was going to the nearest LZ on the riverbank about fifteen miles northeast of the airfield. After sharing the calculations information with Captain Kennedy, we talked about what type of approach he was going to fly and what he wanted me to do to assist him.

We found the LZ without difficulty. Captain Kennedy made a right-hand turn over the LZ to positively identify it. It was a large area near the riverbank that looked like it was used as a soccer field but was clear of any grass or other vegetation.

There was a South Vietnamese flag flying from a pole in the village, which was a good way to determine which direction the wind was blowing. This was important to know so you could utilize the wind's effects to help make safe approaches and landings in confined areas.

After over flying the LZ, Captain Kennedy started a descending right turn while asking me to perform the landing checklist. His approach ended as he rolled out on final, so he had the aircraft heading into the wind passing over the front part of the LZ, then coming to an approximately twenty-foot hover. The crew chief cleared the aircraft tail and sides of the aircraft to avoid any obstruction surrounding the LZ.

Once cleared, Captain Kennedy eased the big bird down to the ground creating a very large dust cloud in the process. We lost forward visibility as the dust cloud totally engulfed the bird in the dust, but Frank was able to maintain visual contact with the ground by looking down through the chin bubble in the nose of the aircraft below his feet.

As we came to a hover, I looked outside my window just before it was completely obscured by dust and watched a small child blown off her feet, then rolling several times across the ground, until an adult grabbed her. *Our rotor wash was a force to be reckoned with*, I mused.

The villagers were used to rotor wash from UH-1s or H-34s flown by the Army and Marines, respectively, and not the very large rotor wash we generated. It appeared the villagers had never experienced winds like we created and ran for cover until the dust had cleared the LZ. Even a new copilot like me could see that this rotor-wash dust problem was going to create challenges for both pilots and people on the ground.

After the dust had cleared, we off-loaded the two passengers. Then Frank instructed the crew chief to make the cargo pallets ready for a taxi drop. The crew chief acknowledged the instructions for our taxi off-loading and, together with one of the gunners, removed all the pallet tiedowns, then pushed the rearmost pallet to the rear of the aircraft, then onto the ramp that had been lowered to a position, which was about six inches off the ground. The rear pallet was connected to the next one by a four-foot-long piece of rope. Then each subsequent pallet was attached to the it, with rope, in a daisy-chain fashion.

Once the pallet was in position on the ramp, the crew chief notified Captain Kennedy that they were ready to taxi. Frank acknowledged the call and started to taxi the aircraft slowly forward while the crew chief pushed the rear pallet off the end of the ramp onto the ground. As Frank continued to taxi forward, each pallet was pulled slowly to the rear of the aircraft on the internal rollers and then off onto the ground. The off-loading operation of all six pallets took about a minute to complete once Frank had started taxiing.

After clearing the loads, we continued taxiing so we could depart the LZ in a direction that would minimize the impact on the nearby village. Once airborne, we headed back to Phu Bai airfield for our second load.

Landing at Phu Bai airfield, we taxied back to the pickup location for the second load.

In order to save time as well as fuel, we shut down the main engines and rotor system leaving the auxiliary power plant operating. The next load was loaded in the same manner as the first through brute manpower. The process was completed in about twenty minutes with the crew chief supervising the loading, and he and I counted the sacks of rice and cargo. When all six pallets were loaded, we closed the ramp, performed the engine starts, and rotor engagement, then we taxied for takeoff. Our second trip was to another LZ located on the same river about two miles from the first.

The same type of approach was used once we positively located the LZ. Captain Kennedy again shot the approach in a precise manner, landing again on a dirt LZ and again generated a large cloud of dust.

I thought, *If there are bad guys out there, they sure will be able to see us based on the dust cloud we generate.*

Off-loading in the second LZ went as smooth as the first one, and we were soon airborne and back to Phu Bai airfield to get our last sortie.

Landing at Phu Bai, we refueled our bird after doing some additional calculations on our ability to carry the last six-thousand-pound load successfully to the third LZ. This recalculation was necessary because the outside air temperature had increased as the afternoon wore on. After the calculation, we still had 15 percent more power available than was necessary to hover out of ground effect at our new LZ location.

Captain Kennedy determined that we needed to shut down completely this time, so we would not have to refuel before heading back to Marble Mountain. We taxied to the staging area again. After we parked our aircraft and shut it down, another South Vietnamese soldier approached our bird. He talked in broken English to the crew chief explaining that additional items had arrive that needed to be taken to the last LZ.

Frank again exited the aircraft and spoke to the South Vietnamese soldier learning that more rice and supplies were needed to support the needs of the friendly villagers at the coastal LZ. He asked the South Vietnamese soldier how much more was required to be moved over and above the current six thousand pounds. The soldier responded to Frank that approximately two thousand pounds of additional materials needed to be moved to the coastal LZ.

Captain Kennedy saw me exiting the aircraft and waved me over as the crew chief was staging the pallets for the loading cycle. He asked me to recalculate the power computations based on the additional weight that could potentially be our load. While we were loading the initial six thousand pounds of cargo, I recalculated the power required to hover out of ground effect at the coastal LZ and determined that we had about 5 percent more power available from our engines than it took to hover.

This calculation showed that if we tried to use more power above the 5 percent delta we had, the engines could not provide the rotor systems enough power to create the additional lift necessary to hover out of ground effect. A roll-on landing would be prudent since our delta between power available and power required was extremely close.

Captain Kennedy made the decision to take the extra supplies, and they were quickly added on the top of the existing pallets.

We headed for the aircraft. The preflight checks, start up, and rotor engagement were again all routine. We taxied, then took off from the runway after again making a hover check to see how much power it took to hover out of ground effect with the speed-control levers in the full forward position. As we finished the power check and started to move forward, I could see, hear, and feel the rotor RPM start to fall as Frank moved the aircraft from a hover to forward flight. The strain on the aircraft was very evident under the heavy gross weight of the aircraft as we made the takeoff. We climbed again to three thousand feet and headed northeast twenty-five miles toward the coastline looking for our third and last LZ.

The third LZ was located about a quarter of a mile from the outskirts of a fairly good-sized village, just behind the first set of sand dunes back from the ocean. The LZ this time was marked with orange panels at the end of a dirt road that led into the village. Captain Kennedy again executed the same type of approach that he used the first-two times before once we positively located the LZ.

He again shot a precision approach but used the road running through the LZ to make a roll-on landing with little difficulty. We were lucky because the prevailing wind was blowing almost directly down the road as we made our approach.

Captain Kennedy's precision roll on landing again created a large cloud of dust that could be seen for miles. A South Vietnamese soldier came from the village area and signaled where we should unload the supplies. Frank taxied the aircraft to the spot, and we off-loaded the third load as smoothly as the first two. We then taxied to the far end of the road away from the village and were about to lift off when the window gunner on my side of the bird said he saw a man dressed in black holding an AK-47 rifle who had just popped up from a hole twenty yards to our left.

He asked Frank if he could engage the target.

Frank answered, "No, do not engage," as we lifted rapidly into the air blowing heavy dust and sand in the man's face and forcing him back in his hole before he could fire on our aircraft, as we made a swift departure over the water to the east. Climbing to a safe altitude, we headed south remaining over the water toward Hai Van Pass.

When the gunner on my side called out the target, I also looked that way seeing the little man dressed in black wearing a pointed straw hat and raising an AK-47 rifle and pointing it at our aircraft. That vision lasted for only a couple of seconds before the man was engulfed in dust and sand-blown by Frank's rapid takeoff. As we climbed away from the LZ, I mused, *Well, I have seen my first Viet Cong on my first day, on my first flight in Vietnam, and did not get shot.*

Captain Kennedy at that point, asked me if I would like to fly the bird.

I responded, "Yes, sir."

He turned the control of the aircraft over to me for the first time that day, and I flew us back the way we came to Marble Mountain, where I made my first landing of a CH-53 on South Vietnamese soil.

Before securing for the day and going to the billeting area, I checked on our weapons that I was responsible for and found them staged inside the hangar with a Marine from the detachment there to guard them. He told me that the detachment ordnance NCO had arranged the staging and guard detail. *Another sharp ordnance NCO* was my final thought as I headed to a jeep that would transport me to the tent area where we would live for the next year.

*****

The next day, the newly arrived squadron personnel and the detachment personnel all assembled at the HMH-463 hangar for a formation. It was supposed to be a welcome aboard by the members of the detachment who had been there for six months, to be followed by an orientation for the newly arrived folks as to how things were done here in Marine Air Group 16 (MAG-16) and HMH-463 Detachment A.

Opening remarks were made by the MAG-16 Air Group commander followed by both our lieutenant colonels. At the conclusion of the formation, an operational briefing was arranged by the Detachment A operations officer and his staff. After the ops brief was completed, we then broke into separate groups and received the orientation briefings from our counterparts.

My counterpart was a young corporal who was responsible for the machine guns, rifles, pistols, and other pyrotechnics that the detachment had deployed with when it went overseas. He had a small cage in the maintenance hangar where the weapons were stored. Ammunition was drawn daily from the Marine Air Base Squadron (MABS) 16 armory at the other end of the airfield for support of the daily flight schedule.

Meeting with the Detachment A ordnance NCO, who was now part of my ordnance shop along with myself plus my two Marine armorers, we listened to how Detachment A had handled the ordnance support mission so far. After listening to his description of his activities, we then turned our attention to the potential changes that we felt necessary to support a much larger organization's ordnance needs.

We continued our discussion at the armory cage and started to reconfigure the cage to accommodate the weapons we had brought with us on the USS *Tripoli*. My two corporals and one lance corporal designed additional weapon racks and built them with lumber they got from MABS-16. Finally, all the weapons were inventoried, cleaned, and secured in the squadron's armory cage.

That night, we experienced our first rocket attack aimed, I believe, at the newly arrived multiple CH-53s now parked on the flight line. They made big targets, but only minor damage occurred to them during this first attack.

The next morning, we turned our attention to the 50,000 rounds of belted .50-caliber ammo, 75,000 rounds of belted 7.62 machine-gun ammunition, and 24 LAW shoulder-fired anti-tank rockets that had been dropped off in front of the logistics hooch on the concrete apron, which was part of the aircraft parking area. It would make a fine target for the enemy rocketeers, and if hit, would make a very big bang.

A custody transfer of 24 LAW shoulder-fired anti-tank rockets was made after a discussion with the Marine Air Base Squadron 16 (MABS-16) ordnance officer. He indicated that they would be happy to have them, as additional weapons for perimeter defense purposes, so we transferred them to the MABS-16 Squadron custody. His MABS-16 personnel arrived quickly and moved the rockets from the flight line to their armory.

Through additional discussion with the MABS-16 ordnance officer, we learned that the MABS-16 armory was willfully too small to hold our squadron's initial issue of ammunition.

My two corporals and I made calls to all the First Marine Air Wing (First MAW) organizations looking for a place that could be used to store this large quantity of ammunition. Our search ended with negative results. We could not find a place that had room to accommodate our ammunition. This meant that we had to look for an alternative solution. Thinking outside the box, we concluded that maybe we could build our own storage facility.

We first got the manual that set the standards for an ammunition storage facility in the field. We then designed a small ammunition storage facility. We looked for a place to put it and determined it could fit next to the logistic hooch.

I went to see the logistics officer, seeking permission to build the facility next to his building.

He said to me frantically, "I do not give a shit where you put it. Just get that ammunition off the parking ramp before the CO chews my ass again. Make it happen, Lieutenant."

"Yes, sir," was my response as I exited his office.

We first found a couple of excess general-purpose tents and used them to cover the pallets of ammunition, so they were not so noticeable. My two corporals, plus my lance corporal, and I then gathered the discarded parking matting materials for the floor and ceiling construction. We also located twelve large-sized wooden beams necessary for the ceiling of the bunker, plus 3,500 sandbags.

Next, we started digging the pit after carefully marking out the outline of our bunker. Since the area was all sand, we used the sand to start filling sandbags we needed for the walls of the ammo bunker. Our crew excavated down four feet, then placed the mat flooring at the bottom of the pit. Next, we lined the inside of the excavation with a single stack of sandbags that had been filled with a mixture of concrete and sand, then water was applied to the bags, creating almost an adobe-type block. Before putting the blocks in place, we lined the outside of the wall with plastic sheeting to protect the blocks from water entry. These blocks were placed from the floor to the surface and kept the sand and water outside the pit from sluffing or entering the bunker floor area. The wall above the ground level was designed to be an interlocking double row of stacked sandbags capable of withstanding a rocket attack.

Work was slow going in the hot summer weather; keeping hydrated was a necessity. We worked twelve hours a day taking time for lunch and dinner breaks and drinking lots of water.

The structure really started to take shape on the fifth day as we finished the exterior double-thickness-sandbag walls. The next day, we placed the eight-by-eight-inch-thick, twelve-foot-long beams in place. Next, we installed the discarded parking matting materials, which was then covered with plastic sheeting to protect the bunker contents. We made sure to slope the roof structure to provide drainage during the rainy season. At the end of the bunker facing the flight line, we put in wooden posts and a metal door for security; plus, we fashioned wooden steps to allow for access to the ammo bunker.

On top of the matting, as part of the final roof structure, was placed three interlocking layers of sand-and-concrete filled sandbags.

Our completed bunker was 20 feet by 10 feet with head clearance of 7 feet inside. Our four-man team completed the work in ten days including the movement of the 50,000 rounds of belted .50-caliber ammo, 75,000 rounds of belted 7.62 machine-gun ammunition into the storage bunker.

We finished the work on the tenth day. I borrowed a jeep and went to the officers' club and purchased two cases of cold beer for our team. We enjoyed a cold one or two while sitting inside the nice, cool ammunition bunker that we had just completed.

The next day, the commanding officer came down to our area looking for the ammunition pallets that had been sitting on the apron for the past twelve days. He was surprised to see our new bunker.

Looking at the bunker and then at me, the CO said, "Who built this bunker, and where is my ammunition that has been sitting on the apron for twelve days?"

"Sir, my team built this bunker since we had no other place to store our initial issue of ammunition that we brought with us," I responded after saluting him.

After showing the CO the inside of the bunker, then explaining to him how we constructed it in accordance with the current munition's storage manual, he smiled and said, "Lieutenant, tell your team they did an outstanding job at solving a problem no one had anticipated we would encounter." He then exited the bunker and headed back to his office.

Having completed our ammo bunker, I pitched in to work with my bunk mates to build a bunker outside our hooch in the officer's area for protection from incoming enemy rockets and mortar rounds.

A week later, my senior corporal came looking for me in the ready room saying there is a major and gunnery sergeant from the wing headquarters waiting in the logistics office who wants to look at our ammo bunker. Hearing this news, I got up and followed him out of the ready room heading for the logistics office.

The major and gunnery sergeant were talking to the logistics officer as the corporal and I entered. The logistics officer introduced me to the headquarters' two visitors. The major, after greeting us, said, "I understand you have constructed a temporary ammunition storage bunker here in your squadron area. We would like to see it, please."

I could tell from his body language and tone of voice that this was more than just a friendly fact-finding visit, this was the equivalent to a wing inspection of our new storage facility. Looking over at my corporal, I saw a look of concern on his face as well. Here we go, I thought, as I moved toward the door leading to the flight line.

The major and gunnery sergeant followed the corporal and me out to the flight line, then around the corner of the logistics office to where the entrance to the bunker was located. The gunnery sergeant almost ran into the back of the major who had stopped dead in his tracks looking at the bunker, which stretched out ahead of him. Looking at me, he asked, "You built this, Lieutenant?"

I replied, "No, sir. My team did. It was built in accordance with the wing and headquarters' orders and the munitions storage manual," which I pulled out of a storage box on the outside of the bunker's entrance.

The major looked at his gunnery sergeant, who nodded, and then he asked, "Can we have a look inside your bunker?"

"Yes, sir," was my response, almost like we might have planned it. My corporal moved to the steps with the key to the lock quickly unlocking and opening the door, then exited the entrance area.

Both the major, along with his gunnery sergeant, entered the bunker. We could hear them talking but not what they were saying to each other. They spent about fifteen minutes inspecting the bunker and the stored ammunition it contained. They both exited the bunker and said, "Thank you for allowing us to visit your newly constructed ammunition storage facility. Tell your team that they have done an outstanding job of following every part of the munition's storage manual in the design, construction, and storage of the ammunitions inside. It was a pleasure to see that your project was done right. Good job, Lieutenant. Now please direct the gunny and me to the CO's office so I can brief him on our snap inspection."

"Yes, sir, right this way," I said, responding to his statement, as I led him and the gunny back out onto the flight line, then told the major that the CO's office was in the last hooch in the line of seven, pointing toward the last hooch in the line. I then saluted as he headed down the flight line toward the CO's hooch.

After the major and gunnery sergeant's departure, the corporal said, "Well, Lieutenant, it looks like we passed the wing ordnance officer's inspection. That could be a first because scuttlebutt has it that he never passes any organization's ordnance operation on the first inspection."

I said, "Corporal, it was a team effort. Thank you for your fine work along with the other two Marines. We made it happen together."

*****

The main body of the squadron's arrival had created a series of major conflicts on who was in charge of what. We had in some cases two majors both thinking they were department heads of the same department. It took several days to sort out the job assignments. During the main body's five-day climatization period, the missions assigned to the squadron were all flown by Detachment A pilots with the exception of one.

Very soon thereafter and almost without exception, the field-grade officers and most company-grade officer pilots from Detachment A were reassigned to duties outside the squadron. Some were assigned to jobs with the ground Marine forces such as forward air controllers (FAC) or aviation liaison officers. In one case, a pilot from Detachment A was transferred to fly fixed-wing O-1C reconnaissance aircraft. Others were transferred to desk jobs at the wing or group headquarters.

In my opinion, these transfers created significant hard feelings and resentments between friends and comrades who were assigned to the former detachment with those of the main body of the squadron. It also deprived the new pilots, like myself, of the opportunity to learn from the combat veterans who had flown the first CH-53s in combat for the past six months.

One lesson learned from the detachment was that it was very advantageous to reduce nonessential items, such as all the centerline troop seats and sound proofing, which reduced the gross weight of the aircraft somewhat, making the loading and unloading of palletized cargo and vehicles much easier to accomplish.

The extremely hot temperatures and high humidity required additional power to lift the loads that the ground commanders so badly needed, so every ounce of nonessential stuff was removed from our newly arrived twenty-four aircraft the first couple of days in-country.

By June 1, 1967, the squadron was up and running combat missions throughout I Corps. We conducted resupply missions from Chu Lai in the south to the demilitarized zone (DMZ) in the north.

As new copilots, the eighteen other lieutenants and I were all competing for flight time and mission experience as the squadron began to see an increased utilization of the CH-53's superior capabilities. One major concern hampered the expansion of our aircraft's use in the more contentious combat environments.

This was the fear of losing one of these new costly helicopters to enemy action. The acquisition cost of a single CH-53A was 2.1 million dollars in 1966–1967 acquisition dollars.

The commanding general of the First MAW was very apprehensive about losing a CH-53 since he had been told it would devastate his career by the commander of the Fleet Marine Forces in Hawaii if his command lost one. This apprehension translated into low-risk missions for our squadron. Flights from one secure airfield or LZ to another secure one was the typical mission flown by our squadron for the first several months in-country.

The Marine ground commanders thought of the situation differently, holding back the CH-53 assets denied them the operational flexibility they sought. They could use a single CH-53 to move an entire platoon into an LZ in one load; whereas, it would take four or more CH-46As to move the same single platoon into the same LZ. The only drawback was that if the 53 was lost to enemy fire, then you would lose an entire platoon all at once; whereas, a 46 loss meant you would only lose about one fourth of one.

*****

On July 1, 1967, six other lieutenants from my flight school class and I, along with several other lieutenants in our squadron, were notified that we were all selected for promotion to captain in the United States Marine Corps Reserve.

This was a shock because all of us had only about six months' time in grade as first lieutenants. Promotions in peace time between first lieutenant and captain in the Marine Corps normally took five years in grade before becoming eligible for promotion. The actual promotion paperwork came along a couple of months later, based, I suspect, on our date of commissioning as second lieutenants. My promotion date was backdated to June 19, 1967, exactly six months from my promotion to first lieutenant. We were still learning how to be Marine Corps Company-Grade Officers at this point in time, but the attrition rate was so great that we were all promoted based on time in grade as first lieutenants. Flying combat missions and doing our ground jobs had taught us some of the leadership traits necessary to perform as company-grade officers, but we still had a long way to go to become "real captains" and not wet behind the ears first lieutenants. Time in grade was one thing, but a lot more experience was necessary for all of us to succeed as leaders.

At the time of my promotion ceremony to captain in the Marine Corps Reserve, I thought, *Maybe I should make this my career?*

Since I was a reserve officer, once my contract was completed, the Marine Corps did not have to retain my services. In order to avoid this situation, I could try to obtain a regular commission in the Marine Corps. I had recently seen a naval message from the Headquarters Marine Corps soliciting application for augmentation. *So why not apply?* I thought, *I have nothing to lose.*

So I submitted the paperwork up through the chain of command to apply for a regular commission in the United States Marine Corps. After I submitted the paperwork, I did not give it a second thought believing it was a long shot at best.

A week later, I got a message from the CO of our squadron office that said I was to report to the commanding general's (CG) office at Da Nang that day at 1500 hours. No reason was stated as to why I needed to see the CG. I borrowed a jeep, after putting on a clean set of utilities, and headed for the First Marine Aircraft Wing headquarters.

After passing through the security checkpoint outside the headquarters, I found a place to park the jeep and went into the building with the two-star flag on top of it. Arriving at the CG's office, I asked his aid, another captain, why I had been summoned to see the CG.

He smiled and said, "He wants to meet you since you're the only Marine reserve officer to apply for a regular commission in the corps in the entire First MAW." At that point, he got up from his desk and indicated I should follow him into the CG's office.

The general was seated behind his desk and looked up at me as I approached his desk.

Coming to attention, I said, "Sir, Captain Wemheuer reporting as ordered, sir."

He told me to stand at ease. He then said, "Captain, I have your application for a commission in the regular Marine Corps here on my desk, but before I endorse it, I wanted to meet you and find out why you want to obtain a regular commission."

Looking him straight in the eye, I explained. "I liked what I am doing, especially the flying, even in combat, so I am applying to stay in the Marine Corps after my reserve contract ended in a little less than three years. I want to continue to serve in the United States Marine Corps as an aviator" was my final answer to his question.

After I had finished, he said, "Captain, you are either the smartest or the dumbest officer I have ever met. Right now, I am not sure which category you fall into," while looking me straight in the eye for a few seconds, then smiling. "I will provide a positive forwarding endorsement on your request for augmentation. Thank you for coming by to see me today. Captain, you're dismissed."

Doing an about-face, I left his office, then departed the First MAW building in my borrowed jeep. I thought on the way back to Marble Mountain, as I returned the borrowed jeep, *I am not sure what he meant by smartest or dumbest officer to apply for augmentation. Maybe he thought it was smart because my chances were much better in being augmented since we were fighting a war, or maybe he thought I was dumb for applying during a war. I could not read his smiling face as to which one of the alternative reasons he favored. Well, at least, the general is going to give me a positive endorsement, so I may have a shot at making regular* was my concluding thought.

*****

We continued to get rocket attacks on our base mostly in the early morning hours on a regular basis as summer turned to fall. Our squadron supported, as the detachment before us had, our Marine brothers, the newly arrived South Korean Marines and the additional South Vietnamese soldiers who were fighting in the area south of Da Nang all the way to the DMZ.

As more South Vietnamese soldiers arrived in the area and with the addition of the Korean Marines down south of Da Nang, as I recall, the Marine ground units were then redeployed to the northern part of I Corps to conduct operations there. They were busy setting up and fortifying combat bases with additional airfields and artillery support bases at places like Phu Bai, Quang Tri, Dong Ha, Camp Carrol, the Rock Pile, Khe Sanh, and Con Thien.

As the Marines moved north, so did much of the helicopter support missions. One of these squadrons that move north was Marine Medium Helicopter Squadron 361 (HMM-361), a medium helicopter squadron flying the H-34 aircraft. It was moved to Dong Ha Combat Base airfield from Marble Mountain, so it was much closer to the action in northern I Corps. This enabled much faster helicopter support for the Marines in the northern part of I Corps.

Our heavy helicopter squadron was also tasked to support our brother Marines and the Naval Mobile Construction Battalion Number 4 as they started to build the McNamara Line along the DMZ.

On August 26, an NVA rocket attack was launched on the Dong Ha Combat Base airfield, hitting it with over 150 artillery and rockets. The attack destroyed two H-34 helicopters and damaged 24 others.

Since our squadron was the only Marine squadron who had aircraft capable of carrying a damaged H-34 externally, we were immediately tasked to retrieve the damaged helicopters from Dong Ha and transport them back to Da Nang for repair or transport back to a rework facility.

The aircraft recovery missions started the next day, and I was flying as copilot for Major Victor M. Lee that day. We were part of a two-plane mission to start to move some of the more severely damaged H-34s back to Da Nang.

Major Lee conducted our NATOPS and tactical aircraft recovery (TAR) mission briefings. After which, we received the intelligence briefing indicating that there was a high probability of continued artillery and rocket attacks focusing on Dong Ha airfield and their environ.

His mission plan was for both our aircraft to fly to Quang Tri and refuel before proceeding the ten miles to Dong Ha for the TAR mission. With the mission planning completed, we launched our aircraft individually, then proceeded to Dong Ha airfield.

Arriving at Dong Ha, we did not shut down our aircraft, which was the normal evolution for a TAR, but we sent our crew chiefs to inspect the aircraft we were going to pick up from the pickup area while we remained turned up and waited nearby. Once the crew chief was satisfied that the bird was ready for transport and had returned, we called the tower for takeoff clearance. After receiving takeoff clearance, Major Lee lifted our aircraft into a hover and moved over the H-34. The crew chief then extended the external pendant through the hell hole where the cargo hook was located for external lifting of cargo, guns, and aircraft. The "hell hole" is located in the middle of the cabin directly under the main transmission.

At this point, I advanced the speed-control levers to the full forward position giving the major command of all the power the engines could put out.

A ground crew member from HMM-361 was in position on top of the H-34 to hook up the external pendant to the aircraft recovery kit, which had been installed earlier along with a drogue parachute. Once the crewman cleared the aircraft, the major made sure he was turned into the prevailing wind as he picked up tension on the pendant until we could feel the H-34 lift into the air.

The major continued to lift the stricken bird off the ground smoothly, coming to a stable hover when his load was at about twenty feet above the ground. He then moved the cyclic forward, the directional control input to the aircraft, moving our aircraft with our load into forward flight. The H-34 streamlined under us was making it possible to fly at between 70 to 90 knots airspeed. We climbed out from Dong Ha to the southeast heading for the South China Sea; I observed our wingman's aircraft getting ready to pick up the next H-34 aircraft TAR.

Coordination and communications between our two aircraft were made by using the FM radio tuned to our squadron's common frequency.

As we reached an altitude of about three thousand feet, I adjusted the speed-control levers as we cruised along at about seventy-five knots indicated airspeed.

Looking down at the engine instruments to make sure everything was within normal parameters; I noticed that the fuel-flow gauges were reading higher than we had planned to burn. It appeared that we were using a lot more fuel than anticipated and our airspeed was not as fast as it should be. Major Lee and I talked about our airspeed restriction, and he concluded that the drogue parachute, while stabilizing the load was slowing us down causing us to use a lot more fuel. After our discussion, I checked the fuel quantities, I did a quick calculation of the fuel required based on our present burn rate necessary to get us to Marble Mountain.

It became very apparent that because of our limitation on our airspeed caused by the drogue parachute, we would not have sufficient fuel to make it directly to Marble Mountain safely.

We would either need to refuel someplace en route or increase our speed significantly, which we could not with the drogue parachute attached. The only way to stretch the fuel and make it to Marble Mountain was to get rid of the drag of the drogue parachute. It was not a good idea when flying over bad guys' territory.

Informing Major Lee of my fuel calculations, he made some quick mental calculations of his own and decided to divert to Phu Bai airfield, get additional fuel, and drop the drogue parachute.

Major Lee called our wingman, telling him he was diverting to Phu Bai for gas and to drop the drogue parachute. He recommended to his wingman that they not use the drogue parachute for their TAR lift since we had experienced airspeed problems with it. He also reiterated to the wingman to be careful and to not push the safety envelop trying to get the load to Marble Mountain. His wingman responded that he understood and would not use the drogue parachute.

We now turned inland, and I was asked to call for save-o-plane clearance and then alert the Phu Bai airfield tower of our intention to divert to their airfield for fuel. I also asked where we could set down our external H-34 load upon arrival. I completed both these tasks while the major flew the aircraft.

At this point in time, I saw in the distance the Phu Bai airfield; we had been given instructions on where to set the H-34 down on the taxiway at the end of the single runway when we arrived.

The only major problem we faced was that the H-34 we were carrying would have to be set down on the taxiway, then picked up again after we refueled. Without a ground crewman to hook us up, we would have to get some help from Marines at Phu Bai to hook us up again. While Major Lee and I discussed the situation, the crew chief jumped into the discussion with a potential solution.

The crew chief, a sergeant (I don't remember his name because he was a member of Detachment A), said, "Major, no problem in picking up the 34 again. I will position our external pendant on top of the 34's rotor system beanie cover after we land, then remove the drogue parachute. Then after we refuel, if you can hold a steady hover over the load and let down slowly, I can reach down and grab the end of the external pendant, then attach it to the cargo hook. Then we will be good to go. We can do it, sir. I have done it a couple times before."

Major Lee thought a few seconds about what the crew chief had said and then responded, "Are you sure you have done this before, Sergeant?"

"Yes, sir," the sergeant responded. "I have done this type of pickup a couple of times when we recovered 34s from the field after they experienced mechanical problems. That was before you people from the main squadron arrived."

I could tell by the tone and selection of his words that our sergeant crew chief did not have much respect for the folks in the main body of the squadron. I understood his feelings since almost all the pilots they worked with had been transferred shortly after the main body of our unit arrived thereby destroying the unit unity that they had established over the six months in-country.

Major Lee finally responded, "Sergeant, if you say you can do it, then we will give it a try."

We approached the taxiway where we were directed to set the bird down. Major Lee made a straight-in approach to the taxiway into the wind and set the bird down gently on the taxiway. We then landed a couple of hundred feet away from it.

Our sergeant crew chief exited the aircraft with the external pendant and a couple of short pieces of wood, which he placed under one of the wheels of the H-34 to keep it from rolling when we were picking it up after we refueled. He also removed the drogue parachute and hooked the aircraft recovery kit again to the external pendant, then positioned it on top of the beanie of the H-34.

After the sergeant returned to the aircraft, Major Lee taxied the aircraft toward the refueling pits. He asked me to recalculate the takeoff and lifting parameters we needed to know to determine if we could safely lift the H-34 with a full fuel load and hotter temperatures. Checking the NATOPS manual, I calculated the power available and power required, then showed my calculations to Major Lee. My calculations indicated that, yes, we could lift the H-34 safely with a full fuel load.

Completing the refueling process, we taxied for takeoff. Major Lee lifted the bird into a hover after getting takeoff clearance from the tower. He then air-taxied to a position about twenty feet above the H-34 with the precise directions provided by the crew chief. Once in a stable hover directly over the beanie of the H-34, the crew chief directed him down slowly over the bird until he could reach through the hell hole and grab the external pendant.

The sergeant then slip the pendant on the external cargo hook and directed the major to start to raise his hover until tension was taken up on the lifting sling and external pendant. Major Lee again checked the prevailing wind and slowly raised the H-34 into a twenty-foot-above-the-ground hover, after I had pushed the speed-control levers again full forward to give the major full power.

The transition to forward flight was made by the major without difficulty. Once in stable forward flight, we headed east, again toward the South China Sea. Our airspeed was now holding between ninety-five and one hundred knots as we climbed with our load to three thousand feet to avoid small-arms fire and getting save-o-plane clearance as we exited the Phu Bai control zone, crossed the coast, and headed for Da Nang.

This was the first time I had seen how close coordination between a pilot and his crew chief could be made in order to perform a difficult and delicate maneuver with a twenty-three-thousand-pound aircraft like the CH-53. It was the first time I had witnessed it, but it was surely not going to be my last.

Major Lee asked me as we made the turn toward the south, now over the water if I would like to fly the bird.

"Yes, sir," was my response.

His next statement was "You have the aircraft, Captain. Don't fuck it up and drop our H-34."

Moving my hand to the cyclic for the first time that day, I found that the aircraft was all trimmed up, balanced, and required only minor movements to keep us on altitude and airspeed with the H-34 suspended beneath us.

This was the first time I had flown with another aircraft attached to mine, so I was a little nervous.

While I was flying the aircraft, Major Lee checked on the status of our wingman, using the FM radio. Listening to the radio transmissions, I learned that our wingman, after receiving the call from the major and not using the drogue parachute was able to maintain an airspeed of one hundred knots and was able to fly directly to Da Nang, drop off the bird, and get to Marble Mountain without having to refuel as we did.

We also found out the destination for the H-34 drop had been changed to a staging area at the Da Nang Harbor to facilitate the loading of the birds on ship transportation to the repair facility. As we rounded the Hai Van Pass, I anticipated Major Lee would take control of the aircraft back, as if he had anticipated the question I was about to ask, he keyed the ICS and asked, "Would you like to make the approach and set the H-34 down at the staging area? I will make all the radio calls, and you fly the bird."

"Yes, sir," was my enthusiastic response to his question.

We continued across Da Nang Bay after descending to five hundred feet altitude in order to stay under the approach corridor at Da Nang airfield. I saw the outline for the harbor containing several large cargo ships. The pad we were to drop the bird on was the same one we used to off-load the heavy equipment from the USS *Tripoli* when we had arrived in Vietnam several months earlier.

Major Lee had obtained all our clearances so we could head directly to the pad for the drop-off of the H-34 where a ground crew would secure the aircraft after we set it down. Since we had burned down half our fuel load, I knew we would have enough power to safely set the bird down on the pad. Planning my approach to the pad so that I would end up turned into the prevailing wind, I asked Major Lee to perform the landing checklist while we were about a half mile from the pad.

He completed the checklist and then advanced the speed-control levers full forward as I had done during his pickups and landings. As I turned the aircraft on the final approach into the wind, the crew chief gave me detailed instructions on how high the H-34 was off the ground as we approached the pad. As we crossed the edge of the pad, his instructions were designed to get the aircraft in a stable hover before instructing me to slowly lower the H-34 to the ground from the twenty-five-foot hover I was maintaining.

Once the bird was on the ground, the ground crew chocked it, and we moved away from the bird and landed in order to retrieve our external pendant. Once the crew chief was back with the pendant, Major Lee got the clearance for us to depart the pad for Marble Mountain to refuel.

To my surprise, I was still in control of the aircraft. Making the most of my stick time, I took off from the pad heading east away from the pad. I did this so I would not overfly any of the ships or buildings that could have potentially been damaged with our rotor wash, then headed out over the sea, and then turned south to enter the landing pattern at Marble Mountain Air Facility. While en route to Marble Mountain, Major Lee talked again to his wingman who was now halfway back to Dong Ha to pick up another H-34.

We landed on Marble Mountain's main and only runway and taxied to the refueling pits. Sitting in the pits, Major Lee went over my handling of the aircraft while we were carrying the H-34. He pointed out several things that I could do differently next time I had the opportunity to do a TAR. His critique was in the form of suggestions rather than snide comments containing no real training value. He said I had work to do before becoming an aircraft commander, but I was well on my way to becoming one.

His positive comments and suggestions bolstered my self-esteem greatly. I knew I had a long way to go, but I knew I would get there.

The remainder of the mission went well with us not having to stop to refuel after picking up our second H-34 without a drogue parachute. Our flight of two CH-53s moved four of the twenty-eight damaged H-34s out of the Dong Ha airfield to Da Nang that day. This mission for our squadron would continue for the next several days, moving the damage H-34s out of Dong Ha to Da Nang.

On September 3, NVA rockets hit the ammunition dump and fuel storage facility at Dong Ha causing a huge explosion.

If my memory serves me right, I was in the refueling pits at Quang Tri when the NVA artillery and rocket fire hit Dong Ha scoring a direct hit on the fuel farm and ammo dump, which exploded in a giant ball of flames, and shrapnel was flying everywhere. When the smoke had cleared and the fires put out, most of the remaining H-34s of HMM-361 were no more. Most of them lay in heaps of burned, smoking wreckage, or they were so badly damaged that they would not fly again. After the attack on September 3, the mission continued until all the salvageable H-34s had been removed from Dong Ha by our squadron.

*****

The TAR mission had showed the generals that the CH-53 was a true asset to the war effort, not something to be used only for non-hazardous missions, so they started to loosen the reins on our combat participation.

By late September 1967, our squadron of CH-53s were not only moving artillery and ammunition in support of major ground operations but were finally engaged in moving troops to the LZs after the first wave of CH-46s carried the troops necessary to secure the LZ. It appeared to me that the CH-53 was finally being utilized properly.

We were there to support the needs of the ground commanders, and we were finally in the game.

As the squadron's operational tempo increased, I had more of an opportunity to fly since I was one of the nineteen copilots all competing for flight time so we could qualify to become aircraft commanders. After flying with a number of aircraft commanders in the squadron like Major Lee, a good one, and evaluating which ones were good and which ones were not so good, I developed a strategy to maximize the potential flight time and experience outside of the normal rotation of copilots on the flight schedule.

The centerpiece of my flight-time strategy was Major George Ebbitt Jr. Having flown with the major a couple of times, I realized he really did not like to fly much. This gave me the opportunity to have a lot of what aviators call stick time.

A lot of copilots did not like to fly with the major and would look for someone to substitute for them if they were scheduled to fly with him. Since I was always looking for the opportunity to fly, I took advantage of these situations whenever one arose. In addition, my strategy included convincing the scheduling officer that volunteering to fill in should not interfere with my normal spot in the rotation on the flight schedule, which I accomplished. I took advantage of this strategy whenever possible.

Returning from one of the flights where I had volunteered to take the copilot's position flying with Major Ebbitt, I was in the ready room filling out the mission debrief, after-action, and statistic summations report forms. While I worked, I overheard two newly promoted captain copilots talking about their experience after just completing an all-day two aircraft resupply mission while they filled out the end-of-the flight paperwork.

One captain said to the other, "I flew with Cinnamon Bear today, and boy, am I glad the flight is over. I am going to see to it that I am not scheduled with him again," the captain said as they worked to fill out their after-action report.

The second captain said, "That's a strong statement. What happened?"

"Let me tell you," said the first captain. "We were on our second lift into the LZ near Hoa An, and I smelled shit. At first, I could not identify where the smell was coming from, but boy oh boy, was it strong. Initially I thought it might be from the burning of the shitters that had been constructed not far from the LZ, but the odor persisted after we departed the zone. We completed two more trips from Hill 55 to the LZ before returning back to Marble Mountain to refuel. By this point in time, I had figured out that the Cinnamon Bear had shit in his flight suit. As we were refueling, I asked the major if he needed to make a head run, indicating we were ahead of schedule, and could afford the time. He looked at me and said, 'Captain, no, I am fine. We will continue our mission.' What could I say to him? I am just a captain."

The second captain went on to say, "You could have said to him, 'Hey, Major, you shit in your flight suit.'"

The first captain, ignoring his comment, continued. "So we continued the flight flying another six hours. I also noticed that the crew chief stayed away from the jump-seat area the entire remainder of the mission. I wonder why," he said, lifting his eyes to indicate a satirical intent to his last statement.

I could tell this story would be out for public dissemination among the officer population very soon.

That night at the officers' club, which was a thatched roofed hooch affair located on the beach near our living quarters, the two captains and their associates arrived, then proceeded to consume way too many beers and shots for their own good. At that point, the captain who had flown with the Cinnamon Bear earlier that day climbed on top of one of the tables and shouted, "Gentlemen, may I please have your attention. I have a question to ask you."

When the club grew quiet. The captain shouted out the question, "Tell me please. Where does the Bear shit?"

The other captains who had gathered together with him, who knew the story, responded in unison shouting, "The Bear shits in the woods."

"No," the first captain responded in a very loud voice and continuing to yell, "the Bear shits in the cockpit of a 53, then sits in it for hours." Then all the drunk captains laughed and hooped it up.

Everyone else in the club remained quiet but continued to look at the captain still standing on the table. After a couple of seconds, he said, just before climbing off the table, "Well, that's what he did, honest."

One of the field-grade officers in our squadron stood up and headed toward the table where all the offending captains were now gathered. He proceeded to escort the captain and his associates immediately out of the club.

Everyone in the club knew who the "Bear" was, and several officers snickered at what they had heard the captain say, and most of the remaining officers went back to talking and drinking.

Interestingly enough, about two weeks later, the Cinnamon Bear was transferred to a wing headquarters' job over in Da Nang and did not, as far as I can remember, fly with HMH-463 as long as I was in-country.

*****

In mid-October, there was a call for volunteers to go to jungle survival school in the Philippines for a week's training. Four of us newly promoted captains volunteered to go. The school was conducted at the Naval Air Station Cubi Point in the Philippines.

We attended classes for three days on base then were turned loose under supervision of a native Filipino to live for three days in the jungle environment outside the base in the jungle. We lived off the plants and animals we found in the jungle, with lots of unusual plants to eat, plus a big snake, some slugs, and the crowning item of gourmet survival food was monkey on a stick.

Once we completed the survival training, we had one night free before returning to Vietnam. All of us went on liberty in town. *Liberty* is a military term for "time off from duty, normally off the base." We all headed to Olongapo, after leaving the base. We walked across a river, which had a very bad, bad smell to it. The local sailors called it shit river because of the visible feces and other bodily waste you could see floating in and on it.

Once past the river, the town of Olongapo lay ahead of us to explore. Our little group walking the length of the main street about twenty blocks was under constant assault. We were constantly pestered to join the bar ladies and to come into their bar and buy them a drink.

Returning the way we came; we finally found a small combination restaurant and bar without the bar girls swarming out front. After entering, the bartender introduced us to the local San Miguel beer and suggested we try some native treats.

I hoped that the beer he was offering was not brewed from the same water as the river we had crossed to get here.

After sampling a couple of his recommended beers, we were introduced to a native custom of eating *balut*, a chicken or duck egg that is almost ready to hatch that is then punctured and put into the ground to age. It is ready to eat in about three weeks. We all tried one and found them to be better-tasting than the slugs we had eaten during training. A good time was had by all on liberty in Olongapo as we walked back across the shit river bridge to the base.

*****

Returning to Vietnam, we started flying a lot more often. I was also able to fly some extra flights because no one else wanted to fly with Major Ebbitt. One operation I remember clearly was a massive Marine assault of a suspected Viet Cong staging and supply center in the Hoa An Valley.

The mission entailed moving a battalion of South Vietnamese soldiers from Hill 55 south of Da Nang to an area in the western part of the Hoa An Valley. Intelligence reports indicated that there was a battalion-sized concentration of Viet Cong, and for the first time, the potential for North Vietnamese Army (NVA) soldiers to be located in the western part of the valley.

The LZ where we were to drop the soldiers was between the Yen River and the town of Hoa Khuong located in a series of dry rice paddies. The mission brief was held at the medium-helicopter squadron's ready room since they would be leading the flight. The flight consisted of twelve CH-46s, four CH-53s, four UH-1 Huey gunships, and one UH-1 medevac bird.

Each CH-46 would hold six soldiers for a total of seventy-two men in the initial landing. Our four CH-53s would be carrying thirty-five soldiers each and would follow the first wave into the LZ. The UH-1 gunships would be used to suppress any fire coming from the area surrounding the LZ. The initial insertion would be completed in one lift using the sixteen aircraft.

Major Ebbitt was on the schedule to lead the second section of our four CH-53s, so I got to fly on this mission since I volunteered to fly with him. Since I had been flying with Major Ebbitt on more than ten missions, he moved me to the pilot seat on the right side of the bird from the copilot seat on the left side. His explanation was that he was preparing me to become an aircraft commander someday, and I should get used to flying in the right seat.

I could tell by his body language and tone of voice that this move was another way of saying, 'I really don't want to fly.'

This was the first time, that I knew of, that a joint mission was planned and executed using both H-46s and H-53s aircraft in a coordinated insertion, supported by H-1 gunships and fixed-wing aircraft as well.

The mission went off without a shot being fired by the gunships or the soldiers after their insertion into the LZ. This was attributed to the heavy pre-insertion LZ preparation attacks by two A-6 attack aircraft. They used napalm and high-explosive ordnance to clear any potential resistance from the LZ and surrounding areas. The South Vietnamese soldiers did discover several bodies in the area just outside the LZ, two of them were confirmed to be NVA soldiers.

Two things struck me about the mission. One was that the NVA had now moved further south than we had previously thought and that the CH-46A model was in the same league as the H-34 in the number of troops it could carry. It was supposed to be much better than the H-34, but in my opinion, in this high-temperature environment, it did not measure up.

*****

Our squadron continued to supply support all over I Corps to our ground Marine brothers, the South Vietnamese Army, and other allied forces from Korea, Australia, and New Zealand.

Our work supporting the construction of the McNamara line on the DMZ was almost a daily event during July through November 1967. We also supported construction of the Khe Sanh and Quang Tri combat bases along with the expansion of the airfield at Phu Bai. All the squadron copilots got as much flight time as they could handle. It was not long before that about eight of the nineteen copilots were found to have sufficient skill and had accumulated enough flight time to be considered ready to become helicopter aircraft commanders, or HAC.

The final hurdle in the process of becoming an aircraft commander was passing a HAC check. My HAC check was schedule with Major Vic Lee, who I had flown with a number of times and who I respected as a good aviator. My HAC check was going to be done in conjunction with a scheduled mission on the southern edge of the DMZ. I knew this because I arrived very early to plan the flight and to look over the mission documents called FRAGS before our briefing. The FRAG indicated we would be moving supplies and equipment from Dong Ha logistic support area to areas on the DMZ.

Thinking, *This is your chance to become a HAC. Don't blow it.* Then I remembered the advice I had gotten after my experience in flight school, "Concentrate on the mission, and the rest will take care of itself." *Mission, mission, mission. Focus on the mission,* I repeated in my head.

Major Lee and I met in the ready room for the mission briefing a few minutes before the operations duty officer's (ODO) weather and mission briefing.

Major Lee explained that I should look at this flight as just another mission that I was going to be responsible for completing. He then told me how he wanted to handle the HAC check; he was going to act as my copilot for the entire flight unless I put the aircraft and its crew in a dangerous situation. Then and only then would he take over the control of the bird. He went on to say, "This is not a training mission. It's a mission whereby I can determine if you have the headwork and physical dexterity to be a helicopter aircraft commander who have the lives of his crew and passengers in his hands."

The ODO briefing covered the intelligence situation, the weather, known arc light (B-52 mass bombing), naval gunfire and artillery-fire mission locations. It also included the general mission profile or FRAG for that day's mission.

I took notes, along with Major Lee, who I had asked my copilot to also do.

With the ODO briefing completed, I went through the standard NATOPS briefing with Major Lee. We manned our aircraft after reviewing the yellow sheet book for uncorrected discrepancies on our assigned aircraft, then Major Lee signed the yellow sheet taking responsibility for the bird.

After we preflighted the aircraft, I briefed our enlisted crew on hostile-fire discipline, emergency procedures, and what we expected to be doing on that day's mission.

Climbing aboard, we entered the cockpit where I took the right seat for my HAC check. The APP start, cockpit checks, engines start, and rotor engagement were all normal. Calling for taxi and then takeoff, I made a departure from Marble Mountain north, then obtained clearance from Da Nang tower to pass under their approach corridor heading toward Hai Van Pass. The weather that day was great. Hot but no rain was forecast since that was the dry season in South Vietnam.

I asked Major Lee to call and check for any save-o-planes for our route of flight. The USS *New Jersey*, a battleship, was currently operating in the waters off South Vietnam, so even over the South China Sea, you needed to be concerned with friendly fire. He called and found none that would affect our flight north.

Staying over the water until about 20 miles from Quang Tri, I turned inland and dropped to 50 feet altitude and increased our speed to about 170 knots, about 200 miles per hour. We had found that this tactic was very effective in reducing the incidents of ground fire from Viet Cong because the noise generated by our aircraft was not heard by someone on the ground until we were almost past their position. By the time they could raise their AK-47 to fire, we were out of range for the most part.

As we approached the control zone for Quang Tri airfield, I called and asked if the fuel pits at Dong Ha were operational again. The tower operator said they had just been put back in service and that they were operational. Hearing this news, I told him we would be transitioning his control zone to the west and then diverting to Dong Ha to refuel and thanked him for his assistance.

Landing at Dong Ha, we refueled the aircraft and then headed for the pickup zone, the Dong Ha Logistic Supply Area (LSA).

That day's mission, as briefed by radio from the LSA liaison NCOIC was going to entail the movement of construction supplies from the Dong Ha LSA to various locations along the south side of the DMZ in front and east of Con Thien. Landing at the LSA, the gunny handed the crew chief a list of the loads we were to move that day as well as the grid coordinates where we were to place each load of lumber that we were going to be carrying. He also told the crew chief that each location would be marked with orange panels to mark the drop locations.

Our job that day was going to be moving large wooden square poles externally. They were very large, eighteen-by-eighteen inches and twenty-eight feet in length each. They would be placed in bundles of sixteen per load. We would have seven loads to deliver. Each load was about eight thousand pounds and was held by cargo slings that were wrapped round two sections of the bundled load and then hooked to a single lifting ring.

Earlier this year, the Marine engineers had been tasked to bulldoze a strip of land from Gio Linh near the coast to Con Thien. The ground Marines referred to it as the Trace or Strip.

The Strip was five hundred meters wide constructed on the south side of the DMZ as part of the McNamara Line construction efforts. The southern edge of the DMZ was about twelve miles from Dong Ha as the crow flies. Because of Viet Cong and NVA snipers and machine gun, mobile crews had infiltrated the area between the airfield and the DMZ; direct flights were not safe from enemy fire.

In performing our mission that day, because we were hauling generally unstable loads externally, our airspeed would have to remain slow as we hauled the lumber. This created an ideal target for enemy small-arms fire. Consequently, we would have to fly over ground that was presently controlled by the Marine and South Vietnamese Army troops. These areas were generally located along and close to major highways. We needed to follow major roadways in order to avoid enemy ground fire.

This meant that we would have to fly parallel to the DMZ following Highway 9 west, which went first to Cam Lo then to Camp Carrol, then turn right, and pick up Highway 561. From that location, we would then fly along Route 660 until we reached Con Thien and then down the strip south of the DMZ where our drop-off points were located in the middle of the five-hundred-meter-wide strip that had been bulldozed south of the DMZ. This was the long way around, but it was safer than trying to go direct.

Concentrating on the mission, I asked Major Lee to locate our first drop position on the map we had of the "Trace" and plot our flight path from Con Thien to its location.

While he was looking at the map, I did some calculations as to our ability to fly with the eight-thousand-pound load that day. Finding we had sufficient power available to do our lifts, I asked the crew chief if he was ready for the external operations we were about to commence. He indicated he was ready.

So I lifted the bird into a hover, checked the engines, hydraulics, and other flight instruments, then asked Major Lee to monitor the speed-control levers as I moved over the first load. Once over the load, the crew chief verbally guided me to a position where a soldier was waiting to hook up our load. The soldier reached up and caught the external pendant and attached it to a lifting ring holding the two sets of slings together. While hovering in the LSA, we generated the normal large cloud of dust, which reduced visibility significantly. Once the load was hooked up, I turned the aircraft into the prevailing wind as the crew chief continued to guide me as we lifted the load off the ground. I again checked the flight instruments and transitioned to forward flight trying to escape from the inside the dust cloud we had generated.

The relative wind helped blow the dust behind us, so I did not lose my visual horizon as we exited the dust cloud and started to climb. The load flew like a barn door. I could not get it to streamline with the aircraft. At best, I could get forty knots airspeed as we climbed to three thousand feet heading west along Highway 9. Flying about five miles west, we found Highway 561, and it turned out to be a partially paved road for the most part. We then turned north toward Con Thien, finding what they called Highway 660, which was more like a jeep trail than a highway, which was hard to follow. We went about two miles following the jeep trail and then saw the Strip or Trace off to our right. Turning right toward the Trace, we spotted the orange panels, which was the first location for our cargo drop.

Major Lee verified the orange panels were located at the grid coordinates shown on the list that we had been given at the LSA.

I would come to find out, making a right-hand spiral approach from three thousand feet and forty knots to the LZ where the orange panels were located was not a prudent move. As we spiraled down to the panels, I could see artillery rounds from the NVA starting to explode north of the LZ. Making my final approach to the area of the panels, I instructed the crew chief to disconnect the load using the release cable that would open the pendant's cargo hook at the loads' lifting ring, thereby not requiring us to land to retrieve the pendant. Major Lee pushed the speed-control levers full forward as I flared the bird, stopping our forward airspeed, then lowering the load to the ground. The crew chief pulled the lanyard on the cargo hook, then told me we were cleared to depart as he struggled to pull the pendant inside the aircraft.

Making a hard right-hand turn away from the LZ, I tried to avoid the area where the incoming artillery rounds had started to impact on the northern side of the Trace. Moving the aircraft along the Trace at low level, I quickly headed back the way I had come, stayed low to the ground for about two miles, then rapidly climbed back to three thousand feet. From that point, I continued to retrace my original route of flight heading back to the LSA.

En route back, I asked Major Lee if he thought we should use the same route of flight and altitudes for our next evolution. He said that if it were up to him, he would change things based on what we had experienced on our first load. Major Lee indicated that our height during the last part of our flight and approach more than likely was seen by the NVA spotters inside the DMZ and that was why we were getting incoming artillery fire in the zone. He suggested that on our next evolution, we should drop down to low level just before we hit Highway 660 in order to mask our final destination from the NVA spotters thereby reducing the potential of artillery fire with our next load.

On our next trip, I used the recommendation he had given me, and we made a successful drop of our second load with no incoming artillery fire being received. Then we had to refuel at Dong Ha airfield before commencing our third load. On our third and fourth loads, we placed about a quarter of a mile further down the Trace from each other each time, using the same tactics, and the drops were made without any problems.

We refueled again and then started the fifth and then sixth sortie, which were again made generally without incident. However, on the sixth sortie, we had received some small-arms fire as we proceeded down Highway 660 at low level. This fire was not returned because the area was supposed to be occupied by friendlies. The drops on the Trace were made without incoming enemy artillery fire. Each load was deposited another quarter of a mile further down the Trace from the previous one.

Needing fuel again, we refueled at Dong Ha airfield, then returned to the LSA for the last pickup. Hooking onto the load, we departed following the same route as the previous six loads.

We had just made the turn and flown about two miles north, along Highway 561, and just as we started our descent from three thousand feet just before reaching Highway 660 on our final trip to the Trace, I felt a big jump in the flight controls with the aircraft shooting upward about twenty feet.

At first, I thought our aircraft had been hit by something, then I realized we had lost our load. The crew chief came up on the ICS and also indicated that we lost our load. Rolling right so I could see the fall of our load, I watched as the huge pieces of lumber fell toward the ground.

They looked like match sticks, I thought. *Hope they don't hit anything.*

As the lumber got closer to the ground, I saw that there were several huts all in a row on one side of the road. It appeared that these huts could be hit by the falling lumber. Sure enough, as I watched, several pieces of the lumber hit the two huts built closest to the road. A couple of seconds later, three large explosions came from the area where the two huts had been located. All I could see was the big cloud of smoke and dust coming from their location. By this time, the crew chief had retrieved our external pendant, which to his surprise, had the lifting ring and several feet of sling materials still attached to it. He informed both Major Lee and I of the recovery of the items and went on to say that it looked like the sling material had been rotten and the sling itself had failed.

At this point, we were still orbiting the area where we lost the load when two more explosions rocked our bird. These were much bigger than the first three that occurred right after the initial impact of the lumber on the huts. Since this was going to be our last load of lumber for that day's mission, we headed back to the LSA.

Major Lee, at my request, made a call to the LSA to let them know that the last load was not delivered, and we would be returning to the LSA to show them the cause of the loss. He also called the mission control center to let them know about the incident.

After landing at the LSA, we were met by the same gunny NCOIC who had provided the listing of drop sights. He came aboard the helicopter and looked at the external pendant with the lifting ring and sling material still attached to it. He shook his head in disgust and asked the crew chief if he could take the lifting ring and sling materials with him. Since I had a polaroid camera in my helmet bag, I told the crew chief to find it, then to take half a dozen pictures of the ring and sling before we gave the lifting ring and sling materials to him. The crew chief took half a dozen pictures of the lifting ring and sling materials, focusing on the failed sling material before he released the items to the gunny.

The gunny departed our bird with the lifting ring and broken sling pieces. Once he was safely clear of the bird, we left the LSA heading to Dong Ha to refuel.

I asked Major Lee to checked in with the mission control center to see if they had any more work for us that day. Their response was that all the fifty-three missions for that day had been completed except for the last lift of lumber to the Trace, but an additional replacement load would not be ready until tomorrow at the earliest. So there was no more work for us that day. We were cleared to return to base (RTB).

As we headed for Marble Mountain on our way home, Major Lee said he would take control of the aircraft for the first time today.

I thought, *Well, what did I do to mess it up?*

Looking over at the major, he smiled and said, "You can relax now, Captain. I will take us home now. You did an excellent job today. I am going to recommend you be designated an aircraft commander. Don't let the dropped load get to you. It appears the loss was beyond our control. It's an LSA problem when they use rotten slings. Now let's go over what you could have done differently to make the mission go smoother and more efficiently."

Arriving back at Marble Mountain, we completed the postflight inspections and wrote up the yellow sheet discrepancies. Back in the ready room, we completed the mission paperwork including the write-up of the circumstance of the lost load of lumber. Major Lee then headed to the operations officer's office to complete the HAC check paperwork.

We would meet later at the O club to have a drink to celebrate my successful HAC check, along with the other copilots who had successfully completed their checks.

A wild celebration was held; shots of tequila, Jack Daniels, and Royal Crown were all included as part of the festivities. We all drank way too much and suffered for it the next day.

*****

Now that I was designated a HAC, I wanted to fly as one. The trouble came when our new commanding officer—we had just gotten a new one—was still not comfortable with new captain aviators on their first tours in combat being responsible for the safety of one of his aircraft. He had decided we were not quite ready to go by ourselves yet. His solution was to have us fly at least five missions with another new HAC before being turned loose with a designated copilot in the left seat. This did not sit well with the new HACs who all were chomping at the bit to get out there and win the war. For the next several weeks, the new HACs flew with other new HACs.

One evening, we received word that one of our aircraft was overdue from a flight returning from northern I Corps. The weather at the time was overcast and rainy. This was one of the HAC-to-HAC flights we were undergoing. The bird had picked up medevacs and filed an instrument flight plan (IFR) for their return to Da Nang.

The two HACs flying the bird were classmates of mine, and one had been my roommate throughout flight school.

Captain Lucien "Lou" Tessier had been my roommate for almost eighteen months, and Captain Bill Deetz was married and was also part of our flight school class that graduated in December 1966 as well.

At first, I had a problem accepting that these two men I knew very well could be dead. My thought was they crashed someplace and were escaping and evading. *They will be found soon*, I thought.

The squadron assisted in the search-and-rescue efforts for the next two weeks, finding nothing. The bird not only had my two friends on it but two of our gunners and a crew chief from our squadron, plus ten medevac'd cases and corpsman to attend them, all being transported to Da Nang for treatment. The air search continued for another week with no results. Ground searches also found nothing but were to continue for several months with negative results.

However, as time passed with no distress signals or other sighting or no evidence of any wreckage, it became more and more apparent that they were not missing but really gone forever. Some extra booze helped make the bad feeling go away for a while after returning from the memorial service, which was held at the base chapel for the pilots, crew, and passengers three weeks after their loss.

Flying my next mission, I had to work hard to push the bad feelings away and concentrate on the mission at the expense of all other thoughts. The training and self-discipline helped dull the pain of the loss of good friends and comrades.

Speculation as to the potential cause of the loss of the aircraft was centered around a report from a CH-46 helicopter flying the same night we lost our bird. It had been flying VFR below the clouds trying to get back to Da Nang at low level. While en route back, they picked up what they thought was the Da Nang TACAN station. It turned out to be providing false location and distance information. Because they could see the lights of the city of Da Nang reflecting off the water and clouds, plus what they could see of the coastline, they disregarded the TACAN station's reading and returned VFR to Da Nang under the clouds without difficulty.

Intelligence reports earlier indicated the Viet Cong and the NVA had the capability to set up false navigation aids. It was their intent to lure with the false signals an aircraft or helicopter flying in the clouds on instruments to lure or draw them off course so they would fly into a mountain or get hopelessly lost and run out of fuel, instead of arriving at the airport. Since no one could find the lost aircraft wreckage, this theory remained only speculation. It was my impression at the time watching the other new HACs in the squadron that a little of the I-am-invincible attitude was gone after the realization of what happened sunk in.

*****

Author's note—the wreckage of this helicopter was found eight months after I left country, as I recall. It had flown at a high rate of speed into the side of the mountain above Hai Van Pass. It appeared that the speculation of the aircraft being drawn off course by a false enemy beacon signal was no longer a speculation.

It took so long to find the wreckage because the front part of the aircraft was embedded into the side of the mountain, which was covered with very thick jungle making the wreckage almost impossible to see, even from the ground, until you were almost on top of it. It was discovered at the autopsy of the crew and passengers that all on board had not survived the initial impact of the crash, fortunately.

*****

Morale in the squadron was low at this point, having presumably lost our first CH-53 crew in combat. It was now late December, and the XO posted a bulletin on the board asking who might be interested in going to Australia on rest and relaxation (R and R) for five days. Seven of us signed up for the trip, which left from Da Nang airport a couple of days later.

Everyone had a good time in Australia during the five days we were there. One story comes to mind about our trip to the big country down under.

*****

We had been airborne in our civilian R and R bird for almost twelve hours in an aircraft that was packed full of Marines, Army, Air Force, and a few Navy personnel who had just left a combat environment and were ready to party. The mood in the big jet was of relief, coupled with when-in-the-hell-are-we-going-to-get-there attitude.

After a quick fuel stop in northern Australia, we landed at Sydney's airport. It was three in the morning. We were processed through the Australian immigration services and then escorted to a building where we all received an hour-long lecture on the dos and don'ts in Australia. All 120 of us were assigned to various hotels around Sydney and then told when we could expect the bus to pick us up for our return trip from our hotels back to the airport in five days.

All seven of us from my squadron were assigned to the same hotel; it was the Menzies hotel located not far from Kings Cross in downtown Sydney. We boarded the bus and stopped at two or three other hotels on our way to the Menzies.

The hotel was a nine- or ten-story building and looked very inviting after living in a hooch for six months. We arrived at the hotel at just before 0600 hours, or 6:00 a.m.

Entering the main lobby, we found no one was at the front desk, so someone banged on the little bell on the check-in counter. About half a minute later, a gentleman arrived from a back room and asked, "Gentlemen, what can I do for you this fine morning?"

One of our field-grade officers stepped forward and said, "We are all here for R and R, and we would like to check in please."

He looked at us and replied, "Gentlemen, unfortunately I cannot check you in at this moment since all our rooms are currently occupied. We were expecting you, but we thought you would all arrive later today. Your rooms will be ready for you by 9:00 a.m. In the meantime, if you like, I can store your bags behind the counter until that time."

The major indicated that we should put our bags behind the counter, which we did. One of the other captains had been looking around the lobby and found the entrance to the hotel's pub, a Closed sign was posted on the bar. He returned and said, "I wanted to buy the first round of drinks, but the bar is closed." We were all standing around the lobby at that point, hot and tired, and hoping to find a cold beer. It was summertime in Australia.

The gentleman behind the desk saw the downcast looks coming from the seven of us and said, "I think I may be able to get someone to open the pub for you gentlemen since you're here on R and R. That is the least we can do since your rooms are not available." He then picked up the telephone and talked to someone. In about ten minutes, a man arrived to open the pub for us.

We were just finishing our first pint when a little old man entered the pub from the outside door. He walked slowly through the pub and took a seat on the last stool. He looked like he was about fifty years old, somewhat hungover, needed a haircut and shave badly. His clothes were shabby, with visible holes in various places where they should not have been, and he wore an old navy-type watch cap on his head. He appeared to be really down on his luck.

Looking at the poor soul who had just entered, I decided to do something kind. I called to the barman and said, "Please give the gentleman sitting down at the end of the bar a pint on us."

The man had not heard what I had said, so when the barman placed a pint in front of him, he looked surprised. He was even more surprised when the barman said we had paid for his pint.

Looking down the bar at us, he raised his glass and said, "Thank you, Yanks. You are Yanks, aren't you?"

"Yes, sir," was our unified response to his question.

"You boys are here on R and R?" he asked.

"Yes, sir. We are Marines and are here for five days of R and R" was again our response to his question.

After a couple of minutes, he asked us, "What plans do you Yanks have for your five days of R and R? We have a lot of activities here in Australia that you might like to try while you're here—water-skiing, scuba diving, deep-sea fishing, and some nice Australian ladies' company if you like. If you are interested in any of these activities, let me know, and I will set them up for you."

Hearing his offer and seeing his clothing condition, we all knew he was pipe dreaming. We all exchanged glances—this can't be serious—but we all smiled at him.

I responded for the group, saying, "Sure, we would all like to participate in some of these activities."

Then we individually responded to the question of what we would each like to do while we were there. Since three of us were bachelors and liked water-skiing, we said we would like to do that with accompanying Australian ladies, of course. The other four opted for SCUBA diving and deep-sea fishing.

The little old man had removed a small notebook from his pocket and asked each of us for our names and when we wanted to partake in these activities.

We three bachelors said, "Tomorrow would be fine. We need to rest today."

Meanwhile, the others stated their preference, knowing these activities would not come to pass but continued to placate the little old man. The little old man then asked the barman for the telephone and made a short call. After he completed the call, we asked him if he would like another pint, and he, to our surprise, declined. He did say to the three of us bachelors to be ready to go water-skiing the next day, and we would be picked up at 9:00 a.m. tomorrow. He then said, "Thank you for the pint, and I hope you enjoy your R and R in Australia" as he left the bar by the same door he had entered.

We had a couple more pints and agreed to meet for dinner and drinks down at Kings Cross while we were waiting to check in.

At 9:00 a.m., the hotel manager came into the pub to let us know our rooms were ready. None of our party gave a second thought to the little old man we met that morning as we checked in to the hotel.

My room was on the third floor of the hotel overlooking the main hotel entrance.

The seven of us all met for dinner at—I think it was—the Red Baron Restaurant in Kings Cross. From there, we hit several clubs and bars. Finally, at around 2:00 a.m., I finished toasting the lives and the loss of my two friends and fallen comrades, went back to the hotel, and fell into bed, having had way too much to drink.

The next thing I hear was a heavy pounding on my door. I opened one eye as the pounding continued, then I heard a female voice saying, "Are you in there? Get up, Marine, if you want to go water-skiing today."

She continued to beat on the door. I finally dragged myself out of bed, headed to the door, and opened it. Standing there with her hands on her hips stood a beautiful young lady dressed in white shorts, a halter top, and scarf. She looked ready to water-ski. Looking me over quickly, she smiled, shaking her head, saying, "You look terrible, Marine! You have a date with me today in case you forgot. We are supposed to go water-skiing. Are you coming or going back to bed? If you're going to join me, you have ten minutes to make yourself presentable and join me in my car out front." She did a quick turn walking away and saying again, "You have only ten minutes."

I was still standing in the doorway as she turned the corner toward the elevator. Closing the door, I went to the window and looked out. She had just arrived at her car parked in front of the hotel. I could also see two other convertible cars parked ahead of hers with the other two bachelor Marines sitting inside each next to a beautiful young lady.

Grabbing some shorts and a shirt from my luggage, I made a quick visit to the *head* ('bathroom' for civilians), downed three aspirin, took a fast shower, shaved, brushed my teeth, and used some mouthwash, then headed out the door toward the stairs, not wanting to miss my water-skiing date.

Running out the front door, I saw her start her car getting ready to follow the other two cars, which had just pulled away from the curb. I caught her attention, and she waved. Getting to her car, a little MG convertible, I jumped in without opening the door as she rolled out following the two cars ahead of her.

She looked over at me, saying, "You sure do clean up well. I must say. I was not sure you were going to make it. What happened to you last night anyway?"

Looking over at her, I noticed her blond hair, which she had tied in a ponytail. Responding to her question, I said, "First, let me apologize for being late this morning. I guess the little old man we met yesterday at the hotel bar was the real thing. He meant what he said about going water-skiing this morning with a beautiful girl. I never thought he was serious, but I am glad he was. I'm Robert since we have not really been introduced."

She looked over at me, responding with her name, and she said she was glad I had made it. She explained that we were all on our way, all three cars, to the White Mountains about a two-hour drive, where we were to meet the boat with driver and enjoy a day of water-skiing. There was also a picnic lunch for everyone to enjoy.

Telling her again that I was glad to meet her, I then asked how much do we all need to chip in to pay for this water-skiing trip and lunch.

She looked shocked at my question, saying, "You Americans are all so laughable. You are not going to be charged for any of this outing. You are the guest of the 'the little old man' you referred to. He just happens to be the owner of the largest rug manufacturing operation in Australia. He fought in the Second World War and likes Yanks, especially Marines, since he served with them. We girls all work for him, and this is our day off, so we agreed to entertain you three Marines today and get in some water-skiing as well. We would not want you Yanks to think badly of Australian hospitality, would we? Now sit back, relax, and tell me why you had too much to drink last night."

I did as she had requested. I told her about the loss of my roommate, and we talked, water-skied, had a wonderful lunch, and then we got back in her car for the return trip to my hotel. She said on the way back, "You are invited to a cocktail party hosted by 'the little old man' tomorrow night if you would like to attend. I, unfortunately, will not be able to attend, but I have arranged to have another lady escort you. She will have your name, so look for her in your hotel at about 5:00 p.m.

"Thank you for your company today. I really enjoyed our time together," she said as we arrived at my hotel. Stopping out front of the hotel, she leaned across and gave me a kiss just before I climbed out of her car.

As she drove away, I thought of the old proverb "Don't judge a book by its cover." Boy, was I wrong. I had not looked past the little old man's clothing and mannerisms. I had not taken him seriously regarding his promise to see we had a good time while in Australia. I thought his water-skiing trip was a fantasy, not so I found out. Another valuable lesson was learned by me that day. *Never judge people based on their looks. Find out about them before making value judgments* was my final thought, as I ran to catch up with my two bachelor Marine friends heading into the hotel.

The seven Marines from our squadron all enjoyed the activities "the little old man" provided, and all too soon, we were back on the bus heading to the airport for our return trip back to Vietnam.

Once on the aircraft, we heard dark rumors circulating from other service members that the NVA were massing several divisions of troops for a potential attack in the area around the Khe Sanh combat base.

The reality of the war in Vietnam suddenly took center stage in my thoughts as we headed back to Da Nang.

*****

Shortly after returning from Australia, I was called to the CO's office and was informed by the adjutant that I was being transferred to the Marine Aircraft Group 16 from my squadron.

After I recovered my composure, I asked him why I was being transferred. He said, I was requested by name by the former CO of our squadron, who was now the executive officer of MAG-16. He had a job for me at the Group and wanted me in it as soon as possible. That was all he knew.

Hearing this, I went directly to the Group XO's office to plead my case that I should remain in the squadron and keep flying.

The Group XO was sitting in his office when I arrived in the Group adjutant's office requesting an audience with the XO. Through the closed door, he heard me making the request to see him and shouted loudly, "Captain Wemheuer, get in here now!"

Entering his office, I came to attention in front of his desk and said, "Sir, Captain Wemheuer reporting as ordered."

He responded by saying, "Captain, stand at ease. I know why you came to see me, but I have an important job for you to undertake, and you are the only person I know who is here at Marble Mountain who can get it done.

"I saw the way you handled the armory and ammunitions storage jobs while I was your CO, so I know you have the desire and drive to get the job that I am about to give you done. You also have a background in architectural design, which no one else around here possesses.

"I know you want to stay in the squadron and fly, but I need you to help me make this place better for all the Marines who have to live here while fighting this war. Recognizing your desire to continue flying the CH-53, I have arranged with HMH-463 to keep you on their flight authorization rolls so you can continue to fly.

"You, effective now, are my new Marble Mountain clubs officer. Not only will you have the management responsibility for all the clubs here at Marble Mountain, but I want you to design and build new clubs for our enlisted men, staff NCOs, and officers. Captain, do you have any questions?"

Still in a state of shock, I finally responded, "No, sir."

"Good, now go to work, Captain," the XO said as he returned to his paperwork.

Resigned to my new situation, but not happy about it, I headed back to the squadron to start the checkout process and then check into the Headquarters and Maintenance Squadron-16 to assume my new duties as the clubs' officer.

*****

My first task was to find the clubs office. It was currently located in the back of the staff NCO club structure. This was where I would find the NCOIC of the club's system here at Marble Mountain. He was running the entire show now since the past clubs' officer had left country several weeks earlier. Staff Sergeant Donald Dewitt was his name.

Having never met him before, I was pleasantly surprised to find him to be an easygoing staff NCO, who was in a job with no help since the previous officer's departure.

Staff Sergeant Dewitt was an avionics professional, who like myself had been pushed into a job that was not what he wanted to do, but like a good Marine staff NCO, he jumped in with both feet and performed well under the circumstances.

I found out from the staff sergeant that the previous clubs officer was medically transferred to a rehab facility stateside for alcohol addiction treatment.

Staff Sergeant Dewitt and I spent the first week going over the books, visiting each club, talking to the current managers and staff of all the clubs we were responsible for. At the conclusion of our week's orientation, Staff Sergeant Dewitt and I formulated a plan on how to handle the challenges we faced. He would continue to oversee the daily operations of the enlisted, sergeants, staff NCOs, and officers' clubs. He had several ideas on how to make the clubs run more efficiently, so I said to him, "It's your call. You are responsible for their operation. It's up to you to make the decisions on how to operate them, but remember, we need to turn a profit in order to justify the moneys from the Morale Welfare and Recreation fund for construction and outfitting of the five new clubs that we are going to build to support our Marines at Marble Mountain.

My challenge was to get started on the design for each of the five clubs, then get them constructed, and still keep flying while doing it. I started by talking at length with each manager and several patrons at each club in order to get their input on what they would like to see at each facility. An example was, the enlisted man's club patrons wanted a stage for shows as a permanent part of their club while the officers at their club wanted to continue to have a clear view of the South China Sea and a covered patio. The design of each club incorporated, to the extent possible, the desires of the managers and patrons.

The next step was finding a local building contractor to construct the facilities. I visited with the military exchange officer asking about how he got his structure built. He sent me to the military and civilian liaison office in Da Nang where I explained the situation and found a South Vietnamese civilian liaison official who would handle the construction contracts. I showed him my basic design for the first two clubs that required construction that would keep the Marines safe while inside them. To do this, his contractor needed to build the walls for all the clubs with stone and concrete walls that would stop shrapnel from mortar or rocket attacks. He looked at me and said he understood the requirement and had someone in mind that could construct such a building.

Next was money that was needed to build and furnish the facilities. It had to come from the Morale Welfare and Recreation (MWR) system who had, in my opinion, boatloads of funding support. I found an Army major, located in Da Nang, who ran the MWR operation, and after explaining what we wanted to do, he said yes to my request for funds. "Just keep me in the loop on how much money you will need ahead of time to construct and furnish each of the five clubs at Marble Mountain. I will handle the contracting for construction after you negotiate a price with your contractor. Please don't spend more than we have allocated for each facility without making a request for additional funds you might need through me. Do you and I understand each other, Captain?" he said.

"Yes, sir, Major, I understand, and thank you" were the words that came pouring out of my mouth, still in shock as to being given a blank check per se.

Leaving his office in Da Nang and heading back to Marble Mountain about four miles away, I thought about how to structure the major construction effort we were about to undertake without disrupting the operation of each club, since space for additional construction of these facilities was limited except for the area near the enlisted club's location. Closing the other clubs was not a viable option because of the use each club experienced daily. Maybe we could build half of the club at a time. Once completed, we could then shift the operation over to the completed side while they finished the work on the second side. That was an option that crossed my mind driving back to Marble Mountain.

Meeting with Staff Sergeant Dewitt when I returned, we discussed the build-one-half-of-the-club concept. Dewitt and I then discussed with the four affected club managers the concept. They all agreed it was a feasible option. Next, we checked with the civilian contractor, who at first balked at the idea, but soon changed his mind when additional funds to do it were offered.

Finishing the design for the sergeants and officers' clubs, I had the contractor visit the two sites. We then met a day later and finalized the price, and he gave me a schedule of when he would start construction at both clubs. He wanted to start construction of the sergeants' club the next day and the officers' club next week. Sending him next to the Morale Welfare and Recreation office to finalize the contracts, which was done that afternoon, we soon had two contracts signed and work scheduled to start on the sergeants' club the next morning.

Staff Sergeant Dewitt and the sergeants' club manager worked through the night to set up the club for continued operation in one half of the club while the other half was being demolished and rebuilt. We also posted drawings of the floor plan and exterior design of the new club so that the patrons arriving could see what the final product would look like.

The next morning, I went to the sergeants' club and witnessed the demolishing of half the club, then the excavation for the footings for the exterior wall, then the placement of the forms for the wall and slab. To my surprise, this was done in one day.

The following morning, a truck with bags of concrete along with several large mixing troughs or mixing boxes arrived. They were accompanied by a large crew of civilian men and women.

The civilian workers went to work mixing the concrete with the sand from the beach area, then they added water and then poured the footing and slab that day. The work was all done by hand. No concrete trucks were used.

The contractor had a very efficient and well-run operation as I watched his men and women mixing and pouring the concrete. The operation reminded me of watching a beehive, as a young boy; every bee worked in unison with all the others to accomplish the task. No wasted efforts, just a single-minded effort to complete the task.

The next day, two large trucks with yellow and white stones—we would call field stone—to be used as part of the exterior wall construction arrived. These large stones were off-loaded by hand and stacked for use by the stone masons the next day.

Staff Sergeant Dewitt, who was the officers' club manager, and I, along with a couple of civilians, worked after closing the officers' club the next Sunday night to prepare the club for construction and continued operation. We again posted drawings of the floor plan and exterior design of the new club so that the patrons arriving could see what the final product would look like.

On Monday morning, a repeat of the events that took place at the sergeants' club construction site occurred at the officers' club. The demolishing of half the club, then the excavation for the footings for the exterior wall, and then the placement of the forms for the wall and slab were completed. Again, this was done in one day.

That evening, as officers arrived at the club, I made myself available along with Staff Sergeant Dewitt to answer questions about the demolition of half the club and to show them what they could expect in the future as we moved forward to give them a new drinking hole.

While I was standing at the entrance of the club, the Group XO, my boss, came in and looked around at the clear synthetic plastic barrier between the construction area and the functioning club side. He started to say something to me until he saw the drawings. He moved toward them and studied them closely, then turned to me, and asked, "Captain, how long will it take to finish the job?"

Responding to his question, I said, "The job should be completed in about a month. We still have to purchase tables, chairs, and outside patio furniture before the job is really complete, but about a month is a good estimate."

Looking at me directly in the eye, he said, "I was wondering if you, in your design for the reconstruction of the O club, had thought of incorporating an officers' mess with its reconstruction."

"No, sir, I did not look seriously into the possibility of incorporating the two functions into one."

I didn't because the operation and funding for the two come from different sources, and mixing them could create problems, but the thought of combining the facilities had crossed my mind. We had room in the back of the new club to accommodate the mess and kitchen facilities necessary to make it work. However, without command direction to make it happen, I had not seriously considered it as a viable option.

After a long pause, I said to the XO, "However, sir, if you like, I will take a look at the feasibility of building an officers' mess directly behind the O club, if you like. A separate building for the officers' mess could potentially be constructed behind the new club. It could be constructed close enough together to be connected by a hallway, doorway, or other structure to keep people out of the weather and still provide security for the operation of both entities. It may be feasible if that is the direction the command wants to proceed. Sir, is that the direction the command wants to take regarding the officers' mess?"

The XO looked at me for several seconds before saying, "Yes, Captain, that is the direction the command wants you to take. See if you can get it done in the next couple of months. If you run into problems, come and see me." The XO took one more look at the exterior picture saying, "The mess should look like the club, don't you think, Captain?" as he headed for the bar for his afternoon cocktail.

I thought, *Boy oh boy, what a new challenge. On top of building five new clubs, now he wants me to build an officers' mess. But what the hell, I like challenges.* Then I started thinking seriously about how to build an officers' mess as I watched the XO, my boss, order his drink.

*****

Mid-January 1968

After being reassigned to manage the clubs system at Marble Mountain, I was allowed to continue to fly combat missions with my previous squadron, HMH-463. As an aircraft commander, I continued to participate in the war in the northern part of I Corps in Vietnam as it continued to escalate. The NVA had, in fact, moved three divisions of troops into the area surrounding the Khe Sanh Combat Base complex including the airfield used to deliver supplies to the Marines, Army, and ARVN fighters in the region.

By continuing to fly with HMH-463, my previous squadron, as my boss promised, I had an opportunity to continue flying missions during the siege of Khe Sanh and then again after the Tet offensive took place. Some of these missions are described in other portions of this memoir as well as the one at the end of this story, which brought my current combat tour to an abrupt end.

*****

Things were going well. The sergeants' club was almost finished, and the O club was halfway done. We had broken ground for the massive, standalone replacement for the current enlisted club, then everything changed.

On January 31, the Tet offensive brought our construction effort to a screeching halt. Marble Mountain was hit with sapper attacks, mortar and rocket attacks off and on for the next month or more. Civilian construction crews were not permitted to work on the base in any capacity.

This offensive in South Vietnam was countrywide and was the largest major operation by the North Vietnamese and Viet Cong in the war to date. It encompassed over one hundred cities, and its goal was to ferment rebellion among the South Vietnamese people against their government.

For the next four weeks, no Vietnamese civilians were allowed on base for fear of sapper attacks, bombing, and potential assassinations. Our ongoing construction work at all the club sites had to be stopped completely.

While we were at a standstill with construction, we still had lots of work to do. I made a trip to the Philippines to purchase plumbing and electrical supplies needed for the various club construction. Lighting fixtures, ceiling fans, and artwork for the clubs were also purchased. I also picked up pictures of tables and chairs that were available for purchase, so the individual club managers could select the type and color they wanted in their individual clubs.

Returning from the Philippines, the gunny and I again turned our attention to the officers' mess problem.

*****

The main administrative problem with trying to build an officers' mess was that the Morale Welfare and Recreation system could not provide funds for an appropriated fund facility; they could only fund things under the law that were deemed to be non-appropriated fund activities like clubs, retail exchanges, and the like. We needed a way to get around that problem.

One approach that we could try was to ask for appropriated funds to build the facility, but that would take at least a year because it would be classified as a permanent facility and fall under the military construction program controlled by Congress.

Staff Sergeant Dewitt, now selected for gunnery sergeant, and I worked long and hard trying to find a way to get the job done, without going to jail.

Remembering an old adage, "It is easier to ask forgiveness than it is to ask permission," we decided on a strategy that stretched legal boundaries to almost the breaking point. Our strategy revolved around two concepts—first, expand the footprint of the building, then find a way to turn it into an officers' mess without going to jail for mixing appropriated and non-appropriated facilities.

Implementing our strategy, I returned to see the Army major who ran the Morale Welfare and Recreation System in I Corps. I told him we needed more funding to provide the additional space for our officers' club facility. "Do you need to see the plans?" I asked.

He indicated that no he did not really care about the drawings and that the additional funds would be no problem to provide. "The increase in the funding level you have requested is approved," he said. "If you need more, come and ask me before you spend above what I agreed to supply like we agreed to before, correct, Captain?"

"Yes, sir, and thank you again," I responded. We now had the funds to enlarge the shell of the structure to accommodate the officers-mess operation.

Next, Gunny Dewitt and I went to see the NCOIC of the mess facility. This was the facility where everyone had their meals. It was centrally located and had a separate seating section for officers.

The master gunnery sergeant had been in the Marine Corps for a long time and listened to us while we told him of our plans. His response at the end of our pitch was a surprise.

He said, "Captain, we have looked at building an auxiliary dining facility in the area behind the existing officers' club since we arrived here at Marble Mountain at the request of the CO at the time. We found it not to be feasible because there is insufficient electrical power to operate the club and mess together. We looked high and wide for a new or used transformer that could satisfy the power-demand problem. The CO at the time tried to get us one, but there were none available in all of I Corps. All the big transformers like we needed were in use, and all the new ones coming into the country were already spoken for.

"Captain, I would like to help you out getting the mess built, but until you can solve the power problem, I cannot justify the expense of the officers' mess you are pushing for. If you can solve the electrical problem, I will support your quest wholeheartedly."

We thanked the TOP (military slang for master gunnery sergeant) for his time and told him that we were somehow going to solve the problem. He just smiled at us as we left his office and started down the hallway in the rear of the dining facility.

As we approached the building's back door, I heard the TOP call out to us, "Wait a minute, Captain."

Turning around, we headed back toward his office. He met us coming out of his office holding several rolled-up and what appeared to be design drawings in his hand.

"Captain, maybe you can use these drawings. I had them produced for the officers' mess when I first looked into building one. You are welcome to them. They show electrical, plumbing, ventilation, wastewater-disposal options, plus the layout inside the facility as we saw it at the time. These drawings will give you an idea of what would be required for the mess if it were to be built."

Taking the drawings, we again thanked the TOP for his help and the drawings. This was exactly what we needed to design and build the mess.

Gunny Dewitt and I went back to our office and looked at what the TOP had given us. It was exactly what we needed to expand the club's footprint and to show the location of the electrical, plumbing, ventilation, wastewater-disposal options, plus the layout inside the facility that we wanted to have constructed.

We copied the plans, and Gunny Dewitt said he would deliver them to the liaison office to be converted into a change order for implementation by the contractor who was currently working on the officers club. They needed these plans to place plumbing and electrical in the slab as they expanded the footprint of the facility.

We were taking a big chance on expanding a building where part of it might never be used, but this was our best chance to get the job done. While engaged heavily in the club's construction activities as well as trying to get the officers'-mess situation figured out, I had to back off from flying with the squadron during the latter part of the Tet offensive as frequently as I would have liked to. Additionally, since I was no longer in the squadron, the missions that I was assigned to were much more administrative in nature, leaving the combat missions for the squadron members to fly. The frequency of my name appearing on the flight schedule also decreased dramatically, which I did not like, but could do nothing to change. I was now an outsider in their eyes.

*****

The next challenge was the electrical transformer problem. I asked, "Who had electrical equipment including transformers?"

Then I remembered, I had flown several missions in support of a couple of Naval Mobile Construction Battalion's operations, better known as Seabees, who were currently working all over I Corps building bridges, roads, and buildings. "I bet they would have some of these types of transformers available," I said.

In my quest to find a large transformer that would handle the loads from both the officers' club and the mess, I decided to visit the one whose current headquarters was close by. It was located at Da Nang Harbor. This specific construction battalion, CB-4, I found out, was split into two parts. One located at the Da Nang Harbor was doing construction in order to expand the harbor facilities, and the other part of the battalion was working south of the DMZ.

Arriving at the harbor, I was directed to the CB-4 headquarters by the sentry. I was driving toward it when I saw a Navy lieutenant start waving vigorously at me. I recognized him as one of the Seabees we had supported south of Quang Tri that were building a replacement bridge over a river that had recently been washed out by heavy rains.

Our bird had been tasked, while airborne on another mission, to Dong Ha to divert and move several pieces of heavy equipment from one side of the river to the other to facilitate the Seabees' continued work.

The lieutenant had been very happy with our work since he did not have to wait a couple of days for a barge to move the equipment across the river. When we were diverted, we were carrying a pallet of beer internally to Dong Ha airfield for the Marines stationed there. However, we lost a couple of cases of the beer to some thirsty Seabees, to the delight of the enlisted sailors. The lieutenant had been in charge of the Seabees working on the bridge replacement and remembered our support and kindness toward his men.

Stopping the jeep I was driving, he continued walking toward it, and as he approached the jeep, he said, "I would like to thank you again for helping us complete the bridge job up north. You left before I could express our thanks. The sailors really enjoyed the beer you gave us. It was a real morale booster for all of us. Thank you again.

"So, Captain, what brings you to visit the Seabees today?" he finally asked.

Exiting the jeep, I guided him toward a shady spot while saying, "Lieutenant, let me tell you all about it." I told the lieutenant all about the project and the need for a larger electrical transformer that would handle the load from both facilities' electrical demands simultaneously. He indicated he was familiar with the O club at Marble and had been in charge of the installation of the original electrical service that was provided for the club when it had been constructed. Then I asked him if there was any possibility that he could find a transformer for our operation. We were willing to help him look for one. We could provide transportation, sea rations, beer, and whatever he needed to help us get the mess up and running.

He looked down at his shoes and said in a low voice, "Your request is a very hard one to make happen. We are critically short on large-capacity transformers all over I Corps, but I will see what I can do. First, I need to talk to my boss about the possibility of getting one for you. It's a remote possibility but let me work on it. By the way, maybe you can help me. My boss has not been able to purchase any Chivas Regal scotch since he has been in-country, and maybe you could help him find a place where he can purchase some."

Smiling at the lieutenant, I said, "I will look into it as soon as I get back to my office."

He said his CO was coming to visit tonight, and if I got any word about where he could purchase the Chivas, please get a hold of him ASAP. He would like to get his boss a bottle if possible.

Thinking back to my initial meeting with the then-Staff Sergeant Dewitt, I thought I remembered seeing a case of Chivas Regal scotch ratholed in the back of his office.

Again, continuing to smile at him, I told him we will see what we can find, as I climbed back in my jeep and headed back to Marble Mountain. I went directly to Gunny Dewitt's office and found him sitting behind his desk, and I asked about the Chivas Regal scotch I had seen when we met.

He said, "Yes, sir, I have a couple of cases of it, but it's almost impossible to get them anywhere in-country, so I have kept them ratholed. Why do you ask?"

I told him about the conversation I had with the Navy lieutenant and the need for a bottle of Chivas Regal scotch right now. He got up and went to the box in the back of his office and brought back two bottles and handed them to me. "Take two of them if it will help us get the job done," he said.

Taking the bottles from him, I found a couple of unused sandbags and placed one bottle each in the bags. I then headed back down to the harbor. Seeing the lieutenant talking to a chief, I waited until the chief had departed and then waved for the lieutenant to come over to my jeep.

"What brings you back so soon, Captain?" he asked.

I said nothing, not answering his question, but reached over to the passenger side floorboard and picked up one of the sandbags and handed it to him. He looked in the sandbag and saw the bottle of Chivas Regal scotch, a look of surprise immediately appeared on his face, followed by a huge smile.

The lieutenant then after a second or two said, "How much do I owe you for the package?"

"Nothing," I said. "Just help us get our transformer is all we ask. Oh, by the way," I said, while I picked up the other sandbag, then handing it to him, "Why don't you send him home with this? If you need anything else for your sailors, just ask." These were the final words I spoke to him.

Taking the second bag and quickly looking inside, his mouth fell wide open as I put the jeep in gear and left him standing there with two sandbags in his hands.

About a week later, I got a telephone call from the Navy lieutenant saying that his CO was overjoyed with his gifts. He, in fact, had taken both bottles back with him when he returned to his quarters. He indicated that the CO had found a potential transformer that could become available that could satisfy our request, but additional supplies were needed to be provided in order to seal the deal. The transformer would also need to be properly installed by his Seabees to ensure its proper installation and operation. He indicated that the additional supplies necessary to complete the job were the delivery of a pallet of beer and a full case of the same items that had been donated to the CO previously. The CO insisted on paying for those specific items he had received earlier as a gift. If we could supply these items, then the larger transformer would magically appear and be installed.

I told the Navy lieutenant to give me a couple of weeks to work out the logistics, and I would let him know when we could deliver the supplies to cement the deal.

Gunny Dewitt and I decided to increase the cost of a beer in the officers' club by five cents, which would provide additional money to purchase the pallet of beer necessary for the exchange. We felt that the officers should contribute to the deal since it was going to be their mess, and after we had enough cash, the price went back down to its previous extremely low level.

While we were getting the pallet of beer paid for, I made a second trip to the Philippines to order the tables and chairs the club managers had selected for their clubs. The tables, chairs, and bar equipment would be held in storage in the Philippines until each of the clubs were ready to accept them after being completed.

In mid-March, the situation with the Tet offensive had quieted down enough to allow civilian construction workers to again start work. The sergeants' club was the first to be finished, then furnished, with the Group XO doing the opening honors.

The second half of the officers' club was again under construction; I watched the crew at work and noticed that several of the previous crew were not present. Asking the supervisor where they were, he indicated that the VC had taken them away and killed them for doing work for the Americans.

After hearing his story, I thought, *This is one hell of a war.*

We had by now gotten the pallet of beer and the Chivas Regal scotch ready for delivery. I contacted the Navy lieutenant to set up the delivery.

The next day, the Gunny and I loaded the beer and scotch on a six-by-six truck and took it to the CB headquarters' compound. We were met by the Navy lieutenant, who escorted us to the back of their club, where a forklift off-loaded the pallet of beer. The Navy lieutenant then took the case of Chivas Regal scotch and headed for the headquarters building, saying as he left, "Don't leave yet. I will be right back."

Ten minutes later, he returned and said, "Thank you," as he handed me the money for the scotch his boss had purchased.

He continued saying, "The other item will be delivered and installed soon. I have been assured by my boss. Thanks again. I have a meeting to get to, so please excuse me," as he turned and walked away.

The Gunny and I climbed back in the truck and headed back to Marble Mountain.

The next morning at around 0500 hours, all the lights in the officers' hooch area including the club went out. This power failure awakened me since we had intelligence reports that sapper teams might be getting ready to hit the base again. Then I heard the sound of a crane, down toward the club area.

Climbing out of my rack, military for bed, I slipped into my flight suit and boots then strapped on my .45-caliber pistol, then walked outside. Looking down toward the club, I saw a couple of men on the power pole working on the transformer, which hung there. A couple of minutes later, the transformer came swinging off the pole and was lowered, then placed in a flatbed trailer. The crane then picked up a much larger transformer from the same flatbed trailer and hoisted it up on the pole where the two men secured it to the pole. I went back inside my hooch and finished dressing and headed for the officers'-club area. About that time, all the lights came back on as electrical power was restored.

Arriving at the rear of the O club, I saw the flatbed trailer containing the old transformer and the tractor that pulled it had *CB* letters and Bee insignia on the door. The CBs had made good on their promise to get us a new transformer. We did not expect it to happen so fast, but here it was—a beautifully new and much larger transformer.

My next stop was made to the mess hall or dinning facility where I went in to see the man in charge. "TOP," I said, as I walked into his office, "you will never guess what just arrived at the back of the O club."

He responded almost immediately, saying, "I already know about the new transformer and have already ordered the equipment necessary to establish the officers' mess. I don't know how you did it, but the important thing is you got it done. Good job, Captain. I estimate it will take about thirty days to get what we need to open the officers' mess. Now if you would please excuse me, I hate to run off on you, but I am late for a meeting at the wing headquarters." He then stood up and headed for the door.

I said, "No problem, TOP, glad to see you are already on top of things, so to speak," I said as I laughed at my own joke.

After eating breakfast in the mess hall, I headed to the gunny's office. We were both happy that we had finally overcome the last major hurdle necessary to get the officers'-mess project into motion.

With the sergeants' club now completed and opened, the construction of the enlisted club was almost completed. The gunny and I knew we were well on our way to having taken care of the needs of the enlisted men's club, except for the staff-club part of our mission.

The officers' club was completed next, including the separate shell structure that would become the officers' mess. The staff-club drawings still needed some work because of a change in location that was required to build additional hooch's for staff NCOs. It was late May 1968, and I would have to work quickly to get everything done before my thirteen-month tour in Vietnam was over in June.

*****

I was working in the office in the back of the officers' club on the plans for the staff club when the XO of my old CH-53 Squadron walked in. The major looked down at me and said, "Captain, you are on the duty section today. See, your name is right here," pointing to the duty-section roster he was holding. Continuing, "We have been ordered to preposition a CH-53 on an LPH off the DMZ in anticipation of a rocket attack on the base tonight. You are on the duty section, so I want you to take the flight."

Looking up at him, I said, "With all due respect, Major, why me? I am not in the squadron, and I have work to do, so please find someone else, sir," pleading my case.

I did not know this officer, having only met him once before since he was new in-country, and I had never flown with him.

His face turned red as he continued to look at me, saying, "Captain, you are assigned to fly with our squadron, and you are on the duty section. You will fly the mission. You understand that this is an order not a request, don't you? Now get your ass down to the operations hooch and go fly the mission." He then turned and left my office. Knowing I had no choice in the matter, I changed into my flight suit, grabbed my overnight bag, and walked into the bar on my way out of the very crowded officers' club.

As I walked through the club, I saw three pilots sitting at the bar drinking. I recognized them as being HACs from the CH-53 Squadron whose names I had seen on the duty-section roster that the squadron XO had just shown me. All were sitting there enjoying their cold beers.

As I passed by them, the realization that the rest of the pilots in the duty section have been drinking hit me, *So that is why the XO came to me to fly.*

I surmised he did not want to try to cancel the mission, and he did not want to confront the squadron pilots who were drinking while on duty, so I became the solution to his dilemma. I was not happy, but I had no choice.

Recognizing I had been given a direct order to fly the mission, I walked past the seated squadron pilots and headed for the shuttle bus stop outside.

Arriving at the squadron operation building, I went inside and retrieved my flight gear and sat down with a copilot whom I had never met before this evening and listened to the briefing given by the squadron duty officer.

After an aircraft was assigned for the mission, I checked the yellow sheet and signed for the aircraft. Once we preflighted the bird, I briefed the crew since we were going to the ship, we did not need to wear our bullet bouncers or armor vest, but we needed to make sure we all wore our Mae West flotation vests instead.

The weather was good that evening, so we filed a VFR flight plan from Marble Mountain Air Facility to the LPH. Departing Marble Mountain as the sun was setting behind the mountains to the west, I again thought, *Why me?* as we headed toward Hai Van Pass, staying over the water east of the mountains. We had climbed to three thousand feet and had locked on to the ship's TACAN station, which showed the ship to be east of the DMZ.

As we proceeded along the coast, we called the save-o-plane agency to make sure that no naval gunfire was going on as we proceeded north, "feet wet" (meaning, over water). No naval gunfire was taking place, but artillery-fire missions on land were numerous. None, however, would affect our route of flight.

It was now getting very dark as we proceeded up the coast with the horizon disappearing quickly. As we continued to fly up the coast, we saw occasional flashes of artillery fire, inland, but nothing that would affect our night vision. We made radio contact with the ship about twenty miles from the ship. At ten miles, we started a gradual descent to fifteen hundred feet above the calm sea.

At five miles, I called the ship reporting, "See me," meaning, "we had the ship in sight." I descended to five hundred feet about three miles from the ship. I asked the copilot to set his radar altimeter to flash at two hundred feet and to let me know if we went lower than his two-hundred-foot setting. I set my radar altimeter to come on at sixty feet since that was normally the altitude, I used to approach the LPH's deck for landing.

We completed the landing checklist at what looked to be about two miles to the port rear of the ship. Over on the DMZ, we could see large flashes of light indicating big explosions were taking place even though we were eight or ten miles off the coast, as we continued toward the ship. There was no horizon, and it was pitch-black as I looked outside except for the lights on the LPH as we continued inbound. Suddenly, there was a large flash of light from the direction of the DMZ. I looked quickly to my left as did the copilot at the flash for a second or two, then moved my head back quickly looking toward the ship's previous location.

I saw a flash from my radar altimeter illuminating, followed almost immediately by an enormous bang, then more lights and noise ensued, then total blackness.

I could feel the harness pressing against my chest. I felt like I was upside down in the water. It was pitch-black. I thought I was sinking, still strapped to my armored pilot's seat. My training at Pensacola took over. I reached toward my stomach and opened my lap belt and pushed myself away from my seat. I was not sure which way was up, so I reached down and pulled the toggle on the Mae West's inflation bottle on the right side. I could feel the bubbles pass my face while I continued to sink. I reached the other toggle and pulled it. This time, I felt my descent reversed, and I started to move toward the surface. Breaking the surface, I took a deep breath and started to orient myself. The what-happened thoughts I had were quickly overcome with the realization we had crashed. I then looked around and saw several crew members also in the water. They were barely visible from a single light on one of the other crew members' Mae West, which we all wore. It appeared that only one of their lights was working. Mine was out too. The bird I was flying seconds before was now upside down with nose down in the water several yards away from me. I swam toward my crew, trying to count the number of crew members bobbing in the water. I could feel and taste the fuel in the water all around us. When I reached the small group, I counted three crew members. The copilot, crew chief, and one gunner were all treading water. They all had their Mae Wests inflated and were gathered around the floating hulk. I looked around for the last crew member, asking if anyone had seen him. The crew chief said the last time he saw him he was by the copilot's side of the bird before we crashed. No one had seen him since the crash.

He must still be inside the bird, I thought.

I knew what the orientation of the aircraft located beneath me was, since I had grabbed on to part of it, but I could feel that it was starting to sink further below the surface. Since my Mae West had lost all its air, I decided to look inside the aircraft for our missing crew member. I dove down, then grabbed the side of the aircraft where the personnel door was located. I grabbed the floor of the bird, then pushed myself down further, then by feel, I went inside the bird. There was no light whatsoever, so I tried to feel my way deeper inside. I felt my way around by feel only. I found nothing while I was in the cabin. Running out of oxygen, I surfaced, took several deep breaths, and dived down again looking inside the cabin for our missing crew member. Without a light, all I could do was feel around for him. Out of air again, I had to head for the surface.

Surfacing, I gulped air for a minute before recovering my wind for a second time. Looking at the other crew members, I said that I had no luck in finding the last crew member. They all looked very dejected as I also felt at the time. Everyone was standing chest deep on the belly of the aircraft, as we all felt it slipping away and sinking. Now everyone was again floating in the water. I used the inflation tube to partially inflate my Mae West to help me tread water while we kept together in a tight circle.

Looking at the face of each crew member in the light of one small flashlight, I asked if anyone was hurt. I learned that the copilot had injured his back but could still move and swim. The crew chief had cuts on his arms and legs as did the surviving gunner. As we all bobbed in the warm waters of the South China Sea, we could see the LPH about a mile and a half away. The ship looked like it was launching a rescue helicopter.

While we were floating around, I felt a bump against my leg followed by a scraping feeling against my flight suit. Thinking back to my days when I did a lot of SCUBA diving in Pensacola, I remembered the touch of a small shark as it swam past me in the water about twenty feet deep. The feeling I had just experienced on my leg was the same feeling. As the bumping continued, I remembered that there was a lot of fuel from our aircraft floating on the water, and there was a good possibility the fuel in the water had provided some dampening of the shark's sensory ability to locate the sources of the blood in the water. I hoped it would not disperse too much before we were rescued.

We all watched the helicopter launch from the LPH and head in our direction. The copilot had opened his survival vest and had gotten a pencil signal flare loaded with a cartridge. Seeing him with the pencil flare ready to fire, I cautioned him to shoot it away from our position because of the fuel in the water. As the helicopter approached us, he fired the flare into the sky, marking our position.

The helicopter turned on his spotlight after spotting the flare and came to a hover over us. The H-34 hovered about twenty-five feet above us, and the crew chief dropped the horse-collar rescue devise in the water about twenty feet from our little group. I signaled the gunner that he should try to grab the horse collar as it was dragged through the water toward us. He caught it as it came into reach but could not hold on because the helicopter hover was somewhat erratic because of the rotor wash spray coupled with the darkness that engulfed us. The pilot tried in vain to get his aircraft into a stable enough hover to get the horse collar to one of us with enough time to get it on before it was pulled away.

Unbeknownst to us, the LPH had also launched a longboat as the backup for the helicopter rescue. It arrived just after the helicopter's final attempt to get one of us out of the water. The boat came alongside of our small group, and a man reached down to attempt to pull me onto the boat. I saw him and pushed the gunner who was next to me toward him. The sailor was a very big man and easily pulled the gunner into the boat. Next, I pushed the crew chief, then the copilot toward the waiting hands on the boat. When they were all safely on board, I finally swam close enough to have him grab me, then hoist me into the boat. The sailor who pulled me in said, "There should be one more of you out here. Where is he?"

My softly spoken answer was "He did not make it."

I looked back at the dark waters we had just been pulled from thinking I wish he had.

On the way to the LPH, a corpsman who was with the rescue party looked me over, and he discovered a deep laceration below my left kneecap. I did not even know it had occurred.

Arriving on the ship, we were all taken to the ship's sick bay for evaluation and treatment. The gunner and crew chief had some small cuts and scrapes treated. My copilot was x-rayed, and no breaks were discovered. He was treated for a badly sprained back and moved to a bed in the sick bay. My wound was cleaned, evaluated, and then stitched up.

The doctor said, "Captain, you are very lucky. Another centimeter deeper, and you would have the nerve to your foot cut."

He then gave me some pain meds as he finished his job. A couple of pilots from the onboard helo squadron came into the sick bay as I was finishing being stitched up. They offered me a bunk in the squadron spaces since they had space in their billeting area rather than staying in the sick bay. I accepted their offer, hobbling along behind them, heading below decks to their group of rooms. Laying down on the bunk they provided, the next thing I remember was someone saying, "You need to get up and head to the flight deck. They are going to medevac you to Da Nang in a few minutes. Better get a move on." Standing up, I found that I could not put very much weight on my left leg. The corpsman who came to get me had to help me get to the flight deck and onto the aircraft.

Arriving at the medical facility at Da Nang, I was again evaluated, and it was determined that I could return to limited-duty status at Marble Mountain as long as I remained on crutches.

*****

Gunny Dewitt and I continued to work on the completion of the enlisted club culminating with a grand opening including a USO show at the facility. The officers' mess was not yet completed, but well on its way to being finished, and my leg was causing me a lot of pain. Looking at my leg, I could see that it was not healing very well, and it looked like it was getting infected.

I went to the doctor only after the enlisted club opening because I did not want anything to stop the completion and opening of the new enlisted club. After it opened, I went to the doctor at Marble Mountain medical facility. He was not happy that I had delayed coming to see him. The doctor determined that a serious infection had set in. He determined that because of the infection, I should be sent to Guam Naval hospital for treatment and to recuperate.

After three weeks in the hospital, they sent me home ending my first combat tour in Vietnam.

*****

Author's note—I originally thought my crash in the South China Sea was the result of being shot down by an enemy missile. However, after the aircraft was recovered from the sea, there was no evidence of any missile damage. The ship had no evidence of a missile attack that evening either.

After the completion of the accident investigation, the accident investigation board concluded that I had experienced spatial disorientation that resulted in me flying the aircraft into the ocean, which was a devastating realization for me.

After reporting to my new duty station in Southern California, I was assigned to the helicopter training group—Marine Helicopter Training Group 30 (MHTG-30)—to serve as part of their headquarters staff. After several months at the group headquarters, I was selected to attend Aircraft Maintenance Officers School in Millington, Tennessee, for sixteen weeks. Upon my return to Southern California, I was assigned duties at the flight line officer at the Marine Heavy Helicopter Training Squadron 301 (HMHT-301), which was the heavy helicopter training squadron. The squadron's principal function at that time was the training of copilots and transition pilots to fly the CH-53 aircraft before they were sent overseas for duty in Vietnam.

During the next two years, I served in various positions in the maintenance department with most of my time spent serving as the flight line officer until I went back to Vietnam for a second combat tour. During my time with HMHT-301, several major events in my life occurred.

One of which indicated that I was going to continue to serve as a Marine officer and a naval aviator. To my surprise, I was selected as a regular officer in the United States Marine Corps and was no longer a reserve officer.

The other was that I met and married Mary Joanne Knox and adopted her two children from a previous failed marriage.

Both of these events would prove to be life-changing events in my life and Marine Corps career.

ROBERT WEMHEUER

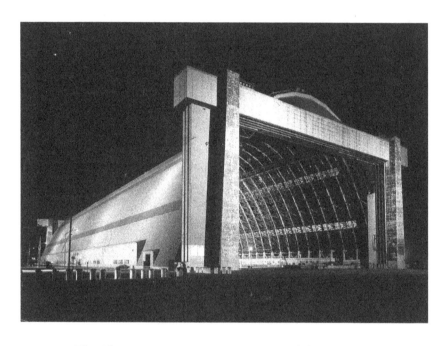

The Blimp Hanger at MCAS Tustin, California. Artist
Paul Gavin and Kimberleigh Web illustration-1993

UNLIKE NO OTHER

Picture of CH-53 loading rice

Marble Mountain Air Facility's billeting area in 1967

Chapter 2

ONE LONG DAY IN LAOS

Northeast Kingdom of Laos

Flying in loose formation en route to Fire Support Base (FSB) Hotel II, I separated my aircraft from my flight leader to provide Major Wasko, our Squadron Operations Officer, flying in another CH-53D Helicopter, call sign "Dimmer 3," by several miles before arriving overhead at the FSB. As my CH-53D aircraft, call sign "Dimmer 4," flew east toward the South Vietnamese border, it was my intention to provide Major Wasko flying his "Dimmer 3" aircraft a distraction or decoy maneuver hoping to convince the enemy machine gunners and mortar crews into thinking that we were calling off our gun-extraction mission. Dimmer 3 called Major Close of the US Army Helicopter Direction Control (HDC), call sign Red Dragon 28, en route back to Hotel II and requested he provide the maximum suppression fire that could be applied to the areas where the incoming enemy fire was emanating around the perimeter of FSB Hotel II.

Major Klose, who was currently directing three additional sections of fixed-wing attack aircraft, acknowledged Major Wasko's request. Approximately a minute later, I saw fixed-wing aircraft attacks begin again on the west and south side of the FSB hoping to suppress the incoming mortar, small-arms, and .50-caliber machine-gun fire that was currently being received by the ground troops inside the perimeter of Hotel II. The major was also using several newly arrived US Army Cobra gunships in his effort to neutralize the incoming fire that was coming from just outside the perimeter.

As we watched Dimmer 3 arriving overhead the FSB, he then commenced his approach to Hotel II. I saw the fixed-wing aircraft attacking the enemy positions directly south of the pickup zone. Seeing him commence his approach, I turned our helicopter back to the west in order to return to an overhead position above Hotel II to await our turn to pick up the last 105mm howitzer.

We continued to watch and listen to Major Wasko flying Dimmer 3 as he again made a left-hand approach to the FSB in an attempt to avoid enemy fire. At the bottom of his approach, as he came to a hover in the gun-pit area, he started receiving heavy mortar fire that reduced the visibility in the entire area making it difficult for him to locate the gun in the red and brown dust and smoke.

Seeing him depart the area of heavy smoke and dust moving to the northeast, he then quickly circled around again moving directly to one of the two remaining guns and coming to a hover over it. As we watched from above, it appeared that he remained over the gun for an extended period with mortars going off all over the area.

Major Klose, along with my crew, worked to identify the areas where the mortars were impacting and to call out the location of ground fire that was being concentrated at the hovering helicopter. Major Klose masterfully directed the Army Cobra gunships to the areas where the majority of the incoming fire was emanating. These efforts appeared not to have lessen the incoming fire into the area very much. My crew and I then observed six to eight mortar rounds, almost simultaneously, impacting directly behind the aircraft Dimmer 3 was flying while he was attempting his pickup.

After a prolonged hover, Dimmer 3 again departed the gun pit without the gun. He again made a hard-left turn inside the perimeter of the FSB and came back to a hover over the gun. He appeared to again be in a hover for an extended period and taking fire all the while. I watched his aircraft as he was starting to lift the gun from the gun pit when a series of mortar rounds (seven to ten) exploded all around and on his aircraft. From our vantage point, they appeared to be directly on top of the helicopter's rotor system and aft of the tail. It was hard to tell because of the smoke and dust. Just after we observed these hits, Major Wasko called over the radio that he was hit and going down in the gun-pit area next to the LZ.

Dimmer 3's CH-53D aircraft was one of two Marine Corps heavy helicopters that were lost while flying in support of an operation called Lam Son 719 in 1971.

His story and mine are told in the following chapter of my memoir. The perspective is from one who was a pilot, a flight leader, and a company-grade Marine officer during the conflict. My recollections are based on the events that occurred over a little less than a five-month time frame. This chapter revolves around that and has a special emphasis on a single day while I was serving in the United States Marine Corps as a CH-53D helicopter pilot fifty years ago. My recollections (sometimes dim) coupled with some old written notes and saved documents along with some research that I did regarding the events that took place during the invasion by the Republic of South Vietnam into the Kingdom of Laos in early 1971 are the basis for this chapter. While the focus of this chapter is on a single day during the conflict, the story needed to be put into a larger context by explaining a number of events that occurred before and after that memorable day.

*****

The late 1960s and early 1970s were times of great cultural upheaval and turmoil within both South Vietnam and the United States. The United States population early on appeared to support the war in Vietnam, but as the conflict dragged on, the sentiment of the country started to change. War protests and riots broke out at various colleges and universities as the support for the war waned.

I can vouch for this dysfunctionality by relating a couple of true stories that impacted me directly. These events took place during my first combat tour in Vietnam starting in mid-1967 and upon my return to the United States after being involved in a helicopter crash in Vietnam. This crash occurred in 1968 late in my first combat tour with Heavy Marine Helicopter Squadron 463 (HMH-463) that took the life of one of my crew members, for which I will always be very sorry.

*****

One of the events began on an afternoon two months before the start of the Tet offensive while I was still working in HMH-463 as the ordnance officer. Since I was not flying and had a little spare time, I went to the base exchange to get a haircut and a straight razor shave. All the barbers in the facility were Vietnamese locals who had sought employment at the base exchange. I had always assumed that all the Vietnamese local employees had been screened and received passes and clearance in order to work in the exchange facility.

After taking a sequence number and having my number called, I took a seat in one of the barber chairs. The barber asked me, in very broken English, what type of haircut I wanted. I told him a short flat top, moving my hands on both sides of my head to show him I wanted it very short on the sides. As he started to cut my hair, I asked him if he could give me a shave.

He said yes he could give me a very, very close shave. I did not respond to him as he continued to cut my hair. He nor I spoke again until he had completed the haircut.

Looking at his facial features while he worked, it appeared that he was not enjoying his work very much.

After he was finished, he turned me around so I could assess his work by looking in the mirror hanging on the wall behind his chair and found it acceptable.

Just before he started to remove the plastic haircut sheet from around my neck, he asked me if I really wanted him to give me a straight-razor shave. As I looked at him, I thought I saw a strange almost sinister look in his eye as he sharpened the razor on the leather belt he held in his hand.

At that moment, I almost said no to the shave but instead pushed the sinister look on his face to the back of my mind.

I said to him, "Yes, go ahead with the shave." He then proceeded to lay the chair back almost horizontally. I closed my eyes, and then he proceeded to give me a nice close straight-razor shave. I felt great as I left the exchange facility to return to my duties at the armory. However, his sinister look in his eyes still stayed in the back of my mind as I worked.

Later that night, around 2300 hours, our base was attacked by Viet Cong insurgents. First, rockets were fired into the base, and then they launched a sapper attack on the facility with the intended targets being the multiple aircraft parked on the flight line. Unfortunately for the Viet Cong insurgents' sapper squad, they were discovered trying to get across the concertina wire by the Marine perimeter guards at the south end of the base. All five of them were killed as they attempted to get into the base with their explosive packages. As part of the intelligence-gathering process, photos were taken of all five insurgents still hanging on the wire, including facial shots.

The next morning, posted on our ready room wall were the pictures of the five Viet Cong insurgents still hanging in the concertina wire. These photos included close-up facial pictures. As I looked at the facial pictures, I recognized one of the men who had been killed last night. He was my barber from yesterday. I could not believe he was also one of the five Viet Cong insurgents. He had been the one who had cut my hair, as well as given me a nice close straight-razor shave!

Thinking back to yesterday, *The sinister look I had seen in his eyes, which I had not taken very seriously, could have very easily cost me my life.* I was shocked and somewhat surprised to see the man who could have cut my throat very easily yesterday was now lying dead across the concertina wire. *The good Lord must have been looking after me yesterday,* I thought.

This drove home a very salient point for me—that in this war, you could never really be sure who were the good guys and who were not. Telling the good folks from the bad was not an easy process in this war. The everyday South Vietnamese citizen could, in effect, be one of the Viet Cong insurgents who were the ones trying to kill you.

After this experience, I thought, *Maybe I need to consider sleeping with one eye open from then on. One thing is for certain, I am not going to have any more straight-razor shaves from the local barbers while I am in Vietnam.*

*****

The second event took place shortly after my first combat tour with HMH-463. I had been involved in a helicopter crash off the coast of Vietnam near the demilitarized zone. Suffering a leg injury in the crash that killed one of my crew members, I was medevacked to Guam to recover from my injury.

After three weeks in the Guam naval hospital, I was sent back to the United States on travel orders. Traveling on orders required me to wear my military uniform. Dressed in my full class-A uniform, I boarded the first commercial flight available back to the States.

The first leg of my flight was to San Francisco, California. From there, I was then on my own for my trip home to Mount Prospect, Illinois. I had been given thirty days convalescent leave before having to report to my next duty station back in Southern California.

Upon arriving at San Francisco International Airport, I stayed in my seat since I was on crutches and was moving slower than most of the other passengers. I let everyone on the aircraft deplane from the big Pan Am 707 before I made my exit. Getting to my feet, I made my way slowly through the plane, then down the aircraft boarding stairs to the tarmac. Crossing the tarmac, I finally arrived at the terminal doors. Pushing open the doors, I stepped inside the terminal, and as the doors closed behind me, I heard someone yelling loudly. Looking in the direction of the yelling, I could see that the person making all the noise was looking directly at me.

I then listened as he yelled at me, "Look at the dirty baby killer! Isn't he a mean and nasty piece of shit! You're not welcome here in the United States anymore. You're a dirty Marine pig!"

The person yelling at me had a smirk on his face while he was yelling these anti-military slurs. Looking at him sitting there with his dirty long black hair, numerous holes in his clothes, and with a beard plus a guitar, I was not surprised to hear his comments. He appeared to me to be the proverbial beatnik.

While we were deployed, we had heard that there were people in our country who were against the war in Vietnam. The Tet offensive had generated a lot of hatred and anti-military sentiment, but I did not anticipate that I would run into one of the haters at the airport on my way home after defending my country from the communists.

What the hell is happening to this great country of ours? I wondered.

Unfazed by his slurs, I just kept moving down the pathway between the rows of seats toward the main part of the terminal. As I moved past his location, he proceeded to spit in my face and uniform.

He again said, "You are a dirty baby killer and a Marine pig."

His actions created a flashback in my mind back to Vietnam; his spittle became the same as a Viet Cong insurgent's bullet hitting me in the face. Surprised! My first reaction was to stop and drop.

Stopping yes but not dropping. I looked at him and wiped the spit off my face with the back of my hand. I then quickly reversed my right crutch and hit him on the left side of his head as hard as I could.

Still seeing this beatnik as a VC insurgent, I thought, *Take that, you VC commie bastard!*

Regaining my composure quickly, I could see the surprise on his face at my actions as he jumped off his stool, dropped his guitar, then swung his clenched right fist at me. I blocked his punch with my crutch, pushing him away from me. He stumbled, lost his balance, and fell on the floor.

The bastard is still surprised and in shock, I thought.

As he started to get up, I leaned down picking up his guitar from the floor where he had dropped it. Looking for something hard, I saw a group of terminal seats close by. I then proceeded to smash his guitar into several large pieces over the back of one of the terminal seats.

I had not said a word to this long-haired beatnik punk since I had originally seen him.

The shocked and angry look on his face indicated that he was very angry and pissed off at me because of what I had done to him and his guitar. At that point, I really didn't give a crap. As he finally regained his footing, he rapidly started forward toward me again.

That is when the first of several San Francisco police officers arrived on the scene.

I thought, *Boy, am I in trouble now having hit him, pushed him, and broken his guitar?*

The first police officer arriving on the seen acknowledged my presence with a nod, then moved into a position between the war protester and me. All the while, the *beatnik* anti-war protester continued to yell out anti-military slurs, continuing to say, "Look at the dirty baby killer. Isn't he a mean and nasty piece of shit? You're not welcome here in the United States, you Marine pig!"

After the *beatnik* anti-war protester was confronted by the police officer, he changed his rants to include anti-police slurs in addition to the anti-military ones, now saying, "Look at the dirty police pigs. Aren't they all mean and nasty pieces of shit? You're here, I bet, to defend that Marine pig."

The first police officer was joined by a second officer. They both moved to quickly subdue the protester, pushing him hard against the wall, then putting him in handcuffs after which they forced him to the floor. He continued to call the police officers pigs and spat on the officer who had cuffed him. This did not make him popular with the police officers at all. They placed him face down on the floor and restrained his legs. After the spitting incident, the police officers handled the anti-military protester rather roughly, which was understandable. Two more officers arrived and took physical control of the anti-military protestor and read him his rights. He was pulled to his feet, then moved to a waiting police shuttle. He continued to scream his anti-police slurs along with the anti-military ones as he left the area on the shuttle.

I was still standing by the terminal seat when the first police officer who arrived on the seen came over to talk to me, saying, "Captain, are you injured? Do you need any medical help?"

I said to him, "I am okay, Officer, thanks. This was not the type of reception I was expecting. That's for sure! I thought this war in Vietnam was to help keep the communists from taking over Southeast Asia, but it looks like they are trying to take over the United States instead. It was President Kennedy who started the Vietnam war back in 1962. I believed he called it stopping the domino effect in Southeast Asia back then. We are just doing our jobs and protecting the world from a communist takeover. I love our country, and I am willing to die to protect it. What the hell are these radicals doing? What is happening to this great country of ours?"

He said, "This is now commonplace here in San Francisco these days because of the Vietnam War. I was also a Marine who had served in Vietnam a couple of years ago. I got out of the Corps so I could go to work for the San Francisco Police Department. Sometimes I question the wisdom of my decision. Having been there, in my opinion, the television and newspaper coverage of the war is completely one sided. They don't report the good things our troops do over there, only the occasional bad ones get any press. It was that way when I served there and continues today. It makes me sick."

While we spoke, he picked up the pieces of the broken guitar putting them in a trash container. As he finished picking up the pieces, he continued our conversation, saying, "I understand your frustrations with the anti-war protesters. I feel the same way. Don't be concerned about the guitar you broke. I will take care of any problems generated by the anti-war protester regarding his broken guitar and the crutch slap you gave him. By the way, he is currently on his way to jail for assaulting a police officer by spitting on him. So you can continue on your journey home. It's just a small thing I can do for another Marine who is bravely serving his country."

I said, "Thank you for your understanding and help today."

As we walked together to the American airline ticket counter, we talked about the war and our perceptions of the state of affairs that our country had retreated into, as well as the lack of accurate press coverage of the war in general.

Arriving at the ticket counter, the police officer and I shook hands, and he said, "*Semper fidelis.*" He then turned and started to walk away.

I called out to him as he departed, "*Semper fidelis.*" I then stepped up to the counter and bought a ticket for home. After purchasing my ticket home, I still had a little time before my flight for Chicago departed, so I went to the "head" (restroom for civilians) to clean up and wash my face. As I washed my face, I thought back to the recent incident. I again became angry, remembering that he had spit on me, yelling, "You are a dirty baby killer and a Marine pig." This again triggered the flashback to Vietnam; his spittle again became the Viet Cong bullet hitting me in the face.

The call for boarding of my flight home snapped me back to reality from my dark thoughts. I finished cleaning up and headed for the departure gate. As I walked along toward the gate, I pushed the dark thoughts to the back of my mind since I was heading home.

After boarding my flight to Chicago, then getting a cocktail, I tried to put the whole incident behind me, as I cruised home. However, the incident continued to echo in my thoughts as I went to sleep, waking only after we touch down at O'Hare field in Chicago.

Semper fidelis. "Always faithful." The Marine motto now echoed in my mind kept me from reliving the recent anti-war incident.

*****

During the Tet offensive in January and early February 1968, I was serving as the clubs officer at Marble Mountain Air Facility as well as flying combat missions with HMH-463, my previous squadron in South Vietnam.

The Tet offensive was a preplanned, sneak attack by the North Vietnamese and Viet Cong that started on the first day of a cease-fire truce that was slated to go into effect the first day of the Tet Vietnamese holiday. The sneak attacks were mounted by the Viet Cong insurgents and their comrades and the *Democratic Republic of Vietnam* (North Vietnam's regular army, NVA) units all across South Vietnam. It surprised both military units and civilian leaders in both Vietnam and Washington. It took the forces of South Vietnam and the American military two months to restore order and push the Viet Cong back into hiding and the NVA to withdraw back to North Vietnam. Technically, the offensive was a defeat for the communists, but it created and fueled disenchantment in the United States and fueled the growing anti-war movement.

As I recall, the Vietnam anti-war attitude continued to propagate in our country for the next several years. The anti-war narrative was continually pushed by the television and print reporters of all nationalities—French, British, Australian, and of course, Americans. I had seen several of these news crews on my first combat tour and had even provided transportation for some of them from one base to another.

On one occasion during the Tet offensive, I remember taking a female French reporter and her camera crew from the Phu Bai airfield to Quang Tri in I Corps of South Vietnam. En route, we flew over the city of Hue at thirty-five-hundred-feet altitude as a major battle to retake the city was underway below. She reported that same day, which was picked up by the Armed Forces news outlet in Vietnam that she had been an eyewitness to the battle at the city of Hue where she saw many women and children were being killed by United States Marines.

I could not believe the reporting from this woman. I found it extremely hard to believe she saw anything from my aircraft at thirty-five-hundred-feet altitude because, for one thing, she was made to sit in her seat in the back of my aircraft for the entire flight. Even if she were able to get up and look out the small windows in the cargo compartment of my helicopter at thirty-five-hundred-feet altitude, it's doubtful she could see anything from that altitude, especially since the city was obscured with smoke and dust from the ongoing battle. This and other incidents of inaccurate and in some cases totally false reporting caused me to not be very impressed with their ethics, competence, or their ability to report events accurately.

The anti-war culture and predisposed negative attitudes of the news reporting in the United States in the late 1960s and early 1970s drove then-presidents Johnson and then Nixon to institute and continue a policy called Vietnamization. This policy of turning more of the war effort to the South Vietnamese was designed to reduce and to minimize the exposure of American service personnel to hostile actions. Troop reductions started under Johnson, then were continued and accelerated under Nixon during this period. It was partly predicated on lessening casualties in the war effort, which it was hoped would dampen the anti-war attitude. It was my belief that under this policy, the military commands faced a problem of how to implement the policy in the air units and still fly aircraft in support of the war efforts. The problem of reporting of aircraft damages, in order to comply with the perceived guidance, required the military establishment to underreport damage to aircraft or to minimize it to the maximum extent possible.

This philosophy, in my opinion, applied to reporting only very major damage to aircraft, not damages that could be fixed at the squadron or intermediate maintenance levels. Holes and shrapnel damage that could be easily fixed by metalsmiths were not generally reported in the Marine Corps' Squadron Command Chronologies. Again, in my opinion, the low reported statistics of battle damage incurred by Marine helicopters directly supporting Operation Lam Son 719 was due to this unofficial edict.

One case in point was the loss of one CH-53D aircraft, which was on its way back from a day of combat operations in Laos.

My memory of these events is also somewhat colored and impacted by the loss of this one aircraft with all on board that was returning from a Lam Son 719 mission in Laos on February 18, 1971.

*****

My recollection of this event starts with Colonel Street, the Marine Aircraft Group 16's (MAG-16) commanding officer (CO), who had previously flown as my copilot on one of a number of my Lam Son 719 missions into Laos. He tasked me to fly the helicopter that retrieved the bodies the day after the crash.

The crash occurred northeast of Hue Phu Bai airfield, and the bodies of the nine lost souls were taken to the medical facility at Hue Phu Bai airfield. Since the two pilots killed were both personal friends of mine (Major Wayne Reuben Hyatt and Lieutenant Strather Franklin Wood), I believe that this was the reason that Colonel Street asked me to fly them back to Da Nang for their eventual return flight home.

The squadron's aircraft accident board originally classified the crash as an accident; their rationale was that they could not detect any significant battle damage during the initial assessment of the crash scene of the aircraft.

The crash impact site was scattered over a large area (one rotor blade was found approximately one mile from the crash site). The condition of the blade and the distance from the impact area supported the theory that the blade assembly departed the aircraft prior to the crash. Additionally, a later JAG (judge advocate general) manual investigation indicated that three occupants of the aircraft were ejected and thrown 1,500 feet; two, as far as 1,700 feet from the aircraft, which could not have occurred on impact of the aircraft.

According to doctors who handled the bodies of the crash victims, all were killed by dynamic cell compression. This type of injury is consistent with ones that are potentially created by the extremely large lateral g-force. It is opined that the force created by the blade loss created a dynamic imbalance in the rotor system that generated the extremely large lateral g-forces that killed the passengers and crew of the aircraft instantly. Since the crash was classified as an accident caused by a mechanical malfunction and not resulting from hostile enemy fire, the crew and passengers were not eligible for Purple Heart Medal Awards.

The rationale for originally classifying the aircraft crash as an accident, in my opinion, was because of the lack of large-scale evidence of hostile-action causation, plus the extreme tempo of operations that were ongoing at the time and possibly the edict cited above. The victims of this crash were therefore initially listed as accident victims and not as casualties of enemy action in Laos.

The subsequent final accident investigation was completed several months after the squadron was redeployed to Marine Corps Air Station (MCAS) Kaneohe, Hawaii, with most of the people who had any knowledge of the events not being redeployed with the unit to Hawaii. The conclusion reached, long after the fact, was that the crash was either a hydraulic malfunction or pilot error. These conclusions were predicated on a flawed initial investigation, inconclusive engineering analysis of several components from the crashed aircraft that were shipped back to the US for analysis after the crash, and lack of people familiar with the crash itself.

This conclusion stood for over forty years until one Marine, William "Whitey" Whitehurst, took on the task of proving the accident was not an accident at all; it was a crash due to direct enemy action. He contacted a number of retired and former Marines (including myself) who were either in the squadron or had specific expertise in evaluating additional evidence and reviewing past reports. Our combined efforts over a four-year period, including several resubmissions of causation analyses, finally concluded with a reversal of the original causation conclusion.

We showed the decision makers that the original evaluations were flawed. Additionally, several persons with specific and critical knowledge of the crash were not even interviewed after the incident. These persons were contacted and interviewed regarding their recollections of the events leading up to the crash. These factors, coupled with a reengineering analysis based on new information, along with additional witness statements, provided enough evidence that the crash was due to direct enemy hostile actions in Laos. Based on this last submittal, the record was corrected by Headquarters United States Marine Corps in April 2018.

After forty-seven years, Whitey and his team had the record of this tragedy corrected, proving these deaths were all, in fact, the direct result of hostile fire in Laos. The eight Marines and one Army Special Forces staff sergeant finally received their well-deserved Purple Heart Medals on April 23, 2018, after a long struggle with the deep-state military bureaucracy.

This flight to recover the nine bodies of our squadron members and the other lost souls took place just three days prior to the date of my Laos story.

*****

One Long Day in Laos

February 23, 1971

My day started like most days at Marble Mountain Air Facility, located just southeast of the city of Da Nang, in the Republic of South Vietnam. I was living in a hooch in the billeting area of the air facility with a couple of hooch mates. Captain Evert Haymore was one of them. He became a very close friend, almost the brother I never had. Even though we had not met before, we both were here for our second Vietnam combat tours. We were brothers in arms, so to speak.

As I lay in my bunk very early in the morning of February 23, 1971, my thoughts drifted back on how I arrived at this place, at this time, and what might lie ahead. I had requested and received orders back to Vietnam because I felt that I needed to prove something to myself. Since the crash that ended my first combat tour, I had felt guilty about losing an aircraft and the death of one of my crew members. I needed to see if I could face the dangers and, again, prove to myself that I could fly in combat. In my opinion, "Flying is inherently dangerous, but flying in combat—that is one of man's ultimate tests."

My flight departed the continental United States the day after Christmas in 1970, from Travis Air Force Base (AFB) in California en route to Vietnam via Okinawa. Arriving in Okinawa, I reported to Marine Corps Base Camp Courtney to await military transportation to Vietnam. Upon checking in to the transportation office at Camp Cortney, I was told by the staff noncommissioned officer (SNCO) on duty that no one was being deployed to Vietnam, and my orders must be a screwup. He went on to tell me that I should expect to have these orders modified to report to the Marine Air Group 36 at Marine Corps Air Station Futenma in Okinawa for duty.

Bullshit, the bureaucrats are at it again was my first reaction in my mind.

I strongly objected to the idea of having my orders modified in any way until approval was obtained for any modification from

Major Phillips, the First Marine Aircraft Wing's (First MAW) personnel officer currently stationed at Da Nang, Vietnam. He was the one who arranged for my orders to Vietnam in the first place. Major Phillips was an old friend and a CH-53 pilot whom I had served with on my first combat tour in-country.

Since I arrived on Friday evening, the SNCO on duty indicated that I should check into the BOQ at Camp Courtney and return Monday morning in order to get things straightened out.

Looking at the SNCO who gave me the bad news, I thought, *I sure am not going to stay here with the ground Marines. If I have to stay in Okinawa, it will be at MCAS Futenma.*

Rather than staying at the BOQ at Camp Courtney, I told the SNCO I would be staying at the BOQ at MCAS Futenma where he could reach me if he got things straightened out before Monday. He arranged transportation for me to MCAS Futenma.

I departed Camp Cortney *really pissed off*, not at him, but at the bureaucratic system.

While checking into the BOQ, I ran into a number of CH-53 pilots from HMH-462 Heavy Haulers Squadron that was permanently stationed in Okinawa, Japan. They suggested I attend happy hour with them at the Futenma officers' club. We all met at the club and enjoyed an evening of good food and drink. The rest of the weekend, I rested, worked out, visited some Okinawa shops, and called my wife to let her know that I was in Okinawa and not yet in Vietnam.

On Monday morning, I was back at Camp Courtney at 0800 hours (8:00 am). The officer in charge (OIC), a first lieutenant, asked me to come into his office to discuss my situation. I told the OIC the same thing I told his SNCO on Friday night. "There was no screwup, and the orders to Vietnam were valid. All you have to do is call the First MAW personnel officer, Major Rick Phillips, to verify their validity. He said he would make the call later in the morning since he was busy right now, and he would let me know the results of the conversation.

I was again, *getting pissed off* about the delay but could do little to speed things up without causing a real scene.

Around 1400 hours (2:00 pm, the first lieutenant called me into his office indicating that he had in fact spoken to Major Phillips and that the orders were in fact valid. Continuing, he said, "You missed the last flight to Vietnam for the year this morning, and there are no additional flights scheduled to Vietnam until after New Year's Day. Since you are a senior Marine captain, as well as the senior man on the flight, you are to be in charge of the military personnel on the flight to Vietnam."

Boy oh boy! One good deal after another. First, another delay. Now I find out that I am the OIC of an aircraft full of military people going to Vietnam. I can't believe this is really happening to me. Murphy's law has struck again—"If anything can go wrong, it will."

I spent the next couple of days working out, resting, and having a few beers while quietly waiting in the BOQ at MCAS Futenma to depart for Vietnam.

*****

Finally, on January 2, 1971, I departed Okinawa for Vietnam. I was in charge of the planeload of ninety airmen, soldiers, sailors, and a couple of Marines on a Pan Am 707 commercial aircraft heading for Da Nang, South Vietnam.

Arriving in-country at around noon, I was met at the aircraft by Major Phillips, who had a jeep at his disposal. After handing off the paperwork for the individuals on the plane that I was in charge of to the Air Force reception team, then after recovering my luggage, I joined Major Phillips in his jeep.

As I climbed into his jeep, I felt the ninety-five-degree temperature and the ninety-eight-percent humidity. I was dripping with sweat. It felt like I was right at home and back in Vietnam.

I rode with Major Phillips to the wing headquarters in order to check in, which was completed quickly. He then took me over to Marble Mountain to check in at the Air Group headquarters, and finally he dropped me off at my new squadron's administration office. Major Phillips said he really needed to get back to the wing headquarters, so I thanked him for his help, friendship, and the taxi service that he provided. We shook hands, and I saluted him as he departed for Da Nang.

Well, I am back in HMH-463. The place looks so familiar. It seems like I am coming home again, despite some dark memories, I thought.

Checking in to the squadron, I met the command people who I would be serving with—CO, XO, and ops O. I also was told that since I was the senior captain in the squadron, I was going to be the squadron logistics officer, a major's billet or job.

After a five-day mandatory acclimatization period, I was cleared to start flying combat missions again in Vietnam. Our squadron, after I joined it, continued to fly support missions for the Marine Corps and South Vietnam's Army units all over I Corps, which was the northernmost area of South Vietnam. We flew resupply missions to ARVN units as far south as in the Hoi An and Chu Lai areas about thirty-five miles south of Marble Mountain. South Korean Marine units south of our base also received support from our squadron, as both of these forces continued offensive operations against both the Viet Cong insurgents and NVA regular army units in their tactical area of operation.

Our support missions continued throughout all of I Corps, but they were gradually being reduced by the American troop reductions along with a new and secret mission whose support requirements could only be satisfied by the use of our CH-53D aircraft. This secret operation was scheduled to start on January 30, 1971.

Our new missions took priority because of the recognition of the critical need for heavy-lift helicopters to support new tactical offensive operations in Laos. This operation had been in the planning phase by South Vietnam Armed Forces for many years. The South Vietnam Armed Forces were finally going on the offensive by attacking into Laos with the goal of disrupting the Ho Chi Minh trail.

This logistical artery was located inside the eastern border of the *Kingdom of Laos*. It had been utilized in the past and would most likely be used again by the *People's Army of Vietnam* (PAVN), *National Front for the Liberation of South Vietnam* (NLF—*Viet Cong*), and the *Democratic Republic of Vietnam* (North Vietnam) for incursions into the *Republic of South Vietnam*. It was estimated that as many as six thousand NVA soldiers, plus supplies and weapons were transported to South Vietnam per month using the Ho Chi Minh trail.[1] The offensive operation inside Laos was designated by the South Vietnamese as Lam Son 719.

US Army and Marine Corps Aviation assets became critical to the operation since the South Vietnamese Air Forces (Army and Air Force) could not begin to meet the helicopter requirements of an offensive operation the size of Lam Son 719. Because they could not do this operation alone, they tasked the United States Army to furnish almost all the helicopter transport assets.

The US Army and Marine Corps aviation units that participated in Lam Son 719 were tasked to directly support the South Vietnamese concept of operations that was utilized during the invasion. The concept was based on the tactics of leap-frogging troops and artillery units into an ever-expanding and overlapping series of fire support bases inside Laos designed to cut the Ho Chi Minh trail. If successful, this tactic would thereby deny Viet Cong and North Vietnam Army's logistics support pathway needed for future incursions into South Vietnam. Operation Lam Son 719 was an all-South Vietnamese ground offensive operation conducted between February 8 and March 25, 1971, inside Laos.[2]

Congressional passage of the Cooper-Church Amendment on December 29, 1970, prohibited any United States ground forces and advisors from entering Cambodia and Laos. The amendment was a congressional reaction to the use by President Nixon of ground troop incursions into Cambodia during the Vietnam War. This amendment did not specifically address the use of American aviation assets to support these types of operations.[3]

---

[1] Nolan, *Into Laos*; Fulghum and Maitland, *South Vietnam on Trial*; van Staaveren, *Interdiction in Southern Laos*; Nalty, *The War Against Trucks*; Cosmas and Murray, *US Marines in Vietnam*.

[2] Van Staaveren, *Interdiction in Southern Laos*; Nalty, *The War Against Trucks*; Sander, *Invasion of Laos 1971*; Cosmas and Murray, *US Marines in Vietnam*.

[3] Sander, *Invasion of Laos 1971*; Willbanks, *A Raid Too Far*; Cosmas and Murray, *US Marines in Vietnam*.

Before the commencement of Lam Son 719 could take place, another operation was required to provide the support infrastructure inside South Vietnam.

Dewey Canyon II would become this operation that was conducted totally within the territory of South Vietnam. The objective of Dewey Canyon II was initially the reopening of Route 9 from Camp Carroll all the way to the old *Khe Sanh Marine Combat Base*, then finally to the border with Laos.

A critical additional objective of this early in-country operation was to reestablish an operational airfield (at the site of the old Marine Khe Sanh airfield) in order to develop a secure forward operating base necessary to support these offensive operations across the border.

The Dewey Canyon II operation coupled the United States Army helicopter units in northern I Corps with our heavy helicopters from HMH-463 in order to provide sufficient aviation assets to perform the mission. Marine Light Helicopter Squadron 367 (HML-367) AH-1G Cobra Attack Gunship Squadron provided gunship support to the Marine CH-53D participating in Dewey Canyon II, which kicked off on January 30, 1971.

The Marine aviators who participated in Dewey Canyon II and then Lam Son 719 were the helicopter pilots and crews from the last Marine Corps' heavy helicopter and light attack squadrons left in South Vietnam.

The day prior to the kickoff of Dewey Canyon II, our squadron flew four Sea Stallions north and hauled heavy equipment for the 101st Airborne Division to staging areas near Quang Tri and Camp Carroll in preparation for the kickoff of the operation. Flying on the first day of Dewey Canyon II, my aircraft hauled load after load of heavy equipment, fuel, fuel trucks, and ammunition from Quang Tri to Khe Sanh. Most of our cargo loads were in excess of 14,000 pounds with some heavy equipment weighing as much as 19,000 pounds. During the first two days of Dewey Canyon II, heavy helicopters from our squadron moved over 177,000 tons of external cargo alone.

Our squadron's external load flights, along with the US Army's flights, continued from February 1 through February 5. Our Marine heavy-lift helicopters provided extensive heavy lifting of aviation and truck fuel, ammunition, and other supplies necessary to ensure that the logistic support base at Khe Sanh airfield and Landing Zone (LZ) Kilo were completed in time to support the kickoff of Operation Lam Son 719, scheduled to begin on February 8, 1971.

On February 7, the Marines established their own forward operating area within the confines of the Army's LZ Kilo, next to the US Army's Command and Control facility, all located two miles from the newly reopened Khe Sanh airfield. The small Marine operating area at LZ Kilo provided a location to stage Marine helicopters and crews that flew in daily from Marble Mountain. They would land, then receive mission briefs and assignments for missions into Laos from the Army's Command and Control unit stationed nearby.[4]

Flying on February 8 as part of eight CH-53Ds in support of Dewey Canyon II, I, along with seven other CH-53Ds carried over 1,035,700 pounds of cargo, ammunition, and fuel from Dong Ha, Camp Carroll, and FSB Vandergrift to Khe Sanh and LZ Kilo. A single day's squadron record.[5]

*****

As stated earlier, helicopter assets became the critical component to both operations since the South Vietnamese Air Forces could not begin to meet the helicopter requirements necessary to carry out either of these offensive operations. That lack of enough helicopter assets to get the job done drove the South Vietnamese military to task the United States Army to furnish almost all the helicopter transport assets necessary to conduct both operations.[6]

The Army also had helicopter-asset shortages and potential helicopter weight-carrying restrictions, which forced them to look at the Marine Corps' helicopter support for these operations. The Army helicopter assets in-country at that time (within South Vietnam) were

---

[4] HMH-463 and HML-367 Command Chronologies for January–March 1971, First MAW Vietnam.
[5] See note 4.
[6] See note 3.

limited at best when it came to lifting and hauling very heavy loads. Lack of mission-capable Army CH-54 "Tarhe" helicopters, called sky cranes, plus the cost to replace these aircraft if lost, were one of several reasons that the Marine Corps' heavy-lift assets were critical to support both these operations.[7]

External loads—such as, lifting 14,000-pound 155mm howitzers and 17,000-pound D-4 bulldozers that were required to be lifted into Laotian fire support bases, with many of them at an altitude in excess of 2,000 feet above sea level—were generally beyond the Army's in-country capabilities.

Additionally, a key element of the Dewey Canyon II logistics plan was the completion of the airfield at the old Marine Corps' Khe Sanh airfield prior to the start of the operation so that the Air Force's C-130s could stock the forward supply base with fuel and cargo necessary for the operation across the border.[8]

The completion of the airfield was delayed over a week because of weather and enemy action, which meant that vital supplies could not be delivered by C-130 aircraft as planned. They would have to be delivered by other means if Operation Lam Son 719 were to kick off on schedule.

Rumors were also circulating that the Army CH-47 Chinook medium helicopters were restricted to loads not greater than 7,000 pounds because of transmission problems. This loss of lift capability added additional requirements to support not only the heavy-lift missions but also to transport large quantities of truck and helicopter fuel and cargo that had previously been relegated to the Army's Chinooks.

While the Army lacked cargo helicopters suited to the requirements of Lam Son 719, the Marines had the capability that they needed. We had 18 Sikorsky CH-53D heavy-lift Sea Stallions in our squadron.[9]

---

[7] Willbanks, *A Raid Too Far.*
[8] Sander, *Invasion of Laos 1971*; Willbanks, *A Raid Too Far.*
[9] Cosmas and Murray, *US Marines in Vietnam.*

The CH-53D aircraft we were flying were the largest helicopters in the Marine Corps at the time and had been developed for movement of most of the Marine Corps' heavy equipment from ship to shore during an amphibious assault. Able to lift external loads of as much as 20,000 pounds, we routinely moved 155mm howitzers and bulldozers, as well as massive quantities of supplies, downed aircraft, and helicopters.

Since our squadron was being tasked to support the heavy-lift mission, at higher-than-normal altitudes in extremely hot temperatures, special permission was asked for and obtained to boost T64-GE-413 engine output above the 3,925-shaft horsepower output per engine to allow loads in excess of 20,000 pounds to be carried externally by our aircraft during Lam Son 719 operations.

The CH-53 was the only helicopter in the free world, at the time, that could perform loops and barrel rolls making it superior to any other heavy-lift helicopter in its maneuverability. These maneuvers were not authorized, but I could attest to the superior maneuverability of the aircraft we were flying.

Our Marine Corps partners in these operations were the pilots of HML-367 who flew the single-engine AH-1G Cobra attack gunships. They provided gunship support for Marine Corps' ground and aviation units in South Vietnam. I and many of my squadron mates had worked closely with the attack Cobras in the past all over I Corps.

HML-367 was also charged with the mission of escorting the CH-53s during Dewey Canyon II, then Lam Son 719. Their aircraft call sign was Scarface. These Scarface Marine Cobra attack gunships frequently came under the heaviest enemy fire and played an indispensable role in protecting the transport CH-53s during their missions.[10]

Weather in South Vietnam played a role in the timing of the attack into Laos. That was a major reason schedule compliance was a critical factor in the operation inside Laos. During most of our squadron's missions in support of both Dewey Canyon II, then Lam Son 719, we had a transitions situation between monsoon weather

---

[10] See note 9.

conditions generally occurring over the northeastern half of South Vietnam while the area across the border in Laos was generally cloud free during the middle of the day with occasional thunderstorms at night.

This weather cycle shifted about every six months so that northern Laos would have monsoon conditions while South Vietnam would be generally cloud free. The operation mostly fell during the transition between the two cycles. The only major weather phenomena not anticipated in the operation inside Laos were the significantly reduced visibility conditions created by brown and red dust in the air from the large amount of artillery fire, B-52 bomb missions, and hundreds of air strikes. All the myriad of factors played into our participation in Dewey Canyon II and then Lam Son 719.

*****

Lam Son 719 kicked off on time on February 8, 1971 with a bang. Prior to the initiation of the attack into Laos, a large group of B-52 bombers were utilized to carpet bomb targets in Laos for the preparation for the ground assault. It was an all–US Army show on the first day of the operation into Laos. The Army's air cavalry provided cover as four thousand ARVN troops crossed into Laos while being supported by the US 108th Artillery Group. The Army helicopters made several tactical insertions in order to establish landing zones, which later became fire support bases.[11]

Lam Son 719, the long-awaited offensive operation into Laos, was underway, and our squadron was in the thick of it starting the day after it kicked off.

*****

Returning my mind to the here and now, I looked at my alarm clock. It read 0400 hours and was ringing loudly. Little did I realize that this was going to be the start of *one long day in Laos*. Climbing

---

[11] See notes 4 and 9.

out of the rack (bed), I cleaned up, dressed, and headed to the mess hall for breakfast. I then proceeded to the ready room (room in the operation area where mission briefing or debriefing takes place) for the morning briefing prior to takeoff.

That morning's mission briefing was scheduled to take place at 0500 hours, so we had sufficient time to complete the briefing, read the yellow sheet, and preflight the aircraft prior to the scheduled 0645 takeoff. Our flight needed to arrive at LZ Kilo near Khe Sanh by 0800 hours for the Army's daily mission briefing and assignments prior to starting work in Laos.

That morning's briefing for that day's mission was conducted by Major Michael Wasko Jr. Major Wasko was our squadron's operations officer as well as the flight and mission leader for that day's flight. His copilot for that day's mission was Lieutenant Colonel Charles Pitman, who was the commanding officer of Marine Air Base Squadron 16 at Marble Mountain (Marine aviation base support and facilities were his squadron's missions).

He was flying that day's mission because he was in the process of being checked out (qualified) in the CH-53D aircraft prior to the dual scheduled change of commands where he gave up his current command and would then become our new squadron commander. The change of command was to take place in three days.

HMH-463 Squadron's aircraft designated call sign was Dimmer. Our squadron policy further designated the squadron's *call-sign* use by aircraft commanders for radio transmission during missions to be based on which billet (job) you held in the squadron. Normally, the side numbers of each aircraft were used as part of the call sign, but not in our squadron. Based on this policy, each of the aircraft commanders had individual designations that were used to easily identify who was the pilot in command of the aircraft. The following were some of the more significant call signs used in our squadron at the time:

- Administrative officer was Dimmer 1.
- Intelligence officer was Dimmer 2.
- Operations officer was Dimmer 3.

- Logistics officer was Dimmer 4.
- Executive officer was Dimmer 5.
- Commanding officer was Dimmer 6.
- Other squadron officers and pilots were Dimmer 7 through 44.

Major Michael Wasko was our squadron's operations officer. That made his call sign Dimmer 3. Since I was the senior captain in the squadron, I was assigned the job of the squadron's logistics officer. My call sign was Dimmer 4.

My copilot for that day's mission was First Lieutenant Dan Silver, who was a new replacement copilot, having arrived in-country and assigned to our squadron a little more than five days earlier. Additionally, this was Dan's first combat flight.

Boy, is Dan in for a surprise today! What a way to start off his combat flying career by being scheduled with me to go into Laos on his first day!

Dan looked a little concerned as we sat down being a little early for the Mission 52 (Lam Son 719) briefing. We spent several minutes, before the formal briefing started, talking about what to expect during the mission and duties that I expected him to complete while we were on the mission. As we talked about the upcoming mission, my mind drifted back to my recent arrival to HMH-463 in Vietnam.

Since my arrival in the squadron on January 2, 1971, I had flown support missions all over the northern parts of I Corps in South Vietnam. Marine Corps ground operations in these northern areas of I Corps were being drawn down, and Marine Corps units were being replaced by US Army units throughout the northern tactical operating area of I Corps. As part of this gradual draw down, our squadron was scheduled to be redeployed to Hawaii from Vietnam in May or June 1971.

In mid-January 1971, I recalled that our squadron had received word that we would be supporting a *top secret* mission that would be launched by the South Vietnamese into Laos. Their incursion would require a significant buildup of supplies, ammunition, and logistical support near the border of Laos.

Our squadron was also tasked to be a participant in the Dewey Canyon II that would support the development of a new logistic base and airfield located in the area of the old Khe Sanh Marine airfield and combat base at the end of the Belong Valley. Being the senior captain in the squadron, having flown the CH-53A in combat on my previous tour, as well as served as an instructor pilot in a stateside squadron, accumulated 850 flight hours in the CH-53, made me sufficiently qualified to be designated a flight leader.

After my five-day acclimatization from flying stand-down, followed by a NATOPS check flight, I was designated to be a flight leader or section leader or both in order to take part in the squadron's combat operations. The other flight leaders in the squadron were all field-grade officers who served previous combat tours, with one exception, that being our present commanding officer.

When I arrived in-country and checked into the squadron, I met the current squadron's commanding officer, a lieutenant colonel.

He, according to scuttlebutt (rumors), had not served a tour or job in a Marine Corps operational squadron prior to undergoing refresher training in the CH-53 and taking command of this squadron. This was almost unheard of in the Marine Corps aviation world. The normal progression of an aviator entails several tours of duty in operational units before being promoted to a senior-officer position. This lieutenant colonel, who will remain nameless, after only refresher training, was assigned as the commander of my squadron—HMH-463.

I could not believe it. A commanding officer with no combat experience was one thing, but no operational experience was over-the-top crazy.

He had been in command of the squadron a little over three months when I arrived in-country. Scuttlebutt indicated that almost all his assignments since leaving flight school were all in Washington, DC, at the headquarters for the Marine Corps or the Pentagon, except for an assignment as a flight school instructor after completing a ground tour as a forward air controller in a ground unit on the East Coast around the time of the Cuban missile crisis. It appeared that he had done very well in the Washington political environment because he had been promoted from captain to major to lieutenant colonel without ever holding an operational job and spent a vast majority of his career in the Washington, DC, area.

It appeared to me and, to most of the officers in the squadron, that this was political payback for his superior performance at *desk duties*.

In my opinion, his lack of any real operational Marine Corps squadron experience, his limited understanding of the aircraft, including its systems, and his political and promotional aspirations made him a poor leader as well as a marginal squadron commander, at best.

Company-grade officers like myself were forced to look to other field-grade officers in our squadron for operational direction, guidance, and leadership. Fortunately, we had two of these field-grade officers in our squadron at the time. They both had plenty of operational experience as well as being second-tour-combat veterans. Our executive officer (XO), Major Myrddyn E. "Red" Edwards, and operations officer, Major Michael Wasko, were these two field-grade Marines.

Coming back to reality and pushing my recollection of the past months out of my mind, I again focused on our mission that day.

My primary job that day was to perform flight duties as the leader of the second section of aircraft in the flight consisting of four CH-53s. I was also designated to be the alternate flight leader if necessary. I was responsible for the operation of my aircraft and my wingman as the second section leader.

My alternate-flight-leader assignment was necessary in case the flight leader had mechanical problems, or otherwise could no longer lead the flight. Then I would take over the mission as the flight leader. As the alternate flight leader, my aircraft was also the only aircraft in the flight that was equipped with a seventy-five-foot-long aluminum rescue ladder. The ladder was attached to the ramp in the rear of the aircraft to facilitate personnel recovery when landing in the area was not possible.

The other aircraft commanders for this mission were First Lieutenant Autrey (Dimmer 2), who was Major Wasko's wingman, and First Lieutenant Gilley (Dimmer 44—squadron pilot), who was my wingman.

The formal mission Lam Son 719 briefing (mission number 52) covered the standard items: mission to be completed, area weather, intelligence, enemy strength, potential threat hazards, radio frequencies, call signs of our Marine Corps HML-367 Scarface squadron partners, who were flying Cobra gunships.

Of note during the intelligence portion of the briefing was the report that the NVA had consolidated troop positions around several fire support bases inside Laos signaling potential NVA infantry counterattacks on these positions. Additionally, more heavy weapons were also observed as well as heavy 23mm and 37mm antiaircraft guns were seen for the first time being moved into areas around several of the FSBs.

After completion of the briefing, Lieutenant Silver and I picked up our flight gear, then proceeded to the line shack to check the maintenance status of our assigned aircraft. This entailed the review of maintenance actions that had been completed on our aircraft over the past ten flights. It's called reading the yellow sheet. Completing our review, I signed for the aircraft, then we proceeded to our bird.

Our aircraft on that day's mission was side number YH-20, which was named Miss Carriage II, whose crew chief was Sergeant Charles "Pogy" Pogany. He was one of the most respected and competent CH-53 crew chiefs in the squadron (potentially the entire Marine Corps). Our two gunners were Corporal R. Garcia and Lance Corporal Arthur "AJ" Pailes. They would be utilizing the hard-mounted .50-caliber machine guns that we carried mounted in the passenger door behind the pilot of the aircraft and in the window behind the copilot.

Lieutenant Silver and I then preflighted and strapped into our pilot and copilot seats. Using our naval aviation training and operating procedures standardization (NATOPS) manual for the CH-53D aircraft, we performed the necessary procedures in accordance with the manual. Lieutenant Silver would read the checklist, and then I would perform the required actions.

Auxiliary power plant (APP), jet engines start-ups, rotor engagement, and other pretaxi operational checks of our aircraft were completed in accordance with our NATOPS checklist. All checklist items were checked and were operating in their normal ranges.

As I looked out the right-side pilot's window, I saw the other three aircraft in our flight engage their rotor systems. When all four CH-53D aircraft had turned up and appeared to be ready to go, Dimmer 3, our flight leader, called for a pretaxi radio check.

The entire flight checked in with him on the radio, and he called for taxi, then takeoff. We all followed his directions for radio-frequency changes. Once all four aircraft were lined up on the runway, we made a formation takeoff heading north toward Hai Van Pass.

Our four Marine Corps escort Cobra attack gunships (two sections of two aircraft) were already en route north, "feet wet," and also heading north toward Hai Van Pass. Our flight would rendezvous with the Scarface birds at the LZ Kilo near Khe Sanh for the Army's daily mission briefing.

Secure communications among aircraft were maintained through the use of encrypted UHF and FM radios that were reprogrammed daily. This allowed for interflight communication among all aircraft in the flight, including escort aircraft, and with other participant aircraft without the enemy being able to hear these communications. Limited ground communications were also possible if the ground units also had the encrypted radios and daily codes.

As we crossed Da Nang Bay, our flight of four encountered the poor monsoon weather that was forecast. We encountered rain, wind, low ceilings, and reduced visibility (less than half a mile) as we proceeded over the water north along the South Vietnamese coastline. Once our flight rounded Hai Van Pass, the visibility improved to about one mile, but the overcast ceiling dropped from one thousand feet to five hundred feet above ground level (AGL) or, in this case, the water.

Our flight proceeded along the coast for approximately thirty miles before the weather started to get better and the clouds to break up. The break in the weather was an unusual occurrence since we were in the monsoon transitory season in this area of Vietnam. Our flight climbed to an altitude that was out of small-arms range, checked for save-o-planes (clearance from friendly artillery fire or air strikes), and proceeded toward Khe Sanh airfield for refueling.

Once our flight had climbed to a safe altitude, I told Lieutenant Silver to relax and observe the countryside below. He looked very worried. So trying to reassure him, I said, "Dan, don't worry about what we are going to do. If you just concentrate on the task we need to complete as we fly our missions, things will be fine. No big deal, just another mission."

I told myself that same thing each time I flew a mission into Laos. No big deal!

Landing at Khe Sanh airfield, we proceeded to refuel all the aircraft in our flight. Once we finished refueling all our birds, we then flew the two miles and landed at LZ Kilo in preparation to receive the Army's daily mission brief and assignments.

Our Scarface Cobra attack-gunship folks had previously arrived and had already refueled and rechecked their store of weapons. The Scarface crews were standing by their aircraft and appeared to be ready to launch on their escort duty after the briefing. After our four aircraft arrived at LZ Kilo, we shut down our aircraft. All the CH-53 pilots and crew chiefs disembarked their aircraft, then rendezvoused with the Scarface pilots, and together, we walked to the bunker to attend the Army's Mission 52 daily briefing.

Our Army briefer started the briefing precisely at 0800 hours. The briefer indicated that we had a two-part mission in Laos to complete that day.

Part 1 of that day's mission was to move external loads (twelve thousand to fourteen thousand pounds each) of ammunition, heavy machinery, food, and construction supplies to the various FSBs inside Laos. He handed out detailed sheets to each aircraft commander that described pickup locations, items to be carried, and where they were to be taken.

The second part of our mission that day was to reposition two 155mm and six 105mm artillery pieces from FSB Hotel II to FSB Delta 1. The two 155mm guns had ammunition loads attached to the guns in a sling arrangement as did the six 105mm guns that also included ammunition packages.

The Army briefer indicated that these artillery pieces were needed at FSB Delta 1 to facilitate the continued ARVN push westward deeper into Laos with the final ARVN objective being the occupation of the town of Tchepone, Laos. Again, the Army's intelligence briefer reiterated what we had heard in our own briefing that morning, that the NVA had consolidated troop positions around several FSBs, including Hotel II and Delta 1. This signaled potential NVA infantry counterattacks on these positions. He further indicated that more heavy weapons and mortars were being observed moving into the area. These heavy weapons included 23mm and 37mm antiaircraft guns that were observed for the first time in areas around several of the FSBs.

After the conclusion of the mission brief by US Army's Command and Control folks, we all returned to our aircraft, briefed the other crew members, strapped in, and started our aircraft.

As we were completing our NATOPS checklist and were ready to take off, I got a call from Dimmer 3. Upon starting his aircraft, Major Wasko discovered that his machine had developed some significant mechanical problems. He did not elaborate what these problems were but indicated that he would be returning to Marble Mountain, our home base, to either have the problems fixed or get a replacement aircraft. He then told me to take charge of the flight and work the mission until his return.

I remembered the Marine Corps' aviation doctrine that states that the *command* of a combined mission force consisting of transport helicopters and attack helicopters is the responsibility of the transport-helicopter commander. This doctrine reminded me that not only was I now in charge of the remaining three CH-53s, but I had now assumed responsibility for the supporting Scarface AH-1G attack gunships as well.

I watched as Major Wasko's aircraft departed for Marble Mountain.

I thought, *Well, it looks like it's up to me now to get this show on the road.*

*****

Getting the show on the road started with my radio call to let the Scarface leader, Captain Crews, know about the change in leadership and that Dimmer 4 would be leading the fight until Dimmer 3 returned. We also confirmed the previously discussed strategy for the first portion of our mission. With our collective strategy confirmed, my aircraft along with my two wingmen lifted off LZ Kilo to start the first part of our mission to resupply ammunition, heavy machinery, food, and construction supplies to various fire support bases inside Laos.

The equipment and supplies we were to deliver were staged just inside the perimeter of LZ Kilo, which was located several miles east of South Vietnam's border with Laos. These pieces of equipment and supplies were to be delivered to FSB's Hotel, Delta, Blue, Yellow, and Delta 1 inside Laos

Each of the loads, which were slung under the aircraft in cargo nets or with slings attached to the equipment, were then attached to our aircraft's external cargo hook or our external pendant. This method of delivery was designed to facilitate fast delivery of the loads to the FSBs. The average weight of each load generally weighed between twelve thousand to fourteen thousand pounds.

The FSBs were located at different distances inside the Vietnamese-Laotian border. FSB Hotel, Blue, and Yellow were located approximately three, twelve, and fifteen miles inside the border of Laos, respectively. FSB Delta was located approximately twenty-one miles inside the Laotian border. FSB Delta 1 was located approximately twenty-six miles from the border. All the FSBs were generally in a westerly direction from LZ Kilo. (See the map at the end of the chapter).

Our planned tactics for that day's resupply mission were to be performed as follows: one CH-53D would pick up an external load and proceed to the Laotian border where the first section (two aircraft) of HML-367 Scarface attack gunships would pick up their escort positions, then accompany them from the border to the designated FSB Hotel, Blue, Yellow, Delta, or Delta 1, and return. The next CH-53D would pick up its load, then head toward the border to be picked up by the second section of Scarface gunships that would escort it to its destination. The third CH-53D would then pick up its load, then head for the border, waiting inside South Vietnam until the first section of Cobra gunships returned to escort them to its destination.

We daisy-chained our cargo lifts into FSBs Hotel, Blue, and Yellow, which were completed without very much enemy resistance being encountered. However, my aircraft and my two wingmen all received light small-arms fire on the first couple of lifts near the perimeters at both FSB Delta and Delta 1.

Our Cobra attack-gunship escorts successfully suppressed the fire at both FSBs Delta and Delta 1 with their miniguns and grenade launchers. They elected not to use their rockets since pinpoint accuracy was necessary in order to not hit friendly troops inside the FSBs. While we could hear and see enemy firing at us during these lifts, no aircraft in our daisy-chain flight nor were any of our four Scarface escorts hit by enemy fire.

I looked over at Dan after we had seen enemy fire at FSB Delta and were departing the FSB after depositing our load. Judging from the look on his face and his body language, it appeared to me that he was handling the fact that someone was trying to kill him fairly well, so far.

Our three aircraft daisy-chain efforts resulted in moving approximately 195,000 pounds of cargo, ammunition, and equipment to FSBs Hotel, Blue, Yellow, Delta, and Delta 1. This took fifteen lifts or trips, which took all morning and into the afternoon, to complete the effort with refueling stops factored in along the way.

I was thinking then, *Today's mission is going fairly well so far. I sure hope the rest of it goes this well too.*

At about 1500 hours, our flight of three aircraft, along with our Cobra escorts, were ready to commence the second portion of our mission for that day. Scarface led, and I again discussed and agreed what tactics we would employ to safely complete the gun-movement lifts.

The gun-extraction mission, according to our detailed mission sheet that was provided this morning, entailed moving two 155mm guns each weighing 14,000 pounds each, plus an attached sling load of ammunition that weighed approximately 4,000 pounds. Then we were tasked with moving six 105mm howitzers each weighing 8,500 pounds, plus attached sling load of ammunition weighing approximately 5,000 pounds from FSB Hotel II to FSB Delta 1. However, things had changed because of our earlier resupply mission to FSB Delta 1. Since we had already taken several loads of 105mm ammunition to the FSB in anticipation of the delivery of the six 105s, the Army changed the mission. The 105mm guns coming from FSB Hotel II would be moved by themselves without the ammunition packages.

Hotel II was located approximately eight nautical miles west of the South Vietnamese border inside Laos and approximately thirty miles southwest of LZ Kilo. The distance between FSB Hotel II to FSB Delta 1 was approximately thirty miles or about twenty-minute flight time. (See map at the end of the chapter).

Since intelligence reports indicated that the NVA were moving 23mm and 37mm antiaircraft guns into the area, we elected to keep the aircraft not directly involved in the gun pickups in an area east of FSB Hotel II and inside the South Vietnam border. Each aircraft would remain in South Vietnam's airspace until it was time for their gun and ammunition pickups. At which time, they would fly approximately eight miles west to the FSB Hotel II.

Per our agreed strategy, the first section of Scarface Cobra escorts sprinted ahead of our flight heading for Hotel II and made several visual-reconnaissance runs around the FSB. The Scarface Cobra leader, radioing back, told me that they had not seen or been fired upon by either 23mm or 37mm antiaircraft guns that had previously been seen around several of the FSBs in Laos. They further stated that they had not seen any of these types of weapons on the ground around Hotel II nor had they received any fire from any type of weapons during their over flights of the area. Our Cobra escort leader also said that they had checked with the Army's Command and Control folks by radio. They indicated, based on direct contact with the ARVN troops on the ground at Hotel II, that no antiaircraft guns were reported around FSB Hotel II. Our Scarface Cobra escorts continued to orbit over FSB Hotel II looking for any potential enemy gun or mortar positions.

As the flight leader, it was up to me to choose the strategy that we would use to protect our flight and our escorts' safety while still getting the job done. Since the antiaircraft-gun threats had not materialized, my main concern became the potential small arms, rocket, rocket-propelled grenades, mortar, and .50-caliber machine-gun fire from around the FSB that could impact our operations in and around the LZ. In order to minimize these risks, I chose to have the flight utilize a high-altitude spiral-approach strategy for our initial attempts in extracting the artillery pieces from the hilltop position. I was familiar with FSB Hotel II's layout, knowing where the LZ and gun pits were located on the FSB since I was part of the flight of CH-53Ds that inserted a bulldozer and then the guns into the gun pits a week earlier.

Since I was flying the lead aircraft, I had the opportunity to test out the strategy by making the first approach into FSB Hotel II that day. Flying above 3,000 feet AGL, I proceeded to FSB Hotel II from the location east of the border. Based on these Scarface reports, I chose to make my approach in a tight right-hand spiral, 80-degree angle of bank, to the hill on which FSB Hotel II was located. The rationale for this type of approach was to fly the aircraft to a position out of small-arms range, normally above 3,000 feet or greater AGL, and once over the friendly position or LZ, then to descend, staying over the friendly position as long as possible before finally entering the lethal range of small-arms and machine-gun enemy fire, which normally occurred at the end of the approach to the LZ.

In my opinion, the unique ability of the CH-53D to perform these types of maneuvers, as well as its extraordinary power, enabled us to climb quickly out of range of most small-arms fire, making the aircraft extremely survivable as compared to the Army's helicopters that were being flown during this operation.

Arriving at FSB Hotel II, we commenced our approach, rolling the aircraft in a right-hand spiral using about 80-degree angle of bank.

Taking a quick look at Dan in the left seat as we spiraled toward the ground, I saw that he had a look of stark terror on his face and had stiffened his body. He had not said a word yet. I felt bad for not warning him that I was going to be using an 80-degree-angle-of-bank approach to minimize our exposure to enemy fire by lessening the duration and profile of our approach. Seeing his reaction, I quickly said to him, "This is a normal approach, Dan, in this environment. We will be fine. Trust me." I then returned my concentration to completing the approach.

I don't think Dan believes me, I thought.

At the bottom of the spiral approach over the FSB, I asked Dan to perform the landing checklist, which he accomplished quickly without difficulty while I focused on my approach to the LZ. As we slowed our approach and headed for the LZ, I spotted one of the ARVN gun crew members in one of the adjacent gun pits next to the LZ who was waving his arms wildly. Modifying my approach toward his location, he quickly directed us to a position over our first load in the gun pits.

As we moved over the load, I recognized that our load was going to be a 155mm gun, including ammunition that the ARVN gun crew had made ready for our pickup.

As we came to a hover over the gun, Sergeant Pogany said to me, "I have the load in sight. Move right five feet," as he worked to direct me directly over the gun.

I saw, then heard the first mortar round of several, hitting on the far side north of the LZ. Our Scarface gunship escorts also saw the impacts and worked to locate the suspected enemy mortar positions. They then attacked the positions, suppressing the mortar fire temporarily.

Sergeant Pogany, undeterred by the mortar fire, continued to direct me to the exact pickup spot over the gun quickly, and we hooked up the gun successfully with the help of the gun crew. Lieutenant Silver increased the power to the maximum on both engines, using the speed-control levers on the overhead quadrant, and monitored the engine gauges while we lifted the heavy gun and the attached package successfully out of the gun pit. A quick calculation of the power required to hover at our altitude indicated to me that the load we were lifting was close to 19,000 pounds.

We climbed vertically in order to get the gun package all the way over the sandbag-and-wooden wall surrounding the gun pits. Sergeant Pogany verified that the load was clear before I transitioned from a hover through the translational lift zone (zone between ground cushion and forward airspeed where helicopters lose lift), into forward flight turning the aircraft northwest initially, then climbing out of the LZ, staying as much as possible inside the perimeter of the LZ in a right-handed spiral climb until we reached 3,000 feet AGL. We were then joined by two of the Scarface Cobras as we completed our spiral climb out from Hotel II and then turned to the west and headed for FSB Delta 1.

While en route to FSB Delta 1, I called Dimmer 2 and Dimmer 44 informing them of the type of approach we successfully utilized to get in, then out of the LZ with the first of the two big-gun packages. They each acknowledged my call, and both said that they would follow my lead. Dimmer 2 indicated that he was inbound to Hotel II for the next gun-package pickup.

First Lieutenant Autrey (Dimmer 2) made his approach to FSB Hotel II in the same manner as I had done. He made a right-hand spiral approach to the hill starting just east of the FSB Hotel II. At the end of his spiral approach, Lieutenant Autrey flared the aircraft, raising the nose of the aircraft to stop forward airspeed and settled into a hover just outside the edge of the area where the 155mm guns were located. Holding in a hover, he saw the ARVN gun crew member who was attempting to direct him toward his load. He followed the ARVN's hand signals, and those of his crew chief to quickly move in the direction of the gun package's location. While in the process of moving over the load in the gun pits, Lieutenant Autrey's aircraft came under renewed mortar fire as well as small-arms fire that appeared to be coming from south of the FSB.

Seeing the mortar impacts and getting a call from Dimmer 2 that he was taking small-arms fire, the two remaining Scarface gunships went into their attack formation and attacked both areas where the fire appeared to be emanating. These attacks did not suppress the small-arms fire into the gun-pit area. The fire, in fact, was becoming heavier and more intense, but Dimmer 2 was still able to pick up his 155mm-gun package and then depart to the northeast, then spiraled up to a safe altitude of three thousand feet AGL.

As I monitored Dimmer 2's progress, as well as the Scarface Cobras' actions supporting his lift, it indicated to me that the NVA had moved in close to the south side of the FSB Hotel II. They had seen our activities and wanted to keep our flight from removing any more artillery pieces out of FSB Hotel II. The Cobra's section leader recommended that they stay engaged with the enemy at Hotel II while Dimmer 44 attempted the first extraction of one of the six remaining 105mm guns to be moved from Hotel II. I concurred with the request of the Scarface's section leader.

With the pickup by Dimmer 2 of the second big-gun package, we still had to move the six 105mm guns from FSB Hotel II.

Two in process and six to go, I thought. Looking across the cockpit at Dan, he appeared to have recovered some of his composure and was looking at the map verifying our course to FSB Delta 1.

The second section of the Scarface Cobras continued their attacks on the enemy positions as Dimmer 44 proceeded from the border toward FSB Hotel II. He was flying the third aircraft in our reduced flight of three. He was also one of our newest aircraft commanders in our squadron, having limited experience, but had flown a couple of missions like this before. His aircraft was to pick up one of the 105mm-artillery pieces without ammunition attached to it. This change in plans occurred because we had earlier resupplied FSB Delta 1 with several lifts of 105mm ammunition in anticipation of the delivery of the six 105s from FSB Hotel II

Dimmer 44 arrived over the FSB Hotel II and located the LZ while at an altitude out of enemy's gun range, then commenced the right-hand spiral approach to the gun pits.

The NVA had seen this flight pattern twice before and were ready when he started to flare at the bottom of his approach over the exposed gun positions. Dimmer 44 reported that he was taking small-arms fire from the NVA south of the LZ. He also reported that the gun-pit area was receiving mortar fire, which was now impacting near and inside the gun emplacements, even while the HML-367 Scarface gunships continued to attack them. The incoming enemy fire did not appear to decrease because of their efforts.

While in a hover over the 105mm gun and trying to get the gun hooked up, his crew chief watched the ARVN gun crew trooper standing on the axel of the gun take several rounds of small-arms fire into his body, then fall off the gun without being able to successfully pass the sling to him.

It should be noted that the ARVN gun crews who manned and fired the howitzers that we were moving were also responsible for their movement from one firing position to another or from one FSB to another. They were exposed to the same enemy fire as we were in our helicopters, but they had no protection from snipers, small-arms fire, or mortars that were directed at us and at them as well.

It was not surprising that when the enemy fire into the gun pits was at its heaviest, some of these troops were reluctant to expose themselves to the enemy fire. However, many of the ARVN gun crew troops paid the ultimate price to get their guns safely out of the gun pits and delivered to their new locations.

Under intense fire and with the loss of the hook up man, Dimmer 44 reported that he was forced to abandon the gun pickup and exit the FSB Hotel II to the northeast. He radioed me that since he had taken a significant amount of mortar and small-arms fire while trying to get the gun out, as well as needing to refuel, he was going to return to Khe Sanh for fuel. He was then going to reposition at LZ Kilo and then shut down in order to inspect his aircraft for battle damage. The two Scarface Cobra gunships also sustained some battle damage during these attacks and returned to Khe Sanh airfield to refuel and rearm and then to proceed to LZ Kilo and shut down to inspect their aircraft.

As Dan and I proceeded west toward FSB Delta 1, at about three thousand feet above ground level, the visibility became somewhat restricted because of the large number of artillery barrages and fixed-wing air strikes that were taking place in support of the ARVN westerly advances. As we approached FSB Delta 1, visibility was dropping to below one mile as we commenced our spiral approach. We inserted the 155mm-gun package into FSB Delta 1. The insert was uneventful, except for taking some small-arms fire from the west side of the gun-pit area, which the Scarface Cobra gunships again suppressed easily.

We set the ammunition down first, then moved over slightly to place the 155mm gun into its preconstructed gun pit and departed the FSB. As we headed back toward FSB Hotel II, we passed Dimmer 2 who was en route to FSB Delta 1 with his 155mm-gun package.

Since his two Scarface escort gunships had remained at FSB Hotel II to suppress the increasing enemy fire around the FSB and cover Dimmer 44's attempted gun pickup, he had no escort available. To ensure the delivery of the gun package to Delta 1, I asked the two Scarface Cobra escorts that were covering my aircraft to pick up Dimmer 2 and escort him to Delta 1. The Scarface lead agreed to the change in plans and broke off as our escort in order to escort him during his approach to FSB Delta 1.

Dimmer 2 also made a successful spiral approach setting the ammunition down first, then moved over slightly to place the 155mm gun into its preconstructed gun pit and departed the FSB. South Vietnamese Army gun crews were swarming all over the gun after the drop, preparing it and its accompanying ammunition to be use against NVA forces further to the west. We had also observed that these activities indicated, to me, that the situation at FSB Delta 1 was becoming more critical. These guns were badly needed by the ARVN forces at FSB Delta 1.

As we proceeded east back toward South Vietnam, it was very apparent that we needed to refuel, so we flew back to Khe Sanh airfield. Calling Dimmer 2 on the radio after his load was dropped, I directed him to do the same.

While sitting in the fuel pits, we observed our section of Cobra escorts refueling, inspecting, then rearming their two aircraft. We needed to regroup and assess the approach we had previously used in order to continue our mission if we were to be successful in extracting the six remaining 105mm-artillery pieces from FSB Hotel II.

Since Dimmer 44 had been driven out of the FSB Hotel II pickup area by heavy enemy fire, it was evident that the NVA were aware of our past ingress strategy.

The Scarface flight leader and I discussed, over our secure radio, the need to modify the tactics we should use to approach Hotel II. We agreed we needed to do a face-to-face discussion and look together at our topographic map in order to formulate our new ingress strategy. I told Lieutenant Silver I was going to talk with the Scarface Cobra leader on the tarmac and gave him control of our still turned-up aircraft.

The Scarface leader and I both exited our aircraft and met on the tarmac near the fuel pits to discuss strategy options. We both agreed that there was no question that a modification in the CH-53D ingress tactics was necessary. Unless we modified our tactics, we would be sitting ducks since the NVA had seen the last three approaches to the FSB and were just waiting for us to do the same thing again.

We needed new tactics that could be used to successfully get into the FSB Hotel II, pick up the load, and get back out without being shot down. Our actual gun pickups had to remain the same because of the need to hover over the guns in order to attach them to the aircraft. We discussed the options available to get up to and into the FSB. After a detailed map review, we came to an agreement on how the Dimmers would proceed and how Scarface would cover our next gun-extraction attempt.

We both manned our individual aircraft and completed the refueling process. At this point, Dimmer 44 came up on the radio from LZ Kilo and indicated that he had received only minor battle damage and could continue with the mission. He indicated that he was ready to start up his aircraft and rejoin the flight. Once positive secure radio communications were again established, we briefed the entire flight on the changes to our ingress strategy.

Once Dimmer 2 had completed refueling, we took off together from the Khe Sanh airfield. Once airborne, we were joined by Dimmer 44. Now as a flight of three again, we flew south inside the South Vietnam border at low level for approximately twenty-five miles. Our intent was to stay behind the low hills near the border and out of sight of the NVA spotters, then continue into the FSB using terrain masking to the maximum extent possible until reaching the perimeter of FSB Hotel II. Since we had not seen or received any enemy fire from the east side of FSB Hotel II nor had the Scarface birds, this strategy appeared to be sound based on our combined observations. Our run-ins from the border would be made on an individual basis with two Scarface Cobra escorts, also utilizing terrain masking, covering our ingress attempt. The other two Cobras would remain with my other two aircraft holding in South Vietnamese airspace east of FSB Hotel II to escort the second aircraft to the hill if we were successful with our extraction.

As we departed to the west, my two wingmen stayed behind and inside South Vietnam's border while I turned and headed in toward FSB Hotel II. As we turned west, my aircraft was again joined by our two Scarface escorts as we entered a shallow valley toward Hotel II at low level and maximum airspeed. This new tactic of maximum airspeed at low level, using the terrain masking where possible to cover our approach, appeared to be working since we received no small-arms fire during our ingress. Upon arrival at the base of the hill east of FSB Hotel II, we popped up over the top of the hill trading airspeed for altitude. We arrived over the gun pits without being spotted by the enemy NVA gunners. That condition lasted about fifteen seconds. As we were getting ready for the pickup of the first 105mm gun, the world seemed to explode around us.

The Cobra leader seeing the volume of fire directed toward us immediately called his wingmen orbiting with our aircraft back at the border, ordering them to fly directly to the FSB and help suppress the heavy volume of fire we were encountering.

In the midst of this explosion of fire, Sergeant Pogany directed me over the closest 105mm gun. Mortar fire, plus .50-caliber machine gun and small-arms fire seemed to come from everywhere, but it appeared to be the heaviest on the south and west sides of the FSB. I directed our two gunners to shoot if they could identify sources of incoming fire. Lieutenant Silver called out a couple of targets, which our gunners fired upon trying to suppress the incoming .50-caliber machine-gun fire.

While we were in this exposed hover over the gun, Sergeant Pogany, Lieutenant Silver, or I could not find any ARVN personnel in or near the gun we were trying to pick up. No one was visible at all in the gun pits. The ARVN troops that had been there to assist on our first loads earlier in the day were no longer there. These troops had previously lifted the gun sling and handed it up to Sergeant Pogany, but this time, they were nowhere to be found. Undeterred, Sergeant Pogany directed me to get lower so he could reach through the "hell hole," which is the location of the cargo hook where the crew chief lies on his belly and directs the pilot's movements so loads can be hooked to the external cargo hook by reaching for the sling that laid on top of the gun barrel.

As we dropped lower over the gun, I had to make a pedal turn, a flat turn of the fuselage done with rudder pedals, directed by Sergeant Pogany, so that the gun's barrel would not strike the aircraft's bottom. While we were doing this, the fire from the .50-caliber machine guns and other small-arms fire was continuing to increase. Mortar fire also was raining down on the entire FSB LZ and in the gun pits.

Lieutenant Silver, Sergeant Pogany, and I could hear bullets and shrapnel hitting the fuselage of our aircraft. Even in a low hover, Sergeant Pogany was unable to reach the gun sling because the rotor wash had pushed it out of his reach. With no help in getting the load hooked up and the increasing hostile fire, we made the decision that the FSB LZ and its associated gun pits were not workable at the present time. We departed without getting the 105mm gun hooked up and extracted out of the FSB.

While we were trying to pick up the 105mm gun from the gun pit, our section of Scarface Cobra escorts were attacking the areas from where we were receiving the .50-caliber machine gun, mortar, and small-arms fire. I observed their attacks, which concentrated their fire on the .50-caliber machine-gun position first. They made multiple attack runs on all the positions they could identify until they had expended all their on-board ordnance, which produced limited results. Even then, with all their ordnance gone, they continued to make attack runs on the enemy positions in order to draw fire away from our hovering aircraft. As I pulled into maximum climb power, I called the Cobra gunships indicating that we were departing the FSB without the gun, and as we climbed to three thousand feet, they quickly broke off the dummy attacks following us back toward South Vietnam.

While en route back to Khe Sanh, the HML-367 Scarface flight leader called the Army's Command and Control folks and indicated that the FSB Hotel II in general and the gun pits in particular were extremely hot and requested fixed-wing aircraft or artillery or both be assigned to suppress the ever-increasing enemy fire from the south and west of the FSB before the next attempt was made to move the six remaining 105s.

As we flew toward the border, I thought, *This mission is going to get one of our aircraft shot down if the enemy fire from the perimeter south and west of the gun pits is not reduced significantly, but we have a mission to complete, and we'll have to find a way to get it done.* I did not share my concerns with Lieutenant Silver, Sergeant Pogany, or the other crew members at that time.

As we approached the border, Sergeant Pogany described the scene behind us. His first words of what was happening behind us were "Wow, you should see this! It looks like the fixed-wing bubbas are kicking the shit out of the bastards back there." He went on to describe what he saw, which was several fixed-wing aircraft working over or attacking the south and west side of FSB Hotel II's perimeter. This was the area where the majority of fire was coming from during our pickup attempt since he could see explosions of high-explosive ordnance and napalm that were evidently being used by the flight of attack aircraft. As Sergeant Pogany climbed into the jump seat between Dan and I, he concluded his description by saying, "I sure would not want to be in their shoes," indicating to Dan and me that it was quite an impressive sight.

After returning to South Vietnam, we were joined by the rest of my flight, and then three of us flew directly to Khe Sanh to refuel and then proceeded to LZ Kilo and shut down.

As the flight leader and aircraft commander, I needed to assess the extent of the battle damage to my aircraft as well as to any of our critical systems and components. I also needed to check on the status of the rest of my CH-53D wingmen as well as the Scarface birds. After my 53's shutdown in LZ Kilo, the Scarface flight leader and his wingman all shut down, then inspected their attack Cobras, now parked on the matting not far from where we had parked. After all his aircraft were inspected, he and I met on the Marston matting near his four attack Cobra aircraft to discuss our next move.

As I walked toward him on the Marston matting, I thought back to the mutual respect that had been developed between our two squadrons. This respect had been created during the lead up to Lam Son 719 through the creation of an inter-squadron flight program. This program was established by Major Wasko, our operations officer, and by Lieutenant Colonel Clifford E. Reese, the commanding officer of HML-367 to promote a better understanding of each other's missions. The program was designed to greatly enhance a *cross-squadron* understanding of transport-and-attack-helicopter tactics necessary for survival on the battlefield, walking in the other man's shoes so to speak. During the program, we took Cobra attack-gunship pilots and flew them as copilots on CH-53Ds during external cargo-transport missions. Conversely, the HML-367 Cobra gunship pilots flew our transport pilots in the front seat on Cobra gunships to demonstrate their attack mission.

I remember one of these missions very clearly because it was the first time, I could personally fight back in a meaningful way at the enemy who had been shooting at me over my fourteen months of combat flying. The opportunity to fly in the front seat of an AH-1G Cobra was offered to me by First Lieutenant Yaskovic, an HML-367 pilot. I jumped at the chance to fly an attack bird. The mission I was to go on was to be a training flight to see how the weapons systems functioned. We were to be the lead aircraft for a flight of two AH-1G on a training mission out over the South China Sea. On that day,

First Lieutenant Yaskovic briefed me on the operation of the AH-1G weapons systems, which were available for my control in the front seat of the aircraft. These included miniguns and a grenade launcher along with twelve 2.75 rockets carried in pods on the side of the aircraft. He briefed me that we were going to go to the practice-range area that had been set up offshore in the South China Sea and shoot at the sea snakes that were currently mating there.

After we got airborne and headed out to sea, First Lieutenant Yaskovic said he had been performing a mission with an ARVN ground unit working the area near Highway 1 in the Hai Van Pass area the night before. He said, "I had received ground fire from an NVA infantry unit while we were there supporting the ARVN troops patrolling along Highway 1 in the Hai Van Pass area. How would you like to see if we can shoot at something other than sea snakes?"

I responded, "That sounds great to me."

He called his wingman and talked about the change in the mission. His wingman was all for it. So we diverted our flight from the sea-snake range and headed for Hai Van Pass. As we approached the area, First Lieutenant Yaskovic called the ARVN ground unit and asked if they had any contact with the NVA troops since last night. Their response was that they had seen some enemy activity in that area that morning, and we could consider anyone in that area as hostiles. They continued to tell him that they had no friendly forces in that area and that we could engage anyone in that area at our volition.

First Lieutenant Yaskovic and his wingman discussed their tactics for the potential attack on the NVA position as he climbed the flight to an altitude of about two thousand feet so it would appear to the NVA that we were going to fly over the pass heading north, not posing a threat to them. Both aircraft then armed all their weapon systems.

When we reached the point where his aircraft had taken fire the night before, we made a hard banking turn and dived straight down on that spot. I looked through the forward wind screen and saw between five and ten NVA troops sitting on a large rock overlooking Highway 1. It appeared to me they were getting ready to set up an ambush on vehicular traffic on the highway. They had not appeared to have seen our flight or had dismissed it as not being a threat since they continued to carry on with their preparations.

First Lieutenant Yaskovic saw the NVA troops as we dove and said, "Get ready, Captain, and use the minigun. Go, shoot, shoot, shoot."

I had placed my hand on the small control stick on the right side of the front cockpit that was used to aim and control the gun turret directly below my feet that contained both the minigun and grenade launcher. Aiming at the troops that were getting larger in size as we streaked toward them, I pulled the trigger mechanism all the way back, and I heard a *kush, kush, kush, kush, kush.* From behind me, I heard First Lieutenant Yaskovic say, "You are firing the grenade launcher not the minigun," as he was firing a series of 2.75-inch rockets at the troops now running for cover. I finally realized that I had been so excited to have a chance to hit back that I had forgotten that the minigun was activated by pulling the trigger only halfway back. I could see several explosions on the ground from both the rockets and my grenades. We pulled out from the attack at about five hundred feet AGL, pulling up and rolling away from the target. The radio came to life at that point with First Lieutenant Yaskovic's wingman stating that he had already commenced his attack on the position. He reported seeing several bodies out in the open, the probable result of our first attack run. He went on to state that he was shifting his attack focus a little closer to the highway where he could still see NVA troop activity. As he pulled off the target below, we commenced our next attack run as we rolled in hot. This cycle provided each aircraft with suppression fire, which helped cover them as they pulled off the target when the aircraft is most vulnerable. We made a total of only three attack runs each since we had not been fully loaded with ordnance because this was supposed to be a training mission. Having expended all the ordnance on both our aircraft, we headed back to Marble Mountain Air Facility.

As we left the Hai Van Pass area, First Lieutenant Yaskovic called the ARVN ground combat unit giving them a report of what we had encountered as well as a warning regarding the potential of an ambush further up the mountain on Highway 1. They responded that they would investigate the situation. After returning to Marble Mountain Air Facility, we debriefed the mission, keeping a very low profile since we were not scheduled for a combat mission only a training flight. I thanked First Lieutenant Yaskovic several times for taking me flying on a real mission and not for a training flight.

Several days later, I saw First Lieutenant Yaskovic in the officers' club where he told me that the ARVN ground combat unit, we had worked with had gone to the area of our attack and recovered six NVA soldiers' bodies. So we got six confirmed killed in action (KIAs) as a result of our training mission. He also said he got his ass chewed by his operations officer for not flying the assigned mission, but what the hell, there were six less bad guys out there because of our mission. I bought him a drink for sharing the news with me.

Looking back on that flight, I felt much better now that I had finally had an opportunity to fight back against the enemy and not just be what Patty shot at.

This exchange program greatly enhanced the understanding and recognition of the problems that the other type of aircraft crew faced in their unique combat roles. This program promoted a greater understanding of our mission by the HML-367 Scarface Cobra attack-gunship pilots, which manifested itself by the fact that almost every CH-53D flight into Laos was escorted by their gunships.

HML-367 Cobra gunships, throughout all of Lam Son 719, steadfastly led our transport helicopters into the landing zones, spotted friendly and enemy positions, and then attacked the NVA antiaircraft guns and mortars with their machine guns, automatic grenade launchers, and 2.75-inch rockets. When the enemy was too close to ARVN firebases to permit actual attacks, the Cobra pilots often made dummy strafing runs to distract enemy gunners from the CH-53Ds, as they had just done for me or maneuvered their gunships between the NVA positions and our transports. These Marines were true warriors who supported our mission totally. Our squadrons were truly bonded together as a "band of brothers."

Meeting their leader on the matting, I thanked Captain Crews, the HML-367 Scarface Cobra gunship flight leader, for their outstanding support during the extraction attempts at FSB Hotel II and, for that matter, the conduct of the whole day's mission. He said that "a thank-you is not necessary since that is our job. One Marine protecting his brothers is what it's all about. Now I have some advice and some bad news to share with you."

He went on to say, "I have not seen that heavy a volume of enemy fire around FSB Hotel II any time in the past, and I have been supporting your squadron in and out of there, off and on for a week. I believe that unless it's significantly reduced, there would be a good chance that we could lose some aircraft in or around Hotel II if the mission is continued."

Finally, he got to the bad news indicating that each AH-1G aircraft had received battle damage. While the aircraft were still safely flyable, their fire-control systems and rocket-launching capabilities had been compromised. This bad news regarding their reduced mission capability made it difficult, if not impossible, for his aircraft to support our continuing gun-extraction mission at FSB Hotel II.

With their safety in mind, as acting flight leader, I released the HML-367 Scarface flight from their support mission. After watching the Scarface pilots man their aircraft, I watched as the flight of four AH-1G attack gunships departed for Marble Mountain so that their aircraft could be repaired.

*****

Returning to my aircraft, I found out that while I was talking to the Scarface flight leader, Sergeant Pogany and Lieutenant Silver had completed the check for battle damage to our aircraft. Seeing no major component damage, outside of holes in the fuselage and other noncritical areas, they indicated to me when I returned to our aircraft that we could continue the mission.

After hearing the good news about our aircraft's mission readiness, I needed to check on the rest of my flight's status. Next, I checked with both Lieutenant Gilley and Lieutenant Autrey to see if either of their aircraft had received significant battle damage. They indicated that they and their crews had checked their aircraft for battle damage finding some, but both indicated that they had no significant damage or mechanical problems that would keep them from continuing the mission. After receiving the report, I headed for the Army's command center to discuss the situation.

Walking toward the Army's Command and Control facility, I was intercepted by an Army one-star general who asked me if I was in charge of the 53s. I answered his question by saying that I was the flight leader of the CH-53s parked on the mat. Yes, I was currently in charge of the aircraft.

He then asked me why I had released the Cobras without requesting their permission. I told him that the four Cobras were no longer mission-capable and could not support my extraction mission, so I as the flight leader sent them home. As he looked at my name patch on the front of my flight suit, he said, "Captain, you realize the mission is now a mandatory mission."

Looking back at him eye to eye, I said, "Sir, unless you can suppress some of the fire coming into FSB Hotel II, I am not going to take my flight back there. If I did, then I am almost positive that we will lose one or all my 53s."

A look of shock appeared on his face, which was quickly replaced by one of anger. Speaking again, he said, "You understand what a mandatory mission is, don't you, Captain?"

Before I could answer, we both heard a helicopter approaching LZ Kilo from the east. I looked up and saw a single CH-53D inbound to LZ Kilo. This CH-53D had to be Major Wasko in his replacement aircraft returning from Marble Mountain.

Looking back at the Army brigadier general, I said in a very calm voice that the general now needed to talk to Major Wasko, the original flight leader, about the mandatory mission when he arrived, as I pointed to the CH-53D that had just landed. Looking at me with a look of disgust, he turned and walked back toward the Army's Command and Control facility.

After his aircraft was shut down and he exited, Major Wasko again assumed command of the flight and the mission. I briefed him and Lieutenant Colonel Pitman on the present status of the mission. I told them how much of the mission had been completed thus far, indicating that the resupply portion of the mission had been completed. Then I detailed the events surrounding the extractions of the two 155mm-gun packages and our failure to get the six remaining 105mm guns out of FSB Hotel II. I then explained the operational loss of our Marine Cobra escorts because of battle damage and system failures that had been incurred by the gunship aircraft and outlined the rationale for sending our Scarface Cobras home. They both agreed with my action. I then told them about my encounter with the Army brigadier general and my concerns regarding continuation of the mission without first dealing with the heavy volume of enemy fire coming from the area surrounding FSB Hotel II.

I strongly suggested that we needed help from the Army in the form of artillery suppression fire, plus additional fixed-wing support and some replacements for our Marine Cobra escort aircraft. If Army AH-1s were available, they could provide in close suppression fire during our approach and departure from FSB Hotel II. Again, as I had told the general only minutes before, it was my belief that without significantly suppressing the incoming enemy fire at Hotel II, we would have a significant chance to lose one or more of our aircraft.

At the completion of my briefing, Major Wasko and Lieutenant Colonel Pitman acknowledged the content of my brief. They then headed to the Army's Command and Control bunker to get an update regarding status and continuation of our mission. I was not asked to accompany them to the bunker.

*****

About twenty minutes later, they returned. Major Wasko then conducted an extensive briefing indicating that the Army command had again stated that the mission to move the guns from FSB Hotel II to FSB Delta 1 was absolutely imperative. It became a mandatory mission as the general had indicated. All six 105mm guns needed to be moved as soon as possible.

Major Wasko looked directly at me saying that he had requested the Army's Command and Control folks provide air support, artillery support, and gunship support before he would take his Dimmer flight back to Hotel II.

I felt somewhat vindicated by his words regarding what I had said to the general earlier.

Major Wasko indicated that Major Klose (US Army), the 223rd CAB S-3 operations officer, had quickly arranged for all requested support.

I believed Major Klose was working directly for the Army general I had spoken to earlier.

Major Klose also indicated to Major Wasko that they would provide an airborne forward air controller and Helicopter Direction Control (HDC, or Army's Command and Control) aircraft to coordinate and integrate all aspects of the support for the Dimmer flight. Furthermore, Major Klose stated that he himself would be flying the HDC mission. His call sign was Red Dragon 28.

It appeared to me that we had gotten the attention of the Army concerning the problems at FSB Hotel II.

Major Wasko also received an updated intelligence assessment from the Army, which he shared with us, and then defined the tactics to be used for the continuation of our mission. He went on to cover the Army's coordinated actions in support of our mission outlining the air, artillery, and gunship activities to be undertaken in and around FSB Hotel II.

At approximately 1745 hours, our four crews manned our aircraft. We departed as a flight of four aircraft en route to undertake the completion of the *mandatory* gun-moving mission starting at FSB Hotel II.

As promised, the Army provided four AH-1G Cobra attack gunships as our escorts. They joined our flight as we crossed the border into Laos. Looking toward FSB Hotel II, we could see the HDC bird and the airborne FAC were already on station east of the FSB. We could also see, orbiting high above, at least two flights of fixed-wing aircraft that were on station to support our mission.

As the four CH-53Ds flew toward the FSB Hotel II, we watched an extensive artillery mission, which had been in progress for some extended time judging by the amount of smoke and dust it had raised south and west of the FSB. The fire appeared to be emanating from FSB Delta and focused on the ridgelines and valleys to the south and west of FSB Hotel II.

Our Dimmer flight, led by Major Wasko, arrived on station above FSB Hotel II at about four thousand feet AGL. Stealth was no longer a consideration in our ingress strategy. The NVA could see our four large helicopters trailing their normal black smoke, along with our four Cobra escorts, from a long way off.

Upon our arrival at FSB Hotel II, the four Army Cobra attack gunships departed our formation and went to work on the target south of Hotel II where most of the enemy fire had previously come from. Meanwhile, Major Klose, the Army's HDC, was flying his UH-1 aircraft in the vicinity of FSB Hotel II coordinating the fixed-wing aircraft strikes and artillery-fire missions through the airborne forward air controller who directly controlled their attacks.

These coordinated attacks appeared, based on reports from inside the FSB, to temporarily suppress some of the enemy fire directly into Hotel II. At that point, just before our arrival at Hotel II, the HDC suspended the artillery fire on the ridgelines and valleys to the south and west of FSB Hotel II so our flight could start the operation.

Dimmer 3 (Major Wasko) as the lead aircraft made the first approach into FSB Hotel II, as the rest of the flight continued to orbit the FSB. He approached the FSB LZ using a left-hand spiral staying away from the south perimeter of the FSB as much as possible and staying over friendly territory to the maximum extent he could. I watched him coming to a hover, then quickly move to the first 105mm gun.

Observing him move quickly over the gun to be extracted, I then saw an AVRN soldier move under his aircraft, I assumed to pass the sling on the gun up to his crew chief.

As Dimmer 3 picked up the gun, and he lifted it out of the gun pit, two mortar rounds exploded directly behind his aircraft. He cleared the gun-pit's containment wall with the gun departing in a left-hand climbing spiral.

The four Army Cobra attack gunships continued to attack the suspected mortar site with rockets and miniguns on the south side of the perimeter of Hotel II.

One gun down and five to go, I thought.

The next Dimmer into the pickup zone was Dimmer 2, Lieutenant Autrey, since section integrity was resumed when Dimmer 3 returned to the flight. I watched from our orbit at four thousand feet as he followed Major Wasko's strategy making a similar left-hand spiral approach to the gun pits. As he entered the gun-pit area, I saw him come to a hover over the gun pit, then quickly move to the 105mm gun he was to extract just as three mortar rounds exploded in the pickup zone along with a hail of small-arms fire that he reported seeing and hearing, again coming from the south and west perimeters of the FSB.

With Dimmer 2 in the gun pits, the escorting Army Cobra gunships continued to bombard and rocket enemy gun positions surrounding the south and west of the pickup area. Again, because of the volume of enemy fire impacting the gun-pit area, Lieutenant Autrey was forced to depart the pickup zone without a gun. He climbed to our original four-thousand-foot altitude above the FSB.

I was the next Dimmer aircraft in the flight to attempt a gun extraction. This time, I made a tight left-hand spiral into the gun-pit area coming to a hover directly over the gun to be extracted.

Glancing at Dan again, as I shot the approach looking through the copilot's window, I saw that he looked very worried since the 80-degree spiral approach had him looking directly at the ground out his side window.

Sergeant Pogany again directed me quickly over the gun and reached down to grab the sling from the ARVN trooper. While he was doing this, I looked out my window to the south for any signs of small-arms fire or the .50-caliber machine gun that had previously been shooting at us from outside the perimeter of the FSB. Seeing only small-arms fire and not .50-caliber machine-gun fire eased my mind somewhat but not that much. Once Sergeant Pogany had the sling on the cargo hook, at his direction, we quickly lifted the 105mm gun out of the pit. Since this gun was significantly lighter than the

155mm-gun package we lifted earlier, our rate of climb out of the zone was much greater. During this pickup evolution, we were under heavy small-arms fire with at least four mortar rounds exploding in our area as we departed.

The Army Cobra gunships continued to strafe and rocket enemy gun positions south and west of the FSB.

The Army's HDC suggested a short delay in our pickup evolution while they worked to suppress the fire we had been receiving. Major Klose and the airborne forward air controller continued to coordinate several flights of fixed-wing aircraft that were massed overhead to provide fire-suppression strikes on the south and western areas surrounding FSB Hotel II. These coordinated attacks appeared to temporarily suppress some of the enemy fire near the Hotel II gun pits.

We monitored by radio the next Dimmer extraction attempt. Dimmer 44, Lieutenant Gilley, was the next bird in the pickup rotation and made his approach following Dimmer 3's and my examples. His approach was made during one of the heavy fixed-wing air strikes, and he successfully extracted gun number 3 of the six that required extraction. He did so while still receiving some mortar fire in the FSB confines.

Three guns down and three to go. We might just pull this off were my thoughts as I crossed my fingers.

While en route to our destination, we again listened to Dimmer 2 as he now made his second attempt to extract a 105mm gun. His approach to FSB this time was made while another set of the fixed-wing air strikes were still in progress. As Dimmer 2 again entered the gun-pit area, he was met immediately with heavy small-arms fire and mortar fire. Because of the high volume of mortar fire, coupled with smoke and poor visibility, it forced Lieutenant Autrey to depart the gun-pit area. This time, he did not depart the area completely but circled around and approached it from a different direction using the smoke and dust to hide his position until he made the successful pickup of gun number 4 of six.

Dimmer 3 was approximately ten minutes ahead of me with his 105mm gun when I left the LZ with my gun. Since he had not flown to FSB Delta 1 that day, he was flying more slowly because of lack of familiarity with terrain as well as the reduced visibility created by the massive artillery barrages and multiple air strikes encompassing the entire area in Laos. It had gotten progressively worse since we had flown our resupply missions earlier in the day. The smoke and red haze reduced visibility to about half a mile, so I did not see Dimmer 3 until we had caught up to him as he approached FSB Delta 1.

Major Klose had also arranged additional Cobra gunship escorts to support our flights to FSB Delta 1. The Army Cobra gunships were on station at Delta 1 when Dimmer 3 arrived. They had already started to bombard and rocket enemy gun positions near FSB Delta 1 on the west side of the FSB perimeter, resulting in suppressing almost all small-arms fire from that area.

Being close to him, I watched Dimmer 3 set his howitzer in a prepared gun pit at Delta 1 and departed east climbing to a safe altitude. He called saying he would wait for me at that altitude and to join him after I made my approach and deposited my gun.

While about a minute behind him, we made our approach to the next gun pit and placed our gun next to the one he inserted. As we climbed out of the FSB, I again noticed that the South Vietnamese Army gun crews were swarming all over the gun after our insertion, preparing it along with the gun Dimmer 3 had just inserted to be used against NVA forces further to the west. I knew these activities indicated that the situation at FSB Delta 1 was continuing to become more and more critical. These guns were badly needed by the ARVN forces at FSB Delta 1, and that is why the mission became mandatory.

Dimmer 44 and Dimmer 2 were now en route to FSB Delta 1 with guns number 3 and 4. We have only two more guns to move. Dimmer 3 requested that the Army Cobra escort aircraft that were covering our inserts at FSB Delta 1 remain on station to cover the arrival of the next four guns—two inbound now and two more that we were going to be picking up. The Army Cobra flight leader agreed to remain at Delta 1 and provide the necessary support. This information was also relayed to Major Klose.

Major Wasko indicated, again by radio, to the whole flight that he and I would move the last two howitzers as we headed back toward FSB Hotel II for the last two guns. He also told all of us that he was planning to send the other two birds home after their gun insertions because of approaching night and the potential of bad weather en route home.

Looking outside, it became very evident that it was starting to get dark in this part of Laos very quickly.

After checking with the HDC, Major Wasko radioed Dimmer 2 and 44 directing them to fly back to Marble Mountain after inserting the guns into FSB Delta 1 and refueling at Khe Sanh. He also told them again that he and I would take care of moving the last two 105mm guns. Both aircraft acknowledged his radio instructions. By this time, I had joined on Dimmer 3's aircraft as we headed back toward South Vietnam.

Flying in loose formation en route back to FBS Hotel II, I separated my aircraft from Dimmer 3 several miles before arriving overhead the FSB. We flew east toward the South Vietnamese border for several miles hoping to decoy the enemy gunners into thinking that we were calling off the gun extraction.

Dimmer 3 called Major Klose en route back to Hotel II and requested he provide the maximum suppression fire that could be applied to the areas where the previous fire was emanating around the perimeter of FSB Hotel II in anticipation of our extraction of the last two guns.

Major Klose, who was currently directing three additional sections of fixed-wing attack aircraft, acknowledged Wasko's request. Approximately a minute later, I saw fixed-wing aircraft attacks begin again on the west and south side of the FSB hoping to suppress the incoming mortar, small-arms, and .50-caliber machine-gun fire that was currently being experienced by the ground troops inside the perimeter of Hotel II. He was also using several newly arrived Army Cobra gunships in his effort to neutralize the incoming fire that was coming from just outside the perimeter.

I watched Dimmer 3 arriving overhead the FSB as he then commenced his approach to Hotel II. I saw the fixed-wing aircraft attacking the enemy positions directly south of the pickup zone. Seeing him commence his approach, I turned our helicopter back to the west in order to return to an overhead position above Hotel II to await our turn to pick up the last 105mm howitzer.

We continued to watch and listen to Major Wasko flying Dimmer 3 as he again made a left-hand approach to the FSB in an attempt to avoid enemy fire. At the bottom of his approach, as he came to a hover in the gun-pit area, he started receiving heavy mortar fire that reduced the visibility in the entire area making it difficult for him to locate the gun in the red and brown dust and smoke. We saw him emerge from the area of heavy smoke and dust, quickly moving to the northeast, and he then circled around again moving directly to one of the two remaining guns and came to a hover over it. As we watched from above, it appeared that he remained over the gun for an extended period with mortars going off all over the area.

We could also see small-arms tracers, and again .50-caliber machine-gun fire from the south and west coming from just outside the perimeter of the FSB. My crew and I assumed that he was also experiencing the same problem we had faced earlier in getting an AVRN hook-up crew to assist with the pickup because of the volume and intensity of fire directed toward the aircraft and the gun pits in general.

Major Klose worked to identify the areas where the mortars were impacting and to call out the location of ground fire that was being concentrated at the hovering helicopter. Major Klose masterfully directed the Army Cobra gunships to the areas where the majority of the incoming fire was emanating. These efforts appeared not to have lessen the incoming fire into the area very much. My crew and I then observed six to eight mortar rounds, almost simultaneously, impacting directly behind Dimmer 3's aircraft while he was attempting his pickup.

After a prolonged hover, Dimmer 3 again departed the gun pit without the gun. He again made a hard left turn inside the perimeter of the FSB and came back to a hover over the gun. He appeared to again be in a hover for an extended period and taking fire all the while. I watched his aircraft as he was starting to lift the gun from the gun pit when a series of mortar rounds (seven to ten) exploded all around and on his aircraft. From our vantage point, they appeared to be directly on top of the helicopter's rotor system and aft of the tail. It was hard to tell because of the smoke and dust. Just after we observed these hits, Major Wasko called over the radio that he was hit and going down in the gun-pit area next to the LZ.

When the smoke had cleared somewhat, my crew and I observed that Dimmer 3's aircraft was sitting upright in the gun pit or very close to it, with its rotor stopped. It looked like he was sitting on top or next to the gun he was trying to extract. Surprisingly, the aircraft was not on fire. We then observed the crew and pilots exiting the aircraft but lost sight of them in the red and brown dust created by heavy incoming mortar rounds impacting all around the downed aircraft.

While we observed these events unfolding from my aircraft, Dimmer 3 had his own problems to deal with as he settled into the gun pit after being hit by multiple mortar rounds. According to his after-action report, Major Wasko had made two previous attempts to hook up the gun under the directions from Sergeant Ford, his crew chief. On the third attempt, Sergeant Ford reached through the "hell hole" grabbing the sling, then putting it on the external cargo hook.

Again, this process was necessary since there was the reluctance of the ARVN troops to hook up and to expose themselves to the increased mortar and small-arms fire. After the successful hook up, Sergeant Ford indicated to Major Wasko that they had the load hooked up and could depart the gun pit. Lieutenant Colonel Pitman monitored the aircraft gauges and applied full power to the engines as they started to lift the gun out of the gun pit.

All this was taking place under a hail of mortar, small-arms, and .50-caliber machine-gun fire. Just after liftoff, Major Wasko felt the aircraft take several direct hits, then it began to shudder badly. At this point, the cyclic controls (used to provide directional control of the helicopter) were frozen in place, and a check of the gauges indicated real problems with directional control hydraulics, and this, along with a large number of caution lights being illuminated, indicated a complete loss of hydraulic power and rotor system control. As the cockpit filled with white smoke, Major Wasko decided this was going to be as good as any place to land, as the aircraft settled upright on the ground.

At this point, it became apparent to Major Wasko that Lieutenant Colonel Pitman had been wounded, and then someone in the back of the aircraft shouted they were on fire. Lieutenant Colonel Pitman opened his escape hatch window on the copilot's side of the aircraft and exited the aircraft landing in the gun pit next to the aircraft where it had come to rest. Still inside the aircraft, Major Wasko then proceeded to shut down the aircraft's number 2 engine (number 1 had already flamed out) and apply the rotor brake to stop the still spinning rotor blades. He then exited the cockpit into the cabin looking around for anyone who may have remained inside the aircraft. Seeing no one, he exited the bird by the personnel door on the right side of the aircraft. Mortar fire in the gun-pit area was increasing, focusing on the downed aircraft, causing Major Wasko to move further away from it and into the next gun pit taking shelter there until the mortar fire eased up a little. Major Wasko noted that the aircraft was not on fire, as had been reported, but was leaking jet fuel all over the gun pit where it landed. Seeing the fuel, he knew he had to find Lieutenant Colonel Pitman, disregarding his personal safety. He returned to the gun pit where the aircraft was sitting and spotted him. He found Lieutenant Colonel Pitman next to the aircraft, and he assisted (dragged) Lieutenant Colonel Pitman into a one-man spider hole he had spotted some distance away from the aircraft and leaking fuel.

He and Lieutenant Colonel Pitman dropped into the hole and found a friendly ARVN already inside. He moved over so that they could all share the small hole in the ground together as another heavy volley of mortar fire impacted the entire FSB.

When the mortars let up again, Major Wasko decided to look for some medical aid for Lieutenant Colonel Pitman's wound and to find a survival radio. He successfully located an ARVN medic in one of the bunkers outside the LZ and took him back to Lieutenant Colonel Pitman so that his wound could be dressed. Major Wasko then started toward his aircraft to get the survival radio, but another mortar barrage forced him to return to Lieutenant Colonel Pitman's location and await a pickup.[12] He and Lieutenant Colonel Pitman then became witnesses on the ground to our rescue attempt.

As our aircraft orbited high above FSB Hotel II (three thousand feet) watching the events unfold below, it was apparent to myself and the rest of my crew that we had Marine squadron mates in trouble on the ground. We all saw and heard Dimmer 3 when they went down on or near the edge of the gun pits. We also observed that his aircraft had also partially blocked part of the regular LZ with his rotor blades.

This meant that there was no place we could safely land our large transport helicopter in the LZ in order to pick up the crew. It was, in fact, fortuitous that we had the rescue ladder on board our aircraft. The entire crew was aware that we had the rescue ladder attached to the back of our aircraft since we had briefed the use of it before takeoff this morning.

The situation on the ground is bad, but I believe we needed to try to get our folks out. We will never leave a brother Marine behind. I am not alone on this bird, so I better see if the rest of the crew sees the situation the same way as I do.

Before making an attempt to pick up the downed crew, I asked the entire crew if they were in favor of making the rescue attempt. To a man, everyone agreed that we needed to try the rescue despite the volume of fire we had previously experienced and had seen again resulting in the downing of Dimmer 3's aircraft.

Hearing positive responses from all the crew, I said, "Then let's go get them," as I then rolled our aircraft into a 90-degree-angle-of-bank turn over FSB Hotel II commencing a tight right-hand spiral approach.

About halfway through the approach, I called Red Dragon 28 and apprised him of our ongoing action as we continued to drop in our tight right-hand spiral toward the gun-pit area. He responded by saying that it appeared that the FSB was coming under increased NVA pressure with incoming mortar, small-arms, and .50-caliber

---

[12] Nolan, *Into Laos;* Wasko Jr., "Michael Wasko's After-Action Report;" Cosmas and Murray, *US Marines in Vietnam.*

machine-gun fire becoming much heavier. It looked as if the NVA were moving ground troops into the FSB perimeter from the south, and there was a possibility that the FSB could be overrun. He strongly suggested that we should wait for additional artillery-suppression fire and more fixed-wing sorties before making a rescue attempt. I indicated that we were already committed as we were fast approaching the gun pits through the smoke and red dust. His response was "Okay, Dimmer 4, I'll do what I can."

During our very steep spiral approach, Sergeant Pogany told me he was going to reposition his restraining gunner's belt so that he could move quickly to the back of the aircraft and drop the 75-foot rescue ladder over the cargo ramp at the rear of the aircraft once we reach the downed aircraft.

Coming out of our spiral, I performed a quick-stop maneuver arriving in a hover about 50 feet over the downed aircraft (*quick stop* is "a radical maneuver that slows forward airspeed from 120 knots [135 MPH] to 0 knots in 6 to 8 seconds by using the rotor system as an air brake in a sliding skid maneuver"). Immediately after I completed the quick-stop maneuver, Sergeant Pogany ran to the rear of the cabin, dropped the rescue ladder, and then positioned himself lying face down on the cargo ramp looking over the edge at the scene below. Since Sergeant Pogany had previously caught sight of the crew exiting the downed aircraft, then entering a foxhole near the rear of the aircraft, he knew where to start looking for them. He quickly located the approximate position and rapidly directed me to start backing up toward the rear of the downed aircraft since that was where he had last seen the crew enter the foxhole. While we were backing up slowly, small-arms and .50-caliber machine-gun fire was again being directed toward our aircraft.

The incoming fire seemed like it came from everywhere; all the while, mortars continued to fall in the gun pits, LZ, and all across the FSB. Again, we all heard the impacts of rounds and shrapnel hitting our aircraft. Smoke and red dust were everywhere, making the job of holding a steady hover over the downed aircraft more difficult, and visibility at times was almost zero in and near the downed aircraft. While the visibility was greatly reduced, I was still able to follow

Sergeant Pogany's instructions while hovering above the downed CH-53. We continued moving back toward the crews' previous known position slowly.

I looked out my side window toward the south and again saw the tracers from the .50-caliber machine gun that had previously been shooting at us before, earlier in the day, were coming at us again. I felt myself subconsciously pushing back slightly in my armored pilot's seat, as I watched the tracer fire and remembered my days when I was the squadron ordnance officer, remembering that only one of four of the machine-gun rounds coming our way were tracers.

The door gunner behind me, Lance Corporal A. J. Pailes, had seen the NVA machine gunner firing at us, and he was firing back with his door-mounted .50-caliber machine gun. I felt better when I heard the door gun open up on the enemy. Suddenly, it became quiet behind me. Something had happened to Lance Corporal Pailes, or his gun had jammed. I was not sure which event had taken place. I keyed the ICS and asked him if he was hit.

He replied, "No, sir, I am okay, but my gun has jammed, and I am working to clear it."

As seconds continued to tick by, it became apparent that Lance Corporal Pailes was unable to clear the jammed machine gun. Hearing my communications with Lance Corporal Pailes, Sergeant Pogany looked over his shoulder while lying down on the ramp, jumped up, and ran back to help. With Sergeant Pogany's help, the gun was quickly cleared.

When I heard the first couple of .50-caliber rounds being fired from the door gun, I was greatly relieved. At this point in the flight, the sound of that big gun firing was music to my ears. Listening to Lance Corporal Pailes continuing to return fire, I again looked to the right out my window just in time to see Lance Corporal Pailes's bullets cutting the NVA machine gunner in half, putting the gun out of action at least temporarily.

Lieutenant Silver looked back into the cabin and saw Sergeant Pogany quickly returning to his previous position on the ramp so we could continue to search for our downed crew members.

The visibility in the entire FSB during this process was greatly reduced by the large number of mortar impacts in the gun pits and LZ, as well as the red dust blown up by our rotor wash. These factors provided some cover from direct fire but also slowed our search for our downed crew members considerably.

As Sergeant Pogany was directing me to move further back to the west, he told me he had just seen several men moving out of a foxhole about twenty meters from the back of Dimmer 3's downed bird. Apparently, they had seen the rescue ladder hanging off the ramp of our aircraft and had decided to make a run for the ladder in spite of the incoming fire. Sergeant Pogany recognized the men and indicated by ICS that they were our downed crew members. Sergeant Pogany watched as the group approached the rescue ladder. He said that the downed crew realized that there was no way our aircraft could continue to stay in a hover while they attempted to climb all the way up to our aircraft because of the ever-increasing incoming fire.

Recognizing the situation was untenable, they did as they were briefed and trained to do. They moved quickly to the rescue ladder, climbed up only a few feet then attached D rings to the steel cables to prevent them from falling off or being shot off the ladder. As they completed the hook-ups, each one of them found a horizontal bar to place their feet on.

When all our folks were attached to the ladder, Sergeant Pogany said, "We have them all. Let's get the hell out of here."

I called Red Dragon 28 to let him know we were departing the pickup area, as I added power and started to climb out of the gun pits. Lieutenant Silver had been closely monitoring the aircraft gauges and applied full power to the engines as we were lifting out vertically. I applied maximum climb power, climbing out vertically and trying to get our crew members hanging below the aircraft out of harm's way as quickly as possible. We went almost straight up until we reached three thousand feet of altitude. We then turned east-northeast heading for the South Vietnam border. The closest safe place I could think of to safely drop our evacuees was the Special

Force's camp at Lang Vei, South Vietnam, approximately thirty miles away.

I kept the airspeed at thirty knots in order to keep the men on the ladder from swinging back and forth too severely. Sergeant Pogany, still lying on the ramp, monitored their oscillations as we flew toward the safety of South Vietnam.

During our very slow flight back, I received a call on the radio from Red Dragon 28. He said that he had picked up the two pilots from the downed aircraft and would rendezvous with us at the Lang Vei LZ, the same location that we were headed to. He further said that this was the first place he could land and transfer the wounded copilot and the pilot to my aircraft.

I could not believe my ears—the call from Red Dragon 28 saying that he had picked up our two pilots was a complete surprise. Our entire crew thought we had all the downed crew members, all five, hanging on our rescue ladder. Sergeant Pogany did another visual check and said that there were in fact five men attached to the rescue ladder.

What the hell is going on? I thought we had everyone on the ladder! It looks like Dimmer 3 had two extra people on his bird we did not know about! Surprise. Surprise.

After a short moment, I responded to Red Dragon 28's radio call indicating that we would rendezvous with him at the Special Forces camp. We proceeded at what seemed to be a snail's pace toward the South Vietnam border. A glance at the fuel gages gave me pause and caused me to be very concerned about our remaining fuel. So while I continued to fly northeast, I asked Lieutenant Silver to make a quick fuel calculation. He made the calculations based on our present ground speed, estimating that we would have just enough fuel to get to the Lang Vei LZ, remain on the ground for three to five minutes (at minimum power), and then fly to Khe Sanh to refuel before we were completely out of fuel. That was assuming that the fuel system had been calibrated accurately.

I crossed my fingers, hoping, first, that Dan's calculations were precise, and second, that the fuel systems and indicators were accurate.

Since it would be well past sunset when we arrived at Khe Sanh airfield, I called the Army's Command and Control Center at LZ Kilo and requested that the fuel pits remain open for our late refuel (Khe Sanh's fuel pits generally shut down at sunset). They responded to my request in the affirmative.

Everyone on board our aircraft was relieved when we crossed the border into South Vietnam and then started a slow descent from three thousand feet toward the Special Forces camp. Our fuel-low-warning lights had been illuminated for a couple of minutes when we crossed the border, and I remained very concerned about our on-board fuel supply.

We flew the last mile into the Special Forces camp LZ in a gradual descent to protect our crew still hanging on the rescue ladder. Sergeant Pogany had remained on the ramp observing the men clinging to the ladder. He had given me updates every five minutes on their status as best as he could ascertain during the entire rescue flight.

As we started our final approach into the Special Forces camp at Lang Vei, he verbally gave me instructions indicating where we could safely set them down on the LZ. Once we were a hundred feet over the LZ in a hover, Sergeant Pogany directed my slow vertical descent until all the men were on the ground and had disconnected their D rings from the ladder. We then moved away from the group and landed on the far side of the LZ. Sergeant Pogany exited the aircraft and started to roll up the rescue ladder. He was almost immediately swamped by the five men we rescued with hugs and handshakes. After the short reunion, Sergeant Pogany directed the men to our aircraft and finished securing the rescue ladder.

As Sergeant Pogany's reunion with the five rescued crew members was taking place, I looked out my pilot's side window and saw an Army UH-1 land on the other corner of the LZ.

Red Dragon 28 called and said that the two pilots were getting out of his aircraft and coming to ours. I watched as two of his crewmen helped our pilots across the LZ and then into our bird.

Keying the radio, I thanked Red Dragon 28 for his outstanding work that day and for rescuing our two pilots. He acknowledged the thank-you, commenting, "It's all in a day's work these days." He then indicated he had more work to do and flashed a thumbs-up. Then as soon as his crew members had returned to his bird, he made his departure from the LZ heading back across the border.

Sergeant Pogany had done a quick evaluation of the five crew members we had picked up, and none of them appeared to have been wounded or hurt seriously; only scrapes and bruises were reported by the five. As soon as Sergeant Pogany had everyone loaded and we were getting ready to takeoff for Khe Sanh airfield to refuel, Major Wasko climbed in the jump seat between Lieutenant Silver and myself.

His eyes appeared to me as large as saucers, and he appeared, to me, to be in shock as he sat down on the seat. He then proceeded to yell over the noise of the helicopter, ordering me to fly directly to Dong Ha airfield to get medical attention for Lieutenant Colonel Pitman. Dong Ha airfield was located more than fifty miles from our present location and not far from the South China Sea. It was named for a Vietnamese village approximately half a mile north of the airfield.

You got to be shitting me, Major. We are almost out of gas, and you want me to fly fifty miles to Dong Ha right now? I thought.

Looking over at him, I yelled back at him, telling him, "We are going to refuel first," and then pointed to the fuel gauges and the low-fuel-warning lights that had been illuminated in the cockpit for several additional minutes. He looked like he was in a total state of shock, which was understandable under the circumstances. However, I again yelled at him, "We are going to Khe Sanh airfield to refuel." He again started to object, but I cut him off, saying, "Major, go strap in now," as I lifted the bird off the ground heading for Khe Sanh airfield, having no more time or fuel to waste.

While this exchange was taking place, Sergeant Pogany went to his crew's box, opened it, and found the unopened bottle of whiskey that he kept there for these types of emergency situations. He kept the whiskey available to help wounded warriors avoid severe shock while he was transporting them to medical facilities. He had been instrumental in keeping several Marines from going into shock while they were transported on his bird. Sergeant Pogany broke out the unopened bottle of whiskey and moved to the area in the cargo compartment where Lieutenant Colonel Pitman was lying. He got Lieutenant Colonel Pitman's attention by kneeling next to him. He then nodded to Lieutenant Colonel Pitman, then looked at the whiskey and back at Lieutenant Colonel Pitman indicating an offer of a drink as he lay on the deck of our noisy aircraft (speech inside the CH-53 without a helmet and intercom was almost impossible). Lieutenant Colonel Pitman looked at him, smiled, then nodded. Sergeant Pogany broke the seal, opened the bottle, and held the bottle so that Lieutenant Colonel Pitman could take a long pull of whiskey before laying back down as we lifted out of the Special Forces camp.

As we lifted off from the Special Forces Camp LZ, fuel was now our most critical concern. We needed to get to the fuel pits before we ran out of gas. It was going to be close. Very close.

We made the four-mile flight and started to refuel before either one of the engines flamed out. I don't know how since both fuel quantity gages read almost zero. While we were in the fuel pits, an Army medic came aboard asking if we had a wounded passenger on board. He had been likely alerted by Major Klose about our wounded copilot. Sergeant Pogany indicated that yes, we had a wounded man on board, then pointed to where Lieutenant Colonel Pitman was lying inside the aircraft. The medic checked out the wound in the upper part of his leg, then rebandaged the wound. As he was departing, he told Sergeant Pogany that was the best he could do for him here at Khe Sanh, stating that Lieutenant Colonel Pitman needed surgery soon and suggested we fly to the medical facility at Dong Ha ASAP. Sergeant Pogany then relayed the message to the rest of the crew as we disconnected the fuel hose from the aircraft and readied our aircraft for an easterly departure.

We departed Khe Sanh airfield following the Quang Tri River toward Ca Lu.

As we followed the river, I took a quick look across the cockpit at Lieutenant Silver. I saw a tired Marine aviator with a look of astonishment, coupled with concern but no fear on his face. He was a good copilot, who had performed all the tasks I had asked him to do.

This was his first real combat flight of his Marine Corps career. I was sure it would go down in his memory as one he would never forget. I remembered my first combat flight as a copilot—first, the adrenaline rush, followed by a this-can't-be-real feeling, and then one-of-you-better-get-the-job-done-correctly-mister attitude.

At Ca Lu, we turned northeast following Highway 9 past Cam Lo to Dong Ha airfield. As we proceeded east, night had fallen, and it was almost completely dark, with a piece of the moon providing some illumination through the broken cloud cover. What ambient light was visible was coupled with the flashes that came from the air strikes and artillery fire to our north along the DMZ. I could just see the monsoon rain clouds that had again gathered over the South China Sea and were moving inland quickly. As we landed at Dong Ha airfield, rain started falling as the cloud cover moved across the airfield.

As we taxied to the parking area, we were met by an Army ambulance. The medical personnel loaded both Lieutenant Colonel Pitman and Major Wasko into the ambulance and indicated that they were going to take them to the Army's medical facility.

After their departure, we proceeded to the refueling pits to refuel. It took about fifteen minutes to complete the process; we then taxied to the parking area. As we started to shut down the aircraft, the ambulance reappeared next to our aircraft. The back door opened and Lieutenant Colonel Pitman, now on a stretcher carried by two medical people, along with Major Wasko, exited it. Major Wasko climbed aboard the bird through the personnel door and again climbed into the jump seat while the medical people loaded Lieutenant Colonel Pitman through the ramp into the back of the aircraft with the help of Sergeant Pogany.

Major Wasko, now on the jump seat, leaned in toward me, yelling that Lieutenant Colonel Pitman had been examined by the head Army doctor at the facility. The doctor told him that he lacked the facilities and operating equipment to properly care for this type of severe leg wound. The doctor further indicated to Major Wasko that Lieutenant Colonel Pitman should be taken to Da Nang ASAP, specifically, directing him to have Pitman taken to Charlie Medical

Facility at China Beach, just outside of Da Nang, for treatment as soon as possible. Sergeant Pogany, with the help of the medical people, made sure the stretcher was properly secured with Lieutenant Colonel Pitman on it in the back of the aircraft.

I gave the thumbs-up to Major Wasko, meaning I understood the content of his yelling over the noise of the aircraft.

Lieutenant Silver and I restarted the one engine we had shut down earlier and completed the checklist for takeoff. We also completed the instrument checklist since it was apparent that we would be filing an instrument flight rules (IFR) flight plan to get back to Da Nang since it was raining harder, and the broken ceiling was now an overcast, and the clouds had dropped down to one thousand feet. The next leg of our flight would be done on instruments as we would be flying in the clouds back to Da Nang.

Light rain was still falling as I asked Lieutenant Silver to contact the base operations, get the weather report for Da Nang at our arrival time, then file an IFR plan from Dong Ha to Da Nang. He did these tasks quickly. We then asked for clearance to taxi for takeoff. We received our clearance and continued to taxi to the runway for takeoff. The tower cleared us, and we departed changing to departure-control frequency on the radio.

After becoming airborne, we called departure control, which acknowledged radio contact and our IFF (information friend or foe) squawk (signal). We entered the clouds at about one thousand feet climbing on our assigned heading. With radar contact established, we continued to climb into the rainy dark clouds as we executed the published departure from Dong Ha.

I was flying the departure on instruments when Lieutenant Silver observed that water was entering the cockpit through several bullet or shrapnel holes above and below the windshield itself. He told me about the problem as I glanced over at the water coming into the cockpit. My first priority was to keep flying the aircraft on instruments and not get distracted by the water problem, as I leveled off at six thousand feet, our assigned altitude. However, my secondary concern was that water coming into the cockpit could short out the electrical instruments and the radios we needed to fly in the clouds under instrument conditions. I knew we needed to get out of the rain quickly as we could.

As water continued to flow into the cockpit, I requested a change in altitude from the Dong Ha departure control. Our original assigned altitude was six thousand feet, and I requested a climb to eight thousand feet. I was hoping to get above the cloud layer and out of the rain we were currently in.

The departure control approved our request, so we continued our climb toward eight thousand feet with water still entering the cockpit. As we passed seven thousand feet, we broke out of the overcast monsoon clouds. The stars and moon overhead never looked so good.

Sergeant Pogany and Lieutenant Silver mopped up the water inside the wind screen and instrument panel as we flew above the cloud cover on toward Da Nang.

With no more water coming into the cockpit, we continued our climb to eight thousand feet. Things settled down a little as we headed south along the airway. We were handed off from Dong Ha departure control to Hue Phu Bai center and finely to Da Nang center for the rest of our IFR flight to Da Nang.

At this point in the flight, we were in a condition that is termed Visual Flight Rules on top (VFR on top), meaning we could see ahead and above us, but we could not see the ground below us.

The weather forecast for Da Nang indicated that it would be overcast at the time of our expected arrival, so I elected to remained on our IFR flight plan. Sergeant Pogany and Lieutenant Silver continued to mop up the water that was still remaining inside the wind screen and instrument panel completing the job in a few minutes as we flew on toward Da Nang. While VFR on top, I turned over the controls of the aircraft, while airborne, for the first time that day to Lieutenant Silver. He acknowledged the control swap and smoothly took control of the bird.

I apologized to Dan for not letting him fly the aircraft sooner. He responded that he understood why I had not let him fly the bird. Looking over at me, he said, "I was happy to have just survived the day's events. Today's flight is truly an exciting way to start my combat flying career."

As he flew down the airway, I relaxed a little for the first time since our takeoff this morning, but just a little.

Throughout the flight to Da Nang, Sergeant Pogany continued to check on the condition of Lieutenant Colonel Pitman and Major Wasko and the other five Marines we picked up in Laos. They all appeared to be, to some degree, in a state of shock. Lieutenant Colonel Pitman and Major Wasko being in the worst shape of all of them.

Again, taking control of the aircraft as we rounded the Ha Van Pass at eight thousand feet, Da Nang center handed us off to Da Nang approach control who directed us to descend to three thousand feet where they turned us over to a ground-control-approach (GCA) controller for a radar-controlled approach to Da Nang airfield.

The weather at this point was not quite as bad as had been forecast; it was partly cloudy with no rain and only a thin broken layer of clouds at around two thousand feet. Looking east, you could see that the monsoon clouds and rain had not yet moved in from the area surrounding Monkey Mountain toward Da Nang, but we could see the heavy layer moving west rapidly toward Da Nang airfield.

The GCA controller picked us up and directed our gradual glide-path descent and compass heading through the broken cloud layer where we broke out in the clear at 1,500 feet above Da Nang Bay.

At that point, I cancelled our approach with Da Nang GCA telling them we were proceeding VFR directly to Charlie Med located on China Beach just north of Marble Mountain.

Our controller was not happy that we did not proceed to Da Nang airfield, but we explained we had wounded on board and had been directed to get them to Charlie Med ASAP. He indicated his understanding as we left his radio frequency.

Changing frequency to the Marble Mountain Air Facility tower, which controlled the airspace around the medical facility, we requested permission to land at Charlie Med LZ. The LZ was located a couple of hundred yards from the north end of the Marble

Mountain Air Facility runway. The tower cleared us to land and indicated that they would alert the medical facility as to our impending landing. As we arrived at the LZ marked with a large red cross, it appeared that they had already been alerted and were ready to accept our wounded officer. As I landed in the LZ, the aircraft was met by several medical personnel who rushed to the aircraft as soon as we touched down to off-load Lieutenant Colonel Pitman's stretcher. He was followed closely by Major Wasko as they entered the medical facility. The other five Marines who were picked up after the crash elected to remain on the aircraft and not seek medical attention. Only after all personnel were inside the medical facility did we call the Marble Mountain tower for clearance to depart the LZ and to enter the landing pattern at Marble Mountain Air Facility.

*****

  I landed on the runway at Marble Mountain, took the first taxiway into the flight-line area. Electing not to refuel the aircraft because it was going to require significant maintenance. Sergeant Pogany exited the aircraft and guided me into an open parking revetment, which is a parking structure designed to separate one aircraft from another thereby keep a single rocket blast from striking multiple aircraft. After coming to a stop in the revetment, I shut the aircraft down myself. I sent the rest of my crew, except Sergeant Pogany, including the rescued passengers inside to start the debriefing process. They all departed the aircraft as I had requested.

  Sergeant Pogany was outside the aircraft starting the postflight inspection as I packed up my gear, then climbed out of the pilot's seat, stretching my back and legs as I entered the cabin of the bird. I was the last person to exit the aircraft intending to perform a postflight inspection of my aircraft along with Sergeant Pogany. As I exited the aircraft by the personnel door and stepped on to the tarmac, I was met by the squadron's current commanding officer.

  He had seen me exiting the bird and moved to stand directly in front of me. He then grabbed the front of my flight suit and yelled in my face, "CAPTAIN, DO YOU REALIZE WHAT YOU HAVE DONE TO MY CAREER? YOU LOST ONE OF MY CH-53S!"

I just stared at him, saying nothing as he reiterated the words again "CAPTAIN, DO YOU REALIZE WHAT YOU HAVE DONE TO MY CAREER? YOU LOST ONE OF MY CH-53S!"

I was completely shocked by his hostile actions and words for a few seconds. *After spending over seventeen hours in the cockpit, being shot at, picking up a crew that had been shot down, flying IFR with water coming into the cockpit, plus a myriad of other events that occurred that day, I had not lost a CH-53 today. This man is losing his mind* were my first thoughts.

I finally started to get angry but still said nothing.

This man standing in front of me (our commanding officer) appeared to know nothing about that day's mission or about bringing our downed crew home. His only concern was his career. He had not asked about any part of our mission that day. He did not ask about either Major Wasko's or Lieutenant Colonel Pitman's condition or even their location. I would have expected, at a minimum, that he would have at least asked about their status, as well as that of the other downed aircraft crew members, but again, it appeared to me, that all he cared about was his future career.

Becoming madder by the second, I was not able to utter a single word to the man who was standing in front of me yelling in my face. I started to move my clenched fist upward but was immediately restrained by my hooch mate who had pushed himself, unnoticed by myself or the CO, close to my right side and had seen my fist start its upward movement.

At that moment, Captain Evert Haymore saved my Marine Corps career by pulling my arm and my body sideways away from our CO, who was shocked to have someone intervene. The shock caused him to loosen his grip on the front of my flight suit as Evert pulled me away from him, saying loudly, "Bob, we need to do an intelligence debrief and after-action report right now! Come on, let's move!"

Captain Haymore continued to pull me away from the CO, pushing me ahead of him toward the ready room before I could say anything or do anything really stupid.

I could not believe how pissed off I had become. Normally, I have an even temper and don't get angry easily, but his lack of concern for the members of his own squadron's Marines got under my skin. His career seemed to be the only important thing in his life.

Once inside the ready room, Captain Haymore and I were joined by Lieutenant Silver. I was still seething mad, but we worked together on the necessary paperwork. Describing the details of the mission in the after-action and intelligence-reporting processes. As we completed the final piece of paper, I finally got my temper back under control again.

We had just finished the paperwork when we heard a jeep arriving outside. It was Major Wasko arriving after being released from Charlie Med. He saw us sitting at the table and walked over to us. I asked him, "How is Lieutenant Colonel Pitman doing?"

He said that Lieutenant Colonel Pitman was undergoing surgery when he left him and would probably be medevacked out of country in the morning. Major Wasko still looked like he was in a state of shock as he sat down on one of the chairs at our table. My thoughts drifted to Lieutenant Colonel Pitman's change of command that had been scheduled for the day after tomorrow, which was now surely on hold, if not cancelled completely. A replacement CO would have to be found for Lieutenant Colonel Pitman since our present CO had a flight date and a set of orders back to Washington, DC.

I was not surprised that his next duty assignment would be Washington, DC. Not in the least. He could not leave soon enough to suit me.

It was not longer than one minute after Major Wasko sat down that Major "Red" Edwards, the squadron's executive officer, entered the ready room. He saw him sitting with us, and Major Wasko stood up, and they exchanged warm greetings. Major Edwards was smiling as he said how happy he was that Major Wasko had made it back home safely. The smile then left his face as he then told Major Wasko that he was to report to the commanding officer in his office ASAP.

I assumed his visit to the CO was to discuss the day's events and the loss of the aircraft. The executive officer, who was also his good friend, accompanied him as they departed for the CO's office. Just before the XO went out the door, he turned and waved to us as we continued to gather up the paperwork at the table in the back of the ready room. He gave us a quick thumbs-up and said, "Thanks to all of you for doing a good job today."

It had been one hell of a day for all of us who were involved in today's mission. That was for sure.

As the XO departed, Sergeant Pogany entered the ready room looking around and obviously looking for me. He spotted the three of us getting up from the table in the back of the ready room. He made a beeline toward us with a stack of paperwork in his hand. Arriving at the table, Sergeant Pogany said he had done the post-flight-discrepancy write-ups, and as much of the rest of the yellow sheet pilot sections that he could fill in, but I needed to complete the rest.

He handed me the yellow sheet that I needed to complete. It included the section requiring the notations—such as, the number of day and night landings, day and night flight time, total aircraft flight time, and so forth. It also had a section with noted discrepancies that Sergeant Pogany had filled out but required my signature. I thanked Sergeant Pogany for his diligence and attention to detail in completing the inspection and discrepancy write-ups. I also apologized for not helping him complete the inspection and paperwork.

He indicated that Miss Carriage II was his aircraft, and he had to take care of her, so she could take care of him on the next flight. He said once the paperwork was completed, they could get his aircraft into the barn (hangar) and start to repair the battle damage she had sustained during that day's mission.

Lieutenant Silver, Captain Haymore, and I sat back down at the table and went to work on completing the remaining yellow sheet forms. Lieutenant Silver had taken many notes during our flight that day. He had taken care of the myriad of logistical details—recording number of lifts that included locations, recording the weight of cargo lifted, number of guns lifted, day and night landings, number and location of landing zones visited, flight time, and so forth.

To my surprise, we had flown more than thirteen hours that day. We had been in the cockpit for over seventeen hours!

I thanked God and Sikorsky Aircraft for the installation of a relief tube in the cockpit. Drinking coffee and water during the all-day flight made it necessary to get rid of the waste products. I would have never made it without the "tube."

I thanked Lieutenant Silver for taking care of the myriad of logistical details. His diligence made the completion of the paperwork both faster and considerably more accurate.

As we completed the last of the paperwork, I looked at Lieutenant Silver, thinking that he had functioned as a model copilot all day long in spite of being somewhat apprehensive at the start of the day. He had functioned well under fire on his first combat mission, totally supportive of the day's mission and was instrumental in our completing it and returning safely to home base. I pointed out this fact to him as we completed the final page of the paperwork. He thanked me for my kind words and smiled.

As we all started to depart the squadron ready room together, I looked at the ready room's clock. It read 2345 hours, still February 23, 1971. We got into the jeep for the ride back to our hooches as we bypassed the officers' club that had closed at 2200 hours, so we could not go there for a cocktail.

On the ride to the hooch, I thought, *This was truly one hell of a day in Laos!*

Arriving back at our hooch, Captain Evert Haymore went to the refrigerator freezer compartment and removed a bottle of vodka, which we kept cool in it. Since it was alcohol, it did not freeze. He retrieved two glasses and poured both of us a tall cocktail. We both sat down at the table in the living area and proceeded to talk about yesterday's mission and the unbelievable conduct of our CO while we drank our cocktails.

While we talked, I thought about the fact that what we did could have gotten all of us killed. At the time I was flying the mission, this thought never entered my mind. I concentrated and focused on the mission almost exclusively, not on the danger it held. Only now as the true reality of what had happened in Laos finally really entered my conscious mind. I then realized that what we had done scared the hell out of me, but it was our job, and I would do it all again if called upon.

After we finished our second cocktail, I went to the shower facility a couple of buildings away and got rid of the red dirt of Laos. Returning to the hooch, I fell into bed and went to sleep only to relive yesterday's entire mission in my sleep.

*****

The next morning on February 24 found me a little hungover from the past day's activities as well as the shots of vodka that our cocktails contained, which Captain Haymore and I consumed in our hooch while discussing and rehashing the mission well into the early morning hours.

Informal squadron policy stated that if you had flown as part of a Lam Son 719 mission one day, you got the following day off. So I got the day off from flight duties and was not on the February 24 flight schedule.

After getting up, dressing, then eating in the officers' mess that I had overseen the construction of on my first combat tour in Vietnam, I returned to my hooch. To my surprise, the monsoon conditions we had encountered the night before had again dissipated, and the morning was bright and sunny.

Since Marble Mountain Air Facility was located on the beautiful white sand beach, I decided to go down and sit on the beach for a couple of hours of sun before going to the logistics hooch, which was my office. I put on some shorts, grabbed my towel and beach blanket, and made my way down to the beautiful white sand beach. The Marble Mountain Air Facility beach was located right next to the China Beach facility, where we dropped off Lieutenant Colonel Pitman and Major Wasko the night before. There were large signs that indicated that we were not allowed to cross into the China Beach medical facility or its beach area. Posted by order of the commanding officer of MAG-16, who was also the commander of the air facility. The two beaches were separated by concertina wire, which reached down to the water's edge. Also located on each of these beaches were large signs that read, "DANGER—Do Not Enter the Water" in large red letters.

These signs had been posted since the influx of breeding sea snakes had arrived in the waters off the beach in early January. These sea snakes were so numerous that you could see the brown mass of breeding sea snakes outside the surf line, moving in a slithering mass of several million snakes, slithering through the water even in the surf close to the shore. Sea snakes live in the water their whole life, but they breathed air and are extremely poisonous and able to bite their prey under water.

I found a comfortable-looking spot in an area down toward the China Beach barbed wire to put my blanket down on the beach and started to enjoy the warm morning sun. As I sat on the beach, I noticed a young Caucasian woman walking to the beach from the nurses' quarters. She wore a white swimsuit, had long red hair, and carried a beach towel. She put the towel down on the beach next to the large red sign, reading "DANGER—Do Not Enter the Water" on her side of the wire, about two hundred feet away from where I was seated.

Forgetting about the red-headed nurse, I lay down on my blanket, tired from yesterday's activities and dosed off.

Hearing several screams awakened me with a start. The screams sounded like they were coming from a female voice on the beach in front of the China Beach facility. Sitting up quickly, I saw the woman whom I had seen earlier in the white bathing suit in front of the China Beach facility. She was standing in the surf, up to her waist and struggling to get back toward shore. Several other women were on the beach now also screaming to her to get out of the water.

Looking closer at her, I saw she was trying to pull several sea snakes off her arms. As she tried to move into shallower water, closer to the beach, I saw a couple of additional snakes had grabbed on to her legs as she continued to struggle toward the beach.

I, along with a couple of other Marines, were up off our blankets running toward the stricken woman. As we rounded the end of the concertina wire and moved into the water, we saw her start to collapse in the surf in about knee-deep water. We could see the sea snakes in the shallow water, as well as outside the surf line, so we had to be careful to avoid them as we raced to help the woman. Two of us grabbed her as she fell into the water and dragged her to shore. She was totally unconscious by this time. After pulling her out of the water, we quickly and carefully removed several sea snakes still attach to her arms and legs. As we finished removing the snakes, several people from the medical facility arrived on the scene. One of these people said he was a doctor and asked what happened while he checked for a pulse. We told him that the woman had gone into the water, ignoring the sign posted right next to her towel, and had been bitten by multiple sea snakes.

The doctor said she was still alive but had a very weak pulse. Another doctor arrived and gave her a shot of something. They then lifted her onto a stretcher carrying her into the medical facility. This all happened in about four or five minutes. After she had been taken inside, we headed back toward our side of the beach.

My fellow Marines and I walked back to the Marble Mountain side of the beach by going into the surf around the concertina wire, again, avoiding the sea snakes in the surf. As we came around the wire, several Marine military police (MP) arrived and wanted to know why we were sneaking on to their base and violating the don't-cross-the-wire order. Since all of us were in shorts with no identification except our dog tags, we knew we were all in trouble. As the sergeant of the guard and two other MPs approached us with guns drawn, we raised our hands trying to indicate to him we were not a threat. The sergeant of the guard asked if we had IDs, and we said we did not. He then told us that we were under arrest until he could get a positive ID on us and find out what was going on. We tried to explain, but he was adamant that we were under arrest and to stay put where we were standing until he could get this figured out.

At this point, Colonel Street, the MAG-16 Group CO, arrived. He had seen the events that occurred from the porch of his beach cottage. The sergeant of the guard recognized the CO and saluted. The CO indicated he had seen all the events that had transpired and that our action may have saved the young lady's life. Further, he said he knew all of us and would vouch for us, and we did not need to be arrested.

He told the sergeant of the guard that he would handle the situation personally. The sergeant of the guard listened to the CO's statements, then saluted, leaving us with the Group CO.

The CO looked at the three of us and said that he was proud of what we had done in trying to help save the young woman, but this was the last time he would overlook the breaking of the don't-cross-the-fence order. "Don't do it again" were his last words as he turned, with a smile on his face and walked back to his beach cottage. We all picked up our beach stuff and left before he could change his mind.

Heading back to my hooch, I had little hope for the survival of the woman on the beach because of the number and size of the snakes that had attacked her. I still could not believe she had entered the water like she had. Being ignorant and not heeding the sign "DANGER—Do Not Enter the Water," probably cost her, her life.

*****

Returning to my hooch area, I showered and then walked to the squadron area. As the logistic officer for the squadron, I had a desk in the squadron's S-4 logistics hooch. As part of my duties, I needed to read the naval message traffic, approve vehicle requests, allocate funds for repairs of squadron facilities, and so forth. Additionally, I oversaw the planning and execution of the squadron's embarkation preparations. The logistics chief and I talked extensively about the status of the planning efforts necessary for the embarkation of the entire squadron out of Vietnam to Hawaii.

Since I had been the armory officer and part of the original HMH-463 squadron's deployment when it arrived in Vietnam in 1967, I was aware of all the original equipment contained in the table of organization (T/O) that came with the initial deployment of the squadron. There was a lot of it. Some of these items were fuel trucks, a fire truck, large military trucks, jeeps, other rolling stock, and ground-support equipment needed to support aircraft maintenance and operation activities. Most folks in the squadron had no idea that we were responsible for embarkation of these items.

All our T/O weapons—such as, M-60 and .50-caliber machine guns, M3A1 submachine guns, rifles, pistol, and so forth were all required to be taken with the squadron as it moved to Hawaii.

Upon arrival in-country in 1967, most of the rolling stock items had been temporarily transferred to the MAG support squadrons. These items were currently held by the Marine Air Base Squadron 16 and Headquarters, and Maintenance Squadron 16. All these items, rolling stock and weapons, were generally not considered by most of the Marines in the squadron to be our squadron's property.

I knew that all these items and equipment would have to be returned to our squadron for shipment to Hawaii. We would be responsible for their cleanup and embarkation of all these items to the squadron's new home base. Further, we would be required to clean up our aircraft thoroughly in anticipation of a complete agricultural inspection by federal and state of Hawaii inspectors both here in Vietnam before departure and again in Hawaii after the squadron had arrived.

Moving a squadron of this size was a major project, which seemed to have been placed on the back burner with the priority going to supporting the operation in Laos and other combat missions. The logistics chief indicated that the squadron's junior officers and noncommissioned officers were not completing the required inventory of all squadron aircraft, maintenance, ground support, office equipment, and supplies (including items held by MABS 16 and H&MS 16) as they had been directed to do.

There appeared to be no senior command interest or priority given to the completion of the inventory, which was the basis for allocation of parking and cargo space on both the aircraft carrier and surface cargo ships that would be necessary to transport the squadron to Hawaii. If we underestimated the need, then valuable items would have to be left behind to be shipped later or destroyed. The logistics chief expressed a real concern that various sections in the squadron were not taking the planning for our departure seriously. He was concerned that since we were scheduled to embark in a little more than ninety days, this lack of concern could pose a real problem to our successful departure if not corrected very soon.

After looking at the inventory completions as of today, I agreed that we needed to make the senior officers, officers in charge, and staff noncommissioned officers in charge in the squadron's critical areas aware of the problem. Hopefully energizing them in order to solve the problem before it became too late to deal with.

In the early afternoon, I received a visit from the XO, who dropped by my office, to talk about the schedule for the change of command that had been turned upside down by the wounding and subsequent medevacking of Lieutenant Colonel Pitman. The XO indicated that a new CO had been designated. He was Lieutenant Colonel Tom Reap, who had a very good reputation, and was a second-tour combat veteran with CH-53 experience. The squadron's change of command had been delayed and was now rescheduled to take place in the afternoon of March 5, 1971. This date was selected by the outgoing CO so he could make his flight out of country and arrive in Washington, DC, on schedule.

Since I was the senior captain in the squadron, I was also told by the XO that I'd be expected to participate in the change-of-command ceremony as a member of the staff.

I said to the XO, "I would rather be flying in Laos." As he started to leave, he shook his head and laughed at me. Quickly before he departed, I said that we needed to talk about the embarkation problems my staff had discovered. He suggested we wait until after the change of command to address the problems with our new CO and himself. I agreed but was still concerned regarding the delay in resolving the embarkation-planning problems.

The operations officer also dropped by my office as the XO was leaving. Major Wasko was on his way to visit the MAG-16 CO, Colonel Street. He also carried a document that he asked me to review and sign. It was a transcribed version of my after-action statement that I had handwritten the night before. It had been transcribed into typewritten form by one of the operation department clerks. I asked him how he was feeling. He responded he was okay.

You still looked like you are in shock to me, I thought.

As he hurriedly started to leave my office to see the Group CO, I indicated to the major that I would be reviewing and signing the statement, posthaste.

Over the next few minutes, I reviewed the newly typed after-action report. I found what I considered to be errors and was concerned that some of the content was not accurate. Going to the operations hooch, I found the clerk who had typed my after-action statement. Since my handwriting was not the most legible, I wanted to make sure what I had written had been correctly transcribed, so I sat down to read the three pages of my original statement again with him. Everything was correct except the number of people who had been rescued by use of the rescue ladder beneath my aircraft.

How the hell did five people end up as three? He must have not read my writing correctly.

I asked the clerk how five people became three people? Did I not write clearly? At first, he did not want to talk about the changes. Then after a minute or two, he said that he was directed to make the changes because only actual people listed on the yellow sheet, flight crew members only, were allowed to be on any squadron aircraft that flew into Laos during Lam Son 719, per the CO's directive. Continuing, he said that the two additional people that were aboard the replacement aircraft that returned to LZ Kilo the day before had not been part of the actual flight crew. Since neither of these two people were wounded or hurt during flight or our rescue effort, the "commander," meaning the CO, did not want any of the unauthorized personnel that had flown into Laos documented as having done so on his watch.

You got to be shitting me. The CO wants to change the facts so he can look good. I guess it does not matter because we got them all back alive from Laos, I thought as I looked at the clerk for several seconds.

The clerk could see that I was not happy about the changes he had been directed to make, telling me he was just doing what he was told. I told him I understood his predicament. Not wanting to ruffle additional feathers of the current CO any further than I already had, I went ahead reluctantly and signed the document knowing it had an error in it.

*****

On February 25, I was on the flight schedule as the squadron's *test pilot* now termed *post-maintenance inspection pilot*. This special flight process was necessary to assure that aircraft that have had significant replacement of components or flight-control adjustments made or changed or had reported pilot discrepancies (not being able to be reproduced on the ground) were safe to fly. These aircraft must be evaluated by a maintenance check pilot who has maintenance experience along with a greater understanding of the critical aircraft systems than normal squadron pilots before they can be released for normal flight operations.

Aircraft that needed test flights had to be evaluated and checked, then signed off by a test pilot before they could be flown on regular missions. The post-maintenance flights were made by designated test pilots using a specialized checklist used to ensure the functionality of the engines, hydraulic, avionics, and flight-control systems of the aircraft.

In our squadron at the time, we had a total of three designated test pilots. The three of us were being asked to fly significantly more evaluation test flights than normal because of a couple of pilots and one pilot in particular who kept reporting problems with vibrations in the aircraft, which could not be duplicated on the ground. Almost all these discrepancies were reported by the same aircraft commander when he was on the schedule to fly combat support missions including Mission 52s into Laos. When he flew normal logistic flights from one airfield to another airfield, he generally completed these missions without experiencing any aircraft vibration problems. On one occasion, he downed (required evaluation by a test pilot before it could be used for normal missions) four aircraft in a row because he said he experienced abnormal vibrations in the rotor system and tail rotor of all four aircraft. He did not complete the mission he was scheduled to fly that day. Another flight crew had to be assigned to pick up and complete his mission.

I specifically remember returning one evening from a Mission 52 flight in Laos, having flown nine hours of flight time already, and being asked by the line chief to fly two evaluation flights before I quit for the day. Both of these two aircraft needed to be evaluated for unusual vibrations. Both aircraft were both downed by the same individual for, in his words, "severe vibrations in the tail rotor." The line chief pleaded with me to fly the birds since the other two test pilots were still out on missions, and he badly needed them to support the next day's flight schedule.

I thought, *One good deal after another, but the line chief and the squadron needs the birds for tomorrow's schedule, so I guess I can help them out. Night test hops [flights] are always a challenge.*

During my test flights of both aircraft, using the test-flight checklist, I found no discrepancies or unusual vibrations during either of my thirty-minute test-flight evaluations. Both aircraft were used for their scheduled missions the next day and returned without incident, and no unusual vibrations were noted in the rotor system or tail rotor by their pilots. It is also interesting to note that several days after downing the four aircraft in one day for unusual vibrations in the rotor system or tail rotor, the individual involved was finally transferred to a ground job at the group headquarters where he would no longer be scheduled to fly any subsequent combat missions in Vietnam.

*****

On February 26, I flew five test hops after major components and engines were replaced. These flights were completed without incident, with all five returning in an up condition after some minor adjustment to engine settings. The maintenance crews and flight crews were performing their duties far beyond what was normally seen at a stateside squadron. They did it right the first time and were operating at their personal peak effectiveness. Combat sometimes drives people to perform far above their normal levels of performance.

I was again assigned as the duty test pilot for February 27, 1971. Three aircraft needed to be flown. All came back in an up condition and operationally ready for any assigned mission.

I started to wonder why I had not been scheduled for another Mission 52 flight. *Something is wrong* was the thought that crossed my mind as I finished the final test flight that was scheduled for that day.

After returning from the last test hop of the day, Major Wasko called me to his office. When I arrived, he indicated in a low voice that we should go outside for our conversation and to have some privacy. We both walked outside his office away from prying ears. He told me that the current CO did not want me to fly anymore Lam Son 719 missions because he believed that I was the cause of the loss of our CH-53 in Laos. Major Wasko indicated to me that he had pushed back saying that he was the pilot of the CH-53 that was lost, and I had nothing to do with it. It was his decision to continue the mission, not mine. Continuing, he said that he had told the CO that unless he was going to relieve him as the squadron operations officer, he would continue writing the flight schedule as necessary to accomplish the squadron's assigned missions. Furthermore, he told him that he would use all the squadron's pilot assets available to ensure the command continued to support the mission in Laos fully. Continuing again, he said that the CO would not look at him while he stated that he would not relieve him of his job at this time since he, the CO, was leaving very soon. However, this was not the end of the issue by any means! He then dismissed him saying nothing more, as the major left his office.

Major Wasko looked me in the eye and said he planned to continue to use me in the Mission 52 rotation as usual. I thanked him for his confidence and support for me with the CO. As he returned to his office, he said over his shoulder that "this is not over yet, Captain. I believe the CO means to make us pay for the loss of 'his aircraft.'"

Later, I would find out how true his words were. "This is not over yet!"

Later that evening and to my surprise, I found myself on the flight schedule as flight leader for the Laos support mission the next day. It appeared to me that our Ops O was driving his point home by utilizing me in the face of command criticism.

*****

On February 28, I was back in the saddle and off to support the Lam Son 719 mission again. That day, I was the flight leader of the four CH-53s in our continuing support of the operation in Laos. My copilot for that day's mission was First Lieutenant Jan Urbanczyk. Jan was a young first lieutenant who arrived in-country a few days after my arrival in January. Sergeant Pogany was again our crew chief, but we were assigned a different aircraft since YH-20 Miss Carriage II was still being repaired.

During the mission briefing, I changed the strategy for our flight somewhat. Since all the work was going to be done inside Laos, I wanted to break up our flight into sections. This would help speed up the movement of loads since each section could carry two loads to the same location covered by two Cobra escorts at one time. It was my understanding from the Mission 52 frag order that we received that morning that all our work would be inside Laos. The rest of the mission briefing, preflight, turn ups, taxi, and takeoff from Marble Mountain were all normal. The weather that day was much better than normal so that our flight to Khe Sanh to refuel, then on to LZ Kilo was rather routine.

We rendezvoused with our Scarface Cobra escorts at LZ Kilo and again attended the Army's Command and Control briefing.

Our flight again was tasked by the Army with moving artillery pieces, equipment, and ammunition between FSBs. The Army briefer indicated that the relocation of these artillery pieces was needed to facilitate the continued ARVN push even deeper into Laos, with their final ARVN objective being the occupation of the town of Tchepone, Laos.

The briefer indicated that there had been several reports that 23mm and 37mm antiaircraft fire had been seen at various locations inside Laos. A number of Army helicopters sustained damage and were lost from hits from these weapons. The Army had requested and gotten support from the Navy to suppress the radar-control features of these weapons that were used against Army helicopters, our aircraft, or fixed-wing attack aircraft. He made a final statement that "the guns are still out there. Even without radar control, they can be deadly. Be careful." He then handed out detailed sheets to myself, my second section leader, and the four Scarface Cobra pilots that described in detail the pickup locations, items to be carried, and where they were to be taken.

On our way back to our aircraft after the conclusion of the mission brief by Command and Control folks at LZ Kilo, I asked the Scarface Cobra leader, "Since we had split the work to be done into assignments by sections, could you see your way clear to split up the four Scarface Cobra escorts into two sections in order to cover each of my sections as they move equipment and guns as indicated inside Laos?"

He agreed to split his flight and said, "This change should speed up the mission considerably."

Our entire flight manned their aircraft. After we had completed our NATOPS checklist and were ready to take off, I called the rest of the flight to check in. My wingman had a small mechanical problem that was quickly corrected, but this delayed our takeoff. Since the second section had checked in and was ready to go. I told them to go ahead now, splitting the flight at this point. I watched the second section and their escorts depart LZ Kilo heading for Laos. Once my wingman was ready to go, we took off on our part of the mission, followed by our Scarface Cobra escorts heading into Laos again.

As both sections went about moving the equipment and guns on our to-do list, neither of our sections had encountered any 23mm or 37mm antiaircraft fire as we moved the guns, ammunition, and equipment from one FSB to another inside Laos. At around 1100 hours, while moving a 105mm gun between LZ Yellow and FSB Delta 1, we encountered what appeared to be an air burst off a couple hundred yards to the side of our aircraft while flying at three thousand feet AGL.

This was the first time, on this tour, I had seen real antiaircraft air bursts at altitude. I immediately initiated a climb, notifying my wingman a quarter mile behind me with another load and our escorts that I was going up an additional five hundred feet, hoping to confuse the gunner who had accurately judged our altitude. Everyone had seen the air bursts and acknowledged my radio transmission.

Thinking back to the television program about World War II bomber raids, the flack explosions that had been shown in the *12 O'Clock High* program came to mind. The real stuff looked just as it had on the television, but I knew that it was far more dangerous here and now.

The Army's Command and Control coordinated the use of carrier-based EA-6B aircraft on station high overhead to suppress the radar that was being used by the NVA gunners to track aircraft in the tactical operation area. This EA-6B jamming of the NVA radars forced the NVA gunners to manually track their targets.

Our two section efforts, broken up by refueling runs to Khe Sanh, took all morning and well into the afternoon to complete. Both sections of our Scarface Cobra escorts continued to perform in an outstanding manner, suppressing small-arms fire and light mortar attacks as we moved our loads between FSBs.

Since we had completed all the assigned resupply and gun lifts, except the last two guns at Hotel II, I elected to send the second section of our CH-53D flight back to Marble Mountain. We kept all four Cobra escorts to cover the final gun moves.

Our final mission for the day was to move the last two artillery pieces out of FSB Hotel II to FSB Delta 1, before it was overrun by the NVA ground forces, which appeared to be again imminent. These were the same two guns that we attempted to move on February 23 when Dimmer 3 was shot down. We were told by the Army's Command and Control that the NVA attack had been driven back the day we lost our bird. Additionally, they indicated that the one gun next to the crashed aircraft had been moved to another gun pit so it could be extracted.

Déjà vu, I thought. *Here we go again.*

Our gun extraction attempts were going to be covered by our four Scarface gunship escorts, not Army gunships this time.

Somehow, I felt better knowing that my brother Marines were covering our asses this time around.

Our two aircraft rendezvoused with our Scarface Cobra escorts at the fuel pits at Khe Sanh. The Scarface leader and I discussed the strategy for the approach and gun pickup over the secure radio that we would use in our attempt to move the last two guns out of FSB Hotel II.

The recent exposure to the antiaircraft fire at altitude that we had just experienced influenced my decision not to come in at a high altitude, instead we would try the low-level strategy we had employed four days earlier. While in the fuel pits, we discussed several important aspects of the upcoming mission. Of specific concern to me was the coordination of fire-suppression activities we needed in order to make our extraction attempt feasible.

Being the mission flight leader, it was my responsibility to coordinate all aspects of the flight. However, I needed some help with the coordination of the fire-support aspect of the mission. Delegating the coordination of these activities to the Scarface Cobra flight leader, in my opinion, was a prudent move. So we agreed that he would assume the role of coordinator of the fire-support aspects of the mission.

I asked him to call the Army's Command and Control center giving them a warning order for our request for artillery and fixed-wing support for the extraction mission. He made the call to the Army's Command and Control center requesting our support based on when we anticipated crossing the border into Laos. Their response indicated that the support would be made available based on our arrival time at the border that he had requested. They also indicated that he should check in with the FAC on station, since they were working several Army missions as well as ours. He needed to call the FAC before our flight departed South Vietnam in order to coordinate the close air-support and artillery-fire missions we needed. The Scarface leader acknowledged the check-in requirements.

After we all had refueled and the Scarface Cobra escorts had rearmed, we departed Khe Sanh heading south along the South Vietnamese border.

Our stealth strategy again entailed a low-level run into Laos from the east of the FSB in an attempt to get into FSB Hotel II without being detected by the NVA. Once again, we stayed inside the South Vietnamese border and behind the hills out of sight of the NVA spotters, then turned west, and continued into the FSB using terrain masking to the maximum extent possible until reaching the perimeter of the FSB. As we had done four days earlier, my run-in from the border would be made by individual 53s with two Scarface Cobra escorts accompanying me.

My wingmen and the other two Cobras would stay behind inside South Vietnam's border and wait until I had gotten my gun out of the FSB. At the specified time, our Scarface leader called and told Command and Control that we were crossing the border toward FSB Hotel II. As we flew west, my aircraft was joined by our two Cobra escorts as we turned into the same shallow valley that we utilized a few days earlier. As we all entered the valley, we proceeded at low level and increased our airspeeds to the maximum. During our ingress flight, none of our aircraft received small-arms fire. I heard the Scarface Cobra escort leader working with the airborne Army FAC coordinating artillery-suppression fire efforts and getting fixed-wing support ready to engage the enemy.

Upon arrival at the base of the hill east of FSB Hotel II, we popped up over the top of the hill again trading airspeed for altitude. As we arrived over the gun-pit area, the first thing I saw was the remnants of Dimmer 3's aircraft on the edge of the gun pit. Sergeant Pogany spotted the first 105mm gun that we were to lift, which had been moved to the adjacent gun pit. He quickly gave me instructions that got us moving toward its location. Surprisingly, we had not been spotted yet, but as we moved rapidly toward the gun, that changed quickly. The NVA mortar crews had seen us and started to drop rounds in the gun pits as we moved toward the pickup location. It appeared to me that they wanted to add another helicopter kill to the one that they had already gotten.

As we approached the gun, the world seemed to again explode around us. Even while we were in the middle of this explosion of fire, Sergeant Pogany directed me over the 105mm gun. Mortar fire, plus

.50-caliber machine gun, and small-arms fire was again coming from everywhere it seemed.

In our pretakeoff briefing, we had already provided guidance to our two gunners that if they saw incoming fire and could identify sources of fire, then they were cleared to fire. Lieutenant Urbanczyk called out targets on his side of the aircraft, which the gunner on his side engaged while the gunner on my side also found plenty of targets to fire upon.

While we were in this exposed hover over the gun, Sergeant Pogany, Lieutenant Urbanczyk, nor I could not find any ARVN personnel in or near the gun that we were trying to pick up. Again, no one was visible at all in the gun pits. Without the ARVN troops to hook us up, we could not get close enough to the gun for a pickup because of the obstacle the crashed aircraft blades still presented, even though the gun was moved to the next gun pit.

The Dimmer 3 aircraft blades would not allow us to drop down close enough for Sergeant Pogany to reach the gun sling lying on top of the barrel of the gun without striking the blade that hung over the original gun location.

Seeing that our gun was not reachable, Sergeant Pogany directed me to the location of the second 105mm gun to be extracted. Once we were over the gun, Sergeant Pogany could not see the sling that should have been placed on top of the gun. It was not visible to him at all, and again, there were no ARVNs to be seen to put it back on top of the gun or to hook us up. As we worked to try to find the sling and get hooked up to the second gun, our two Scarface Cobra escorts were working with the FAC and continued their attacks on the enemy mortar and NVA troop concentrations attempting to suppress their incoming fire. The incoming mortar fire appeared to be increasing its intensity. With no way to reach the gun sling and with the small-arms fire increasing, we abandoned the extraction attempt.

I called the Scarface flight leader and told him that we were aborting the pickup. As I moved up and away from the downed CH-53 and both of the 105mm guns, I started a tight right-hand power climbing spiral in order to get out of the small-arms and mortar fire. We were climbing through the altitude of about three thousand feet when we saw several flashes ahead and above us. The whole crew heard several big pops as the aircraft shook violently. Immediately after the flashes, the caution panel lit up in the cockpit, indicating we had a problem. Recognizing the antiaircraft air bursts, I rolled the aircraft in the opposite direction and stopped our climb diving away from the bursts continuing to explode above us.

Looking down at the illuminated lights on the caution panel, I determined that we had lost hydraulic power in our first-stage hydraulic system, which included half the tail rotor servo, half of all the primary flight-control servos, and part of the automatic stabilization system. If we lost the second-stage hydraulic system, the aircraft would become uncontrollable, and we would crash. At the same time, the first-stage hydraulic pressure gauge was falling to zero. Sergeant Pogany indicated that we had a lot of hydraulic fluid in the cabin along with a three-inch hole in the ramp and in the overhead section of the rear cabin.

He said over the ICS, "You could see daylight through these two holes."

In the cockpit, we followed the NATOPS procedures for the loss of the first-stage hydraulic flight-control systems. The redundant flight-control systems worked as designed, and we were able to continue to control the aircraft as we departed the FSB Hotel II area to the east. As we leveled off heading east, I watched the two Scarface Cobra escorts climb, then joined us to escort us back to friendly territory.

The Army FAC, meanwhile, was working two flights of fixed-wing aircraft in an attack on the gun position that hit us. The weapon that hit us would later be identified as a 23mm crew served antiaircraft weapon. The Army FAC continued to work fixed-wing aircraft into the area that we received mortar and small-arms fire along with the antiaircraft position as we departed the area heading east.

At this point, I called my wingman and the other two Cobras while we were en route back to the border. I alerted them to the situation at FSB Hotel II and my aircraft's condition. As we headed for the border, the Army FAC then called indicating that in light of the antiaircraft fire that I had received as we departed the pickup area, any further attempt to get the two 105mm guns out should not be made until these weapons had been neutralized.

The flight back to the South Vietnamese border was a short one, about eight miles. Once back inside South Vietnam, we turned north toward Khe Sanh. My wingman had now also joined me as we proceeded back to the Lang Vei LZ. He flew in close to us and looked us over for damage, but he saw only the small hole in the top of the fuselage of the aircraft and what looked like some blade pockets missing close to the rotor head.

Extended flight on a single hydraulic flight-control system is not recommended (loss of the second hydraulic system means loss of control of the aircraft), so we were all extremely happy when I set the aircraft down on the ground at Lang Vei LZ and shut it down.

I sure don't want to do that trick again today, I opined.

As we inspected the aircraft, it was evident that an antiaircraft projectile entered the ramp of the aircraft, went through it, then went upward through the top of the cabin ceiling, just missing the tail rotor drive shaft but damaging the first-stage tail rotor hydraulic line. The projectile then continued upward through the main rotor blades and exploded above the aircraft's rotor head.

The antiaircraft rounds normally are set to explode at a specific altitude. Boy, were we lucky they were not contact-fused rounds. We would not be here if they were, I thought.

We observed that several pockets in each main rotor blade had sustained shrapnel holes, with a couple of pockets missing. However, none of the blade spars appeared to be damaged. We climbed down from on top of the aircraft and looked at one another, I said to the entire crew, "Gentlemen, we were extremely lucky today."

The good Lord must not have wanted us to die today, I thought.

If the explosive round had hit one of the main blades, it would have caused it to leave the aircraft and we would have all suffered a similar fate as the aircraft we lost at Hue and Phu Bai on February 18, 1971.

I said and I believed that my entire crew said a prayer or two after looking at the close call we had just experienced.

Our next challenge was to get the aircraft into a flyable condition and then take it back to Marble Mountain for repair. If the aircraft remained at Lang Vei overnight, it was an open invitation for the NVA to shell or rocket or attack the Lang Vei LZ.

Checking the blade inspection system (BIM) indicators for each main rotor blade, we found them all to be white (black BIM indicated pressure loss in the spar, making the blade inoperable for flight). The white showed that the spar pressure in each blade had been maintained indicating that the spars were not damaged. Only the pockets attached to the blade spars appeared damaged. While far from being ideal, we all concurred that we could fly the bird home in this condition.

The tail rotor line was another story. Sergeant Pogany was an expert mechanic who quickly found a way to fix the problem. He took the break line off the nose landing gear, capped off that line, then utilized it as a replacement for the damaged hydraulic tail rotor servo line. The line was the same size and was pressure tested to the same pounds per-square-inch pressure as the tail rotor system.

Some people would call this innovative thinking repair jury rigging, but I prefer to call it an expedient field repair. Once this fix was completed and the first-stage hydraulic system was serviced with fluid, we turned up the aircraft to look for leaks. After several minutes of ground turning, no leaks were found. I shut the aircraft down to make sure all the hydraulic reservoirs were completely full.

My wingman, during this evolution, supported our repair efforts by retrieving a hydraulic servicing unit from the LZ Kilo so we could service the hydraulic systems. He also checked the weather for our return flight home. He indicated it was clear, which was a pleasant surprise for a change. My wingman and I started our birds, then flew to Khe Sanh, refueled, and headed home after returning the hydraulic servicing unit to LZ Kilo. I did not push the damaged hydraulic fix or blade damage aircraft too hard on our return trip. We arrived back at Marble Mountain just as the sun was setting. We shut down and completed the required paperwork.

No commanding officer confrontation occurred after this mission. I was surprised because I had anticipated it would happen. The entire crew had all agreed on our way home, that after being safely on the ground and all the paperwork was completed, we would have the entire crew meet at Sergeant Pogany's hooch for a well-deserved drink.

I made a detour en route to Sergeant Pogany's hooch to purchase several cases of beer along with a large bottle of whisky for Sergeant Pogany who, again, pulled our asses out of a tight jam. A good time was had by all that evening.

One item of intelligence information that was passed along to us at Sergeant Pogany's hooch, by another Marine who stopped in for a beer that evening, was that FSB Hotel II had been overrun by the NVA after we had departed. The guns we had tried to extract had to be destroyed in place along with an air strike to destroy what was left of Dimmers 3's aircraft.

*****

March 1 was no day off for me since we were short on pilots that day and the flu bug was going around. I flew a single aircraft mission in support of the South Korean Marines, as well as continuing to perform my job as logistic officer at the squadron. Our mission for that day involved the resupply of several South Korean Marine units northwest of Hoi An, approximately twenty-five miles south of Marble Mountain.

A section of HML-367 Scarface Cobra gunships accompanied my aircraft. During the mission, which entailed movement of ground troops from one LZ to another, we suffered a casualty. One of the South Korean Marines failed to follow the direction of his NCO and ran into the tail rotor blade of our aircraft. This would not have normally occurred except for the fact that we had to land on top of a slanted rock outcropping high above a valley, which was the designated pickup LZ.

Because of the strong winds, it was necessary to land on the rock with the tail pointed into the upward slant of the rock formation. Our crew chief and I took special care to notify the South Korean Marines about the hazard that had been created by our landing location. The first three sorties or lifts of about fifty South Korean Marines each went as planned, then on the final lift, a South Korean Marine ran around the wrong side of my crew chief and into the path of the tail rotor. He sustained a head injury even with his helmet on. We immediately loaded him on board and flew him to the South Korean Marine medical facility nearby and then returned to finish the troop movement portion and resupply mission for the South Korean Marines. We never learned if he had survived the encounter with the tail rotor. There was no damage observed to any of the tail rotor blades during the postflight inspection we conducted at the end of the mission.

After completing the postflight inspection and the mission paperwork, I discovered that I was scheduled for a nighttime flare-dropping mission the next night.

The next day, being that I was scheduled for the nighttime flare-dropping mission, I went to work a little later than usual. As I passed the HML-367 hangar that day, I watched them receive their first AH-1Js Sea Cobra gunship. This was the first of four aircraft that were to join the AH-1Gs Scarface birds of HML-367.

These twin-engine helicopters, armed with a three-barreled 20mm cannon, as well as machine guns and rockets, had been sent to Vietnam for their initial combat evaluation. The four new birds were temporarily attached to HML-367. These Sea Cobras would join the AH-1G Cobras that regularly escorted the CH-53Ds in Laos and elsewhere in Vietnam. We Marine aviators welcomed their additional firepower, and I was sure the pilots appreciated the greater safety provided by having two jet engines instead of one.

That night's mission, which I had not flown before, prompted me to find out what it entailed, what part my aircraft would play, and who else was going to be involved. Checking in with the operations department, I asked for all the information regarding the flare-drop mission I would fly that night. They gave me the information, which I studied in detail.

Our part of the mission was but a small part of a larger effort to interdict and hopefully eliminate a growing rocket threat to our base and the major airfield at Da Nang. ARVN intelligence had been warning that the Viet Cong and NVA were planning rocket attacks on Da Nang for the past several days, and my squadron had been flying flare-drop missions since the threat had been identified.

The flare mission I was to fly was designed to light up a large area where suspected rocket launch teams may be hiding. There have been numerous attacks on both our base and the large airfield of Da Nang in the past causing significant damage to structures and limited damage to some aircraft. Aircraft damages were significantly reduced by the construction of revetments, where almost all the combat aircraft were parked. These revetments generally shielded the birds from anything except a direct hit.

Our mission that night entailed the dropping of two million candle power flares out the hell hole in the middle of the aircraft. These parachute flares, about four feet in length and three inches in diameter, would be dropped out through a tube that extended a foot below the belly of the aircraft. A team of four people would be added to our normal crew to handle the unpacking, set up, and drop of these pyrotechnic devices.

We were part of a much larger team effort to see that the enemy did not get a chance to set up and launch their 122mm rockets at our facilities.

*****

Our flare mission briefing was to start at 2200 hours. The mission package we were flying in was made up of one Huey UH-1 that carried a million-candle-power spotlight and two AH-1 G Cobra gunships and ourselves.

The strategy was for my CH-53 to drop parachute flares from 3,500 feet in order to light up about one square mile of territory. The Huey with the big spotlight was the flight leader for this mission. He along with the two Cobra gunships would search the illuminated area for the rocket teams and engage them. The most likely areas we were to provide illumination were generally the areas where they had previously launched their rocket attacks.

After the combined briefing, we moved to our aircraft where we briefed the crew, checked the load of flares, and talked to the launch team leader, a sergeant. We then turned up the machine and made our midnight takeoff time. Our flight would work together from midnight until sunrise about 0530 hours with a couple of refueling evolutions being required.

After takeoff we climbed to 3,500 feet and waited for the Huey and Scarface Cobra birds to take off. With radio contact established, we set up an orbit about five miles southeast of the Da Nang airfield, the site where the last rocket attack originated. After we were cleared by the Huey flight leader, we commenced our illumination flare drops. Each flare we dropped was fitted with a parachute that gave the flare a burn time from our altitude of about six minutes, depending on the winds or until it hit the ground.

We dropped flares as we orbited the area for about two hours. No activity was spotted on the ground during this time. Needing to refuel, we called our Huey flight leader requesting to refuel. He suggested we go ahead and refuel along with the two Cobras. He said that he would continue to remain on station while we refueled. This was done so that the flight could continue to maintain an overwatch of the targeted area continually. He would refuel once we were back on station.

After all the aircraft in the flight had refueled, we again took up the orbit at 3,500 feet. After we had been on station for an hour, the Huey flight leader directed us to move our orbit further east toward the river, having a small village next to it, the river ran south in between Da Nang airbase and Marble Mountain Air Facility.

Moving into position, we continued to drop the flares lighting up the river and both riverbanks for about three quarters of a mile. The Huey flight leader came up on the radio saying that he had seen people moving north along the east bank of the river. He and his two Cobra gunships dropped lower to take a closer look. As they dropped to an altitude of about 1,000 feet, the Huey flight leader turned on his million-candle-power spotlight.

Looking out my pilot's window at the site below, from 3,500 feet, I was amazed to see around 50 people carrying what appeared to be long poles; actually these poles were 122mm rockets being moved along the riverbank. Most of these people appeared to be clad in black pajamas and had pointed straw hats on their heads. I also recognized some individuals who appeared to be dressed in NVA uniforms, having seen them up-close and personal in Laos, interspersed among the group.

The Huey flight leader came up on the radio again, saying that they had made a positive identification of the people on the ground as "unfriendlies" carrying what appeared to be 122mm rockets and launchers. He said they would engage the targets as soon as he could get permission from the Vietnamese liaison officer who controlled the approval to fire near this village.

On a different radio, he called the Vietnamese liaison officer who controlled the approval to fire near this village. After a couple of tries, he finally made contact with someone on the ground who sounded to me like they had just been awakened out of a sound sleep.

His response to the request to engage the "unfriendlies" was negative at this time. Our flight could not fire on the assembled group, without the village chief's approval, which he would attempt to obtain.

I could not believe what I had just heard and was seeing. We had them dead to rights moving into position to shoot rockets into one of our airfields, and we could not engage them unless some village chief approved. This is ridiculous, I thought.

The Huey flight leader came up on the radio again, more forceful this time, saying to the Vietnamese liaison officer that they had made a positive identification of the people on the ground as "unfriendlies." He also described to the Vietnamese liaison officer that the group had stopped and were in the process of setting up the launchers and loading the rockets on to them. Again, he asked him to approve the attack on the group. He received the same response—that the village chief would have to approve the mission, and no approval for the mission had been received from him as of yet.

Again, I could not believe what I had just heard and what I am watching. We have them out in the open. They are setting up to fire, and we can't engage. Unbelievable!

As we continued to illuminate the area below, my copilot and crew chief expressed frustration about our flight's inability to engage with what was surely the enemy below. I shared their frustration but said our flight leader had his orders, and he was following them.

About five minutes later, the Huey flight leader came up on the radio again, more dramatically this time, saying to the Vietnamese liaison officer that people on the ground had just launched several of their 122mm rockets at the Da Nang airfield. Again, he asked him to approve the attack on the group. He received the same response—that the village chief would have to approve the mission, and no approval for the mission had been received from him as of yet.

As we watched from above, what appeared to be at least twenty-five rockets were launched toward the Da Nang airfield. As we looked toward Da Nang, we could see the flashes of their impacts but could not see what they had hit.

After all the rockets had been fired from the bank of the river below, we watched as the fifty people picked up their rocket launchers and started dispersing in several directions.

The Huey flight leader made one last attempt to get clearance to engage the fleeing enemy but was again rebuffed. After a couple of minutes, no one could be seen on the riverbank or in the rice fields beyond. It appeared that they had just melted away.

The Vietnamese liaison officer then came up on his radio and notified our Huey flight leader that he had received clearance from the village chief to engage the rocketeers. The Huey flight leader's response to him was "Too little and too late, asshole. They're gone. I hope you are happy."

There was no response to the Huey flight leader's statement was made by the Vietnamese liaison officer. We continued the mission, refueling again as we had before, but encountered no other rocketeers that night. As we landed then debriefed after the mission, there was a sense of utter frustration exhibited by all involved.

It appeared to us, as a group, that the village chief was forced into compliance with the enemy's plan or was part of the insurgent's organization. We should have been able to prevent the attack on Da

Nang airfield but were blocked from doing our job by the politics of the situation.

These types of orders requiring South Vietnam's authorization to fire came after the American press corps in Vietnam broke the My Lai Massacre story in November 1969. The press corps that reported the story portrayed the Americans as cold-blooded murderers and the Vietnamese involved as just poor civilians. There was no question that some atrocities had occurred, but what was not reported was the previous significant losses of Army combat troops that had been incurred at the hands of the Viet Cong, NVA, and their supporters.

After My Lai, the American government, not wanting any additional bad press, continued the policy established by the Johnson administration and modified by President Nixon called Vietnamization. Nixon's policy continued the required withdrawal of American troops that Johnson had started along with the transfer of control of significant portions of ground operations to the South Vietnamese.

In doing so, in my opinion, these administrations went overboard by ensuring that the Vietnamese were the ones calling all the shots before they were ready. The NVA and Viet Cong recognized this policy shift and took advantage of it whenever possible. This policy played, in my opinion, directly into the NVA's and Viet Cong's developing strategy. NVA and Viet Cong now, in a lot of cases, called the shots either through intimidation, murder, or by recruiting of supporters. What I had just witnessed during the flare-drop mission was a case in point.

On March 3, subsequent to my flare mission and having been in bed for a couple of hours, I was awakened in my hooch by the squadron adjutant. His message was that the CO wanted to see me in his office at 1500 hours after the change-of-command practice.

The change-of-command practice started at 1330 hours and concluded about an hour later. I reported to the adjutant just outside the CO's office as ordered at 1455 hours not wanting to be late. There I remained until 1600 hours cooling my heels.

At around that time, I observed that the XO and the Ops O were exiting the CO's office. They both appeared to be very unhappy as they walked past me and out the door. Neither of them said anything to anybody in the room as they departed.

The adjutant received a phone call, then said that I was to report *now* to the CO. I reported to the CO in the standard military manner, remaining at attention. After several minutes, he looked up from his desk and ordered me to stand at ease. He then handed me a piece of paper, which I recognized as my fitness report, telling me to read it, which I did.

The report was cast in terms that equated to a scathing damnation of both my flying ability and my performance as the squadron's logistic officer.

He then asked if I had any questions regarding the grading and text portion of the report.

I looked at the report for the second time, then I remembered the reception that I had received on February 23 from this same individual after returning from Laos. He had confronted me, then grabbed the front of my flight suit, and yelled in my face, "CAPTAIN, DO YOU REALIZE WHAT YOU HAVE DONE TO MY CAREER!" Now it all came into clear focus for me. *This was the retribution for what he perceived I had done to his aspiring career. What a hypocrite,* I opined.

Seeing no sense in arguing with him, I said that I read and understood the contents of the fitness report. He then told me to sign the bottom of the report, which indicated that I had been counseled regarding the unsatisfactory content of the report and had no rebuttal comments to make.

Looking at the report for the third time, I looked him straight in the eye and said, "I will not sign the bottom of the report because I intend to submit rebuttal comments."

He broke eye contact, saying, "Captain, you will have twenty-four hours to provide me with your rebuttal comments. Do you understand, Captain?"

"Yes, sir," I responded. He then looked back down at his papers telling me that I was dismissed.

Coming to attention again, then doing an about-face, I left his office quickly so that I would not give him the satisfaction of seeing the anger on my face that had been building up inside me since the beginning of the counselling session.

While moving through the admin office toward the outside of the building, I thought about his unjustified accusations that would surely end my Marine Corps career.

Going outside the administration building, I headed back toward my office. While en route, I was intercepted by the XO and Ops O. They each took hold of my arms and forcefully escorted me toward an empty revetment on the flight line.

As we walked, the XO said, "We need to talk to you about your recent meeting with the CO. Please accompany us to the empty revetment so we could talk without interruption."

Looking at the XO, then the Ops O, I nodded as we continued to walk toward the flight line. After reaching the empty revetment, the XO asked me what happened in the CO's office. I told them both what had happened in the office a few minutes earlier. After listening to my version of events, the XO and Ops O both said that they had had a similar experience with the CO, and both indicated that they had received marginal fitness reports based on lack of leadership, judgment, and loyalty.

The XO spoke again telling me not to do anything until they could finalize a strategy to address the problem that we all had with the current CO's evaluations of our military and aviation performances.

I agreed not to do anything despite the order by the CO to submit my rebuttal the next day. It appeared we were all in the same boat. Both these Marine officers had a lot more experience in dealing with these types of problems than I did, plus they were both working on developing a strategy to counter the CO's negative and, in my opinion, unfair efforts.

I trusted both of these two Marines implicitly.

*****

On March 4, I again found myself heading north on another Lam Son 719 mission. Lieutenant Dan Silver and I were again scheduled together for the Mission 52 flight into Laos. On this mission,

I was the flight leader. My alternate flight leader was my roommate Captain Evert Haymore (Dimmer 24).

Since I was on the flight schedule that day, thanks to the Ops O, I got to miss the change-of-command practice again that day, which made me very, very happy. I was also not available to turn in my rebuttal to the CO.

The further away from the CO I could get, the better it was for me was my thinking.

Our morning briefing for Mission 52 again covered the standard items—mission to be completed, area weather, intelligence, enemy strength, potential threat hazards, radio frequencies, call signs of our Marine Corps HML-367 squadron teammates, and so forth.

The weather forecast was not very promising for our flight north that day. Rain and poor visibility were forecast from Da Nang to Quang Tri all along the coast.

In the intelligence portion of the briefing, it was again reiterated that the NVA were continuing to consolidate troop positions around a number of the FSBs inside Laos.

Yesterday, FSB 31 had been overrun by the NVA troops and abandoned because the ARVN could not get relief troops to their location. The guns there had to be destroyed in place. The briefer reported that it was anticipated that more NVA infantry attacks on other FSBs were likely to occur in the near future.

Another item of interest reported at the briefing was that an Air Force F-4 aircraft had been shot down on February 25, 1971, while providing air support to the ARVN forces near FSB Sophia II. This bird was likely the victim of 37mm or 57mm radar-controlled antiaircraft gunfire. Also reported was the loss of several more Army helicopters. These Army helicopter losses continued to mount because of the increased antiaircraft fire from more and more NVA forces entering the fight.

Because of the very poor weather, we decided to depart an hour later than planned. As the four aircraft crews broke up into their own briefings, Lieutenant Silver and I covered the checklist items that needed to be discussed before we launched the flight. Dan and I again covered the sharing of duties for that day's flight. Dan appeared much more confident and ready to take on the tasks ahead of us that day.

For this mission, we were again assigned aircraft YH-20 Miss Carriage II, which had been repaired since I had last seen it. It looked as good as new except for the spots of new paint covering the patches here and there, along with a new set of cockpit windows.

Preflight, APP, and jet-engines startup, rotor engagement, and other pretaxi operational checks of our aircraft were completed in accordance with our NATOPS manual. All checklist items for our aircraft were normal. After startup of all four aircraft, I called for a pretaxi radio check. The entire flight checked in on the radio. I then called for taxi then, takeoff for our flight of four.

All four aircraft lined up on the runway, and we made a formation takeoff heading north. Our four Marine Corps escort Cobra attack gunships were already en route north. We were scheduled to rendezvous with the Scarface birds at LZ Kilo near Khe Sanh for the Army's daily mission briefing. Secure communications between our CH-53s and the AH-1G aircraft had been working well through the use of encrypted UHF and FM radios. So positive radio communications were not going to be a serious problem.

After takeoff, our flight of four encountered the weather that was forecast—rain, wind, low ceiling and reduced visibility—as we proceeded north along the coast. Normally, once we passed Ha Van Pass, the visibility would improve. This was not the case today. Visibility, in fact, had decreased to about one-quarter mile, and the overcast ceiling dropped to 300 feet AGL.

As we continued past Ha Van Pass, we received a call from the flight leader of the Scarface flight indicating that the weather had not broken up. They had encountered extremely heavy rain and reduced visibility down to one-sixteenth of a mile as they tried to proceed west toward Khe Sanh. The Scarface flight leader said that they were diverting to the airfield at Quang Tri to wait for the weather to improve and recommended we do the same. As the flight leader, I acknowledged the weather and situation report (sit rep) he had made and agreed to meet the Cobras at Quang Tri airfield.

Our flight proceeded along the coast for approximately thirty-five miles before starting our turn inland toward Quang Tri. Lieutenant Silver handled the radio calls required to check for save-o-planes before we made our turn toward Quang Tri. Dan was much more reassured and confident that day as he handled sometimes tricky communication problems very well.

After receiving the Scarface sit rep, I notified my flight that we were going to divert our flight to Quang Tri because of the weather. I called the other aircraft in the flight and spread our flight of aircraft out horizontally approximately a quarter mile before turning inland. This was done in an attempt to avoid potential ground fire from Charlie, a nickname Americans used for the Viet Cong or NVA, by having each aircraft spread out, not close together, or behind one another.

As we all crossed the coastline, each aircraft in the flight dropped to an altitude of approximately 50 feet AGL and pushed the airspeed to 170 knots (200 miles per hour). Flying at this high speed and low altitude limited the time, amount of noise, and aircraft silhouette that the bad guys had for them to acquire you as a target, raise their weapons, aim, and shoot at you.

This tactic, plus the poor visibility, helped ensure our safe passage from the South China Sea to Quang Tri, a flight of approximately twelve miles.

All four of our aircraft landed safely at Quang Tri and then proceeded to the refueling area to refuel, so the flight would be ready to go to Khe Sanh when the weather cleared. As we proceeded to the refueling area, I saw that our four Cobra gunship escorts had arrived ahead of us and were already shut down waiting for the weather to break.

Quang Tri Air Facility, where we were currently located, was originally established by the Marines in 1965 to support aviation operations in South Vietnam's northern I Corps. It was transferred to US Army control when the Army took over operational control of northern I Corps in late 1970. At this point in time, it had also become what the Army called a base support area (BSA) for the buildup and support of Dewey Canyon II and Lam Son 719.

While we were refueling our aircraft, Sergeant Pogany came up over the aircraft's ICS describing to us what he was seeing as he observed one of the pilots from the third CH-53D in the fuel pits behind us exiting his aircraft in a very rapid manner. Sergeant Pogany continued to observe the movement of the pilot as he broke into a dead run away from his aircraft toward the hangars. This strange activity occurred while his aircraft was still running with the rotor system engaged. Generally, this type of activity is not done while the aircraft is being refueled or while the rotors are engaged. It appeared to Sergeant Pogany that something was wrong. He rapidly scanned the area looking for the cause of the unusual activity. He looked for a fire in the fuel pits, checking to see whether the aircraft involved was on fire or enemy fire or something else was the cause for the quick evacuation from the aircraft by the pilot. Finally, we received a radio call from the copilot of the pilotless aircraft. He said all was well with the aircraft. He said that Dimmer 24 actual, meaning the pilot, needed to make an emergency head call (bathroom visit).

After hearing the radio call, I breathed a sigh of relief.

As I looked to my right out the pilot's side window, I saw my roommate, Dimmer 24 actual, running across the tarmac heading for the head. Suddenly, he stopped dead in his tracks, stood there for a few seconds, then shook his flight suit pant leg several times. As a couple of small objects dropped on the tarmac, he then slowly walked toward the nearest hangar.

My entire crew also observed his activity, then broke into almost hysterical laughter. We knew what had occurred, and it struck all of us as extremely funny. I continued to watch him, and after a couple minutes of slow shuffling along, he disappeared into the hangar building.

Completing the refueling cycles, all our aircraft repositioned to the parking ramp and shut down, waiting for the weather to break.

Exiting the aircraft, I met with the Scarface flight leader for a few minutes to discuss the weather and assess when we might be able to get up to Khe Sanh. He indicated that he had checked the weather at Khe Sanh, by landline, and the Army at Khe Sanh reported that it was still very bad but was expected to clear in the next hour. He said he would do a weather recon flight in about an hour and let us know when and if the weather cleared enough to get up over the hills to Khe Sanh.

While continuing to wait for the weather to clear, I went to the hangar where Captain Haymore had entered. He and I both had cases of amoebic dysentery at the time. Looking around the hangar, I found that he was nowhere in sight. Continuing to look around, I saw a young Army warrant officer (WO) and asked him if he had seen a Marine pilot come to the hangar earlier. He said that yes he had seen him enter the hangar walking very slowly. He, smiling, then pointed to the head, saying, "That's where he went. You can probably find him in there."

Entering the head, to my surprise, I found my roommate sitting stark naked in front of the shower that he had just exited. His clothes, including his flight suit, were nowhere to be seen. Evert Haymore looked sheepishly at me and tried to explain what had transpired.

Upon arriving at the hangar, he had met the Army WO who approached him as he entered. As the WO got close to him, he said to Evert, "Boy, Captain, you smell really bad," so the young WO took pity on him. After ushering him to the head, he asked the captain to takeoff his flight suit and underclothing. He also pointed to the shower in the back part of the head and recommended that he use it ASAP as he handed him an extra towel that someone had left behind. He then departed the head.

A short while later, a *mama-son*, slang for a female Vietnamese worker, came into the head and scooped up all his clothes and started to depart. He said that after chasing *mama-son* and catching her while still naked, she looked at him with disgust and said she was going to wash his clothes. She left the head holding her nose and his clothes at arm's length. That was about thirty minutes ago.

He was concerned about where his clothes were in the washing cycle, so I went looking for the WO or the *mama-son* to check on the cleaning process. I found the *mama-son* in a room off the hangar bay that contained several new washing machines and dryers. To my surprise, she was removing Evert's skivvies and flight suit from the dryer. She looked at me, then handed me his clothes, saying, "Stinky, stinky."

I thanked her and returned to the head, presenting Evert with his clean clothes and told him to move it since we were behind schedule for our mission. His head bobbed up and down indicating he understood the urgency. On my way out of the hangar, I stopped and thanked the WO for his help. We both agreed that Dimmer 24's flight crew would be much, much happier now that he was not, as *mama-son* said, stinky.

As our four-crews returned to each of their aircraft getting ready to take off, we received a radio call from the Scarface leader indicating that they were over the hills, the weather had broken, and they were proceeding to Khe Sanh. He indicated he would be waiting at LZ Kilo for our arrival. By this time, all four of our aircraft were again started, and we departed Quang Tri west for Khe Sanh and then LZ Kilo.

After our arrival at LZ Kilo, we joined the Scarface folks for our specific mission briefing for that day. We were again assigned to move external loads (twelve thousand to fourteen thousand pounds each) of ammunition, heavy machinery, food, and construction supplies to several FSBs inside Laos. Additionally, our subsequent mission task was to reposition several 155mm artillery pieces from Fire Support Base Hotel to Fire Support Base Sophia II.

The Army briefer indicated that these artillery pieces were needed at FSB Sophia II to support the assault on Tchepone as the ARVN continued their push westward and deeper into Laos. Again, the Army's intelligence briefer reiterated that the NVA had consolidated troop positions around several FSBs, including Hotel, LoLo, and Sophia II inside Laos signaling a potential NVA infantry counterattack on these positions. He further indicated that more heavy weapons were being observed moving into the area. These included 23mm, 37mm, and 57mm antiaircraft guns operating in areas around these FSBs.

After the conclusion of the combined transport and escort mission brief by US Army's Command and Control folks at LZ Kilo, we all manned and started our aircraft. The first part of our mission was again resupplying ammunition, heavy machinery, food and construction supplies to various fire support bases inside Laos. These supplies were staged inside LZ Kilo inside South Vietnam to be delivered to FSB Hotel, Delta, Delta 1, and LZ Alouie in Laos.

Our resupply mission again reverted to the previous strategy of having the CH-53 pick up an external load and proceed to the Laos border where the first section of Scarface attack gunships would pick up and accompany it from the border to either FSB Hotel, Delta, Delta 1, and LZ Alouie and return. Then again, the next CH-53 would pick up its load, then would proceed toward the border to be picked up by the second section of Scarface gunships, which escorted it to their destination. The third and subsequent CH-53s would then pick up their loads following the same process until all the supplies, ammunition, and equipment were taken to their respective destinations. This daisy-chain effort resulted in moving approximately 125,000 pounds of cargo, ammunition, and equipment to FSB Hotel, Delta, Delta 1, and LZ Alouie.

Cargo lifts into FSB Hotel, Delta, and Delta 1 were generally uneventful. However, we received light small-arms fire on the first couple of lifts near the perimeters at LZ Alouie. Two of the new Bell AH-1J Sea Cobra gunships were operating as part of our flight today. These twin-engine helicopters, armed with a three-barreled 20mm cannon, as well as machine guns and rockets added a significant enhanced degree of protection for our mission.

These new Cobras, along with the AH-1G Scarface Cobra gunships, successfully suppressed the fire utilizing all the weapon systems available to them. While we took some limited enemy fire during these evolutions, no aircraft in our flight or our four Scarface escorts were hit. The flights, including several refueling operations, took the remainder of the morning and well into the afternoon as usual to complete.

Our subsequent Mission 52 task for this day was to reposition several 155mm-artillery pieces and ammunition from FSB Hotel to FSB Sophia II to support the eventual assault on Tchepone as the ARVN continued their push westward even deeper into Laos. To my surprise, we accomplished these lifts without incident.

At the conclusion of our mission, one of the new Bell AH-1J Sea Cobra gunships wanted to continue to exercise their new aircraft's weapons systems, so they took on a Russian T-34 tank that had been sitting in the same general location in Laos for several days. This tank had previously been impervious to attacks by several AH-1G Cobras in the previous days.

The NVA tank crew saw the Cobras go into their attack formation, thinking this was the same Cobras attacking them as before. They simply closed-up the tank and waited for the rockets to bounce off the tank. To their surprise the three-barreled 20mm cannon of the AH-1J cut the tank into pieces and cause it to explode in a large plume of fire.

*****

March 5 was the day that our delayed squadron change-of-command ceremony was held. It went off on schedule without a hitch. Our new commanding officer, Lieutenant Colonel Tom Reap, was a truly fine Marine officer and superior leader. He would go on to lead our squadron's efforts in support of Lam Son 719, earning a reputation for valor, strength, ethics, and compassion.

At the conclusion of the change-of-command ceremony, I headed back to my office. As I rounded the corner of the hangar, I was intercepted by the XO who guided me to a quiet and private location in an empty revetment so we could talk. He said that the situation concerning the recently written unflattering fitness reports would be handled by Colonel Street, the MAG-16 Group CO, after the departure of our previous CO. Furthermore, I would hear from Colonel Street in a few days and not to worry. Colonel Street understood the situation and would take care of the problem. I thanked him for his intervention, support, and concern as we walked back to our individual offices.

As I approached my office, I saw the previous CO put his military suitcase (B-4 bag) into the back of a jeep, climb in the back, and depart the squadron area toward the main gate.

Remembering what he had done to my career, I thought, *I hope I never run into that man in a dark alley,* as he departed.

He was, in my opinion, going back to a place where he belonged—Washington, DC. He was obviously in a hurry to do so since he was making sure that he was not late for his flight from Da Nang, South Vietnam, back to Washington, DC. I was not at all unhappy to see him depart.

On March 8, Lieutenant Colonel Tom Reap called me into his office, and we talked about the state of the squadron's embarkation efforts. We talked at length regarding the embarkation problems and concerns that both my logistic chief and I both had witnessed. He indicated that the preparation of the squadron's upcoming embarkation should become my number 1 priority. Lieutenant Colonel Reap indicated that he was in the process of getting me some help in the form of a field-grade officer who would take over duties as the logistic officer leaving me to devote my full efforts to the embarkation job. He knew how much I wanted to fly, but getting the squadron ready to go was more important. I could continue to fly local support missions and test hops but no more Lam Son 719 missions. I told him I understood, and I would do everything in my power to get our squadron ready to move. He knew I was disappointed, but the redeployment of the squadron to Hawaii was critically important.

Now I knew what my tasks for the next couple of months would entail. I sure had a lot of work ahead of me in order to get the squadron ready to go.

Our squadron continued to support Lam Son 719 through March 27, 1971, as it was winding down.

HMH-463 continued to fly other support missions for the ARVN troops in north central I Corps, but the tempo of these operations was also steadily decreasing. Our squadron continued to fly combat missions in addition to continuing to prepare for our redeployment to Hawaii.

The Marine helicopter participation in Lam Son 719 support declined significantly partly because the offensive was nearly ended and because after March 11, 1971, Lieutenant General Robertson, at the request of Major General Armstrong (First Marine Air Wing, commander), insisted that the Army use CH-53s strictly for heavy-lift missions only, meaning lifts that could not be performed by Army helicopters—such as, ammunition resupply missions.

During most of February and the first half of March, we normally provided four CH-53s making a total of twenty to forty lifts per day from LZ Kilo alone. Between March 11 and March 18, the daily number of aircraft was reduced to three and then to two, making two to seven lifts per day. Our support activity increased again as our squadron assisted the ARVN withdrawal. On March 23, three of our aircraft made eleven lifts; and on March 27, the last day of operations in Laos, HMH-463 made the last ten lifts with four CH-53Ds.

*****

Finally getting to fly a mission or two in between my embarkation duties, I was assigned a single-aircraft mission on March 30, in support of several ARVN units in the Hoi An area. This area is located about twenty-five miles south of Marble Mountain and was still a hot bed of enemy activities. We had a section of HML-367 Cobra attack birds to support that day's small resupply mission. The AH-1Js job was to fly cover for our transport helicopter operations into the landing zones by spotting friendly and enemy positions near the LZ, as well as suppressing fire from the NVA and Viet Cong ground units in the area as needed. During the last lift of the mission, we suffered a casualty. One of our gunners was shot through his foot and leg through the bottom of the aircraft as we hauled a twelve-thousand-pound load of rice out of a supposedly friendly LZ.

The casualty occurred just after picking up the last external load as I started to transition to forward flight. At about fifty feet of altitude, I glanced out my side window and saw a door to a thatched roof hooch open. As I continued to move the aircraft into forward flight, I saw a man dressed in black pajamas and a straw pointed hat step out of the hooch and raise an AK-47 weapon and point it toward our aircraft. Losing sight of the man, I heard the distinctive noise made by his AK-47 weapon as he fired, hitting the side and bottom of our aircraft. Our crew chief said, over the ICS, that one of our door gunners had been hit and asked the other door gunner to check him out, since he was lying on his belly looking down through the hell hole monitoring the load of rice externally suspended below our aircraft.

I continued the departure, with our load from the LZ climbing to a safe altitude.

I sure hope our gunner is not hurt too badly. We will need to get him help quickly, so he does not lose too much blood, I opined.

I called our Scarface gunship leader on the radio and told him about the fire we had taken from the hooch. He responded that since this was designated a friendly village, he would have to get permission to attack the hooch. The left-hand gunner came up on the ICS, at this point, and said the other gunner, a staff sergeant who was also our administrative chief in the squadron, had been shot through the rear part of his foot with the round exiting the calf of his left leg. The staff sergeant would not have normally been flying on this mission, but he was trying to earn enough points to qualify for combat aircrew wings.

The gunner continued to report that he had made the staff sergeant lie on the floor of the aircraft so he could evaluate his condition, but after the initial shock of being shot had worn off, the staff sergeant, who was conscious and pissed off, wanted to stand back up and shoot back. After a short discussion between the two gunners, the staff sergeant finally agreed to lie down again and have a dressing applied to his left leg at the exit-wound site.

Since the drop zone for the external load of rice we were carrying was in the direction of the medical facility where we needed to take our gunner, I elected not to "pickle the load" (military slang for *dropping the load*) as we continued to climb out of small-arms range.

Our two Scarface Cobra gunships joined us, and we proceeded toward the drop LZ. I asked the Cobras to sprint ahead and check out the drop zone for possible bad guys. They sprinted ahead making a couple of low passes and received no fire in return. It took about ten minutes to reach the drop zone and make a successful deposit of the external load of rice in the LZ where people were waiting to start distributing the cargo almost immediately.

We departed the LZ heading for Charlie Med with our wounded staff sergeant, leaving the gunships behind to look for bad guys. The staff sergeant got back on the ICS complaining that he was not going to have enough points to get his aircrew wings.

I said to him, "Don't worry about it. We will see to it that you get your combat aircrew wings, and by the way, you just won a Purple Heart Medal to go with them. Relax, and we will get you some medical help soon."

Just before we landed at the medical facility, the Cobra gunship leader called me and said he had received permission to engage the Viet Cong in the pickup LZ village. His only problem was identifying the hooch where the fire came from. I suggested we could return and help identify the exact location if that would help. He said it would. I told him I would be there in thirty minutes. After dropping off our gunner, who was carried on a stretcher from the aircraft by the medical personnel into the hospital, we departed Charlie Med. Stopping at Marble Mountain Air Facility, we picked up a replacement gunner and headed south to join our Cobra gunships.

Arriving at three-thousand-feet altitude above our original pickup LZ, I suggested that we make a simulated pickup approach to draw their fire.

The Cobra gunship leader responded rather than doing that, "Why don't you make a gun run with your .50-caliber machine gun on the hooch so we can see which one to destroy? Seeing the wisdom in his suggestion, I concurred by radio as we rolled into a steep angle of bank so the door gunner on my side of the aircraft could open up with the .50-caliber machine gun on the hooch where we had taken fire earlier. My door gunner got ready to fire as we descended altitude. He was assisted by the crew chief who had also seen the location of the incoming fire that wounded the staff sergeant helping him identify the right hooch.

Dropping rapidly through two thousand feet, my gunner opened up on the hooch. I could see tracers hitting the top and sides of the structure, noting that every fourth round of the ammunition we were using was a tracer round, so it made it easy for the Scarface Cobra gunships to identify the target hooch.

I pulled the aircraft out of the tight spiral at one thousand feet, not wanting to hazard my crew by going any lower. As we pulled out of the spiral and started climbing back to a safe altitude, the crew chief heard rounds impacting the rear of our aircraft. Checking the caution panel and seeing no caution lights on it that might have indicated that we had a problem from the hits we had taken, I relaxed a little. As the crew chief looked out the ramp, he could see the same man who probably shot at us earlier was still shooting up at us again.

Boy, that VC has either a real death wish or a giant set of khoonkies. I don't know which, I thought.

The Scarface gunships also saw the man firing at us. They were already in an attack formation and rolled in on both the man and the hooch with grenade launchers, miniguns, and rockets killing him where he stood and destroying the hooch completely.

After returning to Marble Mountain Air Facility, I was met in the revetments as I parked the aircraft by Captain Haymore. The first question I asked him as he climbed on the jump seat while I was shutting down the bird was if they had any status on our wounded staff sergeant gunner. He said that they had received word that he was in surgery. He would recover completely, but he was going to be medevacked out of country after surgery was completed. I thanked Evert for the good news, as we finished our shutdown and then proceeded to do a complete postflight inspection of my aircraft.

I found several holes in the back section of the aircraft, the ramp, and horizontal stabilizer, which I noted on the yellow sheet.

I guess the CH-53D does not make a very good attack aircraft, I opined, *as I noted the holes in the ramp and horizontal stabilizer. It might be just too big a target,* I concluded.

Reading the yellow-sheet discrepancy that I had written, the line chief said, "You did it again, didn't you, Captain?" meaning, there were more bullet holes in one of his aircraft. It appeared that I was getting a reputation for being a bullet magnet.

*****

In early April 1971, a new CH-53 pilot joined our squadron. He was the major named Johnson that Lieutenant Colonel Reap had promised. Upon his arrival, he was assigned to the position of logistic officer, the position I had held since arriving in-country in January. I was reassigned as the squadron's embarkation officer per the CO's direction.

This was a good thing since we needed to provide more direct supervision of our embarkation preparation activities prior to the squadron's departure for Hawaii. With our new CO came a real commitment to get the squadron ready to move to its new home at Kaneohe Bay, Hawaii, as well as completing our current combat missions.

Morale since Lieutenant Colonel Reap took over went through the roof. I continued to fly combat support missions for the ARVN after his change of command but had now switched my focus to the preparation of the equipment, supplies, and aircraft for embarkation to several locations.

Not all the aircraft were scheduled to return to Hawaii. Three aircraft were slated to be loaded aboard surface shipping bound for Naval Rework Facility North Island, California, for rework before being returned to the squadron in Hawaii. Two of our aircraft were to be loaded on surface shipping bound for HMH-462 in Okinawa, Japan.

HMH-462 in Okinawa, Japan, was my next duty station since I had not accumulated a full six-month service overseas to qualify to go with the squadron to Hawaii as of the day that I was scheduled to depart Vietnam. I had to complete a full overseas tour since I did not qualify. I would have a total of five months and twenty-eight days of overseas service when I left South Vietnam for Okinawa.

Close but no cigar, I opined.

*****

One afternoon while working on building embarkation boxes in the squadron armory inside the hangar, I, along with several staff NCOs and troops, listened to Armed Forces radio broadcast a speech that had been televised to the American people on April 7, 1971.

In the speech, President Nixon claimed that "tonight, I can report that Vietnamization has succeeded."

Broadcast later that day also on Armed Forces radio, we heard a translation of a speech that President Thieu of South Vietnam, who was speaking from Dong Ha where he addressed the survivors of the incursion into Laos and claimed that the operation in Laos was "the biggest victory ever." Historical accounts in the future would show that although Lam Son 719 had set back North Vietnamese logistical operations in southeastern Laos, truck traffic on the trail system increased immediately after the conclusion of the operation. It also indicated that the Lam Son 719 operation had exposed grave deficiencies in South Vietnamese "planning, organization, leadership, motivation, and operational expertise."

After listening to the speech, translation, and commentary, I thought that our departure from South Vietnam before the South Vietnamese could completely defend themselves from the north was a recipe for disaster. History would prove my prediction to be accurate.

*****

On May 1, at about 1700 hours, I received a call from the MAG-16 CO, who personally invited me to visit with him in his quarters that evening. His call had caught me by surprise, but I quickly recovered, accepting his invitation to his quarters at 1900 hours, then I thanked him for his invitation.

Since Colonel Street and I had flown together several times and had other interactions, I was not overly concerned or intimidated by his invitation, even though he was a full bird colonel.

His quarters were located next to the China Beach medical facility, just inside the perimeter of our base. His quarters consisted of a small beach cottage with a porch overlooking the South China Sea. It was the designated residence for all MAG-16 commanders since it was constructed in 1967.

Arriving at his quarters that evening, he met me at the door, asked me in, then asked me if I would like to have a drink. I responded that a beer would be great. He got both of us a beer and asked if I minded sitting on the porch.

It was the same porch he had been sitting on February 24 when he intervened in the MP incident regarding the sea snakes.

I said that sitting on the porch was a great idea, as we walked out the screen door on to his porch, and we each took a seat in one of the several deck chairs on the porch overlooking the South China Sea. We talked for several minutes about the progress of the embarkation efforts at my squadron and whether the group headquarters people were supporting our efforts adequately. I responded by saying that everything we had asked for to date we had received from his HQ. He said he was glad to hear that we were getting what we needed. He then steered our conversation to the fitness report that had been written by my previous commanding officer. He indicated that I was not the only one who had experienced fitness report problems with this particular officer. He said the regulations required that these reports be submitted as written, but he, as the reporting senior of the officer who wrote these reports, could write reviewing endorsements to these reports, if he so desired. He went on to indicate that he had completed several of these endorsements, mine being one of them. Furthermore, he asked me if I would like to read the one he was planning to attach to my fitness report.

I answered, "Yes, sir, I would very much like to read it."

He left the porch and returned with the package of three endorsements he had prepared. Mine was on the bottom of the stack of three. As he was sorting through the stack, I glanced over and caught sight of the names of the other two individuals he had also written endorsements on. I saw the names Edwards and Wasko on the other two endorsements. Smiling at me, he handed me the endorsement he had written regarding my performance in which he stated in the initial paragraph that he had personally observed my performance during his tenure as the Marine Aircraft Group 16's commanding officer.

After reading the multiple-page endorsement that he had written, I felt extremely vindicated. He had reaffirmed my belief in the Marine Corps' abilities to police a rogue individual who, in my opinion, was not concerned about mission accomplishments and personal accountability but was only concerned with their personal advancement at the expense of others. After I completed reading the document, I thanked him for his very kind words. He said that he was doing what was, in his opinion, the right thing to do by merely correcting inaccurate reports of several fine officers in his command based on his observations and perceptions of their performance.

We each had another beer and talked about the impact that Lam Son 719 might have on the South Vietnamese' ability to win their war. He and I both agreed that the performance of the South Vietnamese individual units during Lam Son 719 were in most cases good, but the command leadership at the highest levels had a long way to go if they were ever to be successful in defending their country from the north.

As I was leaving his quarters, I had renewed confidence that maybe my Marine Corps career was not over yet.

*****

From May 2 through the 17, we continued to work on embarkation preparations for the squadron's move to Hawaii. Since our squadron had been in-country for over five years, additional items had been procured, scrounged, or in other ways found their way into the various maintenance shops and administrative spaces. These items had to be either added to the inventory or disposed of before we left the country. We had to initiate a squadron-wide cleanout and disposal process along with the continuation of the inventorying, cleaning of the squadron's supplies, ground-support equipment, materials, and not used weapons before they could be packed up for embarkation.

Cleaning of these items was essential in order to not transport insects or other critters to the Hawaiian islands. Progress in cleaning these items was moving along slowly but surely.

Our squadron's last major flying effort was made on May 17, 1971. Our squadron was to be part of the First Marine Aircraft Wing's massive plan for a flyover of all its aircraft present in-country at the time. This flyover would include both fixed-wing and helicopters. The flyover was designed as a demonstration of the air power associated with the departure of the First Marine Aircraft Wing from Da Nang, South Vietnam, to Iwakuni, Japan.

Our squadron, along with all the other MAG-16 aircraft, were to participate in the mass flyover that day. Our squadron had a total number of sixteen aircraft, at that point in time, that we could hopefully get airborne to participate in this mass gaggle that was planned.

Major Wasko had scheduled all our aircraft to fly as part of the big show. Getting all sixteen of our aircraft ready for a flyover was an especially hard job for the maintenance department. All the aircraft had to be safely flyable and airborne all at one time. Our squadron had not had all its aircraft airborne at one time since the main body of HMH-463 arrived in South Vietnam on May 23, 1967, after they departed from the USS *Tripoli* on our initial arrival.

On the morning of the flyover, Lieutenant Colonel Tom Reap briefed the pilots who were to fly our sixteen CH-53s that day. He had earlier attended a MAG-16 briefing for squadron commanders, who would each lead their squadron's aircraft in the flyover. This was done in order to receive final instructions on sequence of events, time, radio frequencies, and so forth.

In order to man all our CH-53 aircraft with pilots and copilots, it was necessary to enlist all the wing and group staff pilots who were qualified to fly the aircraft and to participate in the gaggle. It was an all-hands-on-deck effort that day.

Lieutenant Colonel Reap was our flight leader, and Major Edwards was the alternate flight leader of our flyover effort. After the briefing was completed, the final aircraft assignments were made by the maintenance department. They were based on the skill of each aircraft commander. These assignments were made so that the weakest pilots were assigned to the most trouble-free aircraft, and the more experienced pilots to the problem aircraft. At the appointed time, all thirty-two pilots left the ready room and headed for their aircraft, having already looked at their yellow sheets and signed for their birds.

Since I was a post-maintenance-inspection pilot, I was assigned one of the aircraft that had recently experienced maintenance problems. It was safe and flyable, but not fully mission capable. My place in the flyover was to be Tail-End Charlie (the last aircraft) in our squadron's flight.

At 1000 hours, all our sixteen aircraft were scheduled to start their aircraft. Unfortunately, three of the aircraft experienced difficulties after engine starts and rotor engagements.

After a slight delay, thirteen CH-53D aircraft of the original sixteen aircraft taxied and took off in groups of four aircraft with the third group having five birds. After taking off to the north, Lieutenant Colonel Reap turned the first-four aircraft in an easterly direction over the South China Sea. The second, and third groups of aircraft, after sequenced takeoffs, joined up on our flight leader.

Once all thirteen aircraft were in formation, we flew south down the coast toward the city of Chu Lai. We then turned inland to the west, in order to fly over the base camp of the South Korean Marines that were still in-country. After crossing over their camp, the flight turned back to the north flying toward the Marble Mountain Air Facility at 3,000 feet.

At this point, the other aircraft from the rest of MAG-16 were also airborne. Cobra gunships AH-1Js and AH-1Gs, Huey's UH-1s, and medium helicopters CH-46s were now all in formation circling over the South China Sea. The fixed-wing OV-10s and O-1, to the best of my recollection, did not fly in the gaggle or were added to the fixed-wing squadrons flyover. Our flight joined the assembled group of MAG-16 helicopters led by Colonel Street. When the entire flight had joined up, Colonel Street then flew in a right-hand descending circle so that all the aircraft were lined up to fly down the runway at Marble Mountain Air Facility at 500 feet.

We then flew toward Monkey Mountain to the north, passing west of it. As we headed out over the Da Nang Bay, we could see the massed flights of fixed-wing aircraft performing their part of the flyover, flying down the runways at Da Nang airfield at low level.

Once we were well out over Da Nang Bay, after all the fixed-wing aircraft had made their pass down the runways, Colonel Street made a gradual turn to the left in order to line up the entire flight with the dual runways at Da Nang's airfield heading in a southerly direction. The entire flight then flew down the runway at approximately 200 feet.

What a spectacular show, I thought as I looked at the massed helicopters that made up MAG-16.

As Colonel Street and the first group of aircraft cleared the runway departure threshold, he then turned the flight to the right and flew over Hill 55 (a major debarkation point for ground Marines who fought in the Da Nang region) heading south where we still had Marines on the ground. Once all the aircraft in the flight cleared Hill 55, each squadron flight leader called Colonel Street, in sequence, indicating that they were going to proceed to separate their individual squadrons per the preflight briefing and then proceed back to Marble Mountain Air Facility as individual squadrons.

After the MAG-16 flight separated, Lieutenant Colonel Reap led our thirteen CH-53 plane formation back heading southeast of Marble Mountain airfield, then again out over the South China Sea, so we were positioned to be the last squadron to return to our home base. Once all the other aircraft had landed at the Marble Mountain Air Facility, he turned our flight back toward Marble Mountain. He called the tower and requested an overhead break for our thirteen aircraft (overhead breaks are used to provide lateral separation between aircraft that arrive in formation at an aircraft carrier or airport for safe separation between aircraft upon landing).

It was quite a sight to see twelve CH-53D aircraft in left echelon ahead of me all lined up in a close formation; the leader was on the right with all other aircraft to his left and slightly behind in order. Starting with Lieutenant Colonel Reap, each aircraft at three-second intervals made a hard right turn. Halfway through these turns, each aircraft put down its landing gear to land. Each one in turn was cleared to land. My aircraft was the last aircraft to complete the break maneuver, and I watched the Marines from our squadron standing on the flight line applauding our thirteen-plane arrival.

As we waited to refuel in our fuel pits, I observed that two of our aircraft had finished their refueling and taxied to takeoff.

Heading south, they had the .50-caliber machine guns out the pilot's side window, meaning they were heading out on a tactical mission. It appeared that we were still flying tactical operations and missions that needed to be completed before the official stand-down of combat flight operations the next day.

*****

On May 18, 1971, HMH-463 officially stood down from tactical combat flight operations. All that was left to do was pack up, fly all our aircraft to the ships, and leave the Republic of South Vietnam.

On May 19, 1971, we flew three aircraft to the Da Nang pier (about four miles), which had a LZ clearly marked on the ground at the pier facility. Three aircraft were inspected for insects and critters, then loaded on surface shipping bound for Naval Rework Facility North Island, California. The inspection went well, and I was encouraged by the results.

On May 21, 1971, another two of our remaining aircraft were flown to the Da Nang pier, inspected by both American and Japanese inspectors, then loaded on surface shipping bound for HMH-462 in Okinawa, Japan—my next duty station. I knew I would see them again as soon as they were hoisted aboard the waiting ship.

On May 26, 1971, all the remaining HMH-463 aircraft along with some CH-46s, AH-1G, and the four AH-1J were flown or loaded aboard the USS *Okinawa* (LPH-3).

All CH-53Ds were destined for their new home at Kaneohe Bay, Hawaii. The other aircraft went to various locations in the continental United States after our squadron disembarked the carrier at Pearl Harbor.

I had the opportunity to fly one of our aircraft aboard that last day, almost five years after I had been a copilot on one of the first HMH-463 main body aircraft flying off the USS *Tripoli*.

I felt a little strange because I was now seeing the end of what I thought at the time was HMH-463's involvement in the Vietnam conflict. This was not the case. HMH-463 would be called upon to participate in operation End Sweep. It was an airborne mine countermeasures operation in North Vietnam and on operation Eagle Pull, the evacuation of Saigon.

Standing on the pier as the USS *Okinawa* departed Da Nang Harbor late that afternoon, taking with it all our remaining aircraft and almost all its squadron personnel, I felt a sense of loneliness as it sailed away, then disappeared from view.

*****

Now the real work of embarkation needed to be accomplished. It was time to complete the movement of the majority of the ground-support equipment, rolling stock, supplies, and cargo to the wharf at Da Nang Harbor. All the MAG Squadron's embarkation folks had prepositioned all their cargo and other equipment ready to be moved to the harbor at Marble Mountain Air Facility's unused part of the flight line. Marine shore party personnel used flatbed trucks and forklifts to move the cargo, equipment, and vehicles to the Da Nang pier facility.

Since we were the last squadron to be loaded aboard the attack cargo ship that was tasked with our redeployment from South Vietnam, we were the last group to have our cargo and equipment moved to the harbor. This sequenced staging was because our equipment and cargo was going to be off-loaded first. The Navy concept of first on last off was in play here. Since the other units were going back to the continental United States, theirs would be loaded first.

On May 30, 1971, we were completing the final phase of the embarkation efforts for most of MAG-16's ground support, aviation support, and other materials necessary to run a deployed Marine air group. We were the last of all of MAG-16's units to have their items staged at the Da Nang wharf. As we finished staging the final items, I looked at the wharf and saw the USS *Tulare* (AKA-12) being tied up. That was our ship that was to take the cargo and equipment out of Vietnam.

Loading of the attack cargo ship, the USS *Tulare*, would begin by placing the cargo and equipment that was going back to the continental United States in the lower sections of the ship through the hatches in the front and center of the attack cargo ship since it was to be off-loaded last. Since HMH-463's equipment and cargo was going to Hawaii, it would be off-loaded first.

The MAG-16 group embarkation officer, other units' embarkation officers, and I were dealing with the ship's chief bosun mate. He was a master chief who was the senior noncommissioned officer aboard the USS *Tulare*. He was responsible for and directly supervised the loading of the ship. The ship-loading went as scheduled until the last four pieces of our motor transport gear, a small fire truck, and three aviation ground-support pieces of equipment consisting of two NC-10s electric power generators, and one hydraulic "Gennie" were to be loaded.

The master chief called the group embarkation officer and myself to tell us he had run out of space for the last four items.

The group embarkation officer reviewed his master listing of equipment, cargo, and supplies and found an error in the MAG-16 listings. The Medium Helicopter Squadron (HMM) had made an error in their required cubic-space requirements; their listing showed a requirement of 3,350 cubic feet instead of the real space needed of 33,500 cubic feet. We ran out of space because of that error. The master chief said he was sorry, but no space was available for these items. Since all the HMM materials were already loaded, there was no way to take it off and make space for my squadron's four pieces of equipment before the ship sailed.

I was not a happy embarkation officer at this point. Pissed would not cover my feelings at this point in time.

The group embarkation officer, a major, knew that I was not happy, but he was already late for his flight out of country, so he turned the problem over to me to solve. Saying he was sorry as he departed, he indicated that I should contact the wing embarkation folks and see when they could schedule another ship to pick up the remaining items. He then departed the pier en route to Da Nang to catch his flight.

As the group embarkation officer was leaving, the master chief kept saying that "there was no space available below decks." The ship was scheduled to sail in two hours. The master chief could see what a predicament I was in. As we stood on the pier talking, I told the master chief that it was not necessary to have these items stored below deck, they were cleaned, and then coated with a fiber-glass-type material that was salt resistant so they could travel on deck without harm if only he could find a place for them.

I thought, *Come on, Master Chief, we have to find a way.*

The chief and I talked further about any other potential place that could be utilized in order to solve the problem that I had been left with. Our discussion turned to an area in the stern (back) of the ship that was not used for cargo. We agreed that this area had the potential to solve our problem, but his boss and then the ship's captain would have to approve the proposed solution.

Our idea was to use part of the small helicopter deck at the stern of the ship to accommodate our gear. His concern was that his AKA's small helicopter deck at the stern was to be utilized for evacuation of personnel from the ship if they needed significant medical care greater than the ship's medical personnel could provide. Since the ship was going to Hawaii from Vietnam, after stopping in the Philippines, it might be possible to put these items on the helo deck for transport if we could get his boss, the ship's XO, as well as the ship's captain to approve.

We went up the ship's gangway and up to the bridge. Both the ship's XO and captain were on the bridge making preparations to leave the harbor in about an hour and a half.

The chief introduced me to both officers, then explained the situation that had occurred. The captain at first seemed cool to the idea, but as he discussed it with the XO, the chief, and I, he reconsidered his position. We suggested to him that the four items could be positioned and tied down on the helo deck so that a helicopter could safely evacuate a ship's crew member by rescue basket instead of landing.

If he agreed, we could then load the four pieces of equipment on the helo deck. He reluctantly agreed but stipulated that this loading activity would not be allowed to interfere with his scheduled departure in one hour and fifteen minutes. I thanked the captain and the XO as the master chief, and I exited the bridge. We literally ran down the ladder (steps) and off the ship. Arriving on the pier, we indicated to the Marine shore party personnel that the loading process could proceed and to please expedite it.

The four pieces of equipment were hoisted aboard the ship by a very large land-based crane on rails that had placed the other items in the ship's cargo bays. The four items were carefully placed on the helo pad near its edges, then tied down. The master chief and I watched the last piece of equipment being tied down as the captain came up on the ship's 1-MC (inter-ship communications system) and indicated that they were making ready to get underway. The master chief and I went down the ladder while I thanked him for his help, ingenuity, can-do attitude, and perseverance in getting the job done. He personified the people who really ran our Navy, the noncommissioned officers. I hit the gangway just before it was removed from the ship. I watched as lines were cast off and the ship got underway.

Boy o boy was I relieved. The mission of embarkation of our squadron was completed.

Climbing into a borrowed Army jeep, I returned to Marble Mountain Air Facility for the last time. I went to the officers' club and had a drink with the gathered Army aviator warrant officers. I then ate my last meal in the officers' mess that I designed and had constructed during my first tour. Finally, I went back to my hooch, packed up my gear, and made ready to depart for my flight to Okinawa the next morning.

My last morning in Vietnam, on my way to the Da Nang airfield, I thought back again about the two supposedly nonflight crew Marines that had climbed onto the rescue ladder from the crashed Dimmer 3 aircraft on February 23, along with the rest of the flight crew. They were not supposed to be flying in Laos, but they were. I wondered how the lives of these Marines would have been changed if we had not recovered them that day.

As my flight on the big Pan Am 707 aircraft took off for Okinawa, I wondered, *Is this the last time I am going to see Vietnam?*

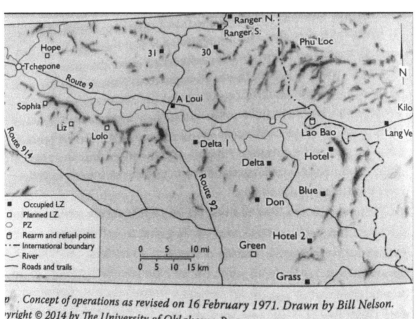

Lam Son 719 Concept of Operation, February 16, 1971[13]

---

[13] Sander, *Invasion of Laos 1971*.

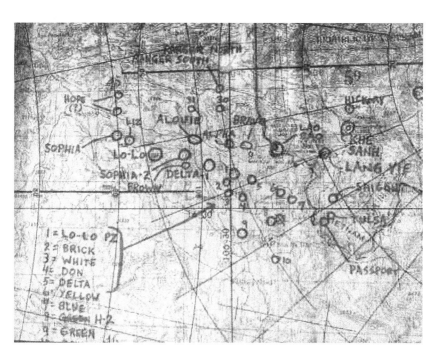

Aviators Lam Son 719 landing zones and fire support bases map

ROBERT WEMHEUER

Marble Mountain, Spring 1971—Marine Air Group-16 en masse

CH-53 picking up a 105mm howitzer, destination Laos

CH-53 departing LZ Kilo with 155mm howitzer

CH-53s' shutdown at LZ Kilo for army briefing

Marine AH-1G attacking enemy positions in Laos

CH-53 making a pickup at LZ Kilo staging area heading into Laos

LZ Kilo staging area
CH-53 making a pickup (middle right of picture)

Enemy anti-aircraft fire (air bursts)

Fire-suppression attack, run by Marine AH-1G

FSB Hotel 1, mid-February 1971

Defensive perimeter of Marble Mountain Air Facility

The last flyover in 1971, Marble Mountain in the background

ROBERT WEMHEUER

What a beautiful machine the CH-53D has become

Chapter 3

FINISHING MY OVERSEAS TOUR WITH SQUADRON HMH-462 IN OKINAWA, JAPAN, AFTER LEAVING VIETNAM

Boy, what a relief! Vietnam is finally behind me. I sure hope this will be the last time I will see Vietnam, I thought as I looked out the window as we took off from Da Dang, Vietnam. I sat back and relaxed reflecting on the other day's successful embarkation of my former squadron to Hawaii.

The flight to Okinawa from Vietnam was a fairly short one, about three hours in length on a nice Boeing 707 civilian airliner. Landing at Kadena Air Force Base, I then went through a check-in process by the Air Force administrative representatives, then went through a customs and baggage check. I was met by my old boss, Major Johnson, who left Vietnam ahead of me by several days. He found me just as I was coming out the door of the reception center. Shaking hands, he helped me with my bags, then we walked out to his car in the parking lot. Opening the back door, he reached inside and produced two ice-cold Kirin Japanese beers. We stood in the parking lot and toasted our escape from the rigors of the war in Vietnam.

Since I had an additional six months and one day in order to finish my overseas tour, I was assigned to HMH-462, the Heavy

Haulers, as the assistant logistics officer working again for Major Johnson. There were also a number of other replacement pilots who arrived in Vietnam after me who were in the same predicament as I was. They were also transferred to Okinawa and HMH-462 in order to complete their overseas tour of duty.

One of the replacement pilots was my roommate, Captain Evert "Ev" Haymore, who had departed Vietnam several days before I had completed HMH-463's embarkation activities.

Since rooms for company-grade officers at the bachelor offices quarters (BOQ) were very limited, Captain Ev Haymore and I again agreed to share a room together in the MCAS Futenma BOQ.

During our time in Okinawa, we both remained in the same squadron and continued to fly the CH-53 aircraft while we completed our overseas tours of duty.

After I had been in Okinawa a couple of weeks, I received a call from Lieutenant Colonel Pitman, which I had not expected. He was the lieutenant colonel whose aircraft was shot down in Laos and required evacuation out of the country. After the incident, he was taken to a naval hospital on the mainland of Japan for reconstructive surgery and recovery. His call came as he and Lieutenant Colonel Frank Peterson were passing through Okinawa en route to the States. We met for a couple of payback drinks at Kadena AFB since I had transported him back to Da Nang, Vietnam, from Laos after he was shot down and wounded. It was nice to see him almost fully recovered as he departed Okinawa for the States after the short layover.

At the time of my arrival in Okinawa, the island was again experiencing a drought. This meant that the entire island was on water rationing, including the military bases. The water for the entire island was turned off by the Ryukyuan government for seventy-two hours, then turned on for twenty-four hours. This cycle meant that you had running water for showers and toilets only for a twenty-four-hour period, then none for the next seventy-two hours. In between these times, you had to carry the water to your room in a five-gallon container if you wanted any water to flush the toilet, wash your face, or any other activity that you needed water to complete. When the water was shut off, you got the water you needed from a trailer parked in the parking lot. It was supplied by the Marine Corps and was called a *water buffalo* (military term for "water trailer," holding about five hundred gallons of potable water).

I thought, *We had better living conditions in Vietnam than we have here, but at least, they are not shooting at us.*

As I remember, in mid-1971, HMH-462 had an overabundance of pilots. Some had chosen to stay in Okinawa rather than go to Vietnam as the war was winding down, so flight time was somewhat limited due to the number of pilots and the lack of missions requested by our ground Marine brothers in Okinawa.

It felt to me like the Marine Corps was taking a collective pause and regrouping after our withdrawal from Vietnam.

The only two memorable events that I recall from my short tour in Okinawa was the island being hit by a large typhoon with winds of over 150 miles per hour a couple of months after I got there. The second was flying relief missions at a group of Ryuku islands several hundred miles south of Okinawa, one of which was named Ishigakijima (*jima* means "island" in Japanese). This mission was mounted to help the relief efforts on these islands after another typhoon with winds in excess of 225 miles per hour hit their islands.

In early September, a series of typhoons had formed a thousand miles to the southeast of Okinawa. The first typhoon was a very powerful storm and was forecast to strike Okinawa head on with the eye of the storm slated to pass directly over the center of the island. MCAS Futenma was located in the center of the island, so we were in the bull's eye of the storm.

With the typhoon still located over 600 miles away from Okinawa, all the military units had adequate time to prepare for its arrival. Aviation units that had aircraft that could fly way from the island departed to other locations. The KC-130 transport squadron flew its big "Hercules" aircraft to locations where the storm was not forecast to hit. Our squadron's maintenance department folded the aircraft we had on the island and put them into several hangars. As the storm approached the island, the last of the preparations were completed. All personnel, except the duty section, were told to go to their quarters and shelter in place until the storm passed that night.

Like all good company-grade officers, Ev and I, along with about 25 other company-grade officers, all immediately complied with the orders that we were given. However, en route to our quarters, we made a small detour stopping at the package store of the officers' club. There, we stocked up on beer, wine, and ice since we knew the power would surely go off. We also included some hard liquor in our purchase in preparation for a "'phoon party" that had been planned to be held in the lounge area of the main BOQ. The party's premise was to thank the typhoon god for creating the storm that brought rain to the island thereby eliminating the water rationing we were currently experiencing. It made for a good excuse for having a party anyway. Since all the preparations were completed to secure the base and the aircraft, the party got underway quickly. One of the CH-46 pilots had found a King Neptune costume, which he had quickly modified to make it King Typhoon. He showed up and officially kicked off the festivities.

We toasted the incoming storm's fury as it slammed into the island. It came directly at us with ever-increasing winds and sheets of rain pounding on the windows of the lounge area. Each blast of rain called for another toast. The party was going full blast when one of the field-grade officers passed through the lounge area in his flip-flops and Bermuda shorts on his way to the vending machine for a Coke. I guess he had not seen the electrical power go off thirty minutes earlier, so the vending machine was inoperative. The party had electrical power since a smart lieutenant from MABS had thought to have an emergency generator positioned outside the lounge area to power the lighting and the boom box that was going full blast. The party had now grown from the original 25 company-grade officers to about 45 or 50 officers as the noise and lights from the party were the only lights currently operating in the BOQ complex. The noise and light seemed to draw them to the party like a moth to a flame.

The field-grade officer looked at the 50 of us and recognized that we were well on our way to having overindulged in too much partying and shook his head as he left the lounge area and headed back to his room, or so we thought. The party continued for another 20 minutes when suddenly 2 of the squadron commanders (CO) showed up at the party. They both entered the lounge area and moved to the tub of cold beer in the center of the room. Each selected a beer, opened it, and took a drink. The partygoers cheered as their leaders joined the party. The perception that the party was going to continue lasted only a few minutes, long enough for both COs to move to the side of the room and turn off the boom box and then called for quiet.

Once the partiers had quieted down, the senior CO spoke to the group. He said, "First, we want to thank you for asking us to join your *party*. It appears that all of you are having a great time. Is that correct?"

A loud cheer went up from the partygoers.

He then raised his hand to again quiet the group a second time. He then said, "We have just gotten word that the storm had become even stronger than forecast. Because of the increased danger to all of us, I am going to have to ask the participants at the party to terminate the festivities until the storm has passed. I know that this is not what you wanted to hear, but it's for all our safety. I ask you to make this sacrifice for safety's sake. Let me also assure you that no disciplinary action will be taken against anyone here as long as you all terminate the festivities right now. Does everyone understand?"

Heads of most of the participants bobbed up and down as the only sound in the room was the rain sheets hitting the windows. Both COs looked out over the group, waved, and then left the lounge area carrying their beers with them. After the COs left, people at the party started to drift out of the lounge area and head back to their rooms. Ev and I were among them as we exited the lounge area into the wind- and rain-swept parking lot for our walk back to our BOQ room. The rain was very warm, and the wind had suddenly dropped off to almost nothing, but there was still plenty of lightning for us to see our way back across the parking lot to the BOQ. As we walked in the rain, Ev said that he had another brilliant idea, which he proceeded to explain to me as we made our way back to our room. I liked his idea, so when we got back to the room, we both shed our clothes, then grabbed a towel apiece, plus a couple of bars of soap, and headed back down to the parking lot for a nice, long shower. Standing in the warm rain in the ankle-deep water in our skivvies was probably not the smartest thing we could have done at the time.

We both had had enough to drink so that we felt invincible. Plus, the water sure felt good, and there was no water restriction on the rain. We could see well most of the time because of the almost continuous lightning bolts streaking across the sky above.

The next morning dawned bright and clear and with lots of sunshine. The typhoon, while being strong, was also fast moving. It had cleared the island in the early morning hours. We still had no electrical service, which meant no air-conditioning, so we opened the door and saw several trees lying in the parking lot and debris all over the area. We looked at each other, and I said to Ev, "I think we were lucky last night when we took our shower." We came to find out later that the time we were taking our showers corresponded roughly with the passing of the eye of the typhoon over the island's center. That was the last typhoon shower for Ev and me.

Thinking back on the afternoon and evening of the typhoon event, it became very apparent that the 'phoon party, while being fun at the time, could have resulted in some serious injuries or even deaths. The CO's strategy for the dispersal of the 'phoon party was a masterful stroke. By using logic and common sense, they had defused a difficult and dangerous situation. If they had come down hard on the 'phoon partygoers, ordering them to go home, there was no telling what type of reaction would have taken place with fifty nearly all drunk Marines. The COs disarmed any real objections that could have been raised by the 'phoon partygoers by introducing new information into the rationale for shutting down the party (the storm is stronger than forecast). They then used the phrase *until the storm has passed*, giving any naysayer the impression that the discontinuation of the party was only temporary, until the storm passed, and suppressing the desire to object to the discontinuation by seeing it only as a delay. Truly a masterful performance from the two COs.

*****

The following week, a series of typhoons were again starting to form about a thousand miles to the southeast of Okinawa. One of these in the series of three was forecast to move in a more westerly direction and could potentially hit the Philippines, Taiwan, or the southernmost of the Ryuku islands 250 miles south of Okinawa. All the others were forecast to move southwest. The one moving northwest was not a direct threat to Okinawa this time, but the typhoon did move quickly and three days later, struck the remote islands of Ishigakijima and Iriomotejima, Japan

The day after the typhoon hit the islands of Ishigaki and Iriomote we were requested by the Okinawa Prefecture government on Okinawa to mount a rescue-and-supply-delivery mission to the islands. The islands of Ishigakijima and Iriomotejima are part of the Yaeyama Islands chain located northeast of Taiwan. These two islands had been almost completely destroyed by the typhoon that had hit the islands.

The hardest hit island was Ishigakijima. It is a little less than 90 square miles in size. The typhoon hit Ishigakijima with winds in excess of 225 miles per hour, washing out all the major roadways, cutting communications, and knocking out all the electrical power-generating capabilities other than emergency generators. The island of Iriomotejima did not fare much better. Ishigakijima had a small airstrip with a coral and unpaved gravel runway with no UHF radio communications, as well as having no jet fuel–refueling capability. Several people were believed to have been killed by the strong winds and storm surge on both islands caused by this very large and powerful typhoon.

Our squadron was tasked to undertake the mission because we had internal fuel tanks that could be placed in the cargo compartment of the aircraft, which extended its range. Each of these tanks added approximately an hour of additional flight time to the range of the helicopter. With three internal tanks, the CH-53 could fly for about four and three quarters hours without refueling. This was far beyond the capability of the CH-46, which is a medium helicopter that would normally be used for such a mission. Additionally, there was no Navy surface ships available to take supplies or helicopters or both to the stricken islands for at least a week. The commanding officer of our squadron asked for volunteers to take on the two aircraft missions. I volunteered for the mission along with First Lieutenant

Jan Urbanczyk, who had flown on my wing on several missions in Laos earlier that year.

We volunteered because we were both bored of the local island flying around Okinawa.

The CO said, "If you two want to go, it's fine with me. Plan the mission and let me know what you need to get it done. Time is critical, so I will get you what you need."

Lieutenant Urbanczyk and I looked closely at the map and reread the mission request for a second time. It became apparent that this mission would require several components to be put in place on the island if our mission was to be successful. We would need to have jet fuel available on Ishigakijima, since no naval ships were available in the area.

This, we thought, could be accomplished by use of the MABS-36's tactical air fuel system (TAFS) that our sister squadron at MAG-36 has available to deploy for such an operation. We needed a method of communications with the ground-support folks to facilitate the movement of badly needed relief supplies as well as our squadron in Okinawa. A communications vehicle with UHF and HF capability could also be obtained from the MABS to provide us with ground-to-air communication while we were working on the island, as well as communications with our squadron. We also needed their Marines to operate both systems while we were operating on the island.

Our largest problem that we saw was going to be getting everything we needed to Ishigakijima. We needed a way to get the fuel system, the radio vehicle, and the relief aid for the typhoon victims to the island quickly. VMGR-152 had six KC-130 transport aircraft that were also part of the MAG-36 organization. The large transport aircraft had the capability to make short field landing and takeoffs from unimproved airstrips, such as the one at Ishigakijima. They also were capable of moving the TAFS unit, providing jet fuel (JP-4) to the unit for our use and to move the radio vehicle and the relief aid to the island of Ishigaki quickly.

We went to the CO's office with our list of requests. He looked at the list and said, "I will arrange to get the MABS-36 TAFS unit and radio vehicle support along with the KC-130 support through the

MAG-36 CO." He also indicated he had just received a call from the liaison officer for the Ryukyu Self-Defense Force (Japanese military) who would be overseeing the distribution of the aid the Japanese government was providing to Ishigakijima and Iriomotejima. He then said, "The government was sending a representative to the island of Ishigakijima that could act as an interpreter and handle the incoming distribution of aid when it arrived on the island. He will be accompanying you when you depart for the islands. Since we were the lead organization on this mission, I will see that you get everything you need. You two better talk to the maintenance officer about getting the internal fuel tanks installed and tested in both birds ASAP. I want you on site working the relief mission tomorrow afternoon at the latest."

"Yes, sir," we replied as we departed his office, heading for the maintenance spaces to arrange the installation of our internal fuel tanks.

The maintenance officer had already received a call from the CO by the time we arrived. He indicated that he had his people working to get the six internal tanks from the warehouse, got them installed, fueled, and tested them in our two aircraft. He anticipated it would take several hours to complete the job, but they were working as fast as possible. He then said, "Both of your birds should be ready for your departure early tomorrow morning at the latest."

We returned to the ready room to continue our flight planning and have copilots assigned for the mission. Captain Haymore volunteered to go as my copilot, and Lieutenant Urbanczyk found another lieutenant to volunteer as his copilot. As we continued to plan our flight, the liaison officer for the Ryukyu Self-Defense Force came up to us and introduced himself. He asked if we were going to depart that afternoon, and I said to him, "No, we will leave very early in the morning since our internal fuel tanks have to be installed and tested before we can depart."

He said he understood but was disappointed because lives might be lost because of the delay. I told him we were making a monumental effort to get our aircraft ready for the flight, but without the operational internal tanks, we could not make the flight to the island at all. We would run out of fuel about seventy-five miles from Ishigakijima. I indicated that I needed to check with the people at VMGR-152 regarding when their aircraft was scheduled to depart to transport our TAFS unit, the communication truck, and the MABS Marines to operate both items to the island.

Picking up the telephone on the duty officer's desk, I called the operations duty officer at VMGR-152 and asked about the flight to Ishigakijima.

He responded, "It is going to leave in about one hour. Why are you asking? Do you need to add additional cargo to our aircraft? We have the MABS-36 TAFS unit and communication truck on board, some MABS troops, plus some just-arrived relief supplies. We also have a mission scheduled for tomorrow to take the initial ten thousand gallons of JP-4 to Ishigakijima for your use. We are scheduling a couple of flights to fly down relief supplies as they arrive for transport to the island, plus additional fuel you may need. Oh, by the way, we are also looking for the liaison officer for the Ryukyu Self-Defense Force that was supposed to accompany the initial relief supply to the island. Have you seen him by any chance?"

I responded by saying, "The liaison officer is standing right here in our ready room. I will send him over to your hangar right away."

"Good," he responded. "We will get him manifested and on the flight to Ishigakijima this afternoon."

The liaison officer for the Ryukyu Self-Defense Force had overheard my conversation and asked where the hangar he needed to go to was located. I indicated it was the one next door to ours, pointing in the direction of VMGR-152 hangar. He said, "Thank you. I will see you tomorrow morning in Ishigakijima at what time?"

"About 0800, since it's about a three-and-a-half-hour flight to Ishigakijima," I said to him as he was heading for the door. He waved in response as he exited the ready room heading for the hangar next door.

Lieutenant Urbanczyk and I checked again on the status of our two aircraft. We notified the enlisted flight crews that "we will be gone for three to five days, at least, so pack your gear accordingly." We and our copilots then headed back to our BOQ rooms to prepare our gear for the three- to five-day mission to Ishigakijima the next day.

Ev and I got up early, then went to the enlisted mess hall for breakfast with Lieutenant Urbanczyk and his copilot, along with our entire enlisted flight crews. We needed to start out well-fortified with food, since we were not sure when we would have another hot meal. Next, we stopped by the base operations building to check the weather, not only for our flight that morning, but for the next five to seven days since we were still in the typhoon season in this region. The weather forecaster check that day's weather between here and Taiwan and said the only weather problems were those that were left from the typhoon that had hit Ishigakijima, which was now impacting mainland China. He looked at the longer-range forecast and indicated that no additional typhoons appeared to be building up in the central Pacific that would impact our operations on Ishigakijima.

The NATOPS briefing, preflight, start-up, taxi, and takeoff were normal. We had filed a VFR flight plan for our two aircraft since the weather looked good for our flight. As we headed southwest from Okinawa, I could see nothing ahead of us but blue, white-capped ocean.

As we cruised in a loose formation at 2,500 feet above the water, I saw a KC-130 passing overhead and heading in the same direction. *It looks like one of the VMGR-152 aircraft is most likely heading to Ishigakijima with our fuel,* I hoped.

We saw the first in the group of three islands in the chain of the Yaeyama Islands at about three hours into our flight. There are three main islands in this chain. The first island was named Miyako, and it had not received major damage from the typhoon. About fifty miles further southwest was the islands called Ishigakijima and then Iriomotejima. They were the second and third major islands and were surrounded by several small islands, most of which were uninhabited at the time the typhoon struck the area. Our initial destination was the second of the three major islands in the Yaeyama Island group named Ishigakijima.

The island of Ishigakijima had a small airstrip that was located on the southeast side of the island just south of the village of Shiraho and several miles north of the town of Center.

The weather was clear, so we had no problem finding the coral and gravel airstrip on the second island since it had a KC-130 aircraft parked at one end of it. We could see the KC-130 as it appeared to be off-loading JP-4 into TAFS blivits, which had been set up next to the strip. As we flew overhead, it appeared the process was being completed since the hose connecting the KC-130 and the blivits was being disconnected. At that point, we got a radio call from the Marine who was manning the communication vehicle that had the UHF radio in it, which was parked near the airstrip. The Marine radio operator asked if we had enough fuel to allow us to delay our landing until the KC-130 departed in approximately fifteen minutes.

I responded, "Yes, we have sufficient fuel to allow us to delay our landing, and we would orbit south of the strip and wait for their departure."

I took a close look at the condition of the airstrip and could see that it was not in good shape, not being designed to have a heavy aircraft like the KC-130 land on it. Fortunately, the Marine KC-130 was designed to operate in conditions like this because it had large balloon tires and a wide footprint. It was able to operate in muddy conditions like we were experiencing at Ishigakijima that day.

While we orbited the area, I had a chance to observe the devastation the typhoon had brought to this island. No power poles were left standing in the village of Shiraho, and most of the wooden structures had collapsed. Only the concrete ones remained standing. Debris was scattered everywhere around the area making our landings and takeoffs dangerous to the people on the ground if we were not very careful.

It sure looked bad. From the air, I could only imagine what the people on the ground had gone through.

About fifteen minutes later, we watched as the big KC-130 rolled down the coral and gravel strip and lifted into the air easily, then turned northeast while climbing to altitude. With the airstrip free, I made my approach to the middle of the landing strip so that

Lieutenant Urbanczyk could land and refuel. After landing, we shut down. I walked back to the approach end of the strip close to the TAFS unit. I found the liaison officer for the Ryukyu Self-Defense Force inventorying the recently arrived relief supplies.

He said that major damage from the typhoon passage occurred on both the islands of Ishigakijima and Iriomotejima. The island of Iriomotejima was the next large island about seven miles to the southwest. He said the roads across and around the island had been washed out and were impassable. There were reported injuries and some fatalities in the towns of Shirahama, Uehara, and Funara, which were cut off from the rest of the island.

There were also some injuries and major damage reported in Ishigakijima. One area on the far northwestern end of the island was a fishing village that was cut off by floodwaters and storm surge from the main part of the island. He handed me a slip of paper with the grid coordinates of the isolated fishing village on it.

Since Lieutenant Urbanczyk had completed refueling and off-loading his three internal fuel tanks, I handed him the slip of paper with the grid coordinates on it and then asked him to take his aircraft and pick up the injured people from the isolated fishing village of Kabira in Ishigakijima. He was then to return here where they would then be transported to the small dispensary for preliminary treatment. The dispensary was located about a half mile from our present location. I also cautioned him about the significant amount of debris that was generated by the typhoon's strong winds and to be careful landing and taking off because the rotor wash could blow the debris around causing additional casualties to the civilians close to the operation. He responded that he would get the job done ASAP.

I could tell by his facial expressions and body language that he was pushing himself and showing concern that any delay could create even more problems for the injured people located at the fishing village he was heading to. I had operated with him in Laos and knew he was a good pilot and could handle the situation with a little guidance.

I cautioned him, "Slow down. Remember, safety first. We could not help these people very much if we crashed one of our birds trying to help them or hurt them further with flying debris. Just be careful."

He looked back at me for a second, then smiled, saying, "I got the message, Captain."

He and his copilot manned their aircraft, started it up, and departed over the broken treetops toward the isolated fishing village on the northwestern end of the island. While this was taking place, I talked to the liaison officer about his next priority for us since we were assigned to him on this mission. He wanted to go and evaluate the impact of the typhoon on Iriomotejima and evacuate any injured or deceased people from the towns of Ohara, Shirahama, Uehara, and Funara, which were isolated due to floodwaters and mudslides.

We moved back to our aircraft, started it, and taxied back to the TAFS unit for gas. While we refueled, we also off-loaded our three internal fuel tanks, now empty, so we could load tents, blankets, food, and water on board before the liaison officer for the Ryukyu Self-Defense Force came aboard. We then, fully loaded with relief supplies, departed for Iriomotejima.

Flying over the southern part of Ishigakijima at about five hundred feet AGL and heading southwest, I could see the devastation to the homes, fishing boats, and farms as we flew toward the water separating the two islands. Our crew chief had an extra gunner's belt that he retrieved for the liaison officer to use as he was very interested in seeing what type of damage had occurred. He also took pictures from each side of the aircraft as we flew over the hardest hit areas. We flew about fifteen miles over the water before arriving over the town of Ohara located on the southeast side of the island of Iriomotejima. The island of Iriomote, at the time, had a population of about one thousand people. Our liaison officer asked us to climb up to two thousand feet, so he could get some pictures of the large-scale devastation to the biggest community on the island.

Climbing to two thousand feet, we again witnessed the result of the devastation that mother nature could inflict on mankind. After several minutes, our liaison officer indicated he had enough pictures and that he wanted to land and distribute the aid to the people here. Since the town was located on both sides of the Nakama River that ran down to the sea where a harbor was located, both parts of the town were connected by a bridge that had failed completely because of severe flooding.

The liaison officer indicated that we should land on the north side of the river first, next to a school on the adjacent soccer field. As we approached the soccer field, we noticed that it had a lot of debris scattered all over it. We also saw several men and women who had splints on their arms and two who were lying on stretchers. After touching down, I asked the liaison officer to have the people try to clear the debris away from the aircraft so that when we departed, they would not be hit by the debris being blown into the air by our very strong rotor wash.

He acknowledged my request, then exited the aircraft at the ramp and moved away from the aircraft so he could talk to the people that were gathered now on the soccer field near the aircraft. After several minutes of discussion, the liaison officer returned to the aircraft telling the crew chief that the residents would help unload the tents, blankets, food, and water as soon as we signaled them it was all right to approach the aircraft. He indicated that most of them had never seen a helicopter before and were apprehensive about approaching it. He had assured them that we were there to help. He also said that the village elders would see to it that the area around the helicopter was cleaned up of debris. He asked me if it was okay to have them unload the supplies.

I responded, "Sure, you can have them start as soon as they are ready."

He went to the ramp and signaled the men and women who had gathered behind the aircraft waiting to see if it was okay to approach it to unload the supplies. Seeing his signal, they surged forward toward the aircraft's ramp. The crew chief and the liaison officer caught the first arrivals at the ramp and slowed them down, then funneled them one at a time into the cargo compartment where the first mechanic pointed to the item that they were to take out off the aircraft. With a steady flow of people taking items off the aircraft, it did not take very long to unload all the tents, blankets, food, and water off the bird.

The liaison officer told the crew chief he would like to take the injured who had been gathered there to the hospital back on Miyako island because of the serious nature of the injuries that they had sustained, which required a full hospital to treat. I told the crew chief to get them loaded up, and we would take them to Hika hospital for treatment. About this time, Lieutenant Urbanczyk's aircraft showed up overhead with a load of tents, blankets, food, and water on his bird. Seeing our other aircraft overhead, the liaison officer came back inside the aircraft and told me to instruct the other aircraft to land at the school's soccer field on the other side of the river and unload the supplies there. He had sent word to the people on the other side of the river what to do when he landed.

Furthermore, he requested that Lieutenant Urbanczyk's aircraft also transport any injured people on that side of the river to Hika hospital located near the Miyako airport. By this time, all the injured civilians had been loaded aboard our aircraft, and we were ready to depart for Hika hospital. The flight of about sixty-five miles took around forty minutes. We off-loaded the injured at the airport where there were a couple of old ambulances to transport them to the hospital across the street from the end of the airport's runway. We departed heading back to Ishigakijima to refuel. En route, we saw Lieutenant Urbanczyk's aircraft heading for Miyako. He called on the radio and said that he had stopped to refuel before making the flight to Miyako so that was why he was delayed.

"No problem," I responded. "Good headwork because I am running a little short on gas myself." I then told him where to drop off the injured civilians at the Miyako airport. My last transmission was "I'll see you back at Ishigakijima."

We landed at the coral and gravel airstrip with both fuel-low-warning lights illuminated but still enough fuel so neither Ev nor I were overly concerned about running out.

Another good lesson here, I thought. *Don't let the mission demands drive you to make stupid mistakes like running out of gas. We need to talk about that at the mission debrief tonight.*

While we were refueling, the liaison officer was signaled to come to the communications vehicle to receive a message. The crew chief finished the refueling and then proceeded to oversee the loading of the next load of tents, blankets, food, and water. About twenty-five people worked quickly to load the cargo.

As it was nearing completion, the liaison officer returned. He came forward and took a seat on the jump seat between Ev and me. He said he would like us to fly to the town of Shirahama in Iriomotejima, which was isolated due to floodwaters, storm surge, and a major mudslide. He indicated that he had just received word that there were more than ten civilians injured and at least two fatalities there. He then told me to have the second aircraft deliver supplies to Uehara, then pick up any injured civilians at the villages of Uehara and Funara on the northwest side of Iriomotejima.

I asked him if he understood that we had not visited the town of Center on the south tip of Ishigakijima yet.

He said, "I set the priorities for the relief mission."

My response was "you're the boss."

I called Lieutenant Urbanczyk's aircraft as we lifted off and told him that we were going to fly to the town of Shirahama and the west side of Iriomotejima that had been isolated because of flooding, storm surge, and mudslides. I then instructed him to refuel and pick up another load of relief supplies to be delivered to Uehara, then pick up any injured civilians at the villages of Uehara and Funara in the northwest side of Iriomotejima. He acknowledged my call with a "Roger, Wilco," meaning, he would comply with the directions I gave him.

We headed for Iriomotejima and passed again over the town of Center in Ishigaki, which also looked almost totally demolished, then headed west toward Iriomotejima. Again, we witnessed the devastation everywhere—trees down, houses leveled, electric poles broken off at ground level, and rice paddies flooded. It was a real mess.

We flew the fifteen miles across the water to the town of Ohara on Iriomote island, then turned west over the spine of the island until we reached Shirahama about fifteen miles from Ohara, which was a very small fishing village right on the water. We made an approach to the only open space available, which was the soccer field near the school. After landing, the liaison officer departed the aircraft and held a short discussion with what appeared to be the village elder. The liaison officer had seen the results of our rotor wash on the debris, so at each of our landing sites, he told the people in charge about the danger they were in from flying debris and to have it cleaned up to the extent possible.

While he was holding the meeting, I looked around the perimeter of the soccer field and saw several stretchers and people with their arms in slings. I then saw what looked to be bodies covered completely with white sheets. I assumed these were the two fatalities the liaison officer had spoken about earlier. One of the sheet-covered bodies appeared to be smaller than the other, so I again assumed it to be a child that had perished in the storm. At that point, I saw a young woman run to the sheet-covered body and throw herself on top of it, obviously in great distress. Then a young man approached the woman and comforted her before pulling her up and away from the small sheet-covered body. *How sad to lose a child,* I thought as I sat there watching the drama unfold.

Once the discussion was over, the liaison officer waved for the crew chief to drop the ramp in order to off-load the supplies we had brought. The process went much slower since a significant number of the villagers were injured and could not help us off-load. Once we got everything off, we first loaded the stretchers, then the walking cases, and finally the two fatalities. Once we were loaded, we departed back the way we came to Ishigaki to refuel before taking the injured and dead to Hika hospital located near the Miyako airport.

After we had completed the off-loading of the dead and injured, we started getting ready to depart for Ishigakijima when Lieutenant Urbanczyk's aircraft arrived and off-loaded the injured people and the fatalities he had picked up in Uehara and Funara on the northwest side of Iriomotejima. We waited for him to complete his off-loading, then we departed together for our return flight to Ishigaki airstrip. We landed and completed our refueling process just as the sun was setting over the small hills west of our airstrip. The liaison officer departed saying he had to try to make some radio calls back to Okinawa to arrange for more relief supplies. We moved our aircraft away from the coral and gravel strip so that the early morning

KC-130 could bring in additional relief supplies and more JP-4 fuel. We postflighted the two birds and serviced the hydraulic systems, as necessary.

That ended day 1 of our mission. We had moved sixty-five injured civilians to the hospital on Miyakojima and distributed about twenty-two thousand pounds of relief supplies to five different locations. No additional relief supplies were left on site for us to distribute that day. In the process, each crew flew approximately eleven hours of flight time. We had exceeded our daily flight time maximum by three hours, but we got the job done, and no additional civilians lost their lives because we did not deliver relief supplies or because of daily flight-time restrictions.

I could not get over the tremendous devastation that Mother Nature could bring to these two islands and their inhabitants. I only wished we could have done more for the people of these two islands today. Well, tomorrow's another day, I opined.

The MABS-36 communication and TAFS Marines had erected a large general-purpose tent where they would be staying. After we shut down for the day, I met the noncommissioned officer in charge (NCOIC) of the MABS-36 Marines, a gunnery sergeant who was the senior Marine in charge of the MABS Marines. He was a big broad-chested gunny whose demeanor and bearing left no doubt in your mind who was in charge of the MABS Marines. His most important attribute was, in my mind, the fact that he liked to drink coffee.

The gunny offered us the use of one end of their tent for a ready room or as a bunk room if we wanted to utilize it. We took him up on the use of the tent for a ready room, but we all elected to sleep in our "Sikorsky Hotel," the cargo compartment of each of our aircraft. We all had dinner of warmed-up C-rations (*C-rats* is the slang military term for the "food," most of which were leftovers from the Korean conflict) and coffee that the MABS Marines had provided. The communications vehicle had its own generator, so we had electrical power for lights, radios, and most importantly, to brew coffee.

After dinner, we gathered everyone at the end of the tent that we had been given to use as a ready room, then conducted our debrief of the day's mission. We talked at length about the tight spaces we were working in with lots of debris that was blown around by our rotor wash. Hopefully, the next day we would be using many of the same LZs as we used today but caution was the by-word for the next day's missions.

We received word by radio that two KC-130s would be arriving the next day with an additional fifty thousand pounds of relief supplies, a rough terrain forklift, and another ten thousand gallons of JP-4 fuel. The arrival of the forklift would greatly speed up the loading and off-loading of relief supplies. We would no longer have to hand-load and unload the supplies. The relief supplies would now be palletized, then placed on the rollers, and pushed into our aircraft cargo compartment on loading rollers. We could also ground taxi to drop the relief supply pallets out of the ramp at each LZ, speeding up greatly the delivery process.

The KC-130s would arrive at 0600 hours and 0800 hours, respectively. After learning this news, we agreed to meet for a C-ration breakfast and coffee at 0500 hours, then brief for the day's missions.

At 0500 hours, the next morning, we assembled at our end of the tent after heating up our C-rations and getting hot coffee. As we were eating, the liaison officer for the Ryukyu Self-Defense Force walked into the tent. He said, "Good morning to all of you."

I asked him if he would like to share our breakfast or have coffee.

He said, "No, thank you. I have already eaten."

Then the liaison officer proceeded to address our whole group, saying, "Thank you for all the work that you performed yesterday to help the people of Ishigakijima and Iriomotejima."

"My Okinawa Prefecture government has arranged for additional relief supplies to be delivered this morning to this airstrip by one of your KC-130s, for you to then take to our disaster-stricken people on Ishigakijima and Iriomotejima." He then handed me, as well as the NCOIC of the MABS unit, a list of cargo and locations where the relief supplies were to be taken. We finished our meal and started to work on how we would divide the supply deliveries between our two aircraft and who was going to go to which destinations.

I noticed the first priority on the list was the town of Center on Ishigakijima, which we had not visited yesterday.

At about 0610 hours, we heard the sound of a big KC-130 landing outside the tent on the coral and gravel strip. The strip had dried out overnight, which had made their landings much less dangerous. We watched them ground taxi to the approach end of the strip, debark several Marines, then we saw a Marine drive the rough terrain forklift out of the aircraft's ramp with a pallet of relief supplies.

This started the process of off-loading of the palletized relief supplies. The forklift driver proceeded to stack them in an area away from the strip. The staging area allowed us to pick up the palletized relief supplies without blocking the strip for the arrival of the next KC-130. The off-loading evolution went very quickly, and the KC-130 was ready to take off in forty-five minutes. The larger KC-130 pallets of relief supplies that were taken to the staging area, then were broken down by the MABS Marines and staged into smaller palletized loads that would fit inside our aircraft. These loads were also staged with a specific village in mind, all directed by the Ryukyu Self-Defense Force liaison officer. This was done to facilitate the delivery to the proper village rapidly.

While the MABS Marines were staging the first two loads, we proceeded to conduct the standard NATOPS briefing and then preflighted our aircraft. Once the first two loads were staged, we started our aircraft and moved to the pickup location. I got six pallets of water, food, and large tents for my first load destined for the town of Center in Ishigakijima. We departed the pickup area as Lieutenant Urbanczyk's aircraft moved into position to be loaded.

Lieutenant Urbanczyk's aircraft was loaded with six pallets of water, food, and large tents destined for the small fishing village of Kabira that he had been to yesterday on his first pickup of injured civilians. As he departed the pickup area, he radioed me that the next KC-130 was on approach to the strip with our much-needed JP-4 fuel.

The day passed quickly as we moved the relief supplies to the six villages on both islands. We each made four flights, each carrying approximately five thousand pounds per trip, to the six locations that had been designated by the liaison officer. Some locations got two lifts. Some got only one since the villages were all different sizes, and some had gotten supplies yesterday. The remainder of the relief supplies were carried by the MABS forklift to the village of Kabira about three quarters of a mile away from the strip. We also refueled four times each from the TAFS unit. We completed all flight operations by 1400 hours when we ran out of relief supplies to deliver.

We shut down our aircraft, then postflighted, and serviced them. We gathered for the debriefing and ate a late lunch of C-rats in our end of the tent. At this point, the gunny in charge of the MABS Marines came by to see if we needed their support services any more that afternoon.

I responded to him, "No, I don't think so, but you are not leaving us, are you?"

As he was getting ready to depart the tent, he said, "No, we were not leaving you, but I am going to take my troops, who had volunteered, up to the village of Kabira and pitch in with the local villagers to help with the cleanup work. Sir, your group is welcome to join us if you like. I have left a radio man to receive any communications for us and a runner to come and get us if we are needed back here."

I posed the idea to our small detachment of both officers and enlisted crew members who were gathered in the tent. All the officers and troops indicated they would like to participate. I responded, "Okay, if you all want to go, that's great, but we need to leave one man back to keep an eye on our birds. The man who stays back will be relieved by one of us in a couple of hours." Looking at the group, I saw nodding, then one young sergeant said he would volunteer to stay and keep an eye on our birds for a couple of hours. I assured him that he would be relieved and could get in on the action. We all left the tent with the gunny from the MABS unit walking toward the village of Kabira about three quarters of a mile away from the strip.

As we walked toward the village, the liaison officer joined our group, asking why we were going to the village. The gunny told him we wanted to help the villagers clean up and start to rebuild their village.

The liaison officer said, "Thank you for your concern, but I am not sure they would like your help. Let me go ahead of you to see if you are welcome in their village," and he headed for the village.

We stopped and sat down on the side of the road while he went to the village to see if we were welcomed. Looking around at ground level, we all got the real sense of how complete the devastation was to these islands from the typhoon. Only a couple of palm trees remained standing where there had previously been dozens of them. Only their stumps remained. Several large fishing boats were sitting several hundred feet inland from the sea, obviously driven up on the sand by the storm surge and high winds. Debris was scattered everywhere.

The liaison officer returned and said he had talked to the village elders, and they were happy to have our help in their cleanup efforts.

As we entered the village, several people stopped what they were doing and looked at us, surprised by our presence in their village. As we walked through the village, the liaison officer guided us to the location of the village elder's damaged residence, then introduced all of us to him. Then the liaison officer explained that there were still people in the village who were afraid of United States Marines; memories of WWII had not faded away completely, even if us Marines were there to help. Continuing, he said, "Do not be surprised if everyone is not hospitable to you and appreciative of your efforts."

We went to work, picking up debris and helping several carpenters in the repair and reinstallation of broken doors, windows, repairing roofs, and any project they were working on. We would pitch in to help. After a couple of hours of work, our small group of Marines seemed to have been accepted by the villagers as friends. At this point, I saw the MABS Marine runner coming into the village looking for the gunny. He found him quickly and gave him a message. The gunny came over to where I was working and said, "We have received orders for the next day's mission, and we should go back to the airstrip and make plans to execute them."

I looked for Captain Haymore and told him he was in charge of our working party, then I found the liaison officer and told him about the radio message. He, the gunny, and I departed the village going back to the airstrip to see what the next day's missions looked like.

The radio operator handed me the message he had written out in longhand along with the printed teletyped orders for the next day's mission. As we finished reading the printed and handwritten messages, the liaison officer made his appearance saying that he had receive word by shortwave radio from Okinawa that his government was sending more relief supplies the next day.

Looking at him, I said, "Yes, we have just received the same information from our headquarters that fifty thousand pounds of relief supplies will be arriving by KC-130 tomorrow morning at the same time as today's shipment arrived. We will also be getting another load of JP-4 fuel tomorrow."

He responded by saying he would get to work on the distribution plan right away as he headed back toward the village.

I sent the Marine sergeant who was keeping an eye on our aircraft to the village with a message for Captain Haymore. I said to him, "Tell the captain to have all our people who are working in the village to work for another hour, then bring everyone back here to the tent since we have a mission for tomorrow that we need to plan for."

*****

Our group of Marines arrived about an hour and a half later, tired, hot, and dirty but pleased that they could help the civilians in the village.

We gathered everyone in the ready room and let them know what the scope of the next day's mission was going to entail. We then all had dinner of warmed-up C-rats and coffee. As the sun was sinking quickly into the western sky, we conducted a mission briefing for the next day's flights. While our crew members made sure the aircraft were ready for the next day's mission, we all went to sleep early in our "Sikorsky hotels."

My entire detachment of HMH-462 Marines were all awake and ready to fly again at 0500 hours. We again had our "gourmet" breakfast of C-rats and coffee while we waited for the KC-130 flights to show up. At about 0600 hours, we heard the sound of a big KC-130 as it landed on the coral and gravel strip. The airstrip had dried out even more overnight. The aircraft now generated clouds of coral dust from the strip as the KC-130 landed. The dust cloud soon dissipated as the sea breeze dispersed it quickly. We again watched the aircraft ground taxi to the approach end of the strip and start the unloading process. The KC-130 also brought some replacement Marines for the current MABS support personnel.

These Marines debarked from the KC-130 and off-loaded some additional MABS equipment, then started to assist the crews who had immediately started to off-load the palletized relief supplies. They stacked them as before in an area away from the strip where we had picked up the loads of palletized relief supplies the day before. This off-loading evolution also took about forty-five minutes to complete. The KC-130 was ready to take off after they had loaded the returning MABS personnel on board.

The larger KC-130 pallets of relief supplies were again broken down by the relief MABS Marines and staged into smaller palletized loads that would easily fit inside our aircraft. Again, these loads were also staged with a specific village in mind where it was most urgently needed. While the MABS Marines were staging the first-two loads, we went to our tent and conducted our standard NATOPS briefing, then preflighted our aircraft. Once the first-two loads were staged, we again started our birds and moved to the pickup location. Again, my load consisted of pallets of water, food, and large tents. My first load was destined for the town of Shirahama in Iriomotejima. We departed the pickup zone as Lieutenant Urbanczyk's aircraft moved into position to be loaded.

Lieutenant Urbanczyk's aircraft was next to be loaded with six pallets of water, food, and large tents destined for the small fishing village of Uehara on Iriomotejima. He had been there yesterday to deliver relief supplies as well as our first day to pick up injured civilians. As he departed the pickup area, he radioed me that he had again seen an inbound KC-130 as it made its approach to the strip, hopefully with our JP-4 fuel.

Again, the day passed very quickly as we moved the relief supplies to the six villages on both islands. I made five trips, and Lieutenant Urbanczyk's bird made four flights carrying approximately 4,500 pounds per trip to the six locations that had been designated by the liaison officer. As it was the day before, some locations that he designated got two lifts; some got only one since they were all different sizes and had different needs. The remainder of the relief supplies were again carried by the MABS forklift to the village of Kabira up the road from the strip.

On my first relief supply flight, we passed over the village of Center on Ishigakijima on our way to Iriomotejima when I saw a large Japanese freighter steaming into the harbor. Several flights later, again flying over Center, we observed heavy equipment and supplies being off-loaded from the freighter in the harbor to small vessels and then taken to shore. We observed another large Japanese freighter arriving at the port of Ohara in Iriomotejima and that it had started to off-load supplies and heavy equipment. It appeared that more help had arrived to start the process of rebuilding the island's infrastructure after the typhoon's devastation.

We completed all flight operations earlier than yesterday because the loading crew had become much more proficient in their operations. Both aircraft again refueled four times each from the TAFS unit. We were done for the day as far as moving relief supplies by 1300 hours.

We shut down our aircraft, then postflighted, and serviced them. We again gathered for the debriefing and had another meal of C-rats and coffee in our end of the tent.

After completing the debriefing and our meal, I received a teletype message from the MABS radio operator. The message said that we were ordered to return to Okinawa the next day after the KC-130 arrived to provide additional JP-4 for our flight home. The message also ordered the MABS unit to stand down and prepare to depart on the KC-130 that was bringing our fuel the next day. The message went on to say that the Ryukyu government would be handling the remainder of the relief mission on both these two islands as well as the other smaller ones that were impacted by the typhoon.

It appeared from the message that the Okinawa government was telling us that our services were no longer needed.

The liaison officer for the Ryukyu Self-Defense Force who was overseeing the distribution of the aid the Japanese government was providing entered the tent where I was standing about thirty minutes after I had finished reading the message.

I can tell by his body language and facial expression that he is not very happy about something. It's most likely about the news we are leaving tomorrow, I thought, as he walked to where I was standing.

He said that he had also been told that we were to depart the next day to return to Okinawa. He went on to say how sorry he was to see us depart so soon with so much work still left to be done, but he understood that his government wanted to take over the job of getting these people back on their feet after the typhoon.

I thought, *Yeah! The Okinawa Prefecture government on Okinawa and its self-defense force wants to save face in the eyes of their people for not being prepared for this emergency.*

He looked me in the eye, with a great deal of sincerity, and said, "Because of your help, together, we have averted a real humanitarian disaster here in Ishigakijima and Iriomotejima. You saved many lives by getting the relief supplies to the villages where they were needed most quickly, as well as evacuating the civilians who needed medical attention to hospitals for treatment. I personally thank you for your efforts.

"The village elders of the village of Shiraho would like to thank your Marines for their help, not only with the relief supplies you brought, but for the help in cleaning up the damage to their homes and businesses that you did since you arrived on their island. They have invited all of you for a thank-you celebration this evening. Will you honor them by attending?" he asked.

"Yes, we will all be honored to attend," I said.

The word that we were going to be leaving the next day was met with mixed sentiment by our team. On one hand, we wanted to go back to Okinawa for a good hot meal and a shower, but everyone saw how much work remained to be done here to get these people back on their feet again, so there was also some reluctance to leave.

Orders were orders, so we reloaded our internal fuel tanks we had brought down with us back into our aircraft. In order to check their operation, we refueled two of them in each aircraft from the TAFS unit and topped off our sponsions fuel tanks. That drained the TAFS unit of their remaining JP fuel and completed the transfer operation. We wanted to make sure we could internally transfer fuel during our flight the next day on our way back to Okinawa in the morning.

This refueling activity helped the MABS Marines by allowing the tanks to be emptied of all their remaining fuel so that the rubber blivits could be rolled up and repacked in their boxes for air shipment the next day.

Having completed our departure preparation activities, we then warmed up our last "gourmet" C-rat's dinner, along with plenty of strong hot coffee, as the sun was sinking quickly into the western sky. After dinner, we conducted a mission briefing for the next day's flight back to Okinawa while our crew members, again, made sure our aircraft were ready for the next day's mission.

An hour after sunset, the liaison officer entered our tent. He said he was there to escort us to the village for the thank-you celebration. We and the MABS personnel—all but one of our Marines who volunteered to remain with our aircraft—departed to walk, under a moonlit sky, to the village about three-quarters of a mile away.

As we approached the village, we could see a fire burning in the center of the village, close to the location where they had erected one of the large tents that we had brought them. Many of the villagers were gathered close to the tent, which had its sides rolled up. Following the liaison officer, we entered the village walking toward the fire and tent.

The village elders greeted us by asking us to join them at some tables that had been set up near the fire. After we were seated, the village mayor stood up and spoke to the gathered group of people. He was one of the village elders whose words were translated by the liaison officer into English for us.

The mayor spoke for several minutes about the typhoon and the resulting devastation that had hit his village. He said, "The Marines gathered here had come to our village with food, water, and tents for our people. These Marines asked for nothing in return for their generosity. Not only did you help us by bringing water, food, and temporary shelter, but you also came to our village to help our people start the rebuilding process. We of the village of Shiraho would like to return your generosity by offering you a drink of our own *sake*, which we have saved from the typhoon."

At that point, several women appeared with hand-blown bottles containing *sake* and small cups, which were distributed to everyone in attendance. These women moved through the attendees and filled each one of the cups with the rice wine they had made themselves on their island. The elder then offered a prayer, and we all drank the *sake*. It was very smooth but also strong.

Our cups were refilled several times before I told our liaison officer that we must head back to our camp so our folks could get some sleep before we depart the next day. I asked him to thank the mayor, the village elders, and the people of the village for their hospitality, along with the honor that they bestowed on us by sharing their *sake* with us. After the translation of my words, I saw nods of understanding as the mayor rose from his seat and extended his hand to me. I took his hand and lowered my head as a sign of respect. Then our entire group headed back to camp waving to the villagers as we departed.

We all went to sleep early in our "Sikorsky hotels" after the *sake*.

As I lay on the floor of the aircraft, I thought, *It really feels good to have helped these people. I wish we could have done more.*

*****

Everyone was up at 0400 hours so that we could have our C-rats breakfast and coffee before the MABS Marines took the tent down to be packed up in anticipation of the KC-130 arrival at 0600 hours. After breakfast, we conducted the final mission briefing and then moved our makeshift ready room field desk and schedule board to my aircraft.

At exactly 0600 hours, we saw the KC-130 starting its approach to the coral and gravel airstrip. After the pilot landed his bird, he taxied to a position where a refueling hose could reach each of our two aircraft. We refueled the two remaining internal fuel tanks in each aircraft in about fifteen minutes. Once the refueling had been completed, he moved the KC-130 to the end of the airstrip and started to load the MABS TAFS unit, com vehicle, the forklift, and other equipment that had been brought to the island to support our mission.

As we were getting ready to start our aircraft and depart, the liaison officer for the Ryukyu Self-Defense Force came up to the aircraft and told the crew chief he would be returning to Okinawa on the KC-130 since another officer of the Ryukyu Self-Defense Force had arrived by boat to take over the relief mission. He said to tell everyone in the crew thank you and then waved to us as he headed toward the KC-130.

Our startup and takeoff were routine. We filed a flight plan by high-frequency radio with air traffic control, in Okinawa, heading back to home base across the calm, beautiful blue Pacific Ocean.

We had a little head wind on our flight, which took three hours and forty-five minutes. Our internal fuel systems on both birds worked as advertised, and we had no problems en route to home base.

Arriving at the MCAS Futenma, we refueled the sponson fuel tanks and left the internals dry so they could be removed. We taxied to the flight line and shut down the birds. Our next stop was maintenance control where Lieutenant Urbanczyk and I each wrote up the minor discrepancies that each aircraft had exhibited on our extended mission. Next, we went to our squadron's ready room to fill out the paperwork describing each day's activities, such as daily flight time, people carried, cargo carried, and locations where we operated on the mission.

At this point, Captain Haymore, Lieutenant Urbanczyk, his copilot, and I were completing the paperwork when the administrative officer, a major, came into the ready room. He saw us, then said, "I am glad you two are back," pointing to Captain Haymore and myself. "You two have just received orders to go stateside. Haymore, you are going to New River on the East Coast, and Wemheuer, you are going to Hawaii.

"You need to pick up your permanent-change-of-station (PCS) orders today, then start the checkout process tomorrow. I am not sure how you two got these orders since you still have not been overseas for your entire year. It's only October, and you should not be leaving here until December or January. You two must know someone in high places to get special treatment like this," as he departed the ready room shaking his head in disbelief.

As the major walked away, I looked over at Ev and saw a big smile on his face, just like the one that was spread across mine.

I thought, *I bet Major Phillips, the Wing G-1, had a hand in getting these orders for our early rotation back to the States.*

Ev and I completed the paperwork, then headed to the administration office, and picked up our orders before someone changed their minds. We then went back to the BOQ. We both made telephone calls to our families back in the States letting them know the good news that we were both coming home early from overseas.

My wife was overjoyed that I was coming home early because she was anxious to get out of Pensacola where she and the girls had been living for the past nine months. They all said that a couple of years stationed in Kaneohe Bay, Hawaii, looked *pretty* good to all of them.

As I packed my footlocker in preparation for leaving Okinawa, I mused, *Here I go again, back to HMH-463 for the third time. There must be something about that squadron that keeps pulling me back to it.*

Ev and I found ourselves both scheduled to depart Kadena AFB on the same military flight, which would take us to Norton AFB in southern California. We sat side by side and talked about our experiences in Vietnam and Okinawa for the entire flight. At Norton AFB, I said goodbye to my roommate and good friend as we both went our separate ways.

Chapter 4

OPERATION END SWEEP— NORTH VIETNAM

HMH-463 Again

My family and I arrived in Honolulu in late November 1971 and checked into an apartment-type hotel that was designated for service families who had been transferred to Hawaii. After getting settled into the hotel, I drove our rental car to Marine Corps Air Station Kaneohe Bay to check into the squadron.

Having never been on the base before, I found the location of my, again, new Squadron HMH-463 by looking for the big green helicopters. As I drove down to the flight line, I saw several of these large green birds parked on the flight line next to the seawall. Looking at the nose of one of the CH-53s parked there, I saw a large pineapple painted on the front avionics access hatch.

This pineapple logo is something new. It sure was not painted on the birds when they left Vietnam. It has to be a Hawaii thing, I said.

I entered the hangar next to the seawall expecting to see some old friends and some friendly faces, but I recognized almost no one. I climbed the stairs and went into the administration office.

A corporal looked at me and took the orders I handed to him. He looked quickly at them, then said, "Captain, have you checked in at the group or brigade yet?" (meaning, MAG-24 HQ and the First Marine Brigade).

Looking at him, I said, "No, I have not checked in at either of these places yet."

He handed me back my orders and said, "Sir, you will have to check in at the brigade and the group before I can help you."

I then asked him who the commanding officer of the squadron was.

He said, "It's Lieutenant Colonel Ledbetter."

Seeing the look of surprise on my face, he went on to say that "Lieutenant Colonel Ledbetter had taken over command of the squadron a couple of weeks after it arrived here from Vietnam."

I asked him what happened to most of the officers who returned with the squadron.

He said, "Almost all of them were replaced once Lieutenant Colonel Ledbetter took command. Some were reassigned to the air group staff and brigade billets, or they were transferred to stateside commands. All the senior command and major department billets that had been filled by officers that left with the squadron from Vietnam had been replaced, but we still have some staff NCOs and enlisted troops from the old organization."

Sensations of shock and being dumbfounded replaced my positive feelings of coming home again. Gone was my positive sense of being reunited with my comrades in arms. All these changes had taken place since the squadron had left Vietnam a little over four months ago. Recognizing change was inevitable, I decided I would have to get used to the changes to the organization that had occurred or look for another job in the group or brigade, but I wanted to continue to fly, so I dismissed these options out of hand.

I thanked the corporal, then headed back down the stairs heading out to my car en route to the brigade headquarters to check in.

On my way out of the hangar, I did see Captains Ron Corner and John Gaynor on the far side of the hangar going up the stairs. I had served with both of them before, so I was not completely alone in my new squadron.

I successfully found the First Marine Brigade headquarters in an old brick and mortar building built prior to the start of World War II. I could tell this because you could still see the holes and pockmark remnants of the .50-caliber machine-gun hits on the side of the building from the attack here on the same day as the attack on Pearl Harbor on December 7, 1941.

Going inside this historic building, I found the brigade's administrative office on the first floor of the two-story building. While I was waiting for my orders to be endorsed, I looked at the pictures of the brigade staff officers hanging on the wall. Major George, now Lieutenant Colonel George Ebbitt, who I flew with many times on my first tour in Vietnam, was now the brigade comptroller. At least I know someone from the old HMH-463 Squadron, as my mind drifted back to my first tour in Vietnam flying with Major George.

*****

I was a young copilot who was trying to get all the flight time I could scrounge. Since there were about nineteen other copilots in the same boat that I was in and all trying to fly enough hours and get enough experience to qualify as an aircraft commander, we all tried to get as much fly time as possible. So I looked for any and every opportunity I could come up with to fly.

Since Major George was known to his contemporaries as Shaky George when it came to flying in combat, not many of the copilots wanted to be assigned to fly with him. I saw this reluctance as an opportunity to fly. So I let the operations schedulers know I was willing to fly with Major George any time. Consequently, I got to fly whenever he was on the flight schedule.

One day, I was scheduled to fly with Major George. Our mission was to deliver externally supplies of water and ammunition from Hill 55, which was located several miles south of Da Nang to our Marines and Korean Marine artillery positions with our aircraft. These positions were located on hilltops between ten and fifteen miles east of the town of Tam Ky. This flight was a normal single-aircraft resupply mission, and we did not expect any problems during the flight, but you could never count on anything being routine in a combat environment like Vietnam.

Since the major and I had flown together before, we had an arrangement about who was going to do what job in the cockpit. I liked to fly the aircraft much more than the major did. He was much more comfortable handling the radios and making sure the paperwork detailing the items carried and the locations where we dropped off supplies and ammunition were properly annotated. As usual, the major handled all the radio calls and kept track of the paperwork functions while I got to fly the aircraft the whole mission.

We were making our third approach to a hilltop landing zone, with a *water buffalo*, which weighed about 4,500 hundred pounds. The weather this time of year produced very hot and dry conditions in this part of Vietnam, so dust kicked up by our very strong rotor wash created huge dust clouds, at times obscuring visibility significantly in the blowing dust. This was a problem at each LZ we visited since ground troops removed the vegetation to create the LZ. To help counter the dust clouds we generated, we flew a faster approach to the LZ and tried to minimize our hover time with the load.

As I made the approach to the LZ, we heard the all-too-familiar sound of an AK-47 rifle, with the accompanying sound of the rounds hitting metal. We were about 75 yards away from the perimeter of the small fire support base when the rounds started to fly. Our crew chief who was looking down at our load through the hell hole, said, "I can see 'Charlie' [slang for Viet Cong fighters] shooting at us, but the rounds were hitting the water buffalo and not our aircraft." Continuing my approach, I came to a low hover over the drop point when the crew chief said, "Captain, the water buff is leaking like a strainer. It's losing a hell of a lot of water out the holes Charlie punched in it. The boys down on the ground could take a shower under it. In fact, I think it may be almost empty right now."

I waved off the approach, knowing that the Marines on the ground needed the water, since I knew it was useless to deposit the almost-empty water buffalo in the LZ in its present condition. Flying away from the LZ, I could feel the difference in how the aircraft handle without the water being inside the buffalo.

Major George looked over at me and said, "I guess we should take this one back to Hill 55 and get a replacement."

I responded, "I concur, sir," as we continued to depart away from the LZ. I could see a squad of Marines heading for the location where the sniper had been hiding that had taken out the water buffalo.

As we returned to Hill 55 with the damaged water buffalo, a Marine on the ground there remarked, "Hey, Dimmer aircraft, it looks like you got a real leaker on your hands," as we set the hole-riddled water buffalo down on the LZ. After refueling, we picked up another full water buffalo and delivered it without incident to the fire support base where we previously had taken fire. The rest of the mission went smoothly as we delivered all the water, supplies, and ammunition to the two fire support bases east of Tam Ky.

Returning to Marble Mountain Air Facility, Major George took care of all the mission paperwork, and I wrote up the discrepancies with the aircraft. We debriefed the mission and secured for the day.

A few days later, I was sitting in the officers' club having a beer when I overheard a couple of field-grade officers talking. Major George's name came up in less-than-flattering terms. From what I overheard from these two was that Major George had a new nickname. It was no longer "Shaky George." It had become "Leaky George."

I flew many hops with Major George and always found him to be a kind, caring, smart, articulate Marine officer who had one basic problem. He was scared of flying in combat and flying in general. Why he became a naval aviator, I could never figure out. He had confided that fear to me during one of our long discussions after one of our flights. That is why he and I got along so well. I felt that some of the unflattering talk he was the recipient of was mostly unjustified.

Looking back again at his picture, I thought, The unflattering talk could not have hurt his career too badly because he is now a lieutenant colonel.

*****

UNLIKE NO OTHER

The young female Marine sergeant spoke to me, bringing me back to reality. She handed me my orders, saying, "Captain, you are to check in tomorrow at MAG-24 where you will most likely be assigned to HMH-463. Do you have any questions?"

"Yes, Sergeant, I do. Where can I find Lieutenant Colonel Ebbitt's office?"

She looked past me pointing down the hall, saying, "Captain, if you will proceed out the door behind you into the hall, turn left, and go up the stairs, then you should see his office about halfway down the hall on the left side."

"Thank you, Sergeant," I replied as I left the administrative office. I walked up the stairs of the headquarters building and down the hallway to a door with a small sign next to the door that read "Lt. Col. G. F. Ebbitt Jr."

I found George's office. As I looked at the big door that had a large, frosted glass window saying "Comptroller," I wondered how he had gotten to Hawaii after his tour in Vietnam several years earlier.

Opening the door, I saw a very attractive woman sitting behind a large desk. As I entered the office, she asked, "Can I help you, Captain?"

"Yes," I responded. "My name is Robert Wemheuer. I would like to find out if it is possible to see Lieutenant Colonel Ebbitt?"

Her next utterance after looking at an appointment book on her desk was "Captain, I don't seem to have you on the schedule to see the comptroller this morning. Did you have an appointment?"

"No, ma'am, I do not have an appointment with the colonel, but I am an old squadron mate of his, and we flew a lot together in Vietnam a few years back. Since I have just been stationed here on the island, I thought I would drop in and say hello to him."

His secretary was about to respond when the door to her right opened and George entered the room, looking toward his secretary, saying, "Helen, I sure could use a warmup on this coffee, please." George then turned slightly toward me, took a quick look, and said, "Well, I'll be damned if it is not the Bull [my nickname]. How the hell are you?" Before I could respond, he walked over to me and extended his hand. We shook hands, and then he said, "I see you have met my secretary. Come on into my office so we can talk. What are you doing here at K-Bay?" as he put his hand on my shoulder to steer me toward his office. He called back over his shoulder, "Helen, is my schedule clear for a while? If not, please clear it. The Bull and I have a lot to catch up on, so cancel any appointments for this morning. Unless it's with the CG, of course. Thanks. Oh, please bring in some hot coffee and another cup for the captain. Thanks."

We entered his very large office, and he ushered me to a large couch and took a seat in an overstuffed chair on the other side of a large coffee table. I told him that I was going to be stationed here at K-Bay and most likely in HMH-463, our old squadron.

He smiled at me as he said, "Since we left Vietnam after our first tour flying the CH-53A, I have kept an eye on how the squadron was performing with the CH-53. That aircraft was ahead of its time. I was very proud to have been in the first squadron to deploy in combat with the machine. As I watched from here after completing my master of science degree in management at the Navy postgraduate school in Newport, Rhode Island, I was glad to see that HMH-463 did such an outstanding job in supporting the Lam Son 719 operation, even if it was a losing proposition. You guys showed what the CH-53 can really do. I am very proud of you.

"Bull, you said you were going to be assigned to HMH-463. Is that correct?"

"Yes, sir," I replied.

"Then as I see it, there are a few things you should be aware of about the current HMH-463. It's not the same unit you served in just over four months ago. It has changed radically. It's now run by a group of CH-46 officers and some East Coast CH-53 pilots. These new CH-53 pilots, to my knowledge, have not seen any combat flying in the CH-53 aircraft. Most of them flew CH-46s in combat. In my opinion, they were all pilots stationed in Hawaii who needed a flying job, that's all.

"The squadron got back from Vietnam in June, and almost immediately, there was a change of command followed by changes of all the department heads and senior staff NCOs in the unit. They stripped out almost all the experience that was resident in the squadron within the first month after their return from Vietnam. In my opinion, the squadron will have to train very long and hard if it's going to get back to the level of experience they had when the unit got back from Vietnam."

Changing the subject, George and I discussed our families and compared notes on what had happened to other squadron mates we had previously served with. Time flew by, and George looked at his watch and said, "I want to take you to lunch at the officers' club, my treat." So off we went.

The next day, I checked into MAG-24, had my orders endorsed, and then proceeded to the HMH-463 hangar at about 1000 hours.

I again climbed the stairs and went into the administration office. The same corporal looked at me, saying, "Captain, I see you have returned," as I handed him my orders. He looked quickly at them, seeing the endorsements from the brigade and MAG-24, he said, "Captain, all you need to do now is check into our squadron," as he handed me a check-in sheet with almost all the boxes requiring a signature highlighted. He also said that he had just received a notice that my clearances had been upgraded from secret to top secret with sensitive access. He said he would annotate the status change in my officer qualification record (OQR) and that I should make sure the intelligence officer knew about the status change when I checked in with him.

I thought back to my interview with two FBI men who had come to talk to me—well, over a year earlier—about my background, my likes, dislikes, and posed other interesting questions. This took place while I was stationed at MCAS (H) Santa Ana at the Heavy Helicopter Training Squadron. My wife, some neighbors, and some fellow Marines were also interviewed by these two individuals. This security upgrade must have been the result of those interviews since I had been involved with the certification of the CH-53 aircraft to carry nuclear weapons off aircraft carriers before they entered port.

"The last stop," he said, "will be an interview with the CO, Lieutenant Colonel Ledbetter."

It took most of the day to complete the checklist down to the last item. I reported back to the administration office at about 1615 hours. I was told that he would see me for not more than fifteen minutes since he had other social engagements to attend.

I was ushered into his office, moving to a position in front of his desk. I reported to my new commanding officer in the standard Marine Corps manner as protocol requires. He acknowledged me with a nod as he completed some paperwork on his desk. Looking at him sitting there, I saw his Navy cross ribbon on the top of a couple of lines of lesser awards. He, in my estimation, possessed an air of arrogance about him that was reinforced when he looked up from his paperwork. It felt like I was interrupting and disturbing him.

Looking up at me, he said, "Captain, you can stand at ease. I see from your record that you have been flying the CH-53 almost all your career. Is that correct?"

"Yes, sir," was my response.

"Good"—as he continued—"we can use some help here in our maintenance department. Captain Rensch will find a position down there someplace. Welcome aboard. You are now dismissed, Captain."

I came to attention, then did an about-face, and exited his office.

The lieutenant colonel was almost on my heels as I left his office, saying to his admin chief, as he walked past me, "I'll be at happy hour at the O club if anyone is looking for me."

So that is the pressing social engagement he had to rush off to. This is going to be an interesting tour of duty, I mused.

Going down to the maintenance spaces located on the side of the hangar, I went to find Captain Rensch, the aircraft maintenance officer (AMO). I found his office, finding the door locked, and the lights turned off. I went to maintenance control and found a staff sergeant behind the desk. I asked him where I could find the AMO.

He looked up from his paperwork and said, "Captain Rensch left for happy hour about forty-five minutes ago, Captain. He will be in first thing in the morning on Monday around 0800 hours."

I thanked the staff sergeant for the information and left the hangar.

Looks like I will come back Monday morning, I said as I got into my rental car and headed back across the island to our hotel apartment. The squadron sure has taken a laid-back Hawaiian outlook on things. It sure was not the old squadron I was familiar with when it was in Vietnam. Lieutenant Colonel Ebbitt was correct in his evaluation of the squadron I had just joined.

As I drove across the island, I wondered why my new CO had not invited me to happy hour at the O club. Maybe it was that I was not a member of their CH-46 clique. My thought drifted back to the seven fellow aviators who graduated with me who went to fly CH-46s and were no longer with us, all killed in Vietnam on my first tour, principally because of aircraft malfunctions and some combat activities. Boy, did I despise the CH-46 aircraft that took so many good people to the other side of the great divide.

On Monday morning, I arrived at the maintenance officer's office at about 0730 hours. The AMO was not there when I arrived, so I went to maintenance control. I found the coffeepot and then proceeded to make myself comfortable.

The person who I later found out was the maintenance control chief, a gunnery sergeant whom I did not recognize, arrived about 0745 hours. As he entered the office, he saw me as he came in the door, and he asked if he could help me.

I told him I was waiting to see the AMO when he arrived.

"Okay," he responded.

"I see you found the coffee. The AMO should be here around 0800 hours."

"Thank you, Gunny," I responded, thinking maybe he did not see my captain bars on my uniform collar or he has a hangover and did not care about being respectful by saying sir after his statement. I sat on a stool near a window that looked out on the hangar floor and waited for the AMO's arrival.

At about 0815 hours, I saw the AMO arrived at the hangar. I got off the stool, then exited maintenance control, and headed for the AMO's office.

As he unlocked his office, I said, "Captain Rensch, I am here to check in with you. The CO told me I was going to work in the maintenance department last Friday, so here I am."

He looked at me and said, "You were with this squadron in-country a couple of times, is that right?"

I responded, "That is correct, Captain."

"Have you been to aircraft maintenance officer school?" he asked.

I responded again, "I have been to AMO school, Captain."

He continued to question me, asking, "What positions have you held in a maintenance department?"

With my temper on the rise, while we both remained standing outside his office, I responded again to his continued questioning. I said, "Captain Rensch, I have served as a flight line officer, ground-support equipment officer, quality assurance officer, ordnance officer, and as an enlisted man, I worked in the ordnance shop loading twenty-millimeter rounds in the cannons of the FJ-4 fighters with the reserve unit VMF-611 stationed at Glenview Naval Air Station."

In my opinion, his next question came out of left field. He asked me what my lineal number as a captain was. A *lineal number* refers to "where you rank on the list of captains." This ranking number changes each year as captains get promoted or leave the service. I gave him my current lineal number knowing that I was senior to almost all the captains in the squadron with the exception of him and Captain Ron Corner, who was the squadron's safety officer.

Having always been told the seniority among captains is just like virginity among whores, so I was not sure why this ranking was relevant to our discussion.

We continued to stand on the hangar deck for several minutes while he appeared to be trying to decide what he was going to say next.

He appeared to make up his mind and finally spoke, saying, "I guess, based on your seniority, you will be the squadron's assistant maintenance officer [AAMO]. Your office is located down the way next to maintenance control. I will talk to you later," as he entered his office, closing the door behind him.

That was my first encounter with my new boss. In my estimation, at the time, he appeared to be a very unhappy former CH-46 *driver* (slang for "pilot"), who appeared to be not very pleased to have a 53 driver as his assistant. It appeared to me that this was going to be a rocky relationship at best.

*****

I started flying missions the next afternoon after my NATOPS check flight with Captain Ron Corner, who was one of a couple of CH-53 pilots that I knew from my first combat tour in Vietnam in 1967–1968, as well as the helicopter training squadron at MCAS (H) Santa Ana. Captain John Gaynor was another.

Most of our squadron's missions were generally military-training-type missions, which provided direct support to the ground units of the First Marine Brigade and other Army and Marine units on the islands. We were tasked several times to move junked vehicles to the island of Kahoolawe to be used for artillery and naval gunfire practice.

Kahoolawe is a small island about ten miles west of Maui, which had been utilized since the Second World War for these types of activities. These missions helped keep our pilots and aircrews qualified in external cargo-carrying operations.

Other administrative types of missions were also scheduled, which provided an opportunity to fly more basic training missions, such as instrument training. An example of these administrative missions occurred every week on Friday. This reoccurring mission entailed a flight to the city of Hilo on the big island of Hawaii to pick up flowers from a florist there, for the senior officers' wives, officers' club, and the staff NCO club functions. This flight, as well as others, were coupled with a training mission, so it could not be classified as fraud, waste, and abuse.

Being one of the senior pilots in the squadron as far as experience, I was quickly made a NATOPS instrument and post-maintenance-check pilot shortly after my initial requalification flight with Captain Corner.

As the new AAMO, I found out quickly that we had a lot of work trying to keep the fleet up and flying. We had only limited supplies and scarce expertise both in the form of pilots and enlisted maintenance personnel.

I settled into my new position and spent a lot of time flying. Learning who was who in the maintenance department was also a priority for me. Things went along fairly well for the first couple of months, allowing me some time to get my family situated in a rental townhouse just outside the gate at MCAS Kaneohe Bay. This rental was necessary because base housing for company-grade officers was not available. The waiting list for housing we found out after our arrival was twelve to fourteen months, which I immediately applied for, since the normal tour of duty here in Hawaii was three years.

Moving to Hawaii, at first, seemed to be a dream assignment. My family and I soon found out this assignment was not a dream assignment at all. It was, in fact, closer to a nightmare for our family. Our dog had to be kept in quarantine for three months at our expense. Our car arrived by ship damaged. Our furniture arrived in wooden boxes with water integrity compromised requiring almost half of our household goods to be replaced. It was a real challenge for my wife, who navigated the bureaucratic morass at every level successfully, so at the end of three months, she had straighten out almost all the problems while I was becoming familiar with my new squadron.

We finally got the dog back, and life started to become closer to normal for our family as we enjoyed the fabulous weather, the fresh tropical fruits, flowers, and the warm, sunny beaches of Hawaii.

*****

On a day several weeks later, back in my office, I looked at the flight schedule for tomorrow. I saw that I was scheduled to give a newly designated aircraft commander an instrument check the following afternoon. This pilot was a first lieutenant who I did not know and had never flown with. His nickname was Space, an unusual nickname. I would discover later why it was an appropriate nickname. He would be referred to in this story as Space M.

The next day, I went to the ready room at our scheduled briefing time and found the lieutenant engaged at the acey-deucey table. Acey-deucey is a board game using dice and checkers. This game is commonly played in the pilots' ready room and is a mechanism for pilots to pass the time when not engaged in flying or doing their ground jobs.

I asked the lieutenant if he was ready for his instrument-check ride. He said he was, but he said, "I want to finish the game first."

My response did not sit well with him, saying, "Our briefing is scheduled to start in three minutes, and we need to depart on time in order to complete your instrument check. You can finish the game after you return."

He looked at me for a few seconds, then slowly got up from the table, and joined me to listen to the operation duty officer's (ODO) briefing.

After the ODO's briefing, I told him how I wanted to handle his instrument-check flight. I wanted him to think of me as just a new copilot and perform the instrument flight as if he were in command of the aircraft. I would do whatever he asked in the cockpit, but it was his show. I then gave him the IFR scenario that I wanted him to fly. He was to plan, file, then execute a round-robin instrument flight plan. The first leg was to Maui airport, where he was then to execute the published TACAN 1, instrument approach, followed by executing the missed-approach procedure, then flying the airways back to K-Bay for a ground-control-radar approach to home field. The GCA would be done under a hood that I would provide him, so he could demonstrate his ability to fly on instruments without looking outside the aircraft. I concluded my directions to him, saying, "This check flight is an evaluation of your ability to fly in actual instrument conditions."

He said he understood my instructions and then proceeded to start the planning process. He first made out an IFR flight plan and handed it to the ODO and told him to file it for him. He did not check the weather en route or at Maui or the forecast back here at K-Bay.

Because the sun was shining outside, it was my guess he did not feel the necessity to get a weather briefing in person at base operations or by telephone. This was an item on the pilot's instrument checklist that I had not seen him use or even refer to. I watched this process but said nothing to him since I was just his make-believe copilot, and he was the make-believe aircraft commander. He then conducted a standard NATOPS briefing, then we headed for the aircraft. I signed for the bird since I was responsible for its safe operation, but put him in the right seat, where the aircraft commander sits.

Startup and taxi was performed normally. At this point, the lieutenant called ground control to activate his IFR flight plan. He was given his clearance, including the heading after takeoff and the altitude to climb to upon departure (this was different from the one on his flight plan). The departure-control frequency was also provided to him so he could contact them after takeoff.

I observed that he had not taken any notes or recorded any of these items on his knee board including the departure-control frequency. He had not asked me to record any of this either.

We were then switched to the tower frequency for takeoff. He lifted into a hover, then departed down the runway. As we passed the end of the runway, he started to climb, turning to the departure heading. He was directed to switch to departure-control frequency. A blank look appeared on his face as he realized that he had forgotten the frequency and had not written it down.

The tower called again directing him to change to departure control. At this point, I put the departure control frequency in the UHF radio for him.

He saw me do that, nodded, and smiled as he called departure control, saying, "This is Pineapple 11 off K-Bay air station climbing to 3,000 feet."

Departure control told him they had radar contact but were not reading his transponder. He looked down at the transponder box, which had been set during the last flight for a VFR code of 1200, plus he then also saw that it had been turned on to the standby-mode setting. He looked frantically at his knee board for the IFR code that ground control had given him when he received his clearance while still on the ground. He could not find it on his knee board. He then looked over at me sitting in the left seat and then asked if I had written down the Identification Friend or Foe (IFF) code.

I had written it down on my knee board, but I said to him, "No, I did not write it down. You did not ask me to write it down, did you?"

He continued to look over at me making no reply, but instead, he keyed the UHF radio and said, "This is Pineapple 11, Departure Control. I have miscopied the IFF code, could you give it to me again or issue a new one?"

The controller read him the previous assigned IFF code to him again, which he put into the IFF box, and turned it to the on position.

The departure controller again said, "Pineapple 11, we have radar contact, turn to heading 180 degrees and climb to and maintain 5,000 feet. Switch to Honolulu Center on frequency 360.10, good day."

The lieutenant turned the aircraft to a heading of 180 degrees and continued his climb toward 5,000 feet and then remembered to switch the radio frequency to 360.10. He called Honolulu Center, which acknowledged his transmission and told him to proceed on his flight plan route and report arriving at 5,000 feet. The lieutenant acknowledged the center's instructions and continued to climb for the next five minutes, finally arriving at 5,000 feet, where he leveled off.

He then relaxed and made the comment to me. "It sure is a beautiful day to be flying," as we flew along the invisible roadway in the sky, called an airway. He, at this point, still had not informed Honolulu Center of his arrival at an altitude of 5,000 feet. The Honolulu Center controller came back on the radio asking him if he was having communication problems.

I could see it in his facial expression that he had now remembered that he was to notify the center when he was level at 5,000 feet.

He replied to the center saying, "This is Pineapple 11. I have not had any communication problems, Center. I am currently level at 5,000 feet."

The Honolulu Center controller replied, "Roger, copy you are now level at 5,000 feet. Pineapple 11, descend now to 3,000 feet. Upon reaching the initial approach fix, you are now cleared for the TACAN 1 approach to Maui airport, report the initial approach fix."

I heard a couple of snickers in the background during the center's transmission back to the lieutenant.

The lieutenant had managed to copy down the instructions he had been given by Honolulu Center and now realized that he needed to have the TACAN approach plate available in order to fly the approach. He found his helmet bag, which also, I assumed, functioned as his navigation bag, and began looking for the book of approach plates for airports in Hawaii. Finding the book, he found the page with the TACAN approach number 1 to Maui airport. He started to read the instructions when Honolulu Center asked if he was going to commence the TACAN approach.

The lieutenant replied, "Roger, Honolulu Center, Pineapple 11 is commencing approach at this time."

At that point, I suggested that he needed to make a 90-degree turn to the inbound radial of the TACAN if he was going to fly the published approach. The lieutenant glared at me, saying, "You have been no help at all," as he turned to the inbound course to the TACAN.

My response was "Lieutenant, as I told you when we started this check ride, I am here to help you. All you need to do is ask."

Seeing that he was now on course, he started to descend to meet the altitude criteria for the approach. Then he asked me to read him the instructions on the approach plate, including the decision altitude and miss-approach procedures contained in the approach chart. I read him the altitude and the miss-approach procedures on the approach plate. He executed them in a satisfactory manner. As he completed the missed approach at Maui airport, he called Honolulu Center telling them that he had executed the miss approach and asked for radar vectors back to K-Bay with a pickup for a GCA at the air station.

Honolulu Center acknowledged his call, saying, "Pineapple 11, radar contact, climb to 4,000 feet, turn right to a heading of 075 degrees."

The lieutenant acknowledged the directions given by the center, turning the aircraft to 075 degrees and leveling his climb at 4,000 feet.

At this point, I pulled a hood from my navigation bag and told the lieutenant that I was taking control of the aircraft. He looked at me with a look of surprise until he saw the hood I was about to hand to him. I took control of the aircraft for the first time that day, then handed the hood across to him. The hood fits over the pilot's helmet and allows only the view of the flight instruments in front of them. The use of the hood allows pilots to train as if they were in actual instrument conditions.

I watched him put the hood over his helmet, then asked him to let me know when he was ready to take back control of the aircraft.

Looking at the lieutenant, I could tell by his body language he was very uncomfortable having the hood in place and not being able to see the horizon outside.

After a couple of minutes, he said he was ready to take back control of the aircraft. I returned the control to him. Things went okay until the Honolulu Center came up on the radio, saying, "Pineapple 11, turn left to a heading of 340 degrees, descend to 3,000 feet, and switch to K-Bay GCA on frequency 290.20, good day."

The lieutenant's attention was diverted from the instrument scan he was using to keep the aircraft on altitude and heading. He looked down at his knee board and tried frantically to record the frequency for the GCA the controller had given him. He did not ask for any help from me to copy any information down or fly the aircraft or do anything to assist him. I assumed again that he wanted to do it all himself, to show his macho status in the Lieutenants Protective Association or LPA.

The LPA was a group of approximately eight to ten first lieutenants in our squadron. They had formed the LPA shortly after the lieutenant I was flying with that day arrived in the squadron soon after he had returned to Hawaii from Vietnam.

The rationale for its creation, I came to understand, was that the lieutenants in the squadron had not gotten the respect they thought they were entitled to. They felt that the captains and majors looked down their noses at them, which was the perception espoused by the officer I was flying with that day. He felt that they collectively, and especially him, were just as competent aviators as these old men who were trying to tell them how to fly the aircraft. He had formed the organization to call attention to their plight.

So far today, his substandard performance had demonstrated to me that this young officer had a long way to go to be a competent instrument-qualified aviator.

After he finally copied the frequency, heading, and altitude changes the center had given him, he acknowledged the call to Honolulu Center, which had already moved on to other aircraft, indicated by the ending phrase *good day*. Hearing him call again, Honolulu Center asked if Pineapple 11 was again experiencing communication problems, or did he have a request?

The lieutenant responded to the center telling them that we had no problem. The center's immediate response was "Pineapple 11, again, I say switch to K-Bay GCA on frequency 290.20 now. Again, good day."

The lieutenant put the K-Bay GCA frequency in the radio and switched to it. He then looked back at the flight instruments and recognized he had drifted 30 degrees off heading and had not made the descent from 4,000 feet to 3,000 feet as directed by the center several minutes ago. He started an immediate 2,000-foot-per-minute descent trying to get back to the assigned altitude. He attempted to get his descent under control and simultaneously tried to bank the aircraft back toward the heading he had been given. He then called K-Bay GCA, saying, "This is Pineapple 11 descending to 3,000 feet heading 340 degrees, over."

K-Bay GCA responded by saying, "We have been calling you for the last three minutes. Are you having communication difficulties? If so, squawk 7700 [lost com squawk] and proceed visually to the airport."

UNLIKE NO OTHER

I could hear and see that the lieutenant was now becoming more frustrated under his hood. I could also see that he was having some problems maintaining his directional control and staying on altitude, indicating that he was potentially having some problems with vertigo.

He responded to GCA saying, "Pineapple 11 reads you loud and clear now. We would like to continue with the GCA."

"Roger, Pineapple 11, we have radar contact, turn right for sequencing to a heading of 090 degrees and continue descent to 3,000 feet," the GCA controller replied.

The GCA controller proceeded to vector the lieutenant around in a 360-degree circle to allow him to reach the 3,000-foot altitude necessary to intercept the GCA glide slope. The lieutenant flew an okay GCA but forgot the landing checklist until the GCA controller asked him to confirm the "wheels were down," at which time, he asked me to perform the landing checklist, which I did as soon as asked. At 100 feet AGL and over the landing threshold, I took control of the aircraft from the lieutenant, switched to tower frequency, and made the landing on the runway. After refueling the aircraft, we taxied back to the flight line, and parked.

After we shut down the aircraft, I told the lieutenant to meet me in the ready room so we could debrief the check flight. He looked at me, smiling, and said, "I hope it will not take too long. The LPA is meeting at the O club at 1630 hours, and I don't want to be late."

Looking back at him, as we climbed out of the aircraft, I said again, "I will meet you in the ready room for our debrief." I postflighted the bird and went into maintenance control to write up a couple of minor discrepancies on YH-11, then headed for the ready room. Looking at my watch, I saw it was 1615 hours as I entered the ready room. I saw the lieutenant talking to several other lieutenants and motioned for him to come over to the table in the far corner of the room, out of earshot of the rest of the officers.

He saw me pointing to the rear table and said something to the others and headed my way. I took a seat and waited for him to be seated. The first thing I did, before saying a word, was to hand him the pilot's instrument checklist, which was part of the NATOPS manual, which he had not used during that day's check flight.

He looked at the manual and said, "I guess, Captain, you think I should have used this for today's instrument flight, right?"

You are damn right you should have used it. It's the bible for how to ensure that you have all the instrumentation and radios set and a myriad of other procedures necessary for a safe and successful IFR flight.

Looking at him, I asked, "Why did you not use the checklist?"

After a minute or two of silence, he responded, "It was not necessary because the weather was *cavu* [aviation term for 'ceiling and visibility unlimited'], and this was just a check flight, not the real thing, not actual IFR conditions."

I could not believe my ears. The lieutenant had not taken this check ride seriously; I now believed that he looked at it as a flight as one where he did not really have to prove his ability to fly in actual instrument conditions. It was just another inconvenient formality even though I told him at the start of the briefing that this was an evaluation of his ability to fly in actual instrument conditions. I guess he did not believe me.

He now looked at his watch and started to rise, saying he needed to get to the O club. I responded to him by saying, "You're not going anywhere until we are finished with the debrief of your instrument-check flight, Lieutenant. Is that clear?" Looking back at me, he saw a look on my face that I believe he knew I meant business. So he sat back down in his seat.

I reviewed the entire instrument-check flight, in great detail with the lieutenant, who appeared to be disinterested in my critique of his performance. It was not until I got to the end of my critique where I told him his performance on today's instrument flight was unsatisfactory. I was going to give him a down. I was going to recommend to the operations officer that he was not to fly as an aircraft commander until he completed remedial training and successfully passed a subsequent instrument-check flight.

Hearing this news, the lieutenant's face became very red. He clenched his fists and looked like he wanted to try to punch me. He said, "I completely disagree with your evaluation of my performance today. I may have made a couple of mistakes, but my performance was far from unsatisfactory. You senior officers are just out to make us lieutenants look bad." He then got up from his chair and departed the ready room.

It took me an hour to write up the lieutenant's instrument-check flight. I recommended that he undergo a minimum of ten hours of remedial instrument flight training with instructor pilots before being given the opportunity to take another instrument check. Contained in my write up was my belief that without significant additional instrument training, he should not be allowed to fly as an aircraft commander until he satisfactorily demonstrated the abilities to fly in actual instrument conditions. I said in my final line of the evaluation that the lieutenant had exhibited an attitude of superiority and belligerence, and if this attitude was allowed to continue, then he will prove to be a liability to the squadron in the future.

I took the write-up to the operations officer who read it in great detail. As he completed his review, I said that "maybe the lieutenant and I may have a personality conflict. I think it would be a good idea if I were not scheduled to fly with him for any of his remedial flights or another check ride. In fact, I don't want to ever fly with this individual again."

The major looked back down at the write-up and said, "I agree with your write-up and assessment of this officer. Thank you for giving him an honest assessment and for bringing it to my attention, Captain."

The following day, the lieutenant pleaded his case to the operations officer, who rejected it saying the he concurred with my evaluation of his performance based on my write-up and a call to the controller who handled the flight at Honolulu Center.

The LPA was at first irate, especially with me, but I really did not care what they thought. The sneers, lack of conversation, and dirty looks continued for some time. Doing some additional research about the background of this aviator, I found out that the aviator in question had had troubles in flight school and almost washed out of the flight program. He also had additional attitude problems and struggled to complete the training syllabus at MHTG-30 (helicopter training squadron for initial qualification of copilots) before being assigned to this squadron. How he became an aircraft commander shortly after he reached the five hundred hours minimum flight-time criteria to qualify for the designation was amazing to me. I could not believe how he managed to fool the senior officers in the squadron and get the designation. This aviator, in my opinion, was a significant liability to the squadron as an aircraft commander. I only hoped he would not hurt or kill people because of his superior, belligerent, and condescending attitude, but only time would tell.

*****

On Monday, February 27, 1972, I got a telephone call from the MAG-24 adjutant telling me that I, along with several other Marines, were to receive some awards at an upcoming award ceremony the following week. The ceremony was scheduled for March 1, 1972, which was also the thirtieth anniversary of the inception of MAG-24.

Colonel Richard Carey was the current commander of the composite fixed-wing and helicopter air group MAG-24. He was an F-4 pilot who had indicated to the adjutant that this anniversary and awards ceremony was a major event for the air group and that all the participants needed to look sharp for the event.

Major General A. H. Adams was going to be presenting the awards that day. He was the deputy commander of the Fleet Marine Forces Pacific.

I had not been told what award I might be receiving, but I had been told unofficially before I departed Vietnam the year before that I had been nominated for a couple of awards based on my participation in the Lam Son 719 operation. I often wondered what became of the recommendations.

I showed up, along with my wife, for the anniversary celebration and awards ceremony on March 1, 1972, ahead of time so I could ensure that my wife got a good seat. I then reported to the MAG-24 adjutant, a major, who was handling the awards ceremony. He had a clipboard in his hand and instructed all the Marines who were going to be recognized as to what order we should line up so we could march on to the field when the awards part of the ceremony was going to take place.

People who receive awards are normally positioned in a line based on the highest award being presented first, then descending to the next highest, and so on. If multiple awards of the same level are awarded, then you are positioned by rank.

I was surprised to be third in line of six participants, and even more surprised to see two people I had not seen since leaving Vietnam last year standing ahead of me. Captain C. T. Crews was first in line; he had provided Cobra gunship support to our operations in Laos. He was followed by Major Mike Wasko, our former operations officer in Vietnam. I was next in line, followed by three more awardees.

The three of us talked for a couple of minutes before the anniversary celebration started. Then the band started to play, and we were directed back to our positions. The anniversary celebration entailed the reading of the history of MAG-24 since its inception and culminated with its current activities. This was followed by remarks from Major General A. H. Adams and Colonel Richard Carey, the MAG CO.

After the remarks were concluded, the commander of troops called for the persons to be recognized to come forward. We marched onto the field and came to a stop in front of the troops in formation. Major General Adams, Colonel Carey, and the MAG-24 Sergeant Major rose from their seats and came forward to a position where the general was standing directly in front of Captain Crews. The adjutant announced the award of the Silver Star Medal to Captain C. T. Crews for action in Laos supporting a flight of CH-53s on February 23, 1971.

As I listened to the citation, I recognized the date; it was forever ingrained in my mind. Captain Crews had been the one who led our Cobra escorts for the morning and early afternoon part of the Mission 52 operation into Laos during Operation Lam Son 719 that day. I had released his flight of Cobras to go back to Marble Mountain in mid-afternoon because his four AH-1Gs had lost their capacity to provide armed escort for the mission that would follow.

He and his Cobras had not been involved in the early evening part of our mission where Major Wasko's bird was shot down. The Army Cobras had that part of the mission. I was happy for him getting the Silver Star because his work that day deserved the award. I hoped the other members of his flight were also going to be recognized.

Major General Adams had finished pinning the Silver Star onto Captain Crews' uniform and had moved on to Major Wasko's position in the line when I came back to the present time. The adjutant again came up on the loudspeaker and announced the award of the Distinguished Flying Cross Medal to Major M. J. Wasko Jr. for action in Laos during the period January through March 1971. He went on to list the actions that justified the award. I watched out of the corner of my eye as the general pinned the DFC on Major Wasko's uniform.

General Adams now moved to a position in front of me. The adjutant again came up on the loudspeaker and announced the award of the Distinguished Flying Cross Medal to Captain R. F. Wemheuer for service as set forth in the following citation:

> For heroism and extraordinary achievement in aerial flight while serving as a pilot with Marine Heavy Helicopter Squadron 463, Marine Aircraft Group Sixteen, First Marine Aircraft Wing in connection with combat operations against the enemy in the Republic of Vietnam. On February 23, 1971 while participating in Operation Lam Son 719, Captain Wemheuer launched as section leader of the second section in a flight of four CH-53 transport helicopters assigned the emergency mission of extracting field artillery pieces and heavy equipment from Fire Support Base Hotel II, deep in enemy-controlled territory, where Army of the Republic of Vietnam units occupying the base had come under heavy pressure and intense fire from a large North Vietnamese Army force surrounding their

position, and the base rapidly became untenable. Arriving over the beleaguered position, he found that deteriorating weather conditions, smoke, haze, and antiaircraft and mortar sites in the area would endanger each approach he made to the extraction zone. Undaunted by the extremely heavy volume of hostile fire directed at his aircraft, Captain Wemheuer resolutely braved the North Vietnamese fire on three separate occasions as he skillfully maneuvered into the hazardous area, safely extracted two 155mm and one 105mm-artillery pieces, and delivered them to Fire Support Base Delta I. When the flight leader's transport was downed by hostile fire and forced to land in one of the gun pits on the base, Captain Wemheuer completely disregarded his own safety as he unhesitatingly maneuvered to a hover above the downed crew and fearlessly remained in his precarious position while an extraction ladder was lowered and three of the crewmen attached themselves to the ladder. With exceptional skill, he then lifted out of the zone and departed the dangerous area.

Captain Wemheuer's courage, superior airmanship, and unwavering devotion to duty in the face of great personal danger were in keeping with the highest traditions of the Marine Corps and of the United States Naval Service.

General Adams pinned the DFC on my chest and shook my hand, saying, "Good job, Captain," then turned and moved down to the next recipient as the awards presentation continued.

Standing next to Major Wasko, I could only think back to what my citation did not say. It had neglected to deal with the fact that I was the flight leader for the vast majority of the mission that day. It failed to recognize that, we, as a flight of three aircraft, had made six additional extraction attempts to get the remaining 105mm-artillery pieces out of Hotel II but were driven out by ever-increasing enemy fire before Major Wasko returned to take over the flight. It failed to recognize that our crew had all thought we had the entire crew of the down aircraft on our rescue ladder that evening. It failed to deal with the fact that I had warned the flight leader upon his return to the mission that unless major suppression of the enemy fire was accomplished, we would have a distinct likelihood of losing an aircraft to enemy fire.

I wondered what had happened to the write-up I had unofficially been told about before I left Vietnam, which had recommended this action for a Silver Star Award. Scuttlebutt also circulated that my award was being considered for upgrade at the First MAW review board. It appeared the scuttlebutt was very wrong. I had no idea why the original submission was changed.

Awards boards at that time were generally made up of fixed-wing pilots. They, I had observed, tended to look down their noses at helicopter pilots as second-class aviators. Maybe one of the F-4 pilots on the First MAW or FMFPAC review boards thought transport helicopters were just like flying C-130 transports and no one flying them ever did anything worthy of a Silver Star, in their opinion. "Oh, but" they surely believed that flying and dropping bombs at two thousand or three thousand feet should get a DFC for an F-4 pilot, which I had seen several of them awarded.

The change could also have been made by the intervention of my previous CO who had thought I had jeopardized his career that day by taking unnecessary chances in order to rescue our downed pilots and flight crews with one of "his aircraft" that day. He had gone back to DC where he still had a lot of influence. I just had no idea why or who made the downgrade.

Looking down at the DFC on my chest, I thought, *I know what I did on February 23, 1971. The people I saved that day know what I did and appreciate it, so don't sweat it. It is, what it is—nothing more or nothing less. I only hope that my crew members and other members of the flight would receive the recognition they all deserved for their work on that memorable day.* My last thought before I heard the command to do a right face and start to march off the parade field was *What hypocrisy!*

I returned to my duties at K-Bay after the short reception my wife and I attended. I looked around for Major Wasko, but I guess he had departed the area right after the ceremony, so I was unable to find him, so the questions I wanted to ask him went unanswered.

A couple of weeks later, Colonel Carey, the MAG-24 CO, was selected for promotion to brigadier general. He subsequently turned over command of MAG-24 to Colonel William G. Crocker. As I recall, after the change-of-command ceremony, Colonel Crocker awarded the Silver Star Medal to Major M. J. Wasko Jr. for action in Laos on February 23, 1971. The medal was in recognition of his heroism and complete disregard for his own safety as he rescued Lieutenant Colonel Charles Pitman from a downed aircraft in Laos. Colonel Crocker also awarded a Gold Star in lieu of the second Distinguished Flying Cross to me. The DFC was again for action during Operation Lam Son 719 in Laos. This award was a compilation of a number of flights I made into Laos from January through March 1971.

At this awards presentation, my wife said she was proud of me; that was all that counted in my mind.

*****

As the assistant maintenance officer for the squadron, I got to fly most of the post-maintenance inspection flights because of the amount of experience I had in flying the machine. I loved the big, heavy but sleek and maneuverable bird. It could do loops and barrel rolls where no other helicopter of the period could. The maneuvers were not authorized but were sometimes performed in a combat-training scenario far from any ground observation.

During the spring and summer of 1972, while I was enjoying my flying assignment in Hawaii, events in Vietnam were still playing out. The final withdrawal of the last Marine units from Vietnam was contingent on negotiations being conducted at the Paris Peace Accords meetings in France. The major part of these negotiations revolved around the release of American and Allied prisoners of war (POW) held by the Communists as well as clearing the mines that the United States had planted in North Vietnam's harbors, rivers, and waterways. Negotiations surrounding the removal of these mines became a lynchpin in the determination as to whether or not to release the POWs and the Marines' eventual withdrawal.

For anyone following world events and the news, it was apparent that the United States would have to find a way to remove, explode, or otherwise neutralize the mines that had been planted in North Vietnamese harbors, rivers, and waterways in order to win the release of our POWs currently held in the North.

I remembered back to a time, several years ago, when I took a training class on the CH-53, which included some Navy helicopter pilots from the East Coast. We had an opportunity to talk to them informally. I found out from them that they had just received modified CH-53As that had been specially modified to pull mine-sweeping apparatuses behind the helicopter to cut loose moored mines. I suspected these folks would be pressed into service to get the prisoners released if the negotiations were successful. I also was made aware that the CH-53D had mine-sweeping capabilities that the Marine Corps had never utilized. So being called on to deploy our squadron, to perform the minesweeping mission came as no great surprise to me.

On the second of June 1972, Lieutenant Colonel Ledbetter relinquished command of the Squadron to Major John van Nortwick III. I believe van Nortwick was Ledbetter's executive officer prior to the change of command, but I was not sure since things like that were far above my paygrade at the time. I had never met or heard of van Nortwick prior to coming to Hawaii. The basic routine and tempo of operations in the squadron did not change much by changing commanding officers. I saw no real differences until the squadron received a top secret (TS) message from FMFPAC Headquarters located across the island.

*****

The TS message received in late November 1972 directed us to pack up our gear and prepare to deploy overseas in four days. We were told by our command that we would deploy aboard an aircraft carrier whose name was classified.

We again had eighteen CH-53D aircraft assigned to our squadron after it returned from Vietnam with the replacement of the two birds that were destroyed in Vietnam. These aircraft were manufactured with hard points specifically designed for attaching equipment that could be used for airborne mine countermeasures equipment. That made these aircraft capable of performing this specialized airborne mine countermeasures mission. Marine Corps CH-53As were not so equipped. We had only a total of sixteen aircraft available to deploy, since one was currently at NAS North Island undergoing periodic rework and the other was involved in a crash on the island and was being repaired.

Because our squadron and HMH-462 in Okinawa had the most CH-53D aircraft available to support the minesweeping mission, it was not difficult to guess where we were eventually heading. That had to be *North Vietnam* doing a mission none of us ever expected to perform.

*****

Our maintenance department worked very hard to get all the aircraft up for the flight to the carrier, making sure that all the blade and pylon folding systems were operational. These systems were not normally exercised on a regular basis, so many problems were encountered when they were put to the test. Because of the importance of the mission, supply shortages immediately disappeared, along with back-ordered parts we needed were air-shipped to us overnight.

Two days before we were to deploy, ground-support equipment as well as internal fuel tanks for all our aircraft were loaded on flatbeds and disappeared. We assumed it was being taken to the USS *Inchon* (LPH-12), which just happen to be in port at Pearl Harbor. It was to sail the next day for destinations unknown according to the ship's crew members. It was all supposed to be a hush-hush operation.

Our deployment-flight schedule was published early in the afternoon the day before our departure. It showed the CO leading the first wave of eight CH-53s taking off at 1000 hours, followed at 1300 hours by the next six birds. The last two birds would depart at 1430 hours for the ship.

As one of the Marines in the squadron with the most CH-53 flying experience and a post-maintenance test pilot, I was directed by the CO to fly one of the last two birds going to the ship. Captain Ron Corner, the safety officer, another pilot with lots of experience, and I would bring the last two aircraft, the ones with the most problems, to the carrier. After the schedule was published, the CO sent most of the pilots and aircrews home to get ready for the next day's departure. While the remainder of the squadron's personnel continued to work on the aircraft and to load cargo for the deployment, I, however, stayed behind to fly a test hop on one of our aircraft that had engine problems on the previous flight.

The next morning, my wife drove me to the base since we were living in a rented town house in Kailua outside the base. I said goodbye to my wife for the second time, again heading for what I was sure was going to be North Vietnam. I told her not to worry, and I would be back; I then took my gear inside maintenance control.

*****

I watched as the first group of aircraft were signed off by their crew chiefs, followed by the arrival of the first group of pilots starting with the CO. He looked at me and said, "I did not expect to see you here this early, Captain."

"I was just making sure all our aircraft are ready for the deployment, sir," I responded.

He said nothing more as he finished looking at the yellow sheet book, signed for the aircraft, and headed for his bird.

I watched as the first eight aircraft turned up, taxied, and took off for the carrier, heading east out over the water in an attempt to keep their departure secret. I could not believe that they thought our departure for the carrier was secret because the Honolulu newspaper that morning had a full-color picture of a CH-53D with the headline: HMH-463 Departs Oahu.

The location of the carrier had been kept a secret until this morning's operational briefing. It was currently located north of Oahu about seventy-five miles from any landmass.

The second wave of pilots arrived at maintenance control at about 1215 hours in order to meet their 1300-hour departure for the boat. This wave was led by Major Smith, the squadron's executive officer. I had never met or heard of him until I arrived in Hawaii. He and the CO must have been East Coast Marine aviators, I surmised.

I watched as the second wave of six aircraft turned up, taxied, and took off for the carrier, again heading east out over the water, still attempting to keep their departure secret.

We had been successful launching fourteen of our sixteen aircraft and having none of them return to the air station. Captain Corner and I went to the ready room and completed our NATOPS briefing with our two copilots. We then headed for maintenance control and signed for our aircraft. We loaded the last of our squadron personnel onto our two aircraft, started them, taxied, and took off. Captain Corner led our flight because he was senior to me and because his last name started with *C* and mine started with *W*.

I mused, remembering the old proverb, *Seniority among captains is like virginity among whores,* as the old saying went.

We launched at the designated time with Captain Corner electing to go west instead of east as the other two flights had done. We both knew the proverbial "the cat was out of the bag" regarding secrecy of our departure from the island, so we both thought *What the hell?*

Captain Corner took us around the south part of the island, then turned west initially, then northwest past Diamond Head. He called and got permission to fly under Hickam AFB/Honolulu International Airport approach corridor along the Waikiki Beach past the entrance of Pearl Harbor at about a hundred feet AGL. We flew in a nice tight formation about a quarter of a mile off the beach giving the beachgoers a little show.

We cleared the north end of Oahu and then passed the island of Kauai. By this time, we had locked on to the USS *Inchon*'s TACAN signal and headed further north to intercept the carrier, which was still twenty-five miles away.

Captain Corner contacted the ship at about twenty miles out and told them we were inbound. The ship responded that they had been waiting on our arrival and were going to change course heading west, and we had a green deck for landing upon arrival.

Arriving at the *Inchon*, Captain Corner called for an overhead break for our two aircraft. This maneuver provides separation between us so we could land on the ship individually.

The air boss of the carrier came up on the radio, identified himself, then he cleared us for the break. He went on to say, "The ship is pitching five to ten degrees and rolling between ten and twenty degrees.

This sea condition was created by a very large hurricane in the Pacific Ocean called a typhoon.

The air boss continued to tell us over the radio, "Use caution when landing, follow the LSE signals closely. Once on the deck, you will immediately be chained down. You will fold your blades immediately, and both the aircraft will remain on their spots until we reach calmer waters. These are unusual conditions, so stay alert."

We both acknowledged the air boss' directions as we approached flying up the starboard side of the aircraft carrier. As we flew past the ship, I looked at the *Inchon*'s flight deck and saw all fourteen of our squadron's aircraft had their rotor blades and pylons folded and were positioned in two areas of the ship. Three of our birds were on the starboard side (right) of the ship forward of the island, and the remainder were arranged in a herringbone at the stern. Captain Corner called the break, and we then executed the standard carrier-break maneuver. I held my heading a full minute longer than normal in order to give Captain Corner time to land on the pitching and rolling deck before I came aboard.

Captain Corner and I were the only two aircraft commanders who were currently carrier-qualified, so it was a good thing that the other fourteen aircraft had come aboard when the sea was a hell of a lot calmer.

It should be noted that the CO had authorized each of the unqualified aircraft commanders a special authorization to make the single shipboard landing without being currently qualified. This was done to expedite the departure for the now critical mission. It was also necessary because there were no ships available prior to our departure to carrier qualify our pilots before we departed K-Bay.

After I finally completed my break maneuver, now on the downwind leg of my approach, I caught several glimpses of Captain Corner maneuvering his aircraft over spot 3 on the deck. As we completed the landing checklist, our aircraft was cleared by the air boss for a landing on spot 5 next to the island.

Acknowledging his instructions, I responded to the air boss, "Cleared to land spot 5, three down, and locked, twenty souls on board." I then turned off the 180-degree position to make my approach to the flight deck. As I turned, I saw green water coming over the bow of the carrier. Knowing that the flight deck of the *Inchon* was approximately 54 feet above the water, I knew the landing was going to be challenging.

About 200 yards out from the ship, I saw my designated landing-signal enlisted (LSE) director. These Navy enlisted men were experts in getting pilots onto the deck regardless of weather conditions, provided you followed their directions exactly.

At this point, I asked the copilot to give me full power, which he did by advancing the overhead speed-control levers to the full forward position. We approached about a hundred feet from the flight deck in the standard forty-five-degree-angle approach. I purposely made my approach a little high. The LSE recognized what I was doing and nodded as a signal that he concurred with my approach being higher than normal. As we crossed the side of the ship, I followed his directions as rapidly and smoothly as possible. He maneuvered me over spot 5, then worked to keep me steady until the ship's pitching and rolls were at almost the midpoint of its gyrations, then he signaled me to set the aircraft down on the deck as it was dropping down. We landed on the deck a little hard but firmly, just a fraction of a second before the ship's deck started to pitch up again. Immediately, the Navy deck hands had chains attached to the aircraft, and I was signaled to shut down. I breathed a little easier being safely tied down to the deck of the ship as it moved up, down, and sideways.

The LSE wanted the aircraft shut down ASAP, so I executed the shutdown checklist from memory, starting the APP, then shutting down both engines, and applying the rotor break. With the blades stopped, I finally looked at my copilot sitting across from me. He had been strangely quiet ever since we had landed.

To my surprise, he was sitting in his seat, barfing in his helmet bag. Seasick already. I suggested to him that he exit the aircraft, and he might feel better, which he quickly did.

During this time, we also off-loaded the passengers and their personal gear from our aircraft. Since the deck was dangerous for them to be on, they were quickly ushered inside the island, then directed to our squadron spaces below deck. I reviewed the shutdown checklist to make sure I had completed all the steps as the exit process was taking place.

The crew chief said the LSE wanted to get the bird folded up as soon as we could since we were going to be sailing into the more severe part of the storm soon. The crew chief and I used the checklist to fold the rotor blades and the pylon while Navy deck crews assisted us by installing the blade and pylon restraints necessary for securing them in severe winds and pitching seas. As they worked to secure the aircraft for bad weather, I continued to see green water coming occasionally over the bow of the *Inchon* accompanied by rolls of fifteen to twenty-five degrees.

I thought, *This could be a rough night.*

Once all these activities were completed, I exited the aircraft, picked up my personal gear, and went into the hatch (door) on the side of the island. Having been deployed on this type of ship on my first trip to Vietnam with this same squadron five years earlier, I knew where the squadron spaces were located, so I went down to the ready room straight away.

As I entered the ready room, no one was there. I had expected to find at least a couple of squadron mates or the duty officer, at least.

I was shocked to find no one; not even the duty officer was present. I looked around and found the stack of paperwork that needed to be completed for our flight out to the ship that day. Looking at the big schedule board in the front of the room, I saw a note as to the location of the duty officer if I needed him. After completing the paperwork and having seen no one come to the ready room, I went looking for the maintenance chief since I was concerned about our aircraft on the flight deck.

Heading to the area where maintenance control had been located on my previous crews, I found the maintenance control chief, a gunnery sergeant who was waiting there for me. I told him, as I filled out the flight time and other items on my yellow sheet, that I had no new discrepancies to write up. After completing the yellow sheet, I then asked him if he had checked the security of our aircraft yet. He said he had just come back from checking all of them, including mine and Captain Corner's aircraft. Everything looked secure, and only one blade tiedown had come loose so far, but it had been caught before any damage could occur to the blade it had broken loose from.

The gunny looks a little green around the gills to me, so I thought, *I better find out if he is all right.*

"You all right, Gunny?" I asked.

He responded, "Sir, I am okay."

Looking at him again, I said again, "Are you sure you are okay, Gunny?"

He again replied, "Sir, I am fine just a little seasick, and nothing I can't handle. Thank you for your concern."

Hearing his reply, I returned to the ready room.

Back in the ready room, I found another large whiteboard where the names of our squadron officers along with their room assignments were posted. Finding my name and room number, I gathered up my gear heading for the room I was assigned.

Entering the room, I saw my bunk mate was Captain Ron Corner, who was lying in his *rack*. Stepping further inside the room, I found he had just finished barfing in our government-issued wastebasket.

Seeing the results of his action, then smelling it, I knew that we needed a quick fix to the smelly problem, so I took action. First, I put my gear on my bunk, then I took the trash can out to the head (ship's toilet) to clean it. While cleaning the trash can, I could feel the ship becoming even more unstable because of the increase in the severity of the pitching and rolling motions. I returned the clean trash can to the room, then looked at my wristwatch, discovering that it was dinnertime, so I made my way to the wardroom or officers' mess for dinner.

Arriving at the wardroom, I expected to see it full of Marines and naval officers. To my surprise, I saw only four other officers in the mess. All the other assembled officers were naval officers. It appeared that the severe motions of the ship had made, not only my squadron mates sick, but had affected a significant number of the ship's officers as well.

Normally, there are about forty to forty-five members of the mess at the evening meal, including embarked Marine officers, but not tonight, I mused.

At the appointed time, we five officers moved to the table to have what turned out to be a very interesting meal.

The Filipino steward brought out a large bowl of chicken noodle soup and placed it in the center of the long table where we were all standing behind our seats waiting to be seated after the chaplain's blessing.

The officers' mess table was constructed of stainless steel, with a slightly curved lip that ran the length of the table on both sides. It was welded to the deck and extended lengthwise across the beam of the ship. This positioning created a condition where the rolling action of the ship had the least impact on the items placed on the table. The standard tablecloths that normally covered the stainless-steel table had been removed because they were already soiled from earlier food spills. These spills were from bowls containing food that had been placed on the table in preparation for this evening's meal.

One of the five officers at the table that evening was the chaplain, who normally conducted a short blessing before the officers partook of their meal. As he launched into his prayer, the large china bowl with our chicken noodle soup in it that was sitting in the middle of the table started to slide down the table as the ship rolled to the port side. Everyone at the table, except the chaplain who had closed his eyes, watched the china bowl moving down the table. The officer sitting down toward the port end of the table was hesitant to take action as the bowl slid in front of him, not wanting to interrupt the chaplain's blessing, as the bowl headed for the end of the table. At the last second and just before it would have gone off the table, the ship rolled back the other direction, and our dinner was saved for the moment. The china bowl once again started to slide back the other way it came and went past all of us who were watching with our mouths hanging open, as the chaplain continued his blessing. No one wanted to interrupt the blessing as our dinner returned to a position in front of us, then continued its slide toward the other end of the table. Again, at just the last second, the ship rolled back in the other direction, and our dinner was again rescued from being deposited on the deck of the ship. The bowl again reversed direction and headed back to the middle. As it passed in front of the chaplain, he concluded his blessing, opening his eyes, and grabbing the china bowl as it slid in front of him. Then saying, "Gentlemen, I believe it's time to break bread," as he reached out and stopped the travel of our dinner in front of him. At that point, the four of us were still standing there with our mouths open in *awe* as to what had just taken place.

Perhaps divine intervention has saved our meal, I thought.

We must have looked like the *Keystone Cops* to the Filipino stewards, who had watched the entire show. They, like us, had not wanted to interrupt the blessing, having just arrived inside the mess from the kitchen with individual serving bowls for our soup, a large ladle to serve it, and a large plate of toasted cheese sandwiches, which was the only thing they could cook in the turbulent seas we were experiencing.

After the completion of our china-bowl-dinner-slide demonstration, the head Filipino steward entered the mess and apologized for the meal, saying it was the best he could do under the circumstances. We all told him we understood and were happy with what he and his crew were able to provide for us. We all dived into our soup and sandwich meals with great gusto.

After dinner, they generally showed a movie in the wardroom, but that night's movie was cancelled because the movie projector would not stay upright on the table because of the rolling and pitching movements of the ship. With no movie to watch, I headed back to the ready room and again found it empty. While I was sitting in the empty ready room reading some of the ship's periodicals, it appeared to me that the seas were getting a little rougher, so I headed up to check on the security of our aircraft.

My first stop was to maintenance control, which was also empty, as I had expected it to be. No one could be expected to perform maintenance in these conditions. My next stop was to go up to the "crow's nest," as the air boss called it, where I could look down on the aircraft on the flight deck without going outside into the weather.

Looking out at the windswept flight deck, I could see my bird parked where I had landed it and the ramp section of Captain Corner's aircraft, along with the first two aircraft that we stacked toward the stern of the ship. When the rain would let up a little, I could see green water was still occasionally coming over the bow. Since I was not able to see much from the crow's nest, I went back down to the area where the LSEs and green shirts (Navy aircraft handlers) were stationed during flight operations. I entered the room through the hatch and found a senior chief petty officer sitting next to a large coffeepot smoking a pipe.

He waved me inside and asked, "Captain, can I help you?"

Responding, I said, "Chief, I need to check on our aircraft's security," as I move toward the hatch going out on the flight deck.

He responded by saying, "Captain, hold on there. No need to go out there and get yourself all wet. Your squadron's flight-line gunny and I just returned from a walk around and found everything secure. I suggest you grab a cup from the ones on the wall and join me in a cup of good old Navy coffee."

Looking at the chief for a few seconds, I said, "Thank you, Chief. I believe I will accept your invitation to join you."

The coffee, as the chief had promised, was good, hot, and strong. I spent a good portion of the night talking with the senior chief, checking the security of our aircraft with him, and drinking coffee. As the night wore on, the storm became less intense and diminished as we sailed out of its reach en route to the Philippines and not North Vietnam as I had originally thought. Then I headed for my rack. It was about 0300 hours.

*****

At about 0600 hours, I was awakened by the duty officer saying that the CO wanted to see me in the ready room ASAP. Pulling on my flight suit I wore yesterday and a pair of boots, I dutifully followed the duty officer to the ready room. While making our way there, I noticed that the ship's motions of rocking and rolling had decrease to an almost imperceptible level.

Amazing what a few hours of sailing time can make in the sea state, I thought.

The CO was sitting in a chair up front, saw me, then motioned to me to come forward. The major looked directly at me with fire in his eyes, he asked, "Captain, how did you get a top secret sensitive clearance?"

Still half asleep, I was caught off guard by his question, thinking, *What does my clearance level have to do with our deployment?*

I recovered my composure and started to answer his question, but he stopped me waving his hand, indicating he did not want to hear my explanation. The CO continued by saying, "You and the captain of the USS *Inchon* are the only two people on this entire ship who have a high-enough clearance to read the naval messages that have been sent to our squadron and this ship."

He slammed his fist down on the arm of the chair he was sitting in while shouting. "How in the hell can that have happened?" he barked, more to himself than to me.

He was obviously very pissed off, at whom, I was not quite sure.

Calming down a little, he then said, "Captain, take your ID card and go to the communication center. You will be granted access to the comm center, then review the top secret, sensitive message traffic for our squadron, then report the content of these messages back to me."

"Yes, sir," I responded, as I turned around heading out of the ready room for the comm center.

How could they let this happen? A lowly captain is the only Marine on this ship who can read the message traffic. Someone overclassified this operation, or someone in the squadron screwed up. The CO will not look good for not paying attention to details like this. It is what it is, I mused.

Arriving at the message center, I showed my ID card and was granted access to the comm center and then handed a folder of top secret, sensitive messages. I looked at the bulk of these messages that were sent to the squadron, and they were requests for information regarding the status of our aircraft, supply shortages, and normal operational stuff a squadron would do in an unclassified manner under normal circumstances. But this was no normal circumstance since we were part of the potential solution for getting our prisoners of war released from North Vietnam.

I wrote notes to myself regarding the information that was requested and took my notes and went back to see the CO in his small office.

After entering his office, I explained what was contained in each of the messages that I had reviewed. He listened to my description of the contents, saying nothing. I continued to talk suggesting that he, as the CO, had two alternatives in order to answer the higher headquarters' messages. First, he could have me go to the various department heads and collect the information to be sent back to FMFPAC Headquarters and put together the necessary messages since I was the only one of his people who could release the top secret, sensitive messages. Or second, he could have the squadron's department heads gather the information and put together the messages for him to hand carry for release by the ship's captain. These were his only two choices that I could come up with to solve the problem.

His face became very red showing signs of great anger as he stood up, saying, "I want to talk to the comm officer myself. These people should have told me this before we departed K-Bay. There is no excuse for this morass. Captain, I don't like either of your proposed alternatives," as he walked out of his office area.

I was left standing there in his office, thinking. *The only person he should be upset with is himself. It is his responsibility to ensure that communications protocols are in place to allow easy and smooth transition from a shore-based operation to a shipboard one. He and his senior staff knew this mission was going to be top secret but failed to ensure his people had adequate clearance to operate in our current ultra-high-security environment. Excuses are like assholes. Everyone has one, and prior planning prevents piss-poor performance,* I mused.

*****

Since I had not been on deck since the storm had moved on, I headed for the flight deck to check the security and status of our birds. Passing through maintenance-control spaces, I found the maintenance-control chief who said he had been looking for me. He briefed me on the damages that had occurred because of the high winds and heavy seas. We had suffered damage to several main rotor blades that had broken loose from their blade restraints. Most of the damage was superficial and could be repaired without having to replace the rotor blade completely, which would require blade tracking and a test hop.

About an hour later, the duty officer was again sent to find me. He found me on the flight deck with the maintenance crew that was repairing the blade damage, saying, "The CO wants to see you right away in the ready room."

I accompanied him back to the ready room where the CO sat up in the front of the room in his usual chair. He saw me enter and waved me over. Speaking in a very low voice, he told me that he had talked to the comm officer about the situation and that the two options that I presented to him earlier were in fact the only alternatives currently available until we reached the Philippines, where he could get the classification problem assessed and corrected.

The CO then said to me, "Captain, I want you to go to the various department heads and collect the information to be sent back to

FMFPAC Headquarters, put together the necessary messages, then see that they have been released as top secret, sensitive messages."

"Yes, sir, is there anything else?" was my immediate response.

"No, that will be all, Captain," he said while looking away from me.

As I left the ready room, a big smile broke out on my face as I considered the instructions that the CO had just given me. I would have liked to have said, "I told you so," but that would not have helped the situation. However, I felt totally vindicated, nevertheless.

Learning later that the comm officer, who was a lieutenant commander (same rank as the CO), had told the CO the same thing I had said to him earlier. That, in his opinion, the CO should use his Marine captain with the clearance to put together the necessary messages since the captain is the only one of his Marines who could release the top secret sensitive messages. The lieutenant commander also indicated that this was the only way he (the CO) could avoid the embarrassment of having to take routine messages to the ship's commanding officer for release (Navy captain is equivalent in rank to Marine colonel).

It took the USS *Inchon* six days to sail to the Philippines, during which time I did the message drafting and released them. This work was necessary to keep the FMFPAC folks happy and off the CO's case for not responding quickly to their messages. I also continued to do my job as the assistant maintenance officer. During the cruise, I also got a new boss, another senior captain whom I did not know, named Ernie Knoll.

*****

We arrived in the waters of Subic Bay in the Philippines on a warm and beautiful day. The CO's plan was to start flying all the birds off the ship to Cubi Point Naval Air Station (NAS) located above the Subic Bay Harbor. He started this process at about fifty miles out from the harbor. Since we had exercised the birds en route, we were able to accomplish this fly off with only a minor number of problems.

As we proceeded to the Philippines, we had exercised each of our aircraft by individually operating all the systems. This was accomplished by running the APP, then moving the aircraft to one of the takeoffs and landing spots, spreading the pylon and blades, starting both engines, engaging the rotor system, and ground turning each machine for approximately ten minutes. After the ground run, the aircraft would again be folded up and repositioned in the pack and another one brought up. This evolution was repeated until we had exercised all the aircraft and repaired any discrepancies found during the process. We did this exercise routine twice while we were en route.

The CO led the flight, which was structured in the same sequence as the arrival flight to the carrier, with Captain Corner and I being the last to depart the ship. Arriving at NAS Cubi Point, Captain Corner and I parked our aircraft next to the other fourteen green CH-53s.

Looking across the harbor, we saw a gray RH-53 being craned off another LPH tied up to the pier in Subic Bay Harbor. These were the modified CH-53As that belonged to the Mine Countermeasures Squadron 12, I surmised.

*****

The next day, we were all required to attend a briefing given by the commander of Task Force (CTF) 78 and his staff. The admiral in charge of CTF 78 was the overall commander for the minesweeping efforts in North Vietnam. After his presentation, we were briefed on the operations and conduct of mine countermeasures to be used in the harbors, rivers, and other areas where we had laid mines. The CTF 78 briefing went into detail as to the type of mines we were facing during our sweeping mission.

As I recall, there were over 11,000 mines that had been dropped in ports and coastal waterways at various locations in North Vietnam. These mines were really various-sized bombs that were planted during the previous air campaign against the North. The bombs utilized were all high-explosive munitions of 250-, 500-, 1,000-, and 2000-

pound bombs that were rigged with different kinds of triggering mechanisms. These very high-explosive mines were designed with some very unusual triggering mechanisms. The unique triggering mechanisms used in these mines fell into three categories—acoustic, magnetic, and acoustic coupled with magnetic types.

The acoustic mines' triggering mechanism are designed to listen for sounds that are created by a ship's propeller and other mechanical sounds generated by a large cargo-type ship passing the mine's location. The acoustic triggering mechanism can be further set to not be triggered on the first sensing of a passing ship. It could be set up to allow up to five ships or acoustic noises similar to that of a ship to pass its location before being triggered.

The magnetic mines' triggering mechanism are designed to sense the magnetic influence created by a large steel hull ship when a large cargo-type ship passes the mine's location. The magnetic triggering mechanism can also be further set to not be triggered on the first sensing of a passing ship. It could be set up to allow up to five ships to pass its location before being triggered.

The last type of mine triggering mechanism used a combination of both acoustic and magnetic input before it can be triggered to explode. This type of mine was designed to sense the magnetic influence created by a large steel hull ship when a large ship passes the mine's location, as well as the acoustic sounds generated by a ship's propeller. The acoustic and magnetic triggering mechanism can also be set to not be triggered on the first sensing of a passing ship. This type of mine could be set up to allow up to five ships to pass its location sensing both the magnetic influences and acoustic noise or any combination of the two inputs before being triggered.

These types of triggering mechanism, coupled with the sketchy location where the mines were planted (mines were found as much as five miles from their intended dropped locations), made the minesweeping operation complicated and time-consuming at best.

We were not told about the self-destruction function of the triggering mechanism until the operation had almost been completed more than eight months in the future. It was our real saving grace because when the mine's battery senses its life was about to end, it would self-detonate the mine. That made the element of time a critical factor in conducting the minesweeping activities.

The most effective of the mine countermeasure devices that were to be utilized in the operation were the MK-105 hydrofoil sled, which contained a small jet engine to power a set of floating electrode cables to influence the mines and generate acoustic noises. The other sweeping devices were known as the magnetic orange pole (MOP) used in conjunction with acoustic rattle bars, which were dragged behind the MOP again to influence both magnetic and acoustic triggers. The MOP was a thirty-foot-long pipe filled with Styrofoam that was magnetized before use to create the desired magnetic influence. In order to maximize the minesweeping efforts, three MOPs were put together and separated by eight hundred feet of tow cable between each MOP with the rattle bars at the end of the last MOP. This setup was called the triple MOP and was generally the device the Marines were tasked to utilize.

During the two days of detailed briefings, some of our aircraft were being fitted by a special team from Naval Air Station North Island for our minesweeping mission. The cockpit underwent a modification that installed the minesweeping system gauges and control systems. External mirrors were attached to the front of the aircraft so the pilot and copilot could see the minesweeping gear behind their aircraft. Also, there was the installation of a large boom and cable storage reel, to which the tow cable was to be attached, in the rear of the cargo compartment. Internal fuel tanks were also positioned forward of the boom and cable storage reel so the fuel could be transferred to the MK-105 from inside the aircraft using a tow cable refueling feature as well as to provide fuel for the aircraft operations, thus allowing a longer time in the minefield.

At this point in the process, we had only seen pictures of the MK-105 hydrofoil sled in operation. Scuttlebutt was that the Navy had scheduled a big media demonstration of the Navy's minesweeping capabilities using the MK-105 in Subic Bay once all their aircraft were off-loaded. The news event was supposedly scheduled in the afternoon the next day.

The maintenance crews continued to assist in the installation of minesweeping equipment in our aircraft. The installations and the exercising of the birds made it necessary to fly test hops on each one as they completed the cycle. I liked to fly, so I volunteered to do most of them since I had been to the Philippines before and was not overly interested in visiting the sights of Olongapo, the town just outside the base perimeter.

If my memory serves me correctly, the Navy's HM-12 had ten RH-53s (refitted CH-53As) in their inventory. All these aircraft had been craned off the ship, and three of them had been flown to the air station's parking area just below our location. I was getting ready to fly a test hop on one of our birds and had a clear view of what was going on at the HM-12 bird's location. All three of their aircraft were preflighted and ready to launch. The press people had been escorted to the three aircraft and were being given a tour of the inside and inner workings of the minesweeping gear. At the rear of the last aircraft was positioned an MK-105 hydrofoil sled. After the tour of the aircraft, the press people were escorted to the MK-105. I assumed they were told how it operated as one of the aircrew members spoke to them. The press was then put into vans and taken to a location; I again assumed they were being transported to watch the Navy aircraft demonstrate the airborne mine countermeasure (AMCM) process.

As I started my post-maintenance inspection test hop, we ran into a problem with the operation of a newly installed mirror on the pilot side of the aircraft, which needed to be fixed before we could continue the flight. Quick troubleshooting by my maintenance crew indicated that an electrical harness was the cause of the problem, and they went to get a replacement so we could continue.

Sitting in the cockpit waiting for the replacement harness, I continued to watch as the HM-12 aircrew closed up and manned the first of their aircraft. I saw the fire guard standing next to the aircraft but did not see any indication that it had started. After a couple of minutes, the crew chief climbed up on top of the aircraft and opened the doghouse that covers the APP unit and started to work on it. At this point, the pilots exited the aircraft and moved to the second open aircraft. They quickly closed it up and again tried to start the APP; this time, they were successful.

I continued to watch them knowing generally what the sequence of the starting cycle they were trying to complete should be. The next step in the sequence was for them to start their engines. I watched them as they tried twice to get the number 1 engine started. The lights on the aircraft went out indicating that the APP was shut down. Again, the flight crew exited the aircraft heading for the third one. They moved quickly to get it closed up and the APP started. It appeared that they had successfully got both engines started this time. I watched as the rotor break was released and the blades started to spin. About fifteen seconds after rotor engagement, I saw a large discharge of what appeared to be hydraulic fluid coming from the vent on the bottom of the bird. It was again shut down. It appeared to me that the number 1 hydraulic system that was driven by the accessory gear box after rotor engagement had developed a major leak.

I thought, *Boy oh boy, does the Navy have maintenance problems?*

Seeing the crew chief waving at me, then giving me the thumbs-up signal, meaning that the repairs had been completed, I returned my thoughts to the job at hand. My copilot and I continued to complete checklist items and were just about to start the engine startup sequence when the crew chief told me over the ICS that the Navy crew wanted to come aboard the aircraft. I told him it was okay to let them come aboard.

A lieutenant commander climbed on to the jump seat and yelled to me that they were going to commandeer this aircraft for the demonstration flight of the AMCM mission, so climb out of the seat, and we will take over.

I looked at him with a look of disbelief, and said, "There is no way you are commandeering this aircraft. It's on a test hop, and you are not authorized to commandeer it," I shouted back at him.

He stepped back down into the cabin and had a short discussion with a Navy commander who had also come aboard. The commander then climbed up on the jump seat after asking to use one of the crewmember's helmets so he could talk to me without yelling over the APP noise.

He said he was with the admiral's Command Task Force-78 (CTF) staff. He said the demonstration of the AMCM mission for the Press Corps was an absolutely critical part of our missions. Could I find a way to accommodate the use of this aircraft so it could be used to perform the AMCM flight without further delay, since the three previous birds had all gone down?

Listening to him and having seen the three birds go down, I thought about how we could make the flight happen. It would be a real black eye for the task force if the AMCM process show was a failure. What would the folks back home think if our failure negatively impacted the ongoing negotiations that were currently taking place? They were counting on the task force to successfully facilitate the release of the POWs.

I had signed for the bird. It was my responsibility to see that it was flown safely, but I was not trained to fly the AMCM mission. However, maybe we could find a compromise. *What the hell? Yes, we will do it,* I said.

I would stay in the aircraft, along with my crew chief. The Navy pilot and his crew chief who had done this mission before could fly the AMCM part of the mission after we completed the test hop checks.

The commander listened to my plan and said it worked for him. His concern was getting the mission moving. He then got off the jump seat and talked to the lieutenant commander who started to argue with him but was told to just do it.

I received a thumbs-up from the lieutenant commander. At this point, I explained the plan for the AMCM flight to my copilot, which meant he would not be flying the test hop with me. After which, I exited my cockpit seat, which made the right-hand pilot seat available for the lieutenant commander. He got in quickly to the right seat and hooked up his helmet and strapped in. I then replaced the copilot in the left seat as we prepared to start the mission. The lieutenant commander said very little to start with. He looked very frustrated but soon warmed up to the idea that together we could make this demo happen. I finished the test hop ground checklist, and he completed the AMCM ground checklist items working together with both our crew chiefs.

With all aircraft startup and ground checks completed, we then taxied for takeoff. The test-flight items that needed to be completed were quickly done with a short hover check and a ten-minute flight. I then turned over control of the aircraft to the lieutenant commander who flew over to an area near the seawall. He set the aircraft down next to the MK-105 on the ramp next to the seawall. Next, his crew chief unreeled the tow cable from the back of the aircraft and attached the end of it to the MK-105. With this step completed, he lifted into a hover, then moved to a position above the sled, and the crew chief moved to the hell hole and extended the external pendant out so that the ground crew could hook up the MK-105 to it. He then lifted it up and flew about a mile away from the seawall.

Pulling into a high hover out in the bay, he set the MK-105 in the water and released the external load, then recovered the external pendant. He then moved forward slowly and away from the device, and his crew chief started streaming the tow cable out the back of the aircraft. Once it was almost fully extended, the tow ball was seated in the tow boom and the aircraft took up the pressure of the device being moved through the water. The next step was to have the crew chief start the jet engine on the sled, then extend the hydrofoil struts, which the Navy crew chief executed flawlessly. The crew chief then notified the pilot that the device was ready to be towed, and the pilot applied forward speed to move the MK-105 up on the step or up on its struts. He pulled the device at about twenty knots and at an altitude of seventy-five feet in front of the gathered Press Corps, and television people gathered on the seawall. After the sled had passed the press people's location, the lieutenant commander started to explain the basics of the tow process to me.

He told me that the two primary gauges for minesweeping that had just been installed in our aircraft were the tension meter and the skew gauge. These were the primary tools to keep the device operating properly and not damaging the helicopter. The tension gauge showed the force applied to the tow cable, measured at the tow hook.

The skew meter tracked the location of the tow boom in the back of the aircraft. He cautioned me that making too sharp of a turn could cause the tow boom to make contact with the side of the ramp area, causing potentially severe damage to the aircraft.

"You need to relearn how to fly the aircraft in the minesweeping mission using flat, uncoordinated turns. It's the only way to keep the skew for the boom under control," he said to me. He demonstrated the turn as we headed back around toward the seawall for another demo pass. At the conclusion of the demo, we retracted the hydrofoils, then pulled the MK-105 back toward the aircraft using the towline to put it close to the bird, then we pulled it up onto the seawall launch area, where the ground crew set the breaks on the wheels of the MK-105, then unhooked the tow cable, and then his crew chief retrieved the cable by using the winch in the cabin and placed it on the storage reel. We then moved away from the device, performed the landing checklist, and landed back on the helo spot we had departed from earlier. That completed the mission.

I returned the aircraft to the flight line after letting the lieutenant commander and his crew chief off at their flight line. I expected to be met by a pissed-off CO like I had experienced in Vietnam the year earlier, but no one showed up at the aircraft as I exited it. I post-flighted the aircraft and then wrote up the minor discrepancies and indicated that the aircraft needed to be freshwater-washed since it was hovering close to the water for an extended period.

Going to the ready room, I found the operations officer, who looked at me and shook his head from side to side, then finally saying, "Captain, make sure you log the tow time on the yellow sheet and in the after-action report," before turning away and exiting the ready room. I completed the paperwork, checked our aircraft-modification status, and headed for the BOQ since the workday was over.

The BOQ at NAS Cubi Point has a very nice bar on the lower deck (floor) of the building, so I stopped in for a cold beer. Ordering a San Miguel, a locally brewed beer, I took a seat at the bar. Glancing up at the TV screen suspended behind the bar, I saw the armed forces broadcast of the news on the screen. The commentator started talking about the Navy's demonstration of minesweeping conducted that afternoon. As I listened to the reports of how the Navy was going to be on the forefront of the mission's evolution, a picture of a big green Marine Corps helicopter towing an MK-105 appeared on the screen.

Hot damn, so much for Navy blue leadership, I thought as I enjoyed the cold beer.

*****

In early January 1973, our squadron undertook extensive training with the pilots and aircrews from HM-12. After basic orientation flights using the MK-105 sleds, the focus changed to utilizing the MOP and rattle bar devices in our training scenarios. A new element was also introduced to the training evolution; it was the incorporation of the buoyed-mounted Raydist navigation system that would help us navigate in the minefield and also help document the minesweeping tracks we made as we moved through the minefield. We were also joined by another Marine Corps aviation unit from Okinawa, HMM-165, a composite squadron that had CH-53D aircraft in the unit

While we were conducting this training with HM-12 and then practicing it on our own, we had a visit from the commanding generals of both First MAW and Third Marine Amphibious Force that watched the training efforts.

We also went back out to sea qualifying all our pilots for day and night operations on the USS *Inchon* an LPH and the two landing platform dock (LPD) ships that were in our task force, qualifying all our pilots in both day and night carrier landings.

During the first part of February, we continued AMCM training and added Raydist minefield navigation into the training cycles. The squadron achieved 100 percent aircrew and pilot qualification at the completion of this phase of training.

On February 15, 1973, CTF 78 embarked on several Navy ships and sailed for North Vietnam waters after the North Vietnamese started to slowly release the POWs they held starting on February 12, 1973.

As part of this task force, our squadron deployed nine aircraft on the LPH, USS *Inchon* (designated AMCM Unit Charley) and three on the LPD, USS *Cleveland* (designated AMCM Unit Delta). I was assigned to the LPD *Cleveland* as the unit's maintenance officer. Our departure from Subic Bay was a couple of days after AMCM Units Alpha and Bravo (HM-12 and HMM-165) departed because of mechanical problems with one of our ships.

During the month of February, meetings were taking place in the city of Haiphong, North Vietnam, to establish procedures and the sequence of areas to be cleared. The negotiations were not going well because of the North's continued push to make them mostly political and not technical. The North's demands were accompanied with veiled threats that there would be severe consequences if their demands were not met. This, we were told, included the termination of the release of our POWs.

On February 23, AMCM Units Alpha and Bravo (Navy HM-12 and HMM-165 units) reached the anchorage outside of Haiphong Harbor. However, disagreements escalated, creating an impasse that dictated the sweeping activities that were about to commence to be terminated because the North was slowing down the release of our POWs. The admiral in charge then ordered the Task Force 78 to leave the anchorage on February 28, demonstrating that the continuation of minesweeping was dependent on the continued release of our POWs.

On February 28, we arrived in the waters south of Haiphong Harbor to join with ships that housed units Alpha and Bravo to await orders to finally commence minesweeping activities.

Navy RH-53As and Marine CH-53D aircraft from HMH-462 attached to HMM-165 carried out the first of the Marines' towing operations on March 7 in the Haiphong channel using MK-105 equipment.

As I recall, it was on or about March 12 when we finally commenced minesweeping operations in Loch Huyen minefield off our LPD. Our initial sweep activities were held in abeyance, awaiting the Raydist installation to be completed, which did not occur until that date.

Each morning's minesweeping operation would be commenced from the LPD *Cleveland* using the triple MOP and rattle bars with its buoy.

The ship had a major responsibility in the launching of the minesweeping gear. Their operation first entailed the magnetizing of all three MOPs that were located in holders on the well deck of the LPD. Once magnetized, the MOPs would be moved to and placed in additional open top racks covered with rubber and located on the stern gate, which had been lower to the water level at the rear of the ship.

When the tow aircraft was ready to launch, the LPD would lower the rear end of the ship by taking on water in special ballast tanks that flooded the well deck in a controlled manner with sea water. The ship's whaleboat would be launched, then proceed to the stern of the ship, and pick up the towline that was attached to the first MOP in the series of three. The whaleboat would pull about 400 feet of towline out away from the stern, then attach a floating buoy to the end of the towline, placing it in the water at the back of the ship. The aircraft would then launch from the LPD and hover over the towline buoy having the crew chief, using a grappling hook, snag the towline and buoy, bring it up to the ramp, attach the tow ball to the line, then set the tow ball in the tow boom, and then disconnect the floating buoy. Once this was completed, the aircraft would slowly move away from the stern of the ship pulling each MOP out of the partially submerged well deck in order, until all three MOPs and the rattle bars with their float were in the water clear of the stern of the ship. Each MOP was separated from the previous one by 800 feet of tow cable, making the triple MOP device well over 2,500 feet long when fully deployed.

The recovery operation was basically a reversal of the launch sequence with the exception of a winch and tractor that were used to pull the sweeping gear back into the partially submerged well deck after the aircraft had dropped the buoy attached to the tow cable into the water at the stern of the LPD at the completion of the days sweeping activities. It was a complicated operation, but the ship's crew made it look easy. We flew these missions daily without difficulty.

*****

The first minesweeping operation conducted off the USS *Inchon* was made by the HMH-463 CO on March 17. These operations were either made using the MK-105 sleds or a single MOP with rattle bars and float. All the sweep activities took place at various locations in the Loch Huyen and lower Hon Gai, which were part of the Haiphong shipping channel's complex.

On March 18, I observed the crash of one of our CH-53D aircraft. I had just completed the first mission of the day, a four-hour tow evolution in the minefield located outside the entrance to Haiphong Harbor.

My triple MOP and rattle-bar sweeping gear had been left just outside the minefield boundaries with the end of the towline attached to the buoy about one thousand yards from the LPD. The next scheduled aircraft in this evolution was to launch from the USS *Inchon* and continue the sweep mission in this minefield.

After finishing the tow mission, we returned to the LPD *Cleveland*. Upon landing, I quickly folded the bird's blades and had the ship's aircrew move me off spot 2 so that Pineapple 11 could land to top off their fuel tanks in preparation for continuing minesweeping operations with the minesweeping gear that I had left for them just outside the minefield. We exited our aircraft after Pineapple 11 landed and started to refuel.

After refueling, Pineapple 11 was supposed to fly to the area where I had left the buoy, find it, then pick up the towline I had left drifting just outside the minefield that was attached to a triple MOP and rattle-bar rig and resume the sweeping mission.

I stopped for a few minutes to watch Pineapple 11 complete its fueling operation, then lift off the deck into a hover and start to move away from the LPD stern. As it was turning away from the fantail, the aircraft started to spin wildly.

It appeared to me that he had lost tail rotor control as the aircraft spun into the water about thirty yards off the stern of the ship. As the aircraft hit the water, the main rotor blades started to disintegrate, throwing pieces of blades in all directions. Fortunately, no one was injured. After what was left of the blades stopped turning, I saw the two pilots and the aircrew exiting the aircraft, and they were almost immediately rescued by the boat crew from the LPD *Cleveland* as the aircraft sank into the dark waters outside Haiphong Harbor.

The entire aircrew came aboard our ship, were screened by the ship's medical personnel, and then transported back to the USS *Inchon*. We received word that all sweeping operations were going to be suspended until the cause of the mishap could be determined.

Thinking, *I'm sure this delay in mine-clearing operations is not going to make the North Vietnamese very happy. I bet the powers that be will expediate the recovery and evaluation of the cause for the mishap quickly. If the cause is mechanical, then a fix will be needed quickly before the whole negotiated prisoner-release process is adversely impacted.*

Later that same afternoon, Navy divers arrived to attach a marking buoy, then a recovery line to the sunken aircraft. Late that night, two large barges, one with a very large crane, appeared off the stern of our ship. At dawn, they started to lift Pineapple 11 out of the water, then placed the damaged bird on to the adjacent barge. Several civilian engineers along with our accident investigation people arrived and went on to the barge to inspect the aircraft. After they had finished their inspections, the barge was attached to a seagoing tugboat, which took the barge with the aircraft away. I assumed it was going to be taken to the Philippines for further engineering evaluation.

The next day, a message was received that the preliminary findings of the engineers along with the accident board was that a tail rotor pitch link assembly had failed causing the crash.

The failure of the tail rotor pitch link assembly was believed to be the direct result of the added stresses created by the towing of the minesweeping gear along with the exposure to the saltwater spray on some of the titanium and stainless-steel components of the assembly. This failure was thought to be created on our aircraft during the towing operations we had undertaken in the training and minesweeping activities to date.

In order to continue minesweeping, a mechanism needed to be developed quickly to allow the task force to continue the minesweeping process. To this end, the engineers at Naval Air Systems Command (NavAirSysCom) and Sikorsky aircraft developed a specific set of inspection protocols to check the tail rotor pitch links for corrosion and replace anyone that exhibited excessive wear. At the same time, they were already well along in the development of a new much heavier tail rotor pitch link assembly for use on our aircraft and those of HM-12.

On the LPD *Cleveland*, we inspected our three aircraft using the inspection protocols and found that all three of our aircraft met the criteria for continued operations. I attributed that positive inspection results to the fact that our maintenance crew freshwater-washed each of our aircraft including the tail rotor after each mission and then again after the day's flight operations had been completed.

*****

The weather in North Vietnam at that time of year was generally overcast, and visibility was greatly reduced in low clouds and fog. One morning, I was already in the minefield under tow with a single MOP and rattle-bar rig working the Loch Huyen minefield when I heard a call on the guard radio frequency. The call was to a Pineapple aircraft. The number was garbled in transmission, which had recently launched off the USS *Inchon* heading to pick up a triple MOP and rattle-bar rig that was located just outside the minefield in the lower Hon Gai area.

The radio broadcast on guard stated that the Pineapple aircraft, its number again garbled, was off course and was headed into the Communists Chinese waters. If it continued in that direction, it would violate the Chinese airspace. The transmission further directed the aircraft to make an immediate left turn and reverse its current heading by 180 degrees so that it did not cross into the Communist Chinese waters. I heard no response to the call.

About two minutes later, again on the guard frequency, I heard a more frantic transmission, saying again, "Pineapple aircraft, you are within half a mile of violating Communist Chinese airspace, make an immediate 180-degree turn now!"

I heard a very weak transmission from the Pineapple aircraft saying he had become lost and would make the turn of 180 degrees as instructed, but he was having trouble with his directional compass (called an RMI) but would turn around now.

Hearing nothing more on the radio about the aircraft, we completed our four-hour mission in the Loch Huyen minefield. Returning to the LPD *Cleveland*, we refueled the aircraft, then shut down, and postflighted the aircraft. I returned to our small ready room, where I heard that a Pineapple aircraft off the USS *Inchon* had come very close to causing an international incident.

The Pineapple aircraft involved in the incident had flown to within fifty yards of sovereign Communist Chinese airspace. It had almost entered their airspace before it finally responded to multiple turnaround calls just seconds before it would have violated their airspace. This task-force aircraft had come extremely close to causing an international incident by almost crossing into Communist China's control airspace and their territorial waters.

Communist China had stated that if the aircraft had entered its airspace, it would be dealt with very severely—meaning, most likely it would have been shot down.

The after-action report, which I had an opportunity to read, indicated that the weather at the time of this incident was not very good. Cloud ceiling varied between 500–800 feet, and visibility was about one mile in light rain showers.

The after-action report further indicated that the RMI instrument (primary directional compass) had not been properly aligned before takeoff from the *Inchon*. The misalignment was over 45 degrees off from the actual magnetic heading of the ship at the time of the aircraft's takeoff and departure. This deviation was not noticed by either pilot before or after their takeoff from the *Inchon*.

They thought their aircraft was heading in the right direction to find, then pick up the triple MOP and rattle-bar rig. The gear had been left just outside the minefield by the early morning mission aircraft.

After flying at 100-feet altitude and heading in the wrong direction, they started to try to figure out why they had not seen the sweep gear yet. They should have sighted the sweep gear about fifteen minutes after takeoff, but so far, they had seen nothing. They continued to fly the same heading while trying to figure out what had happened to the sweep gear. They had now been flying in the direction of Communist China for a little over thirty minutes.

Scuttlebutt from the Lieutenant Protective League later indicated that the UHF radio had not been fully turned on to include the guard channel before takeoff. With the guard part of the radio not on, they could not hear the calls that were made on that frequency trying to turn them around. It had been only pure luck the copilot had seen the switch was in the wrong position and corrected the error, they were less than a half mile from the Communist China border. If they had continued to fly on the same heading, there was a significant likelihood that they would have been either shot down or at least intercepted and forced to land in Communist China.

As I completed reading the after-action report about this incident, I was not at all surprised to see that the pilot in command of the aircraft involved in this incident was Space M. I predicted this pilot would have problems back at K-Bay after his failed instrument-check ride with me many months earlier, and he had just proven me right. To my knowledge, Space M was not assigned to fly as pilot in command for any of the subsequent flights in our squadron while I was assigned to it.

*****

One morning during one of our minesweeping missions, I was pulling the triple MOP and rattle-bar rig in the Loch Huyen minefield when I encountered a couple of problems—one created by a North Vietnamese soldier and the other by my own stupidity trying to push my aircraft and myself too hard in order to complete the mission.

We had been flying at our standard seventy-five feet above the water using the radar altimeter hold feature on the automatic flight control system (AFCS). We had been in the minefield working perpendicular to the shoreline for about three and a half hours. It was very apparent that the distance between the first line of shrubbery and the water's edge had grown much greater as the tide receded. The entire time we were sweeping, I could see an NVA soldier standing just outside of the wave patterns furthest extension onto the beach. As the tide receded, he moved forward getting closer and closer to our aircraft's turnaround point as established by the Raydist navigation system. He had moved to what I estimated to be about two hundred yards closer to our turnaround point established by the Raydist system.

I assumed he had his orders to not allow the Yankee aircraft to cross over the surf line, and he was making sure we did not violate the order by moving further out and away from the shrubbery as the tide went out.

We were on the final leg of our sweep evolution for this period as we approached the newly defined surf line. The Raydist system indicated we needed to continue another fifty yards in order to get credit for the sweeping of this tract in the minefield. I looked out the chin bubble and saw the NVA soldier waving at me. His gesturing indicated I was not to cross the position where he was standing. I checked the Raydist again and saw we needed to go just a little further before making the turn to get credit for the sweep.

Looking back down at the NVA soldier again, he was becoming even more animated in his gestures and now waving his AK-47 rifle at me. Glancing at the Raydist again, I saw that we had finally reached the turnaround point, glancing down again, I also saw him chamber a round in his rifle and start to raise it toward me. At the same time, I had initiated the flat left-hand turn to reverse our course back into the minefield. As the nose of the aircraft almost passed over him, I watched as the water and sand spray engulfed him as he held his rifle pointed directly at me. I waited for the sound of the AK-47 round to strike the aircraft, but none came. We finished our turn and headed back out into deeper water with our triple MOP and rattle bars trailing behind us.

Looking over at my copilot, I said, "We may have cut that one a little too close."

He responded, "I agree. Let's get the hell out of here before he changes his mind."

We had completed the final sweep run for our mission and were in the process of attaching, then dropping the marker buoy so that the next aircraft could continue the mission. I had been watching the fuel consumption for the last thirty minutes and had pushed the endurance envelope to the limit. We were looking at a fuel warning light that had been illuminated for several minutes as we dropped the buoy and headed for the LPD five miles away.

Switching to the *Cleveland* tower frequency, I called them and requested a straight-in approach to spot 2 and that I was in a low-fuel state. They asked me how many souls were on board and cleared me for the approach. At a half mile, we completed the landing checklist, and at about three hundred yards, I saw the LSE who would direct me to the final landing. I kept my speed up on the approach to spot 2, which I could see caused some concern with the LSE. Crossing the stern, the LSE positioned me over the spot. As I was lowering the aircraft to the deck, with only a foot to go, number 1 engine flamed out. We landed a little hard but with no problem. We were quickly chained down, safely on the deck, and at that point, we lost number 2 engine. The electrical power also failed as the rotor system started to spin down. I reached over and started the APP and regained electrical power, then applied the rotor break. The LSE signaled he wanted to fold our rotor blades. I shook my head no and sent the crew chief out to tell him we needed to fuel first. He was in the process of telling him when the APP also ran out of gas.

I looked over at the copilot who said to me, "Boy, was that cutting it close, Captain?"

Just shaking my head in disgust but saying nothing in return because I was too embarrassed to respond. Poor headwork on my part had almost cost an aircraft and potentially hazarded my crew. This close call highlighted my obsession with getting the job accomplished, pushing the envelope to the maximum. I promised myself from that day forward, I would not allow myself to be put in that position again. The *six Ps* became my new refrain—prior planning prevents piss-poor performance, I swore.

I knew I was in trouble as I exited the aircraft because the air boss wanted to see me in the tower ASAP. As I walked away from the bird, I asked the copilot to postflight the bird, which was currently being refueled. He said he would take care of it, as I headed for the LPD tower. The lieutenant commander air boss was really upset. The task force had lost one aircraft already, and now I had almost lost another. He went on to chew my ass for piss-poor headwork and said he would talk to the CO about the incident. I said very little, knowing I had screwed up. As I left the tower, I observed that my aircraft had been refueled, blades folded, and pulled forward into its parking spot next to the small hangar.

The CO wasted no time in coming to the *Cleveland* for a little chat. He arrived by longboat from the *Inchon* at the air boss's request. Seeing me on the flight deck, he screamed at me to follow him to our small ready room. Again, I got my ass chewed by the CO who was really irate. I said very little since I knew I was at fault.

He chewed my ass for about thirty minutes. It would have gone on longer, but he was scheduled to fly, and he needed to get back to the *Inchon*. Before he departed, he said, "Captain, you are grounded for one week in order for you to think about what you almost did. You almost lost one of my aircraft is what you did. Captain, am I crystal clear about no flying for one week?"

"Yes, sir," was my only response.

My week of not flying passed very slowly as I watched the daily activities transpire. At the end of the week's grounding, I again found my name back on the flight schedule, indicating that I could fly again. I was back in the daily rotation of minesweeping activities.

No more was said about the close call until fitness report time.

*****

With final departure from North Vietnam of the last known POWs on March 29, 1973, we were ordered to depart the North Vietnamese waters early on April 2, 1973, heading back to Subic

Bay in the Philippines. This marked the end of the first period of minesweeping. HMH-463 had successfully swept the minefield of Loch Huyen and the lower Hon Gai areas. No mines had been detonated by our squadron, but the sweeping activities verified that no active mines existed in those areas. HM-12 detonated one mine during the period. We still did not know, at the time, that most of the mines in the North Vietnamese waters had already self-detonated. Furthermore, time was on our side as the remainder of most of the mines in North Vietnamese waters continued to self-detonate.

The port period in Subic Bay lasted only a few days, then we headed back to North Vietnam to continue our sweeping mission. We had rejoined the rest of CTF-78 at their anchorage very early on April 14. We again started our minesweep tasks.

At about 0600 hours, on April 17, I was standing on the flight deck performing the preflight check on my aircraft for that day's mission when I heard a surprise announcement coming over the ship's 1-MC.

"General Quarters, General Quarters," the captain of the ship announced, "General Quarters, General Quarters, this is not a drill. MIG attack is imminent, stand by to get underway." He repeated the message a third time. I watched sailors heading for the gun positions as the ship was preparing to get underway. Looking out across the water, I could see the other ships also responding to the emergency and were rapidly preparing to get underway. We, the squadron pilots, were assigned to our ready room if the ship went to general quarters. Climbing down off the aircraft, I was told to clear the flight deck by one of the ship's crew members, so I headed for the ready room. A few minutes later, I could feel the ship getting underway and moving rapidly away from our anchorage.

We were later informed that a breakdown in relations between the North Vietnamese and the United States negotiators in both Hanoi and Paris created major disagreements over mine clearance requirements, along with the issue of US aircraft overflights of North Vietnamese territory. It appeared that these disagreements escalated into threats of attack on United States forces in North Vietnamese waters. These were the two explanations we were given for our immediate departure from the Northern anchorage. We steamed south quickly out of North Vietnamese waters and waited further direction.

While we were underway south, I received word that my mother-in-law had suffered a stroke, then had passed away on April 14 in California. I was granted emergency leave, so I could return to Hawaii to watch our children in Hawaii while my wife flew to California to attend the funeral and settled the estate.

I was transported back to Hawaii, via helo flight to the carrier USS *Enterprise*, then COD supply aircraft flight to Okinawa, followed by a C-141 flight back to Hawaii. My wife had just left the same day for the funeral in southern California when I arrived.

After three and a half weeks at K-Bay, I was headed back to rejoin my squadron, which was en route back to Subic Bay. The squadron arrived in Subic Bay on the *Inchon* and *Cleveland* on May 19 for replenishment of supplies and equipment. The negotiations were still continuing as to the extent of the minesweeping activities that were required to meet the vague language laid out in the Paris Peace Accords. A stalemate over the extent of the mine clearing and access to fly over the North Vietnam territory continued, keeping us from finishing what we had started.

Our squadron continued to train to keep minesweeping competency sharp and performed other missions in support of Marine and Army training in the Philippines for almost a month. Most of these activities were of a routine nature, but one stands out in my mind as one of my most significant peace-time brushes with death.

*****

It all started when several Navy and Marine Corps officers took a ride on a Navy C-12 aircraft that was heading for Taipei, located on the island of Taiwan. They went because they had heard that there were very good deals on handmade furniture to be had from the artisans in Taipei. After they returned, the word about the good deals spread. Roll top desks were on the top of the list to be purchased in Taipei.

Since both Captain Ron Corner and I were both interested in purchasing a Roll top desk to take home, we decided to make a trip up there to check out the desks. We put the paperwork into the approval process requesting to fly two birds on a cross-country flight to Taipei.

Captain Corner would lead the flight, and I would be his wingman. Our aircraft would require four operational internal fuel tanks in each bird in order to make the flight of a little less than five hours with sufficient fuel in reserve. To my surprise, the cross-country was approved, probably because Ron put in the paperwork and the XO, along with several other people, wanted to have us bring back their furniture rather than having to pay for it to be shipped to Hawaii.

The day before the cross-country flight, Ron and I planned out the flight in great detail. We originally were going to make it a navigation-and-formation training flight for our copilots, but a look at the weather forecast forced a change in plans. There was a weather low moving down from the north that could impact our trip with low ceilings and poor visibility, so we changed the plan to make our single navigation-and-formation flight into two instrument training flights. We would be filing separate IFR flight plans with a request for a ten-minute separation between our departures.

We were scheduled to take off at 1200 hours local time with our anticipated arrival in Taipei at just before 1700 hours local time. At around 1030 hours, we met with our two copilots, both newly designated aircraft commanders and performed the standard NATOPS briefing, then went to the NAS Cubi Point weather office for a weather briefing before filing our two flight plans. We also agreed to keep in contact with one another by means of the squadron's common frequency on our FM radios.

A Navy chief was on duty in the weather office. He looked at our flight plans, then filled out the weather briefing paperwork covering our route of flight. He went over the forecast for the weather for our departure from Cubi Point, our en-route weather, and the forecast weather at our proposed arrival time at our destination.

Our departure weather was forecast to be great, unlimited visibility and ceiling. However, the Navy chief indicated that the forecast low was moving rapidly south and more rapidly than previously anticipated. However, he said that the low was a weak one and that we could anticipate broken layers of clouds and rain at our requested flight level, starting after we left the north end of the island of Luzon in the Philippines. He forecast that the turbulence en route would be light to moderate, and the ceiling over the entire island of Taiwan was not to be less than one thousand feet. At our arrival in Taipei, the weather was forecast to be broken clouds, with visibility five miles and occasionally reduced to two miles in rain showers.

The forecast was acceptable for our flights since we both had special instrument-qualification status, so we proceeded to base operations to file the two flight plans. That completed, we manned our aircraft and prepared for our individual IFR departures, making sure to complete the instrument checklist before takeoff.

Neither Captain Corner nor I liked the call sign that had been adopted by the commanding officer, which was Pineapple. Additionally, we did not want to confuse the IFR controllers who would be handling our flight today, so we decided to use the side numbers of our aircraft instead of Pineapple as our call signs. Ron was flying YH-05 and I flew YH-07, as I recall.

Captain Corner's takeoff was ten minutes before mine, but since the weather was clear and we had no ceiling, I could see him in the distance as we made our takeoff after activating our IFR, International Civil Aviation Organization (ICAO) flight plan to Taipei. Departing NAS Cubi Point, we were switched to Manila Center. Making contact with Manila Center, we were told that we were in radar contact and to report when reaching eight thousand feet, which was our en-route altitude. We reached eight thousand feet and informed the center that we were level at that altitude.

The initial part of that day's flight took us up along the west coast of the island of Luzon, at eight-thousand-foot altitude. The weather was beautiful, and we could clearly see the larger cities as we crossed over them. The city of San Fernando and Laoag City were the two largest we could identify along the way as we flew north.

Our two aircraft were in frequent communications using the FM radio as we proceeded further north. About twenty miles north of the island of Luzon, Captain Corner called on the FM radio saying, "I can see a wall of clouds ahead of us, and it appears to stretch from the *deck* [military for 'the ground'] to about thirty-five thousand feet. We anticipate entering the cloud formation in about ten minutes." He commented further that this was not what the weather forecaster forecast by a long shot.

I then heard him call Manila Center on the UHF radio and asked for an update on the weather he was about to enter that lay between Luzon and Taiwan.

The center responded, saying that "the low previously forecast has turned into a cold front. We have no pilot's reports as to the conditions between the two islands currently, but if we receive any, we will pass it on to you."

Ron thanked the controller and then came back up on the FM radio saying he was entering the wall of clouds now. As he was speaking, I lost sight of his aircraft as he entered the clouds.

As we flew toward the wall of clouds, I could hear only intermittent and mostly garbled transmission from YH-05 on our FM radio. Just before we entered the cloud bank, I heard a faint transmission saying something about experiencing severe turbulence and slowing down.

As we entered the clouds, both my copilot and I both transitioned to instrument scans as we also started to experience moderate turbulence. About five minutes later, YH-05 was called by Manila Center saying that they had lost radar contact, and they should contact Taipei Center frequency, then the rest of the transmission was garbled and unreadable.

The turbulence was increasing as we encountered heavy rain, hail, and lightning flashed all around us. I was looking at the pilot's attitude direction indicator (ADI), a gyro-driven instrument that provided the artificial horizon during instrument flight. This instrument is the primary instrument for nonvisual-flight reference.

The pilot's attitude direction indicator and the vertical velocity indicator both showed we were climbing at 2,000 feet per minute, even though the collective was bottomed—meaning, no engine power was driving the rotor system. We climbed up, with no power on the aircraft, to an altitude of 8,900 feet, 900 feet above our assign altitude before the bottom felt like it had dropped out from under us. We were now in a severe downdraft. We passed through our assigned altitude; we could not control our descent even with the application of almost full power. Our aircraft finally stopped its descent at about 7,000 feet, then the cycle started all over again. It was like riding a bucking bronco. We were also pushed around horizontally, making it hard to stay on course.

I thought, *We must have penetrated a thunderstorm that's imbedded in the clouds,* as I struggled to maintain control of the aircraft. *This sure is not the weather that was forecast!*

We went through five or six evolutions of these up and down drafts. I called YH-05 asking his location from the TACAN station on the northern tip of Luzon and what airspeed he was maintaining. He responded that he was at 45 miles distance from the station, maintaining 110 knots, and experiencing severe turbulence as the rest of the transmission faded and became garbled.

I assumed the large amount of lightning that we were currently experiencing was the main cause of our communications problems.

Checking our position from the same TACAN station, I saw, to my surprise, that we were located at a distance of 43 miles; we had closed the distance between the two of us from more than ten miles to less than two. He had slowed down his airspeed when he entered the clouds, and we had not slowed but continued at 120 knots. I immediately reduced our airspeed to 100 knots to provide some separation between our two aircraft as we continued to fly blindly through the clouds.

A few minutes later, I heard a faint call from Manila Center saying that they had lost radar contact with us and that we needed to contact Taipei Center frequency on 290.10.

I attempted to acknowledge the transmission but received no reply, only static. At this point, I needed to change frequencies and asked the copilot to take the controls. He acknowledged the request and said, "I have the aircraft," while I dialed in and set the new frequency in the UHF radio. I then attempted to call Taipei Center on the UHF radio, but all we heard was static. About this time, I saw that our angle of bank was about 30 degrees to the left and asked the copilot if he was all right.

His response was "No, I have vertigo really bad. You better take back control of the aircraft."

My next thought was *This situation is turning into a Murphy's-law event*—meaning, that if it can go wrong, it will.

Taking back control of the aircraft, I righted the bird, worked to stabilize our altitude, course, and airspeed. The rain and lightning had increased again as had the turbulence. I worked hard to stabilize our bird once again. I looked at my pilot's ADI.

It was showing a 25-degree angle of bank turn to the right, but all the other instruments showed we were straight and level. I looked across the cockpit at the copilot's ADI and saw it showed we were in a wing-level attitude. This meant one of two things—the gyro powering my instrument was failing, or the indicator was failing.

One of the troubleshooting procedures for diagnosing this type of failure was to switch the input to my current ADI to the other one that provided inputs to the copilot's ADI. This was done by switching the gyro input and selecting the other gyro from the two separate gyros in the back of the bird as the input to my ADI indicator. I moved the switch, and nothing change on my ADI indicator. That meant that the indicator was malfunctioning and was unreliable for IFR flight. I now recognized that I would have to depend on a partial panel scan to keep us straight and level.

Boy, has Murphy struck again, I mused.

Switching the gyro inputs back to their original setting, I asked the copilot if his vertigo had gotten any better.

He said, "No, not really." So I settled into my partial panel scan with an occasional look over at his ADI as a secondary check—trying to keep us on course—airspeed, and altitude as the turbulence subsided in severity but still bounced us around a lot. Fortunately, the crew chief was able to successfully transfer fuel from our internal tanks, so that was not one of our growing list of problems. We continued to fly, still unable to contact either Taipei or Manila Centers on our UHF or high-frequency or guard radios.

We had been airborne for about four hours when I tried again to call Taipei Center but received no response on the UHF or HF radio or guard. At this point, I switched to the FM radio and tried to contact YH-05 again. He responded, but his transmission was faint and almost unreadable. I took a chance that he was going to hear my transmission, so I told him I was having radio problems and could not contact Taipei Center on UHF or HF or guard radios and to let them know I would be proceeding NORAD (loss communication procedures), squawking 7700, then 7800 on my transponder while proceeding to the initial approach fix. There, we would then enter holding until my expected approach clearance time and then shoot the published approach.

I thought I heard him responding, but again, his transmission was unreadable. I hoped he had received my message and that he would relay it to Taipei Center. The FM radio came to life once again when I heard him faintly say that he was currently starting his descent for a radar approach to Taipei International Airport, and he would see us on the ground, as his radio transmission faded away to static.

I now felt really alone in the world with no communications with the ground or my wingman. *Murphy is really having fun with us today. I sure hope our IFF transponder is operating, or we may have even bigger problems.*

My copilot had recovered enough from his severe vertigo to read the specific arrival procedures for Taipei International Airport and to review with me the TACAN, holding location, and procedures, as well as the published approached procedures to be used for a lost-communications situation. The last item we needed to verify was to make sure we knew exactly when our expected approach clearance time was, so we could start our approach on time. He, my copilot, double-checked it since it had been filed on our ICAO flight plan. This time was very important for two reasons—first, so that air traffic control could clear airspace for our holding and subsequent approach and then to alert the military air defense crews not to shoot us down as unidentified intruders, trying to attack their airfield. Taiwan military was extremely strict about unidentified arrivals.

Arriving at the holding location, we entered the published holding pattern until our expected approach clearance time, and then I shot the published approach after completing the landing checklist. As we approached, then passed through the decision height on the TACAN approach, we continued the approach busting through minimums and continuing until I could make out the runway lights at an altitude of 50 feet on the radar altimeter and with a horizontal visibility of about 50 yards. I eased the aircraft down toward the runway making a landing and came to a stop on it without difficulty despite the pouring down rain.

Almost immediately, a military vehicle bristling with .50-caliber machine guns and a follow-me vehicle appeared directly in front of us. The follow-me truck turned on its lights showing the big "Follow Me" light sign illuminated above the truck's cab, and we followed the truck to the parking ramp, with the military vehicle in trail behind us. We arrived in the parking area and were guided to a position next to our sister aircraft.

Our crew chief deplaned and monitored the shutdown of our aircraft. I had the feeling he was a happy Marine to be back on solid ground. My copilot was up and out of his seat quickly. He also appeared to be very happy to have solid ground under his feet once again as well.

I continued to sit in the cockpit for a couple of minutes trying to absorb all the events that had just taken place in our five-hour flight. *We have been very, very lucky,* I thought, *but we made it despite the obstacles thrown in our path. We beat Murphy this time.* I exited the aircraft, and making sure no one could see me, I kneeled down next to the aircraft, thanking God we had made it as I kissed the wet pavement, then I proceeded to postflight our aircraft in the driving rain.

We found that the hail and water from the storm had damaged the seals in the avionics compartments, allowing a significant amount of water to enter the two compartments and may have caused the radio problems we had during the flight. We compiled a list of things we needed to replace including the pilot's attitude direction indicator, the failed radios, and the avionics' compartment seals before going to the base operations building.

There, we met the crew of YH-05 and talked at length about the events that had transpired. It had been a long and harrowing flight for both crews. Captain Corner's aircraft had not had any major problems, so since YH-07 needed the parts, I was going to have to get the replacement parts ordered. My aircraft could not return to the Philippines without being fixed.

I called back to the squadron's duty officer and notified them of our arrival in Taipei and passed on the list of parts needed before we could depart. I also indicated that we needed the parts before we could return. We were originally scheduled to be in Taipei for one day, but we might have to stay longer if the parts needed for repair of my aircraft did not arrive the next day. He said he would pass on the information and asked where we could be reached if they needed additional information. I gave him the name and telephone number of the hotel where both of our crews would be saying. Ron and I always made it a point to take good care of our enlisted crew members, even if they were short on funds.

We all checked into the hotel, dropped off our gear in our rooms, and then met at the hotel bar for a much-needed drink. Ron and I talked about the flight, and I went into detail on the events as I recalled them.

He said he had barely gotten my transmission about the lost-comm situation but had been able to pass the information along to Taipei Center. He said after he had parked his aircraft, he went back to the Taipei Center's frequency and was monitoring the center's radio transmissions as they tried to contact you.

He said, "The center's transmissions indicated that after you entered holding, they understood and confirmed, in their minds, that you would be shooting the TACAN approach intending to commence it at your expected approach clearance time on the ICAO flight plan, so just prior to that time, they waved off one Japanese Airlines 747 commercial aircraft that was about to commence the ILS approach to the same runway and put a second one in holding out over the ocean. That enabled you to make the TACAN approach safely. One of the controllers made a comment as they were clearing the traffic out of your way. He said, "At least, that Marine pilot knows how to follow the ICAO lost-comm procedures and has his shit together."

About that time, the hotel bartender's phone rang; the bartender answered it and said, "Is there a Captain Corner here? It's your XO."

Captain Corner raised his hand, and the bartender gave him the phone. After an extended conversation with the squadron's XO, he came back and said, "The parts would be sent up on the next scheduled C-12 flight, the day after tomorrow, so enjoy your time in Taipei, since this will be the last cross-country flight approved to go there by our squadron. The XO initially thought we were trying to delay our return on purpose, then I told him about your aircraft flight and the problems you experienced. After hearing the entire story, he calmed down and accepted the fact that we were lucky to have made it there safely and said to come home when you had your aircraft fixed."

We all had a couple more *hooks* (military for "drinks") on me, then headed for our rooms. The next day, we went back to our birds and looked them over closely in the day light. All we discovered was some of the paint on the top of the cockpit, the horizontal stabilizer, and on the rotor blades had been worn off by the hail we had flown through. Other than that, both birds looked to be in good shape.

The enlisted crews were not interested in looking at furniture, so we split up and agreed to meet for dinner back at the hotel. Ron and I, plus our two copilots, caught a taxi and headed for the furniture district of Taipei. Ron had the address, which he gave to the driver who said he knew the place. He said, "Many American military people go to do business there. Good deals for you," as he smiled at us over his shoulder.

It was interesting how the cities in the Orient—such as, Taipei—laid out their business districts. The people of Taipei had elected to group the merchants by the commodity they sold together. An example of this commodities grouping was seen as we drove past an entire city block that had nothing but fish displayed in the stalls that faced on the street. We asked our driver, and he explained that both the inside and outside of the entire block were devoted to the sale of fish. As we continued to drive along, we saw an entire block that was devoted to the sale of pork, then beef, et cetera.

Reaching the furniture district address that we had given the driver, we paid him and went inside. The shop was located next to several other cabinet and furniture makers in the same commodities sales grouping. The gentleman who met us at the door was the owner of the shop, and when Ron told him we were there to pick up some completed furniture for the XO, Major Smith, he recognized the name immediately. He said that all the items the major ordered were ready, along with the other orders that had been placed at the same time. The owner then looked at the four of us with a gleam in his eyes, saying, "Are you gentlemen interested in purchasing some of my fine furniture? Please step this way. Oh, may I offer you all something to drink while you look around my shop?"

To make a long story short and, as I remember it, Captain Corner and I each purchased roll top desks along with each of us getting a Pop-I-Son chair. Captain Gaynor, Corner's copilot for this trip, bought a Pop-I-Son chair, and my copilot resisted the sales pitch but enjoyed the several beers that accompanied it and bought nothing.

We made arrangements to have all the furniture we and our predecessors had purchased delivered to the base the next day. The owner then offered to have one of his employees take us back to our hotel, which made the return trip very pleasant.

The next morning, our parts arrived via C-12, along with the furniture that had been delivered to our birds early in the morning. My crew chief and an avionics technician who had accompanied the new parts for my aircraft quickly installed and tested the radios and new attitude direction indicator. After checking the weather and conducting our standard NATOPS briefing, we loaded all our cargo onto the two birds. We filed an ICAO VFR flight plan for our return trip to Cubi Point in the Philippines.

Our return trip to the Philippines was made in almost perfect weather since the low-pressure system we had flown through coming to Taipei had moved a thousand miles south. The trip back was uneventful. We delivered the cargo of furniture, which was stored on the *Inchon* for our eventual return trip to Hawaii.

As negotiations continued to be stalled, the rest of the task force had withdrawn from North Vietnam waters returning to the Philippines. Our squadron, during this period, continued our support of various Marine and Army exercises in the Philippines. We also participated in a couple of minesweeping exercises in preparation for our eventual return to the minefields of North Vietnam and Operation End Sweep.

On June 3, John van Nortwick III passed the squadron's commanding-officer responsibilities to his XO, Major William J. Smith, in a change-of-command ceremony on the hangar deck of the USS *Inchon*.

*****

With the entire task force waiting for a break in the negotiations, the admiral moved the entire task force out of the Philippines and took the entire fleet to Singapore, arriving on June 12. Several of us used the time in Singapore to explore the beautiful city and stayed in the famous Raffle's Hotel, the proverbial birthplace of the Singapore Sling drink.

Ron Corner and I stayed in the same room at the Raffle's Hotel on the night of June 14 because of the room's cost. At 0500 hours, the phone woke both of us up with its persistent ringing. Ron answered it and then said, "We had been recalled. We need to get moving back to the ship ASAP since it's going to sail at 0700 hours, with or without us."

The task force pulled out of Singapore Harbor, then headed north to North Vietnamese waters to continue minesweeping after a new provision of the peace agreement had been signed. I was now assigned to work off the USS *Cleveland*'s replacement LPD, the USS *Ogden*.

We were now officially told that our mission was now one of verification. No longer one of minesweeping and detonation. We were now there to assure the North Vietnamese that the minefields were no longer a threat to North Vietnamese shipping. Most of us had figured that out several months earlier because only one mine had been detonated during the whole mission to date, but now it was official.

After, in my opinion, some unnecessary training, we again finally started the in-minefield verification activities on June 20. The USS *Inchon* aircraft worked the minefield at Hon Gai while our aircraft stationed on the LPD *Ogden* worked the minefield in the area off Cam Pha. Having completed the two minefield-verification operations, our two ships sailed on to our next assigned minefields off the coast in the Vinh area.

On June 2, YH-09, after refueling on the LPD *Ogden*, crashed in the minefield off the coast at Vin. The crew was rescued sustaining no injuries, but the aircraft was not recovered.

On July 5, minesweeping verification activities in our area of responsibility were deemed completed, and our squadron went into a standby mode.

Minesweeping-verification activities continued in the Haiphong Harbor area, but our squadron was not tasked with any additional verification sweeping operations. Operation End Sweep for all intended purposes was over for our squadron.

As we left the North Vietnamese waters for, what I hoped would be the last time, I thought, *This minesweeping mission is the best way to significantly reduce the usable life of these superior flying machines we have been operating. The constant exposures of salt spray and the flat turns required for the mission created overstressed conditions on the tail rotor components and contributed to early failure of critical components of these helicopters. To say it succinctly,* This mission sucked! *This mission should be left to the Navy. They should be equipped with specially designed aircraft to do this type of mission. In my opinion, a twin or tandem rotor helicopter such as the CH-47 would make a much superior platform to do this type of mission because it does not have a tail rotor. If the mines in the North Vietnamese waters (really bombs) had not had self-detonating settings and had not almost totally destroyed themselves before we really got started with the minesweeping process, we would have been in the unpleasant position of making the hours of minesweeping boredom into ones that were broken up by seconds of stark terror as we detonated these large munitions.*

We sailed to Subic Bay and then made the trip back to K-Bay on two LPDs. En route back, I found out that my requested humanitarian transfer to MCAS El Toro had been approved based on the death of my mother-in-law and the requirement to provide care for her eighty-five-year-old mother, who had lived with her prior to her death and was her sole caregiver.

Three days after my return, I checked out of HMH-463, packed up the family, and headed for a new duty assignment at MCAS El Toro.

As we departed Hawaii in a big PanAm 747 jet for Los Angeles Airport, I thought, *Sure hope I never have to do another minute of minesweeping in the future.*

CTF 78 task force sailing in mass at the end
of Operation End Sweep-1973

Pre-Press Conference showing Mine Sweeping demonstration in Subic Bay by Marine Helicopter-1972

Marine CH-53D towing mine sweeping gear in
Hanoi Estuary, North Vietnam in 1973

Chapter 5

COMMANDER OF MARINE CORPS AIR BASES, WESTERN AREA (COMCABWEST)

Marine Corps Air Station in El Toro, California; Essential Subjects Training; Officer's Story (1973–1974)

Two months after returning from Hawaii

As I stood before the two commanding generals after telling them that a twenty-seven-year-old gunnery sergeant in one of their commands could not read above the third-grade level, an expression of shock appeared on both their faces.

"That's impossible," the air station commander said. "A staff NCO of that rank could not advance that far and not be able to read above the third-grade level. That's really next to impossible or just an individual anomaly. This single case does not explain the failure rate of over 70 percent of our Marines in the written portion of the Essential Subject Test (EST) that was conducted by the inspector general's (IG) last inspection, does it, son?"

Since when did I become his son? I muttered under my breath.

The air wing commander then interrupted saying, "How could these failures happen, and are these events connected?"

I responded by saying, "Sirs, both of these events could have happened in a couple of different ways. I am sure that both of you, Generals, remember that all Marines have been taught to adapt, improvise, and overcome obstacles placed in their paths in order to accomplish their missions. This had been the Marines' philosophy and has been in place since its inception at Tun Tavern in 1775.

"In the case of this gunnery sergeant, he wanted to make a career in the Marine Corps, so he found various ways to hide his reading deficiency effectively until this last IG inspection. We believe he was successful until now because the written EST test had not been modified or rewritten until just before the latest IG inspection, three months ago. We believe this rewrite revealed a potential widespread problem.

"My staff and I wanted to find out why he and the rest of both commands did so poorly on the last IG inspection.

"Our first thought was to look at a potentially common reason why so many Marines of all ranks failed the written portion of the new EST test. Seeing lack of reading comprehension as a potential common thread connecting these failures, we wanted to look at reading skills first. We took the opportunity to administer reading comprehension tests during the next EST training session. The results were very revealing. We discovered that the average reading comprehension level of the class was at the third-grade level. Some Marines scored higher, 5 percent at an eighth-grade level, and some scored lower, 25 percent at a first-grade level, but 70 percent scored at the third-grade level.

"As you gentlemen can see from the IG inspection results, along with our testing results, the gunnery sergeant was not the only one who appears to have reading problems. Since the IG inspection was a newly written examination, it is now understandable why the failure rate was so high. My staff and I believe that the Marines in both of your commands have an excellent to outstanding knowledge of the military essential subjects. The problem is how to prove to the IG that these Marines possess this knowledge using our short-term solutions. These facts highlight why my staff and I have recommended that we take a different course of action to solve the short-term problem of how to show the IG inspectors that our Marines are not deficient in essential-subject-training skills. This short-term solution has to be implemented quickly if we are to pass the reinspection that is scheduled in four months from now.

"Our new testing program, if you two approved the plan, will be the key to demonstrating that each Marine possessed the knowledge, skills, and abilities required to function as an enlisted Marine who could perform their fundamental duties as Marine infantrymen. This will enable the commands to pass the IG reinspection," thus I concluded my presentation.

The two generals' facial expressions and mannerisms appeared to show a degree of skepticism that our recommended short-term process could be put in place fast enough to produce the results that would be acceptable to the IG; however, they agreed to support the project. They agreed that the longer-term problem of the lack of reading ability was to be considered later. I was not convinced that they believed my explanation, but their approval of our short-term plan was all we needed to go forward.

It was very evident that these two generals wanted a positive result from the IG reinspection, now just four months away. They did not say it directly, but a repeat failure of the IG inspection of the EST program could potentially and would most likely adversely affect their commanders' evaluations (meaning, limiting their long-term career opportunities).

These two generals did not state this specifically, but it was implied that they wanted the previous failure to disappear, and my team was tasked to make that happen.

After leaving the general's office, our team met and agreed that the short-term success of the new testing program was going to be the key to demonstrate that each Marine possessed the knowledge, skills, and abilities required to function as an enlisted Marine who could perform their fundamental duties as Marine infantrymen. We needed to get started on the development of the testing program ASAP.

As I listened to my master gunnery sergeant start to make assignments to our team, I could not help thinking back to how I got myself into this predicament. After returning to Hawaii, having participated in Operation End Sweep (airborne clearing of mines in North Vietnam's shorelines, harbors, and rivers by helicopter), my mother-in-law passed away in mid-1973. Because my mother-in-law's mother was still alive and needed special care, I was given a humanitarian transfer to MCAS El Toro so my wife could provide it.

Reporting for duty at the MCAS El Toro base located in Southern California unexpectedly, the chief of staff had to find me a job. Initially, I was assigned temporary duties in the community planning and liaison office where I functioned as a glorified clerk for two senior officers for approximately one month. Getting coffee, answering the telephone, and taking notes was not my cup of tea. Watching what went on in the office was very interesting but getting coffee for two colonels was not very challenging for me after my past combat assignments. As I was continuing to do coffee and phone duty, I found out that the Headquarters Marine Corps' inspector general had performed an overall command-inspection program of commands located at MCAS El Toro including the air station command the month before my arrival at MCAS El Toro. As part of these inspections, the Marine Corps' IG conducted an inspection on the EST program administered by the MCAS El Toro Training Department. This IG inspection found the EST program to be unsatisfactory. This finding was based primarily on the excessive failure rate of those who took the new EST written test.

Hearing about the unsatisfactory results of the IG inspection and being in a position that was not at all challenging, I volunteered to be reassigned to the training department in hopes of finding a more challenging and fulfilling job. I talked to the chief of staff of the air station who indicated that there may be an opening in the training department that would certainly be a challenging job if I took it. As I was leaving the chief of staff's office, he said, "Are you sure you really want to do this, Captain?"

"Yes, sir," I replied on my way out.

He arranged for me to be scheduled to meet the head of the training department, another full colonel who was biding his time waiting to retire, for an interview.

I met with the colonel in charge of the training department who was surprised that I would want to take on such a daunting challenge in light of the recent results of the IG inspection. He told me during my interview that if I got the job, my primary task was to find out why the EST program was having so many failures. Then I would need to find a way to get it fixed. The colonel also said it needed to be fixed quickly and prior to the IG reinspection that was scheduled four months from now.

After our discussion, he asked me if I was still interested in the job. Recognizing a good challenge, I said to him, "Yes, sir," and took the job.

My current bosses were very understanding of why I was seeking a more challenging position and did not object to my move. I was transferred to the training department the next day.

The first step after checking into the training department and finding my office was to meet the Marines that I would work with in my new assignment. As I placed my briefcase on the desk of my new office, I heard a knock on the door. Looking up, I saw a sharp-looking master gunnery sergeant standing in the doorway. He stepped forward and said, "Sir, you must be our new EST training officer. We heard you were coming to help us with our problems."

"That is correct on both counts, Top [Marine slang for 'master gunnery sergeant'], and you must be the noncommissioned officer in charge [NCOIC] of our EST program," I responded.

"You are correct, Captain, and welcome aboard," he responded. "Do you mind answering a question before I take you to meet the rest of our team?"

"I would be happy to, Top," I said.

He asked, "Sir, why would a young officer, such as yourself, volunteer to take on a task like this deteriorating and troubled operation?"

Looking him in the eye, I responded by saying, "Top, I have two reasons for volunteering for this job. First, I like challenges, and

I believe this job will be one. Second, I like to fix difficult problems. I have had both of these afflictions since I was a child. That is why I volunteered."

As I watched the reaction to my explanation for why I volunteered for this job, I saw a very big smile spread across the master gunnery sergeant's face. At this point, my mind drifted back to my youth. I was about five years old, if I recall correctly, when I watched my father fixing a toaster in our utility room. He told me that the way you looked at a problem had a great deal to do with the way you went about solving it. I remembered him saying, "If you see a problem as a challenge and not something that is insurmountable, you are halfway there in finding a good solution." He applied this philosophy to all the jobs he undertook, whether it was fixing a toaster or to starting and running his moving and storage company. Coming back to reality, I heard the Top speaking to me.

He said, "In that case, Captain, again, welcome aboard, and now let's go meet the rest of your new team," as he ushered me out of my office to a large conference room where my new team was gathered.

The master gunnery sergeant introduced me to my new team that consisted of himself, nine staff noncommissioned officers (staff NCOs), and twelve noncommissioned officers (NCOs). I walked around the room and shook each Marine's hand as they were introduced. After the completion of the introductions, I took a seat and listened as they briefed me on the current operation of the EST program from its inception until that day.

Our program was borne out of the directive promulgated by the commandant of the Marine Corps. In this directive, the commandant of the Marine Corps directed that all enlisted Marines, regardless of their grade or military occupational specialty (their primary job), shall achieve and maintain proficiency in certain essential military subjects. After recruit training, all enlisted Marines will be evaluated annually by their commanders to determine if essential-military-subject proficiency is being maintained by their Marines.

The Marine Corps' philosophy was that regardless of their technical job specialty, they were first and foremost infantrymen. This

United States Marine Corps headquarters' directive was the driving force in the development of the EST Evaluation Program in each command. The directive authors recognized that some Marines may require refresher training to remain proficient. Once the necessity of additional refresher training was recognized and that the testing program needed to be standardized, a program that covered all enlisted Marines was established across the Marine Corps by its headquarters.

One such program was instituted per the Marine Corps' directive at MCAS El Toro, MCAS (H) Santa Ana, and MCAS Yuma. It additionally encompassed units of the Third Marine Aircraft Wing (Third MAW), which was a tenant unit located at all these facilities.

The Marine Corps' Essential Subjects Program was designed to measure the ability of enlisted Marines to perform their fundamental duties as Marine infantrymen. This program included the following subject matter areas: (1) code of conduct, military law/Uniform Code of Military Justice and conduct in war; (2) Marine Corps' history, customs, and courtesies; (3) close order drill; (4) interior guard; (5) first aid and field sanitation; (6) uniform clothing and equipment; (7) physical fitness; (8) nuclear, biological, and chemical (NBC) defense; (9) service rifle and marksmanship; (10) individual tactical measures; (11) security of military information; and (12) substance abuse.

The MCAS El Toro Training Department was charged with the responsibility of annually conducting essential-military-subjects testing and training for all enlisted Marines located at MCAS El Toro, MCAS (H) Santa Ana, MCAS Yuma, and its tenant units of the Third MAW.

My next step was to evaluate the EST program. Since the current EST program was divided into two parts—a hands-on demonstration of proficiency and a written test—we would evaluate each part separately.

The first step we took was to schedule and make a visit to the hands-on EST demonstration areas. The NCOIC and I visited the rifle and pistol ranges and the physical-training field, watching the conduct of the training exercises. Next, we visited the classrooms and observed some of the remedial EST training that was taking place.

If a Marine failed any part of the EST test (a two-hundred-question written test covering all the subjects, including the ones requiring demonstration of skills), they were required to undergo remedial studies until they could pass the failed portion of the test.

We looked at remedial study guides, lesson plans, and other materials to assess if the necessary information for successful passage of the tests were being provided to those who failed the test.

Remedial training could last up to eight weeks for multiple-subject failures. Instead of a Marine being away from his primary duty, for example, an aircraft mechanic, for two weeks, he could be away for eight to ten weeks. These extended absences were having a significant negative effect on aircraft readiness and morale at all the air stations and the Third MAW.

These briefings, tours, and reviews of all applicable orders took about a week to complete. During this time, I also reviewed the department-posted *passing and failing* rates since the establishment of the combined air stations and Third MAW EST training program.

My initial observation after a week was that the health of the program was poor from the start and became worse and worse to the point where it failed the last IG inspection with only 30 percent passing their annual EST written examinations. Meanwhile, the program was continuing to process Marines that came because of their annual evaluation. The program's pass-through rate had to be fixed while we still maintained an inflow of approximately two hundred additional enlisted Marine personnel per month that were required to go through the training. The class size of approximately fifty Marines each week was necessary in order to meet the requirements of annual testing at the air stations and their tenant units.

Morale of my EST team at this point was extremely low because of the program's failure at the last IG inspection. We discussed, at length, what the staff believed was the reason for the failure of so many staff NCOs, NCOs, and enlisted troops who should have known the answers to the test questions cold. No one on the team could fathom why senior Marine staff NCOs, NCOs, and enlisted troops were failing these tests. The senior staff NCO of my EST team indicated that he had observed several remedial training sessions and found that these Marines could answer a previously failed test question when asked verbally. Several other instructors indicated they had similar experiences.

These observations led me to wonder whether the individuals taking these written tests could comprehend the substance of the test questions. I asked my team if we had any data regarding the reading comprehension levels of the Marines taking the EST test. They indicated they had no reading-level data, and it was not required to be kept by any regulation they knew of.

After our team meeting, I asked my NCOIC to arrange two interviews—one with one of the most senior staff NCOs who had failed significant parts of the EST written test and the other with an NCO who had also failed several parts of the test, both of whom were currently undergoing remedial training.

After the interviews were scheduled, I used the original tests they had taken in preparation for my conduct of the interview of each Marine in order to see which questions they had missed. My review of these two tests that were a multiple-choice written test revealed that the senior staff NCO had missed 50 percent of the questions while the NCO had missed over 90 percent of them.

In the first interview, the staff NCO and I discussed in detail the specific EST test questions he had missed. After talking to this staff NCO for more than an hour, it became very clear that he knew the answers to all the EST questions he had missed on the test when they were asked verbally. After thanking him for his participation in the interview, I asked my NCOIC to send a young sergeant who had also failed almost all the parts of the EST exam into my office to see me.

Upon his arrival, I read him questions taken directly from the EST exam he had not passed. He correctly answered all but two of the fifty questions asked. At that time, I handed him the exam and asked him to read question number 6 (one of which he answered correctly earlier verbally). He managed to get partway through the question but was unable to finish reading it. He left my office after I thanked him for his participation in the research process.

After his departure, I again met with my staff and shared the results from my interviews. We all agreed that it appeared that the young sergeant and senior staff NCO were experiencing a great deal of trouble reading the questions on the written EST exam. It became apparent that the individuals knew the material but were unable to read or understand or both the questions on the EST written exam.

Our next step was to determine the comprehensive reading grade level the EST exam was based on. A telephone call to the headquarters of the Marine Corps' (HQMC) Training Department revealed that the EST exam was written for the eighth-grade comprehension level. At this point, I asked the folks at the HQMC if they had reading comprehension tests available that we could administer to our students. They indicated that they had the tests and would send them to us. We received the reading tests a couple of days later.

After receipt of the reading tests, my staff and I scheduled the current remedial EST class to take the reading comprehension test during one of their study periods. After administering the test, we graded them and discovered that the average reading comprehension level of the class was third grade. Some were higher (5 percent was eighth-grade level), and some were lower (25 percent was first-grade level).

Next, my NCOIC and I reviewed the personnel files of each Marine in the remedial EST class in order to determine the education level of each one, as documented in their personnel record. Fifty percent of these records indicated that these Marines had a high school education or GED, and 50 percent indicated that they had completed at least sixth grade.

Our team gathered together and discussed in great length the results of the reading tests, the review of student records, and EST failures. Most of my team were shocked to see the disparity in reading comprehension levels and education. A consensus by the team was reached regarding the fact that these and other Marines were not educationally equipped to master the current new EST written exam based on their lack of reading ability and comprehension.

"What can we as a team do now to fix the problem?" I asked my team.

One idea the team discussed was to test all Marines coming through the EST program to determine their actual reading comprehension level. This would be done in connection with the development and administering of remedial reading programs.

This approach would take an extremely long time to administer and would require the individual to accept that they had a problem. It appeared that this strategy for long-term improvement would help those individuals, but it would not solve the short-term problem of continued failures currently exhibited by these folks taking the EST written exam.

Our team recognized that the command was under pressure to show the IG reinspection team that we were dealing proactively with the problem of EST failure rates. Additionally, the aviation commands were putting additional pressure on our training department because their Marines were in training and away from their primary jobs for extended periods. We needed a strategy that quickly fixed the short-term problems first, and then we could deal with the larger reading problem failures.

Our team developed a short-term strategy that utilized the concept of the demonstration of practical EST knowledge. We would need to develop a process to measure the ability of the individual Marine to demonstrate physically or verbally their knowledge of the EST materials. This mechanism, it was hoped, would eliminate the reading problem on a temporary basis and portray the real EST knowledge possessed by these Marines.

This radical concept of practical evaluation was going to require a significant amount of command support to be both viable and acceptable to units participating in the program, including the Headquarters Marine Corps IG inspectors.

Our next step was to formulate a briefing and presentation to my boss. We needed to explain the reading problem and outlined the new approach to solve the current EST failure problem.

The briefing consisted of statistics that showed the number of failures in the current remedial EST class and the reading comprehension scores for each member. A specific comparison was made between the two Marines who were interviewed that included the test results for the written exam and for the same questions when asked orally. This was designed to show that the knowledge required for successful completion of the EST test was resident in the mind of the individual Marine, but it was beyond his capability to pass the written test because of his poor or nonexistent reading skills. The last part of the briefing consisted of a recommendation for the development and implementation of a practical examination of the EST subjects that were previously only tested by written examination.

With the briefing package completed, my team and I scheduled the presentation the following day with my boss. He was skeptical of the process at first, but after hearing all the evidence we had compiled, he agreed to have us present it to the commanding generals of both the air stations and air wing.

The following day, our team made the presentation to these two general officers. At the conclusion of the presentation, a discussion was held to evaluate the options presented and then to approve or reject our recommendations.

While these two generals were still somewhat skeptical that the recommended short-term process could be put in place fast enough to produce the results that would be acceptable to the IG, they again agreed to support the project.

The longer-term problem of the lack of reading ability was to be considered later. It was very evident that they wanted the results of the IG reinspection, now just four months away, to be positive. Again, the concern of a repeat failure of the EST program could potentially and most likely adversely affect their commanders' evaluations (meaning, their long-term career opportunities) must be resolved.

As in the first meeting with the two generals, they did not state this specifically, but it was implied that they wanted the previous failure to disappear, and my team was tasked to make that happen using the new testing program.

Our team met after the briefing and agreed that the short-term success of the new testing program was going to be the key to demonstrate that each Marine possessed the knowledge, skills, and abilities required to function as an enlisted Marine who could perform their fundamental duties as Marine infantrymen.

The testing protocols that were required to undergo major redevelopment under our plan were code of conduct; military law/UCMJ and conduct in war; Marine Corps' history, customs, and courtesies; interior guard; first aid and field sanitation; uniform clothing and equipment; nuclear, biological, and chemical (NBC) Defense; individual tactical measures; security of military information; and substance abuse.

Areas such as close order drill, physical fitness, and service rifle and marksmanship were already being evaluated by the practical performance of each Marine during their temporary assignment to our organization.

As our team worked to develop each of these key EST areas, it was suggested that we assign staff NCOs to each area to become a subject-matter expert for that area. As subject-matter experts in each of the new key areas were assigned and started, their development work. They quickly developed tasks, assignments, and projects that Marines could utilize to demonstrate their mastery of the specific subject areas. In order to support the subject-matter development, other NCOs were assigned to support their efforts.

One example of the practical examination concept that we developed was to demonstrate knowledge, skills, and abilities in the area of first aid by asking a Marine to perform CPR on a manikin and evaluate his technique and competence. This was used to test the Marine's skill rather than asking him, in writing, on the EST exam, to identify written steps that are necessary to perform CPR.

Our team continued to work overtime and weekends for the next three weeks in order to complete all the protocols, practical exams, and to obtain all the equipment, as well as the facilities necessary to start testing.

One of our largest challenges was to make sure that all the areas that were tested on the written EST exam were evaluated with the same rigor as they were going to be by the new practical examination methods.

Since our classroom space was limited, we asked the facilities management organization for additional space needed to house the practical demonstration testing necessary to implement the new testing program. The Navy Captain in charge told us that there was no space available in existing facilities but suggested we might be able to utilize tents to get the space necessary quickly. We asked the Third MAW for two general-purpose field tents, which they supplied, that were put up outside the training department building.

As a longer-term solution, the captain did assign an old warehouse, which required rehab before we could utilize it. Rehab was started while we utilized the tents for our interim space. These temporary facilities met our immediate training needs but were far from an ideal training environment.

Things were moving very rapidly as we obtained materials from the supply system to be use for field sanitation projects and nuclear, biological, and chemical drills. Storage became another problem, but our team solved it by using a Conex box for storage of these hazardous materials after receiving the blessing of the station fire chief.

Everything came together so quickly that we had only a limited time to review and modify, as a team, each practical examination test. Our evaluation processes had to be completed and checked prior to being used in the evaluation of the next incoming EST class.

Our final modification of the practical evaluations was completed Sunday afternoon of the third weekend. We were now ready to test the new EST practical evaluation process on the Marines.

Bright and early on Monday morning, the next class of fifty Marines arrived, as scheduled, to undergo the first half of their annual EST evaluation. Previously, this evaluation entailed the administration of the written EST examination. Now they would be using the new practical examination testing program. In their second week, these fifty Marines would receive rifle and pistol range and physical fitness exams to complete their EST annual training.

My first task was to welcome these Marines to the training department and to explain the new EST testing program to them. As I explained the new EST practical examination process, faces on almost all the Marines showed signs of relief. It appeared to me that most of the Marines were dreading the written examination.

The EST class was broken up into groups of ten Marines each and assigned to various EST practical testing locations. Each group would be tested on the assigned subject at that designated location. Throughout the five days of testing, each group of Marines would be rotated to other areas of EST practical testing until all Marines in the class had completed the entire exam circuit.

At the end of the first day, my staff and I met to discuss and evaluate the testing that had taken place so far. Each subject-matter-expert staff NCO presented the results for his area of EST testing.

After each report, the master gunnery sergeant tabulated the results and kept a running total of pass and fail statistics. At the end of the first day of testing, the fifty Marines had passed 91 percent of the practical examinations administered.

While we had only the first one-fifth of the new practical testing completed, we were all very encouraged. On each of the subsequent four days, we repeated our discussion and evaluation process after completion of the day's testing.

Late on Friday afternoon, the results of the final day's training completions were discussed and tabulated. The Top then tabulated all test results from the previous four days of testing and incorporated them into a final summary for the entire week's EST practical evaluation testing. I then double-checked it to ensure it was accurate before we passed the results on to my boss.

Our first day pass rate of 91 percent had not been maintained throughout the entire testing cycle. It had fallen slightly to 89.5 percent when all the Marines in the class had completed all EST practical examinations as part of this portion of their EST annual evaluation (rifle and pistol range, close order drill, and physical fitness exams still had to be completed).

The 89.5-percent pass rate was a far cry from the previous written EST exam pass and failure rates that had caused the command's previous IG inspection failure earlier in the year (30-percent pass rate).

After the final week's tabulation discussions were completed, my master gunnery sergeant NCOIC and I held a private meeting in which we discussed how we could win command approval of the EST practical testing protocols that our staff had created.

We agreed to delay briefing my boss or the CG as to the progress that had been made in our program because we had not gotten the results of the rifle and pistol qualification, close order drill, and physical fitness exams for our first class, which could affect the passing statistics.

While we waited for these results, we tackled the problem of the IG perception of our process. The IG used written testing scores exclusively to evaluate the Marine's mastery of a large portion of the EST program. Our practical evaluation method was different from what they would expect to see.

Our approach to solving this problem was to provide written documentation of our practical examination process completion to the IG.

We put together forms that were filled out by the subject-matter experts for each area being tested at the time the actual evaluation occurred. These forms indicated that each Marine had completed the specified evaluation, documented by the use of written check marks, thus providing documented evidence by the subject-matter experts that the individual Marine had correctly or incorrectly demonstrated their knowledge and ability to complete tasks, projects, and assignment of the specific EST items or had not.

In order to pass the upcoming IG reinspection, we needed a way to convince the IG and the HQMC training department that our practical evaluation method was in fact a valid measure of these Marines' abilities. After some brainstorming, we decided to use a movie camera to document each of these practical examination tasks, projects, and assignments that had been developed to evaluate EST proficiency.

These pictures would be worth a thousand words in trying to describe our testing protocols. We also discussed the possibility of filming each Marine coming through the program as they took their tests. We ruled it out because of the cost of the filming process, the space required to store all the film, and the repetitive nature of the process (the annual testing).

On the following Monday, the current class moved on to the rifle and pistol qualification, close order drill, and physical fitness portion of the testing while we welcomed another fifty Marines into the practical examination portion of the EST evaluation. These results may change the passing rate significantly, so we waited for all the testing results to come in before claiming victory.

As the new class started the EST process, we again continued to utilize our subject-matter experts to test each Marine using the new EST practical evaluation protocols. During this testing period, we had each of the practical examination tasks, projects, and assignments filmed by a professional photographer from the photo lab.

The practical exam testing results were like the first week's, with a 90.5-percent passing rate for all the EST subjects tested. We also received the results of the rifle and pistol qualification, close order drill, and physical fitness exams for our first practical exam class.

These results increased our passing rate for the first EST class using the practical evaluation process to 92.1 percent from the 89.5 percent. This was truly good news, but it was just the start of the program, and more data would be necessary before we could present a case that the program was really succeeding.

We had only about two months before the IG reinspection, so it was time to make another presentation to my boss and then to the CGs.

Our presentation again outlined the new process we had developed, and again, we sought support for the continuation of the new program. The presentation we put together consisted of statistics that showed the number of failures in the previous written EST evaluations and compared them to the new scores of the practical EST examinations.

We then showed part of the movie that documented Marines taking the practical examinations. Our intent in showing the movie was to show that the knowledge base required for successful completion of the EST annual evaluation was present in the minds of the individual Marine taking the test.

We would place our emphasis on the problem of poor reading skills, which made it very difficult for these Marines to pass the written EST tests. We would then conclude the presentation by suggesting that additional practical examinations would be necessary in order to document that this program accurately evaluated the individual Marine's military skills and knowledge.

We were going to recommend that a summarization of the practical examination program be sent to the IG prior to their reinspection. This summarization would be accompanied by the movie that we had produced. We hoped that this heads-up to the IG before the reinspection would lessen the shock of not looking at completed written tests when their team arrive for the reinspection.

After the briefing package was completed, my team and I scheduled the presentation for the following day. After his briefing, my boss became an instant advocate for our new process. Immediately following the briefing, he picked up the telephone and called the staff secretary to request time in both the commanding generals' schedules when we could make our presentation. He got us on their schedule quickly because of the serious nature of the problem.

The following day, our team made the presentation to the two general officers. We initially planned to show the generals and their staffs only part of the practical examination tasks, projects, and assignments that had been filmed by the photo lab. However, during the presentation of the movie, we were asked by the generals to show the entire film because they became very interested and impressed with our new practical examination process. At the conclusion of our presentation, the two generals indicated that they were satisfied with the progress we had made fixing the big problem.

They agreed to approve our recommendation for the development of a package that summarized the practical examination program (including the supporting film). This package would be sent as part of the command's corrective action report to the IG prior to their reinspection. In addition, it was strongly suggested (ordered) that the HQMC Training Department be provided copies of everything that we were going to send to the IG.

Over the next two weeks, we developed the summarization submittals and had the film reproduced. During this same time frame, our subject-matter experts continued to administer the practical evaluation to additional Marines. The test results were very similar to the first two classes and further reinforced our contention that we are on our way to solving the short-term problem of the EST failures.

Another significant by-product of the implementation of our new process was that many more Marines were returned to their units after the two-week training period instead of being required to complete remedial EST training. Only about 9 percent of the Marines tested using the practical evaluation process required additional remedial training. This result made the aviation unit commanders very happy along with commensurate raising of operational readiness of their units.

The command submitted the materials we created, along with other corrective actions for other command deficiencies, to the Headquarters Marine Corps IG.

We, per the CG's directive, sent additional copies of the summarization materials and film to the Headquarters Training Department (HQ). My staff and I waited several days for reactions from HQ. We were told that both submittals all arrived at HQ approximately two weeks before Christmas.

Since we had not received any feedback from HQ, we continued to process Marines under our new program until the command shutdown for the Christmas holidays. Both commands observed the Christmas and New Year's holiday routines over the next two weeks. After returning to normal duties after the holidays, we still had not received any feedback from either of the HQ organizations. We needed to know if we were headed in the right direction, or was this process not going to be accepted?

I decided to call Washington and try to find out. My informal telephone communications with the Headquarters Training Department indicated that the package had been received and was being processed. No feedback would be provided from the HQ Training Department until they had finished processing and assessing the package.

The HQ major I had talked to was not supportive of the process at all. He told me that he believed it violated the HQ order on EST evaluation processes.

He is bullshitting me now; he has not looked at it. It does not fit his HQ-driven agenda and concepts, so he wants to automatically reject it, I thought.

I asked him a question regarding what specific section of the EST order that he believed we were violating. His answer was that he would get back to me. This led me to believe that he had not really looked at the order in depth and would have to do some homework before he could respond.

After my discussion with the HQ major, I assembled my staff and asked them to do additional in-depth reviews of all applicable orders with special attention to the HQ order on EST evaluations. I hoped that when we had done our original review of these orders, we had not missed anything.

Two days later, my NCOIC informed me that the staff had completed the requested reviews and that nothing was found in the orders that would prohibit the utilization of our practical examination process. He indicated that the key to the compliance with the orders was adequate written documentation of each Marine's subject-matter-experts qualifications, as well as separate written documentation for each Marine undergoing evaluation in each specific EST areas tested.

Our current lesson plans for remedial EST instructions were found to be in compliance with all applicable orders. He and the staff also recommended that we develop a joint air station and Third MAW EST order outlining our new process and articulating the required documentation requirements.

It was crystal clear to all of us that we needed to have the order in place before the IG reinspection.

I asked my NCOIC and my staff to develop the joint order as soon as possible. The NCOIC indicated to me that he wanted to take personal responsibility for the order's development as well as to ensure that we had the necessary documentation for all the enlisted Marines who had undergone the practical evaluation examination to date.

We also developed résumés for each subject-matter expert who was being utilized as an evaluator during the EST practical evaluation process. This large task needed to be done quickly as well. Once the résumés were completed, I personally reviewed each and every one of them.

My staff completed the writing of the joint order in record time and pushed it through the review process so that it could be issued as a joint air station and Third MAW EST order. My NCOIC completed his tasks as directed and I reviewed the products he produced. Throughout this period, we continued to process additional Marines through the program. We obtained the same results, approximately a 91-percent passing rate. The IG reinspection was quickly approaching, and I had confidence that our program would meet the spirit and intent of the headquarters' EST program.

As the IG reinspection got underway, I was surprised to see the major from the Headquarters Training Department that I had talked to earlier. He was heading up the IG team that would be reinspecting our EST operation. He appeared to have brought half his training organization with him for the inspection. During the in-briefing process, he indicated that he had received the package outlining our process and that he and his team were willing to keep an open mind regarding its acceptability. His concern again was compliance with the HQ EST orders.

The IG reinspection team review of our operation took a full four days with the morning of the fifth day devoted to development, finalization, and conclusions reached for the reinspection. I met with my staff each day after the inspection team had finished for the day. They indicated that no comments were made regarding the documentation that was presented or processes that were being reviewed.

We had no idea if our new process would survive the reinspection or not. The IG team presented the formal reinspection results for all areas that were reinspected at a presentation on Friday afternoon in the air station gym. This large venue was selected in order to accommodate the large number of people potentially impacted by the IG reinspection results.

Our EST area was the last area to be discussed and critiqued. The major from HQ got up to brief the audience and reviewed the problem that generated the unsatisfactory inspection earlier. He then went into specific documents that he and his team reviewed. The major took additional time to discuss the joint EST order we had written in order to implement the new practical evaluation process. He indicated that the order provided the needed clarification regarding the interface between the HQ EST order and our new practical evaluation process, and it also provided the necessary compliance with the HQ EST order that he had originally questioned. He further stated that "This EST practical evaluation processes implementation has highlighted the problem of reading comprehension that had not been heretofore officially recognized. While the practical evaluation process is a good short-term solution to the EST failure problem, it will be necessary to tackle the larger problem of reading comprehension in the future."

The major concluded by saying that all the areas inspected by his team passed the inspection and that the practical evaluation process we had developed would be considered as a viable alternative to the written EST evaluation in the future.

Both generals, my boss, my NCOIC, and I were extremely pleased with our Headquarters Marine Corps' IG reinspection results. After the conclusion of the review and critique, the CG called my boss asking him to gather all the officers and staff who directly contributed to the development and implementation of the new EST evaluation program. We assembled all concerned in our training building. The CG made a special trip to our building to address the group. He thanked all the Marines for their ingenuity, common sense, and hard work. He rewarded everyone a ninety-six-hour pass (a *ninety-six-hour pass* is "time off that is not counted against accrued leave").

Having completed the EST practical evaluation implementation process, I continued to oversee the positive results for the next several months.

While the EST work was continuing, I had totally forgotten that I was in the selection zone for major. I had no preconceived notions that I would be selected, primarily because of my amateur performance in the eyes of my CO during my Lam Son 719 tour of duty and again during the End Sweep Operation.

I tried to learn from the mistakes that I made, and I made many, but it was my intent on learning from them and not to repeat them again. I had hoped that I had learned to be a good company-grade officer in the nine years I had served on active duty.

To my surprise, in mid-July 1974, I was notified that I was selected for promotion to the rank of major. This promotion would make me a field-grade officer. The promotion would move me from the ranks of senior captain, a company-grade officer position, to a position of a field-grade officer, which offered several benefits. One benefit was that I could, at the time, remain in the Marine Corps for twenty years and had a guaranteed retirement. The other benefit, in my mind, was that this promotion could open more opportunities to take on bigger and more challenging jobs.

On September 1, 1974, I was officially promoted to major in the United States Marine Corps ending my company-grade service.

With this promotion to major and to a field-grade officer in the United States Marine Corps, my memoir of the remaining fifteen years of my twenty-five-year career is set forth in chronological order in book 2 of *Unlike No Other*.

CHAPTER 6

ESCAPE AND EVASION FOR DUMMIES

(An Excerpt from Book 2)

Book 2 of this memoir describes and traces my career as a field-grade officer from my promotion to major, lieutenant colonel, and then colonel until my retirement after a successful completion of my final command of the Marine Corps' Air Station Tustin, California, in 1989.

Below is an excerpt from one of the stories contained in book 2 of my memoir.

Gathering my survival gear and knowing time was not on my side, I decided to use a couple of backtrack deception strategies first in an effort to confuse the enemy tractors. Then a concealment strategy to try to keep out of sight of the "Red Team's" enemy exercise capture force.

Approaching the rice paddy, I noted the presence of four or five large water buffalos. Each of these black and brown animals had large menacing-looking hooked horns three feet or longer sticking forward from their heads. These two-thousand-pound buffalos were walking slowly in and around the rice paddy leaving a large number of tracks along the shoreline and in the muddy water of the rice paddy itself.

I had seen these types of buffalos all over Vietnam. They were used to pull a plow in the rice field there, so I knew that some of these animals were probably domesticated. All the buffalos seemed to be paying no attention to me, further convincing me that they were, in fact, domesticated.

Since the buffalo's actions appeared to be nonthreatening, it occurred to me that I might use these buffalo tracks to cover my trail and slow down the Red Team's search effort somewhat.

When I reached the edge of the rice paddy, I looked for buffalo tracks that were headed in the direction I wanted to go across the rice paddy. I found five or six sets of tracks that were close to my location that led across the rice paddy in various directions. Before selecting a set of tracks to use for my crossing, I moved quickly back and forth along the bank, leaving visible footprints in order to confuse my pursuers. As I was doing this, something caught my eye in the grass next to the rice paddy. It was a large snake lying in the grass a couple of feet from me. I quickly stepped away from it a couple of feet.

I looked again at the rice paddy, a little closer this time, seeing several even larger snakes swimming on the rice paddy's surface near the tall elephant grass and bamboo that I had seen on my way coming down the hill. These snakes caught my attention for only a few moments because I realized that I needed to keep moving fast.

I first heard, then saw one of the water buffalos as it passed very close by my right side on its way into the water. The buffalo's passing made me jump. Its approach and passing had surprised me. Regaining my composure, I watched the buffalo walking away from me in the direction I wanted to go, heading for the opposite side of the rice paddy. Seeing my opportunity, I stepped into the rice paddy following those buffalo's tracks as it headed across the paddy. As I followed it into the mud, I was careful to step into each of its hoof tracks as it crossed the paddy.

My rationale for selecting this track was that since it was a new track, the churned-up mud and water I created as I went across could be directly attributed to the buffalo's crossing the paddy. *Walking in this track will help camouflage my footsteps,* I thought.

Carefully exiting the rice paddy behind the buffalo on the far side of the paddy, I continued to follow it, as it walked on top of the bank surrounding the paddy toward the road. Following it, I walked carefully in the hoofprints of the water buffalo as it continued to head for the road. My footprints were not noticeable to me because of the size of the water buffalo's hoofprints. Carefully walking in its newly generated hoofprints, I hoped that this action would be effective in slowing down my pursuers.

Once I reached the road that I had seen from across the rice paddy, the water buffalo that I was following turned sharply and reentered the rice paddy. I turned the opposite direction walking down the right side of the road, away from the Quonset hut, making sure that I was leaving clear tracks in the dust, by design, as I headed up the road toward the stream.

The stream crossed the road at a ninety-degree angle approximately four hundred feet from the end of the rice paddy that I had crossed and that the buffalo reentered.

The stream looked like it was about thirty feet across and two to three feet deep in places. It appeared to be very fast-moving running water (north to south) and flowed over many slippery moss-covered rocks. The stream on both sides of the road was covered by dense overhanging layers of jungle canopy, which in several places extended down into the water.

As part of my developing strategy of deception, I saw another opportunity to further confuse the Red Team's capture force by using the river as a deception ploy.

I moved into the center of the stream on the north side of the road, then walking up stream, I entered the jungle overhang. I found myself almost immediately in the middle of hundreds of spiderwebs that were attached to the overhanging branches and bushes that protruded into and over the stream.

Trying to avoid the mass of spiders, I found a stick I could use to break up some of the webs as I moved up the stream. Moving upstream, employing my deception strategy, I moved several rocks and broke off small branches on trees and shrubs as I proceeded approximately 150 feet up the stream bed. As I moved upstream, I also exited the stream at several spots on both sides, intentionally leaving noticeable signs, before reversing direction and moving downstream in the opposite direction.

Proceeding downstream, I crossed the road, then proceeded about 200 feet, repeating my exit and reentry of the stream strategy, moving rocks, breaking branches, disturbing spiderwebs before reversing my course again. Keeping an eye out for snakes and spiders, I quickly returned to my original entry point into the stream on the north side of the road that came from the rice paddy.

At my original entry point, I again employed another evasion strategy to conceal my exit from the stream and cover my exit point from the road into the jungle. I carefully exited the stream walking backward in my own dusty footsteps, moving back up the road toward the Quonset hut.

I learned this form of backtracking strategy in Okinawa with the Hash House Harriers. It would, I hoped, allow me to exit the road into the jungle at a point that was not easily discernable by the trackers that I knew would be pursuing me soon.

Proceeding backward in my own footsteps was time-consuming, but necessary if my deception and concealment strategy were to be effective. Moving back up the road walking backward, I looked for a place where I could enter the jungle without leaving too many signs of my jungle entry. As I reached an area several feet from the outside bank that surrounded the rice paddy that I had originally crossed a few minutes earlier, I found what looked to be the best location for my attempt to enter the jungle.

Making the decision that this was the place and having to move quickly, I carefully threw the rubber water container into the dense jungle to my right and then proceeded to jump as far as I could into the jungle myself. Landing on my hands and knees but safe in the jungle, I turned back around and then used a piece of fern that I found to reach back out into the road and lightly smooth the dust I had disturbed in my jumping process. My intent was to camouflage my jumping-in-entry-point footprints as best I could. That task completed, I then camouflaged the hole in the foliage where I entered the jungle using a combination of small palm and fern leaves, dirt, and sticks.

Looking at my watch, I realized that 21 minutes had passed since the start of the escape and evasion (E and E) exercise. Needing to keep moving quickly, I recovered my rubber water container, which I found without difficulty. Again, the realization hit me that I was running out of time, but also thinking that if I rushed and made errors in executing my strategy, they would find me.

Carefully moving deeper into the jungle, I looked for a suitable location to hide myself where I was not visible to someone passing close to my position. I needed to find a place that provided good natural camouflage while still allowing me to observe the movements of the Negritoes and other Red Team members who were going to be looking for me very, very soon.

As I moved deeper into the jungle, I saw a location that could be suitable. However, a close inspection of the hideout showed that it was too thin on top to provide adequate concealment.

As I continued to move deeper into the jungle along the bank of the rice paddy, I saw another location that could be suitable. Moving forward again toward the location, it appeared more and more promising as a potential hiding spot.

Looking closely at my potential hideout, I observed that it was made up of closely spaced groups of four-foot-high fan ferns that overlapped one another and hung down to the ground in places. These ferns were covered with a heavy tangle of vines with large spikes sticking out of them.

My quick evaluation of the potential hideout location showed me that it met almost all my requirements for concealment and provided good natural camouflage. *This is the place,* I thought as I parted some of the fans on the fern and put my water container under the canopy.

Having selected my position for the hideout, I again returned to my original entry point into the jungle. I then began working from that point back to my hideout making sure my jungle environment had not been visibly disturbed. I worked hard to try to erase all signs of my movements into and through the jungle. In the time I had available, I wiped away as much of these telltale signs as I could all the way to my hideout's location.

My hideout was located approximately six feet in from the bank of the large rice paddy that I originally crossed and approximately thirty-five feet north of the road where I had entered the jungle after my backtrack movements from the stream.

Having returned to my hideout, after working to cover my tracks as best as I could, I entered it making sure not to break or bend any of the fans on the ferns as I entered.

The next task was to camouflage myself. The term *camouflage*, according to *Webster's Dictionary* means "to hide its wearer or mislead a pursuer," which was what I was attempting to accomplish. It was my intent to use the hideout and personal camouflage together to, I hoped, make myself almost invisible to my adversaries. I knew that I needed to become *one* with the environment to stay focused on the job at hand just like the ornithologist I watched as a boy. Being shrewd and focused were two of the keys to be successful in my mission to evade my pursuers and then escape.

Noting the time, I realized that I had just three minutes left to complete my personal camouflage application and drink some water before the Red Team's capture force started their search for me.

Quickly opening my survival vest, I removed and then applied camouflage paint to my face, neck, and exposed hands. Donning a mosquito head net, then my boondock hat, which I had kept hidden in my flight suit's pocket, completed my personal camouflage.

Satisfied that I had done all I could do in the time I had to prepare, I retrieved my water container and took a long drink of water, then covered the water bottle with a fern leaf to hide it.

There was only one thing left for me to do. Wait.

Looking out from my hideout at exactly 0600 hours, the E-and-E exercise start time, I saw the first of the Negritoes' exit from the Quonset hut. He moved quickly toward the top of the nearest hill just as I suspected he would. Then I watched and heard the other Negritoes moving to the top of every major hill that overlooked the E-and-E exercise valley.

I now understood why the Red Team's capture force had such a superior capture record. If participants in the exercise were out in the open or moving after the head-start period, they would have been spotted almost immediately and captured very quickly.

It was exactly thirty minutes to the second since the official start of the exercise. Safe in my hideout, I continued to observe the Negritoes on their hilltop observation points. I could see them searching for the slightest movement in the jungle below, and they were all looking for me. I watched them closely as they looked for my movements. All the ones I could see stayed in their hilltop positions searching unsuccessfully until after sunrise.

Then approximately 0645 hours, what sounded like a bird whistle emanated from one of the Negritoes I was observing on the hilltop closest to me. This sound appeared to be a signal of some sort. As I watched, the majority of the tracking party came down from their hill locations and gathered together at a location near the Quonset hut. Not all the Negritoes moved to join the gathering. It appeared to me that some of the hilltop observers remained in place to continue looking for any movements that I might be making.

The recalled Negritoes gathered near the Quonset hut for what looked to me like an assignment or strategy meeting. After what appeared to be a short discussion, the Red Team's capture force started what looked like the tracking process. Using only hand signals and bird sounds or whistles, the Negrito trackers followed my footprints down the hill into the lower valley toward the rice paddy.

As I watched them, they easily followed my tracks to the edge of the large rice paddy that I had crossed. It was very interesting to observe the Negritoes' detailed process that they used to determine where I had entered the rice paddy and what direction I had taken to cross the paddy.

One Negrito tracker moved ahead of the others to the very edge of the rice paddy bank, reached down into the water, and started to examine each of the tracks that had been made by the water buffalos' hoofs as they moved into and around the rice paddy. At the third set of tracks that he examined, he indicated by hand signals to his team that this was the set of tracks that I had followed in crossing the rice paddy.

Sure enough, it was the set of hoofprints I had used to cross the rice paddy. After watching these activities, my appreciation for the skill and knowledge of the Negrito trackers was even more enhanced.

Another thought slowly crept into my mind. *Maybe they are so good that I may be caught after all.*

I did not know at the time but found out later that the Negrito trackers had used their knowledge that the water buffalos' hoofs, which are split in front, to check where I walked in hoofprints that eliminated the ridge created at the front of the split hoof to determine which set of tracks I utilized.

After determining my entry point, one of the Negritoes entered the rice paddy and followed the buffalo's track that I had used. He stopped and stooped down at each of the buffalo's hoofprints and examined the hoofprint for the eliminated ridge until he reached the far side of the rice paddy. He then signaled his team, using only hand signals, for the rest of his team to join him at my rice paddy exit point to continue their search and tracking process.

As the Red Team's capture force passed my hideout position, I visually observed that each of them carried an AN/PRC-90-2 airman rescue radio strapped to their belts.

They had not had these radios at our initial briefing in the Quonset hut earlier. This observation confirmed my suspicion that all my radio communications were going to be monitored during the entire exercise. This was the same tactic that the Viet Cong and North Vietnamese used during the Vietnam War to locate and capture downed pilots.

As the capture team moved along the rice paddy bank toward the road tracking my movements in the buffalo's hoofprints, I listened closely to their unusual form of nonverbal communication.

The Negritoes were utilizing a series of bird calls and whistles to communicate their intent, progress, as well as any discoveries their team was making. They used this type of communication to direct the search for me with no words being spoken between any of them.

Interesting that they used stealth in their search for me just as I was using it to evade them.

I listened to the Negritoes' communication and watched them from my hideout in the heavy jungle until they reached the road. Because of the jungle structure, I could see mostly legs and boots of the Negritoes searching for me. Losing sight of them, I then heard them as they turned up the road. I again heard them communicating among one another as they worked the road to find my not well-hidden footprints heading up the road toward the fast-moving stream.

Sitting in my hideout quietly for over twenty-five minutes, I again heard bird calls and whistles indicating to me that the Negritoes had moved up the fast-moving stream and undoubtedly had located some of my exit points and found nothing. A short time later, more calls emanated from the area downstream of the road indicating that they had found nothing there either. After that flurry of calls and whistles, these noises just seemed to fade away into the distance.

Sitting in my hideout, I heard nothing but *dead silence* except for what noises the small birds and other animals that live in the dense jungle were making.

Things are looking good so far.

All of a sudden, I felt something stinging or biting me on the calf of my left leg, then on the same area on my right leg, then my hands. Looking down on my left hand, I saw several red and black ants that were in the process of biting me. Looking down at where I was sitting, it was then that I discovered that I had made a big mistake in the selection of the hideout location.

My hideout was located directly on top of a larger red and black anthill.

What's next? I thought.

Quickly scanning the area and listening for the presence of the birds and whistles of the Red Team' capture force, I opened my survival kit, found, then applied my entire supply of insect repellant to as much of my body that I could reach without disturbing my camouflage. I also quietly applied some anti-infection cream to the bites that I could reach.

Reevaluating my situation, I thought, *My anthill hideout location is not a good place for an extended nonmovement position in the jungle, but now I am committed. To move now will mean almost sure capture. It looks like I will have to make the best of my current location despite the ants.*

Resolved to my fate, I drank some additional water and checked to see that my camouflage was in place while I waited for both the ants and Negritoes to return.

About an hour later, I again heard the Negritoes communicating with bird calls and whistles. This time, the noise was emanating from the area of the fast-moving stream and very slowly getting louder, indicating to me that they were moving toward my location.

It sounded like maybe eight to ten Negritoes had formed some sort of search line moving toward me. It appeared as though they were searching the jungle that covered the north side of the road, moving through the jungle from the stream toward the rice paddy and my location.

Listening as their search progressed very slowly, it sounded like each Negrito took one or two steps, then stopped. It again appeared to me like they may be looking, listening, and communicating with bird calls and whistles, before they moved again.

If I had not been listening to these sounds earlier and watching them communicating, there would have been a good chance that I would not have heard the search line advancing toward my position. Since I was aware of their progress, I was able to prepare myself for their arrival, hoping my camouflage and hideout location would make me hard to detect.

Not moving anything or making any noise was my paramount task now. If I moved, I would be caught. I focused on my training as a bird watcher as a boy back in Wisconsin and did not move a muscle. My only problem was that the ants were back! They had found another point of entry to get into my flight suit and were biting me again. Still, I needed to remain perfectly motionless for the duration of the search line advance and passage, or I was going to be caught.

Since my back was toward the stream where they were coming from, I could not see the approach of the Negritoes search line. Not daring to move anything except my eyes, I saw a boot of one of the Negritoes' out of the corner of my right eye just outside the fern cluster I was under.

He was approximately three feet away from me and had come to a stop. I could almost feel him looking, listening, and starting to communicate. ...

To be continued in book 2 of my memoir.

BIBLIOGRAPHY

Cosmas, George A. and Terrence R. Murray. "Chapter 11: Marine Helicopters Over Laos" in *US Marines in Vietnam: Vietnamization and Redeployment 1970–1971*. Washington, DC: History and Museum Division Headquarters, US Marine Corps, 1986.

Fulghum, David and Terrence Maitland. *South Vietnam on Trial*. Boston: Boston Publishing Company, 1984.

HMH-463 and HML-367 Command Chronologies for January–March 1971. First MAW, Vietnam.

Nalty, Bernard F. *The War Against Trucks*. Washington, DC: Air Force History and Museum Program, 2005.

Nolan, William K. *Into Laos: Story of Dewey Canyon II/Lam Son 719*. Novato, California: Presidio Press, 1984.

Sander, Robert D. *Invasion of Laos 1971*. Norman, Oklahoma: University of Oklahoma Press Publishing Division, 2014.

Van Staaveren, Jacob. *Introduction in Southern Laos*. Washington DC: Center of Air Force History, 1993.

Wasko, Michael Jr. "Michael Wasko's After-Action Report." Personal Copy. First MAW Vietnam, February 1971.

Willbanks, James H. *A Raid Too Far: Operation Lam Son 719 and Vietnamization in Laos*. College Station, Texas: Texas A&M University Press, 2014.

About the Author

Dr. Robert F. Wemheuer is a retired colonel in the United States Marine Corps. After serving in the corps for twenty-five years, he became an environmental remediation project manager who managed remediation projects for Fluor Daniel and Bechtel Corporations culminating with thirteen years of work on the Yucca Mountain High-Level Nuclear Waste Repository Program in Nevada. He is currently now living in Georgetown, Texas, with his wife of fifty-three years.

CPSIA information can be obtained
at www.ICGtesting.com
Printed in the USA
LVHW101510090822
725521LV00004B/38